AND THEN THERE WAS FOOTBALL
FOOTBALL
MERSEYSIDE FOOTBALL:
A HISTORY 1878-2025

PHILIP ROSS

AND THEN THERE WAS FOOTBALL MERSEYSIDE FOOTBALL: A HISTORY 1878-2025

PHILIP ROSS

MOUNT VERNON
PUBLISHING

First published by Mount Vernon Publishing in 2025.

First Edition

Mount Vernon Publishing Group Ltd,
71-75 Shelton Street, Covent Garden, London, WC2H 9JQ.

ISBN: 978-1-917064-92-7

A CIP catalogue record for this book is available from the British Library.

Cover design by Thomas Regan of Milkyone.
Typeset by Steve Foot of epubknowhow.co.uk.

TO ANDREW,

THANK YOU FOR YOUR HELP AND SUPPORT
THROUGHOUT WRITING THIS BOOK, BUT MOST OF
ALL FOR BEING MY WONDERFUL BROTHER

CONTENTS

FOREWORD

'Some people think football is a matter of life and death.
I assure you it's much more serious than that.'
– Bill Shankly

THIS BOOK CAME ABOUT AFTER A DISCUSSION WITH MY FRIEND AND mentor, the author James Corbett. He had mentioned that Gary James had written *Manchester: A Football History* in 2008, which he had updated in the years since. Although there was a Merseyside football history book by Percy Young, it had been written back in 1963, and therefore it was high time Merseyside had an updated version. The Manchester football history book was written with a love for Manchester and its football. On Merseyside we very definitely have the same love for the game, and I would say even more so.

The idea of the book was to concentrate on Merseyside/Greater Liverpool area clubs, but it does stray over borders. Liverpool and Wirral clubs often played in each other's leagues and cups, so Wirral clubs and competitions are shown in the book. Wigan Athletic are included due to winning the Liverpool non-league Senior Cup on a few occasions, and to continue their story.

In such a big book with many moving parts, mistakes will happen. Some are down to simple oversight on my behalf, but others are down to newspapers not reporting that teams or leagues have dissolved. Many club and league secretaries were implored by local newspapers to send in their club or league reports, but many times they failed to appear, meaning a league table didn't appear in the newspaper or the disbandment of a club was not shown. Teams and leagues also changed their names, either by adding 'Town' or 'United', and in the case of New Brighton they simply changed their name from South Liverpool. In the case of leagues, they added 'Amateur' or 'Alliance' and so on. Newspapers also called leagues by different names. The I Zingari League and its offspring, I Zingari Combination and I Zingari Alliance, often became mixed up, especially their individual cup competitions. So please accept my apologies for any mistakes found.

Women's football proved a particular challenge. Early match reports were few and far between, and there was also the need to navigate the sexism of the particular times they were written in. Hopefully the book has pulled together enough of the information on the teams and leagues that do exist, and there is a narrative and history of sorts about that part of the game.

It could be argued that football on Merseyside took off in the 1960s when John Moores took over the ownership at Everton with the help of manager Harry Catterick, and Bill Shankly became manager of Liverpool and started to win trophies. Later, Shankly built Liverpool's Boot Room of the 1970s with the help of Paisley, Fagan and Evans, who produced their own trophy haul in the 1980s. Although room doesn't allow for an in-depth analysis of these times, I think just a look at the success Everton's Moores/Catterick partnership and Liverpool's Shankly, together with the Boot Room, brought to Merseyside tells its own story. The Moores family, of course, owned or had controlling interest in the big Merseyside clubs of Everton and Liverpool, and their influence as a whole plays a large part in the success football has had in the area. Tranmere Rovers had successful times under managers Johnny King and John Aldridge. The same restriction applies to other teams such as Waterloo Dock and Marine, who had fabulous trophy hauls themselves under long-time managers Jimmy Davies and Roly Howard respectively.

Room also doesn't allow for an in-depth look at each individual club, so the trials and tribulations of the Moshiri years at Everton or the Gillett/Hicks time at Liverpool, and the various problems at Southport, Tranmere Rovers and Chester, can only be given a glancing mention.

My thanks go to my family: my brother Andrew and my late mother Wendy for putting up with me throughout the hours and years spent writing this book, and James Corbett for the massive help given, especially the editing, and also putting up with me. My main thanks go to my late father, the Reverend Harry Ross, Goodison Park's chaplain from the early 1980s to 2019, who took me to my first football game aged ten, which helped instil a love of the game.

Thanks also go to the various people who have helped with information. Hyder Jawad helped with the many iterations of South Liverpool FC, Greg Mclean with Cheshire FA information, Kevin Mighall with Wirral District FA information, and Iain Munro with I Zingari League information. Gill Wallworth provided invaluable information on the league and cup winners of local Merseyside and Wirral women's football. Gary Berwick, Iain and Mick of the Liverpool Premier League provided information on that league. Major Ian Riley and Dennis Reeves helped with information regarding the Liverpool Scottish Football team. The staff at Crosby and Liverpool libraries also receive my thanks.

Although that Bill Shankly quote was certainly not meant to be taken in any way seriously, his point was that football means a lot to the people of Liverpool and Merseyside. As someone once said, 'If football didn't exist it would have to be invented.' Well, if it did have to be newly invented, it couldn't find a better birthplace than on Merseyside.

Philip Ross
August 2025

CHAPTER 1

THE BIRTH OF A GREAT CITY

CHESTER WAS FIRST ESTABLISHED AS A ROMAN FORT NAMED DEVA Victrix in 79 AD, and there are reports suggesting a form of football was played during that period. A football game using a Dane's head was thought to have been played annually and the Roman game similar to Rugby called Harpastum was also played at that time.

In 1085, various areas of Merseyside appeared in the Domesday Book, including modern day Ainsdale, Allerton, Altcar, Aughton, Bootle, Chester, Childwall, Crosby, Formby, Halsall, Heswall, Huyton, Ince Blundell, Kirkby, Kirkdale, Knowsley, Litherland, Lydiate, Maghull, Melling, Meols, Neston, Newton-le-Willows, Roby, Sefton, Skelmersdale, Smithdown, Speke, Tarbock, Thornton, Toxteth, Wallasey, Walton, Wavertree, West Derby and Woolton.

Garston was named after previously being known as Gerstan meaning great stone or grazing town. Wirral was old English for Myrtle corner, Myrtle was a plant that covered the area. Bromborough was Anglo Saxon for Bruna's fortification. Heswall in the Doomsday book was owned by Patrick de Haselwall.

Comprising just seven streets arranged in the shape of the letter 'H', Liverpool was granted borough status in 1207 by a charter from King John of England. Birkenhead was first developed around the same period when Benedictine monks constructed a priory, subsequently operating a ferry across the River Mersey from 1330 onwards.

In 1229, Liverpool received a second charter from King Henry III, permitting the formation of its own guild, complete with its own seal. This seal introduced what became the city's prominent symbol – the Liver Bird – which was adopted centuries later by Everton and, subsequently, Liverpool Football Clubs. The bird depicted in the 1229 seal is now believed to be a poorly drawn copy of an eagle, symbolising John the Evangelist, the patron saint of King John. By the time of Edward III (1312–1377), Everton had a population of 95. St Helens was first recorded in 1552 as a chapel dedicated to St Elyn.

Anfield means a field on a slope and started as Hongefield in the 1600s and was mainly cattle grazing and quarrying area until the mid-1800s when the gentry started to build villas in the area.

During the English Civil War, Liverpool Castle was besieged by Prince Rupert's Royalist troops in 1644. Prince Rupert had stayed in a cottage in Everton, close to what became known as Rupert's Castle or Tower, a structure depicted on Everton Football Club's badge and built in the 1800s as a lock up.

Liverpool's first commercial docks opened in 1715, built using stones and bricks from the demolished castle, which never recovered from the siege. In 1753, Molly Bushell began producing what became known as Everton Toffee in the Everton area. The district of St Domingo, Everton, traces back to 1757 when sugar merchant George Campbell established an estate named after St Domingo in the West Indies, where capturing a ship reportedly made Campbell wealthy. The town of Southport originated as a single guesthouse, constructed by William Sutton in 1792.

In 1817, a steam ferry service commenced between Tranmere and Liverpool, and in 1824 William Laird founded an ironworks in Birkenhead, launching its first ship in 1828. Pilkington's Glass Company, originally named St Helens Crown Glass Company, opened in St Helens in 1826. By 1829, Bootle was vastly different from today, described then as a place where 'writers and artists came to refresh their minds and gather inspiration,' briefly flourishing as a seaside resort with caravans along the beach during summer months.

The Liverpool to Manchester Railway opened in 1830, eventually running through or near areas such as Edge Hill, Broadgreen, Roby, Huyton, Whiston, Rainhill, St Helens, Parr, Sankey and Newton-le-Willows. In 1835, Liverpool expanded to incorporate Kirkdale, Everton, parts of West Derby, and northern Toxteth Park. Liverpool's modern police force was established in 1836, with a local newspaper advertisement stating, 'Three Hundred Men are wanted immediately for the Day and Night Police of Liverpool,' offering 18 shillings weekly pay along with required uniform clothing.

In mid-1840s the Bath Hotel in Waterloo with its well-aired beds and no effort spared attitude and panoramic view of Seaforth was run by Mr. Brining and his sister Mrs. Sillitoe complete with its own Private Omnibus for removing families, thanked the Nobility, Gentry and public for their patronage of the hotel since it had opened. Fifty years later and a change of name, it would play its part in the naming of Merseyside football team.

In 1847, Birkenhead opened new commercial docks and Birkenhead Park. The following year, 1848, saw the inauguration of the Liverpool, Crosby and Southport Railway. The route eventually would start at Sandhills and passed through Bootle, Seaforth & Litherland, Waterloo, Blundellsands & Crosby, Hightown, Altcar, Formby, Freshfield, Ainsdale, Hillside and Birkdale, before reaching Southport. This line would help the formation of the local Cricket Liverpool Competition, with local sides forming in communities along the railway line. That same year a new dock opened in Liverpool Bramley Moore named after the then Chairman of the dock committee Bootle gained municipal status in 1868.

During the Irish famine in the mid-1840s, Liverpool's port experienced increased immigration from Ireland. While many immigrants moved onward to America or elsewhere in Britain, a significant number remained in Liverpool. By the 1851 census, over twenty per cent of Liverpool's population was Irish-born, the highest proportion in England and Wales, with many families residing along Scotland Road or near the docks. By 1871, Liverpool's Irish community represented just over 15% of the city's total population, numbering approximately 76,000 out of 493,000 residents. By 1891, the Irish population had slightly decreased to around 47,000 out of a total of 513,000, just over 9 per cent.

Although Scotland and Wales did not experience famines that prompted significant migration, Scottish and Welsh families gradually settled in Liverpool. Welsh communities primarily settled in Everton and in streets off Stanley Road. It is thought that the name Liverpool derives from the Welsh spelling and pronunciation. Scottish families often moved to more affluent areas in North Liverpool. Both the Welsh and Scottish communities were predominantly Protestant and together made up just over five per cent of Liverpool's population by the turn of the 20th century. Welsh builders Owen and William Elias constructed terrace houses in Walton, which eventually became home to Everton Football Club's Goodison Park. To mark their involvement, they used their initials to name streets situated between County Road and Goodison Road. Additionally, it is believed that the phrase 'Jerry-built' originated from Liverpool's building trade, associated with the Jerry Brothers.

The rise of a sporting culture

Before team sports became prevalent, Liverpool hosted horse racing at Aintree Racecourse, which opened in 1829. Nearby Chester had the historic Roodee Racecourse, dating back to the 1500s. Merseyside also hosted blood sports; the last recorded bear-baiting event took place in West Derby in 1853. Hare coursing events, notably the Waterloo Cup, named after Liverpool's Waterloo Hotel whose proprietor provided the trophy, began in 1836 and continued at Great Altcar until 2006.

In the early 1800s, cricket and rugby were the predominant team sports in Merseyside. Cricket is thought to have begun in Liverpool in 1807 with the formation of 'The Original and Unrivalled Mosslake Fields Cricket Society'. Mosslake Fields occupied an area bordered by Hope Street (west), Crown Street (east), Oxford Street (north), and Parliament Street (south). The cricket club, located between Chatham Street and Crown Street, partially overlaps the present-day site of St Catherine's Church in Abercromby Square. This club, possibly the predecessor of Liverpool Cricket Club, was formally established around 1811. In 1820, the club relocated to Falkner Square, formerly Crabtree Lane, and moved around the Edge Hill area through the decade. In 1847, the club established a more permanent location near Edge Hill Station, staying until railway expansion in 1877. After a three-year stay at Croxteth Hall, thanks to the patronage of the Earl of Sefton, the club finally settled permanently at Aigburth/Grassendale in 1850. The Liverpool Competition, established in 1892, involved eleven prominent cricket clubs across Merseyside: Birkenhead Park, Bootle, Formby, Huyton, Liverpool, New Brighton, Northern, Ormskirk, Oxton, Rock Ferry and Sefton.

Bootle Cricket Club was formed in 1833, followed by Ormskirk Cricket Club in 1835. Birkenhead Cricket Club was established in 1845, with St Helens Cricket Club founded two years later, in 1847, as part of the St Helens Recreation Club. New Brighton Cricket Club was founded in 1857, Southport Cricket Club in 1859, and Sefton Cricket Club in 1860. Huyton had a cricket club from around 1860, Wallasey Cricket Club was formed in 1864, Formby in 1865, Chester in 1873, and Birkdale Cricket Club in 1874.

Liverpool Rugby Club was founded in 1857, with its first recorded match played between former Rugby School pupils and local youths. Initially playing at Liverpool Cricket Club in Edge Hill until 1879, the rugby club then moved to Brook House Hotel on Smithdown Road. In 1882, they relocated to Aigburth Road, before moving again in 1884 to another Liverpool Cricket Club ground at Riversdale Road, Aigburth. The Wirral's first rugby club, Birkenhead Park, emerged in 1871, while New Brighton Rugby Union Club was established in 1875.

In 1878, a rugby team became part of the St Helens Recreation Club, initially set up in 1847 by Pilkington Glassmakers. The Recreation Club was pioneering in its commitment to workers' welfare at a time of poor labour conditions, influenced by parliamentary reforms like the Factory Act of 1833. Waterloo Rugby Club started as Serpentine RFC in 1882, formed by Merchant Taylors' pupils, and Liverpool Gymnasium founded a rugby club in Tuebrook. In 1884, a meeting at the Liverpool Gymnasium led to the creation of the West Lancashire and Border Towns Union, aiming to counter the growing popularity of association football, which was increasingly overshadowing rugby as the region's main sport.

English baseball officially began in Liverpool, with origins predating the formation of the Football League in 1888, arising from local rounders and baseball teams. The rules for the English variant were drawn up by a Freeman of Liverpool, with official matches starting in 1892.

Football's Origin Story

Football in various forms has existed in England since at least the 12th century, notably in Shrovetide games involving entire villages attempting to move a ball towards rival goals. One such game in Derby, played between St Peter's and All Saints, may have given rise to the modern term 'Derby matches' referring to local football rivalries. In medieval times, football was banned by Edward III in 1365 and by Richard II in 1388 because it distracted people from archery practice. Similarly, Scotland's Parliament banned football in May 1424 by royal decree.

Football's historical roots in Chester date back significantly. In 1564, football was played on the River Dee, and earlier still, an annual Shrove Tuesday tradition involved shoemakers presenting a ball to drapers at the Rodehee Cross, overseen by Chester's mayor, to be played towards the city's Common Hall.

There is also reference to a football game played on the frozen River Dee in the late 1500s. William Shakespeare mentions football in his play King Lear, written between 1605 and 1606. Women are also recorded as playing football during the 1700s. By the mid-1800s, football was predominantly played and further developed at public schools and universities. In Scotland, teenager John Hope established a Foot-Ball Club in Edinburgh in 1824, drafting some basic rules by 1833.

Rugby School published rules for their version of the game in 1845, and Eton produced rules for the Eton Wall Game in 1847. However, there were no universally accepted rules or standards. Matches could last several hours, pitch sizes varied significantly, and rules such as offside differed widely. Tackling frequently led to injuries, as players could hack, charge, or hold opponents. The ball could be caught by any player, who would then call 'mark'. Handball was permissible if the ball was knocked backwards rather than forwards.

Cambridge University introduced the first recognised set of football rules in 1848, rules that were referenced by FA Secretary Charles Alcock fifty years later. By the 1850s, the concept of Muscular Christianity emerged, coined in 1857 by Thomas Sanders in his review of Rev. Charles Kingsley's novel 'Two Years Ago'. This philosophy emphasised discipline, self-sacrifice, masculinity, physical fitness, and athleticism, significantly influencing the formation of many church-based football clubs in both football codes.

The oldest existing English football club, Sheffield Football Club, was founded in 1857, playing both rugby and association football. Sheffield Football Club and the Sheffield FA frequently clashed with the Football Association (FA), established in 1863, regarding rules, until their differences were resolved in 1877. Other early clubs included Notts County (1862) and Stoke City (1863).

In October 1863, the FA was formed by representatives from eleven schools and clubs responding to an advertisement in *Bell's Life*, a London newspaper, aiming to create a unified set of football rules. Meeting at the Freemasons Tavern in London, these groups agreed upon thirteen initial laws of the game by December 1863. Subsequent clubs were established, including Wrexham (1864), Nottingham Forest (1865), Sheffield Wednesday (originally The Wednesday Football Club, 1867), Chesterfield (1867) and Scotland's Queens Park Club (1867). The Rugby Football Union were both founded in 1871, definitively separating association football and rugby union into distinct codes. Wigan Cricket Club created a football team in 1872, later becoming Wigan & District in 1876, before reverting to Wigan Football Club, now known as Wigan Warriors Rugby League.

By this period, football was becoming more standardised. Pitch dimensions were capped at 200 yards long and 100 yards wide, goals measured eight yards wide without crossbars, and teams switched ends after each goal. No specific goalkeeper role was defined; rather, the closest defending player to their goal could claim a 'fair catch' as a 'mark,' allowing an unimpeded kick from any chosen spot. Corner kicks did not exist; when the ball went behind the goal, the defending team would restart play from the touchline if they reached it first, whereas an attacking player gaining the ball first resulted in a free kick fifteen yards from the touchline. Notably, the original rules made no mention of match officials.

In 1866 the *Sportsman* newspaper commented on the absence of football activity in Liverpool, expressing hopes that Mr W. D. Hogarth, a renowned local athlete and honorary secretary of both Liverpool Gymnasium and the Athletic Club, would succeed in acquiring land on Belmont Road for athletics and potentially establish a football club. Although this particular aspiration may not have immediately materialised, football began emerging in the early to mid-1870s. The journalist O'Whatmore, writing for Liverpool's *Porcupine* magazine, recalled the earliest matches in Stanley Park, noting the participation of local churchmen Rev. Jackson and Rev. Marsh. Initially, players lacked tactical concepts like passing or dribbling, simply kicking the ball far ahead and chasing after it. Early goals were improvised using coats and tape, later evolving into portable goalposts carried to and from the pitches.

On 20 July 1871, FA Secretary Charles Alcock proposed the establishment of a Challenge Cup at an FA committee meeting, leading to the creation of the FA Cup. The first round began on 11 November 1871, featuring twelve of the FA's fifty member clubs. Wanderers Football Club defeated the Royal Engineers 1–0 in the first final at Kennington Oval on 16 March 1872, in front of 2,000 spectators. Northern English teams participated from 1873 onwards, with Sheffield being the first. Lancashire clubs Darwen and Manchester joined the competition in 1877. Football expanded rapidly across the Midlands and North; Aston Villa and Bolton Wanderers formed in 1874, Birmingham City (originally Small Heath Alliance) and Blackburn Rovers in 1875 and Middlesbrough in 1876.

In September 1871 James Wade laid the memorial stone for a new Methodist Church in the St. Domingo area of Everton near to St Domingo vale. The Church would soon prove synonymous with the formation of Everton Football Club.

That same year another quite different building was opened, The Sandon Hotel on Oakfield Road, Anfield was opened by John Houlding, a Liverpool businessman. As well as being a pub it had bedrooms, billiard room, a function room and bowling green with club house. The Hotel would go on to play a part in the history of Merseyside Football.

In 1874, an association game was played in Chester in which King's College lost 4–0 to Chester College, largely due to unfamiliarity with the rules. Two years later, *The Athletic News* reported an association match in Liverpool on 15 January 1876, between the Manchester Association team and Liverpool Casuals. Played on slippery ground, the match was scheduled for 2:45 p.m. but started at 3:20 p.m., likely due to Manchester arriving with only six players and borrowing three from spectators. The game was balanced for the first twenty minutes before Hassall scored for Liverpool Casuals, adding another just before half-time. Gilbert scored a third in the second half, securing a 3–0 victory (though some reports list the score as 2–0, with Gilbert scoring twice).

That same month, a team of Old Boys named Claughton played New Brighton at Claremont School in Wallasey, in what is believed to have been another early association game, ending in a draw.

In February/May 1876, the Welsh Football Association was founded at the Wynnstay Arms Hotel in Wrexham. One attendee, Robert Lythgoe, would go on to play a significant role in Merseyside football. The first Welsh Cup was held in 1877, although no Merseyside clubs participated initially. That year also saw the formation of Crewe Alexandra and Wolverhampton Wanderers (then known as St. Luke's Football Club).

By this time, football goals included crossbars or tape, and corner kicks were taken from within a yard of the corner flag. Matches were officiated by two umpires, typically one from each team, with some also featuring a referee.

In August 1878, the Cheshire FA was formed at the at the Hartford Station Hotel near Northwich. The first meeting of the Lancashire FA was held on 28 September 1878 at the Co-operative Hall in Darwen when over twenty clubs from the Lancashire area both big and small agreed twelve rules for the new Association. Although no Merseyside clubs had taken part in the new organisation, football was about to change in Liverpool.

Football arrives in Liverpool

From the early part of nineteenth century an area of Walton would be set on a path to play its part in Merseyside football history. It was called Walton Stiles and a part of it was a flower and vegetable nursery owned by a William Skirving. When he died in December 1878 his family put the 6130 square yards of land up for sale. Most of the land was bought for housing by the Walton Board. They used a Mr George Goodison to do the surveying of the land and they promptly named a road after him, Goodison Road.

That same year a Methodist Church cricket team predominantly from the New Connexion Chapel, built at the top of St. Domingo Vale, Breckfield Road North, Everton, called St. Domingo began to play football during the winter months. This local team would change its name at a meeting at the Queen's Head pub in November of the following year 1879 to Everton Football Club. Everton's first recorded game was against St. Peter's a fellow church team from the Everton area. Everton beat St. Peter's 6–0 at Stanley Park in December 1879.

Liverpool became a city by royal charter in 1880. According to the 1881 census, its population stood at 682,000, comprising the areas of Liverpool, Toxteth Park, and the West Derby Union. The Everton area had a population of 110,000, as did West Derby itself. Birkenhead's population was 81,000, followed by St Helens with 57,000 and Wigan with 48,000. Chester had 37,000 residents, Southport 32,000, Tranmere 30,000, and Bootle 27,000. The Wirral had 25,000, and Wallasey 21,000. Walton recorded a population of 18,000, Runcorn 14,000, Garston 10,000 and Formby 4,000. Birkdale and Kirkby had populations of 1,500 and 1,400 respectively.

By this time, local newspapers were emerging as sources of sporting news. The *Birkenhead News* began publishing in 1871, the *Bootle Times* in

1878, and the *Liverpool Echo* in 1879. In 1880, Liverpool dockers earned between 4s 6d and 5s per day, while sailors received 15s to 20s per week. Casual porters at the docks earned around 15s weekly. A joiner earned 7½d per hour, and Lancashire loom workers about 5s per week. A collier in St Helens earned 10½d per ton of coal, and at Prescot Colliery during a strike in 1881, colliers were paid 1s 2½d per ton. By the start of the 1880s, Liverpool's police force had grown to 1,200 officers. Southport, which had maintained a police force since 1870, added a Police Court, while Bootle and St Helens formed their own police forces in 1887.

Everton's first entry in the Lancashire Senior Challenge Cup came in the 1880/81 season with an away match against Great Lever. After a 1–0 defeat and a dispute over the winning goal, Everton secured a replay – only to lose 8–1.

In February 1881, *The Field* newspaper reported on an association match between Birkenhead and Liverpool. The article opened: 'Association football has made great strides in these parts. Three years ago, it was scarcely, if ever, heard of; now we can name a dozen clubs or so, the most prominent being in possible order of merit – Bootle, Birkenhead, Everton, Liverpool, with Everton United Church, St Peter's, and several of lesser note. All these societies put at least two teams in the field every Saturday, and some venture even to the 'A' team combinations....'

Liverpool witnessed its first women's football match on Friday, 3 June 1881. The two teams, representing England and Scotland, were touring the country and had played their first match in Edinburgh the previous month. After appearances in Blackburn and an aborted effort to play in Manchester, they relocated to Liverpool. The match, which ended in a 1–1 draw, took place at the Stanley Athletic Grounds with a 7:30 p.m. kick-off. Press reactions were mixed. The *Athletic News* (8 June 1881) praised the event, despite modest attendance. A second match was held later that month, again at the Stanley Athletic Grounds behind the Cattle Market Inn, and drew a larger crowd.

Other papers, however, were dismissive. The *Liverpool Daily Post* described the event as 'merely a showman speculation, the women being all engaged by the same people.' Some reports, including in the *Manchester Evening News*, suggested the game may have blended elements of association and rugby football, referencing touchdowns. Whatever the code, it offered only a brief glimpse of the women's game in Merseyside. It would take over a decade – and the influence of an adopted daughter of Merseyside – before women's football returned.

Meanwhile, football itself was undergoing significant changes. Referees became more formalised, though they typically stood off the pitch and primarily kept time, making decisions only after consulting with umpires. Crossbars were now made of wood, replacing tape. The touchline became the standard boundary of play, and goalkeepers were restricted to handling the ball within their own half.

By October 1881, the Association game on Merseyside had grown enough to attract the attention of the *Liverpool Daily Post*, which observed that it was slowly overtaking the Rugby version of football: 'Taking it altogether,' it said, 'the winter pastime shows much vitality; and one thing noticeable is the growing favour of the Association and the consequent decline of the Rugby game.'

That same year, a team known as Tranmere Rovers emerged. Originally a cricket club, they began playing football around 1881, featuring in matches against Anfield in October, St George's on Stanley Park in November, Birkenhead Argyle in December, and St Peter's in February. These seem to have been their final matches under the Tranmere Rovers name. At a meeting held in January 1882 at the Bee Hive Hotel in Tranmere, the club decided to drop the 'Rovers' from their name. Present at that meeting was J. H. McGaul Esq., who would later become an influential figure in the future of another club named Tranmere Rovers.

Elsewhere on Merseyside, football was also developing. In Southport, as in Liverpool, rugby had initially been more prominent. However, the poor performance of the town's rugby club in the early 1880s led to the creation of its first Association team. Southport Rugby Club, founded in 1872, made the switch to Association football, playing its first match under the new code in November 1881.

Bootle became the first Merseyside club to enter the FA Cup in November 1881, drawn at home to Blackburn Law. Two players in the Bootle team, Lythgoe and Sloan and one from the Blackburn Law side Rylands (Rylance) went onto play a major part in both Liverpool Football history and Southport Football history.

Coincidentally, on the same day, Bootle were also scheduled to face Preston North End in the Lancashire Challenge Cup. Bootle won the FA Cup match, coming from behind to win 2–1 thanks to an overhead kick by centre forward Turner. Immediately after, the same exhausted team took on Preston North End, where Bootle's captain, Heaton, scored an equaliser in the fading light. That match ended in a 1–1 draw.

There had been speculation in the press for some time about forming a local football association for the Liverpool district. In early April 1882, the *Liverpool Daily Post* reported that the leading Association clubs had met at the Royal Oak Hotel at the invitation of the Stanley Hospital Sports Committee to organise charity games. Two matches were arranged to be played on Stanley Park, including one between a visiting team and a team representing Liverpool and District. Clubs in attendance were St Mary's, Bootle, Everton, St Peter's, and Liverpool, with T. Evans of Everton elected chairman. This gathering marked the origins of the Liverpool Football Association.

Southport's first entry into the Lancashire Senior Challenge Cup came in October 1882, when they hosted and defeated Stacksteads Working Men 4–0.

On 25 October 1882, Robert Lythgoe – as mentioned then playing for Bootle Football Club – wrote a letter to the press advocating the creation of a formal football association. His letter appeared under the heading 'Liverpool and District Football Association' in the *Athletic News* (1 November 1882):

> 'Sir – Having observed in some recent issues correspondence advocating the advisability of forming an Association in this district, and being also of the opinion that the time has now arrived for the formation of such an organisation here (similar to those of

33333

333

Birmingham and Sheffield), which will not only enable us to put a thoroughly representative team - playing under the Association rules - on the field, but will also in large measure benefit the local charities... it has occurred to me that the time for action has already arrived, and there is nothing to prevent our forming an Association at once, and selecting a Committee, so that we may have our first draw for the Charity Cup competition at the end of this season...'

Lythgoe concluded by inviting all local clubs and associations to a meeting at the Tarleton Hotel, 30 Tarleton Street, Liverpool, on 2 November at 8 o'clock.

As advertised on 2 November 1882, twelve clubs from the local area – Bootle, Everton, Liverpool, Wirral, Birkenhead, Stanley, St Peter's, St Mary's, Liverpool Rovers, Anfield, St Benedict's and St George's – met at the Tarleton Hotel on Tarleton Street in Liverpool city centre. The hotel, which described itself in an advert as the 'Football and Cricket Club's Resort,' hosted the meeting that led to the formation of the Liverpool and District Football Association. By the end of its first season, the association had grown to include Bootle Wanderers, Stanley Rovers, and Toxteth Wanderers.

Liverpool's newly formed FA quickly organised a representative team to face opponents from the Manchester and District FA. In the 1882/83 FA Cup, Southport and Liverpool Ramblers played their first fixture, a 1–1 draw at Southport's ground. Ramblers won the replay 4–0.

In an effort to further promote football in the city, the Liverpool FA requested to host the international match between England and Ireland. This request – likely influenced by Liverpool's significant Irish population – was granted, and the match took place at Liverpool Cricket Club's Aigburth Park ground on 24 February 1883. A crowd of 2,000–3,000 attended, with the *Liverpool Mercury* noting a fair number of women in attendance. England won 7–0 in a dominant performance. Following the match, a dinner was held for both teams at the Bear's Paw Restaurant on Lord Street.

At the end of 1882 and into early 1883, the FA introduced new laws: crossbars on goals were now compulsory, and ends were only to be changed at half-time, rather than after each goal. In January 1883, the Liverpool and District Challenge Cup – later known as the Liverpool Senior Cup – held its first round of fixtures. Liverpool and Everton met in what may have been the first competitive derby between clubs bearing those names. Everton won 8–0.

Other results from that round included Bootle beating St Mary's 2–1, Liverpool Rovers defeating Wirral 8–1, Liverpool Ramblers beating Toxteth Wanderers 8–1, St Benedict's overcoming Anfield, and Stanley defeating St Peter's. The first final was contested by Bootle and Liverpool Ramblers at Liverpool College's ground in Fairfield. The match was level 1–1 at half-time, but Bootle scored twice more in the second half to win 3–1.

In the mid-1870s Liverpool had reportedly over two thousand pubs which was more than any other city in the country and at the end of 1883, the *Liverpool Daily Post* published a series of reports under the title 'Squalid Liverpool,' detailing the harsh living conditions in some of the city's poorest areas. Scotland Road was described as 'a great stream of rough, inodorous, more or less intoxicated humanity, travelling to and fro' between public houses. The journalist noted that during their evening on Scotland Road, they saw only one sober woman.

In September 1884, John Houlding – by now a club member of Everton since 1881 – offered his Sandon Hotel in Anfield as Everton's new headquarters. In return, he became club president. Which he added to that of being President of Everton Coits Club and Everton Bowling Club and just a couple of years later President of Everton Baseball Association.

By the 1883/84 season, Everton had moved from Stanley Park to Priory Road, but this arrangement proved unsatisfactory. Houlding then purchased land on Anfield Road from local landowner Joseph Orrell, spending £6,000. The Everton board agreed to repay the sum at 4% annual interest, although Houlding accepted less in practice. While the club had secured a new home, the financial arrangement and future dealings with John Orrell (Joseph Orrell's son), who owned adjoining land, would create complications.

On the Wirral, football continued to grow. Alongside Birkenhead FC, other clubs emerged. Birkenhead Argyle was one, and another – Belmont FC – was formed by players from two local cricket clubs: Belmont (formed in 1881) and Lyndhurst Wanderers (formed in 1883). Seeking a winter sport, the clubs merged and played their first reported match at Steele's Field, off Borough Road, on 15 November 1884, defeating Brunswick Rovers 4–0.

Towards the league era

The Football Association was struggling to address professionalism they had become increasingly strict about the use of professional players, this wasn't going down well in Lancashire, which was often seen as a stronghold of professionalism –with clubs like Bolton Wanderers and Preston North End facing accusations of ignoring FA rules. Meetings were held which failed to come to an agreement between the clubs and the FA. Prompting some Lancashire clubs to establish the British Football Association in October 1884. No Merseyside clubs attended the meeting.

After further deliberation and additional votes, the matter was finally resolved in July 1885, when professionalism was officially legalised, and the FA amended its rules accordingly.

Everton were quick to adapt to the new era of professional football, signing their first paid players in 1885: George Dobson from Bolton Wanderers, Alec Dick from Kilmarnock, and George Farmer from Oswestry. All were paid double the wages of the club's amateur players and in general, a footballer in 1885, earned a weekly wage of about £1 compared to the ordinary workers 13 Shillings a week. Chester became the first regional club to compete in the Welsh Cup in 1885 but were defeated 3–0 by Crewe Britannia.

In May 1885, the Wigan area established the Wigan and District Football Association, open to any Association club within an eight-mile radius. With the expansion of the game across Lancashire, the Lancashire FA introduced a Junior Challenge Cup for the 1885–86 season. This competition allowed newer clubs to compete without facing established senior teams. Winners and runners-up would qualify for the Senior Cup the following season. Five teams from the wider region participated: Earlestown Wanderers (home to Gillibrand Rangers), Southport Wanderers (home to Brinscall), Liverpool Stanley (home to Chipping), Liverpool St Mary's (home to Great Lever Wanderers), and Southport High Park (away to Lostock Hall).

In September 1885, Belmont Football Club changed its name to Tranmere Rovers. Shortly thereafter, the Tranmere Rovers board-initiated steps to form a Wirral Football Association. At a follow-up meeting in late November 1885, nine clubs agreed to establish the new body: Birkenhead Argyle, Birkenhead Rovers, Bromborough Pool, Highfield Park, New Ferry, Seacombe St Paul's, Tranmere, Tranmere Rovers, and Wallasey Village. The Wirral FA quickly created a Challenge Cup, now known as the Wirral Senior Cup, first contested in January 1886.

Early matches that were disputed often went to the local FAs to rule on the matter or sometimes by the clubs themselves tried to get a result in bizarre ways. In 1886, Wigan saw a match thwart with difficulties, complaints and various enquiries and suspensions. Three clubs claimed their right to play in the final, Wigan, Hindley and Westhoughton, two finals were actually played for just one cup with the first final seeing two teams playing against one and the Wigan Chief Constable having to step in to sort things out, before the first Wigan Association Cup was won by Hindley 1–0 against Westhoughton. Earlier that year the Birkenhead News were corrected by the Secretary of the Liverpool & District Amateur Football Association about the result of the Amateur Medal Competition. The newspaper had mentioned St Benedict's were runners-up to Oakfield Rovers but the Secretary told them that St Benedict's had in fact won. The result was actually Oakfield Rovers 2 St Benedict's 0 which prompted the newspaper to surmise that St Benedict's had won on appeal.

In November 1886, the *Cricket and Football Field* newspaper commented on a friendly between Stanley and Everton, stating: 'The Liverpool Association clubs are unfortunately all situated in one locality, that is, the Liverpool clubs of any calibre. Bootle, Everton, and Stanley are located in the north end of the big seaport and hence it is but natural that all three cannot be liberally supported.' This observation would prove prescient in the coming years.

Chester played their first FA Cup match in November 1886, defeating Goldenhill 4–0. However, they were disqualified for fielding four unregistered players. Everton entered the FA Cup for the first time in the 1886/87 season and were drawn to face Rangers. The match was awarded to Rangers after Everton fielded an ineligible player; it was instead played as a friendly.

That same season, the Cheshire Amateur Cup began life as the Cheshire Junior Cup. The Liverpool FA followed suit in 1887, launching its own Junior Cup alongside what was now termed the Senior Cup. The first Liverpool and District Junior Cup Final took place in May 1887 at Anfield, with Earlestown defeating Southport 1–0.

The Mersey Railway linked Liverpool and Birkenhead in 1886, enhancing transport across the region. In 1887, Lever Brothers purchased 56 acres of marshland on the Wirral Peninsula to construct a village for workers producing its Sunlight soap. The first sod was cut in March 1888 for the Port Sunlight factory in Bromborough Pool. Initially occupying 13,000 square yards (around 3 acres), the factory expanded to cover over 160,000 square yards (approximately 4 acres), and the adjacent village also began development.

Everton's first proper FA Cup match occurred in the 1887/88 season against Bolton Wanderers. The initial game, played away, ended in a 1–0 defeat for Everton but was voided due to Bolton fielding an unregistered player. Two replays followed, both drawn (2–2 and 1–1), before Everton won the fourth match 2–1. They then lost 6–0 to Preston North End. However, the FA later voided the Bolton match entirely, ruling that Everton had fielded seven professional players registered as amateurs. As a result, Everton were suspended and Bolton reinstated, ultimately facing Preston North End.

By the end of the 1880s, several key rule changes had helped unify the game. England, Ireland, Scotland, and Wales had all agreed to adopt the same rules, bringing consistency to the sport. However, clubs across the country were grappling with financial sustainability. Up until this point, most clubs generated income through friendly matches, but with the increasing number of local and national cup competitions, these friendlies were often cancelled or postponed. Between 1872 and 1888, cup competitions had grown from just the FA Cup to nine prominent tournaments, not including numerous local and charity competitions.

Additionally, friendly fixtures were often manipulated, with clubs arranging matches they were sure to win, resulting in dull, one-sided affairs. Spectators were losing interest, and as one writer observed, fans would not pay to see their team lose. The professional game, still in its infancy, was beginning to struggle.

The solution came in March 1888 from William McGregor, Chairman of Aston Villa. McGregor, along with others, had long argued that the existing system was unsustainable. Inspired perhaps by the newly established Cricket County Championship in 1887, he proposed the idea of a structured league. He wrote to Blackburn Rovers, Bolton Wanderers, Preston North End, Stoke and West Bromwich Albion, suggesting that ten to twelve leading clubs create a schedule of home and away fixtures. He proposed calling the organisation the Association Football Union.

On 23 March 1888, representatives of these clubs met at Anderton's Hotel in London. They were joined by Accrington, Burnley, Derby County, Notts County, Wolverhampton Wanderers and Everton. At this meeting, seven key principles were agreed:

1. A league or union of twelve clubs would be formed.
2. Matches would be played home and away.
3. Games would follow the FA Cup rules.
4. Clubs would field full-strength teams in every match.
5. Gate receipts would be shared, though admission prices would be set by the home club.
6. League positions would be determined by an average of wins, draws, and losses, not goals scored.
7. The four lowest-ranked clubs would retire but remain eligible for re-election.

Fixture arrangements were made among the clubs themselves. The league was formally named 'The Football League' at a subsequent meeting on 17 April 1888 at the Royal Hotel in Manchester. The founding members were: Everton, Accrington, Aston Villa, Blackburn Rovers, Bolton Wanderers, Burnley, Derby County, Notts County, Preston North End, Stoke, West Bromwich Albion, and Wolverhampton Wanderers.

The *Cricket and Football Field* newspaper ran the headline: 'The Twelve New Apostles – Another League Proclaimed'. The article opened with: '... No more debts. Both ends to meet. Plain Sailing. These, we suppose, are the ideas of the promoters of the New Football League.' The same publication commented on the inclusion of Everton and the exclusion of Bootle. It argued that Everton had earned their place through financial backing and performance but noted that Bootle had reason to feel aggrieved. Clubs such as Notts County, Derby County, Stoke, and Burnley had been admitted ahead of them, despite Bootle's comparable stature. This perceived injustice sparked swift action.

The following week, representatives from clubs that had been excluded from the Football League met at the Royal Hotel in Crewe. There, they formed a rival competition: The Football Combination. Bootle took a leading role, with Mr Sloan of Bootle appointed chairman. It was proposed that the league would consist of no more than twenty clubs. Bob Sloan was one of the original first team members of Bootle Football Club when it first formed who became its Captain.

Initial member clubs included Walsall Town Swifts, Derby Midland, Notts Rangers, Burslem Port Vale, Leek, Small Heath Alliance, Crewe Alexandra, Newton Heath, Witton, Blackburn Olympic, Long Eaton Rangers, and, via correspondence, Derby Junction, Halliwell, and Mitchell St George's. By June, the fixture list had been finalised with some alterations. Bootle's first opponents in the new league included Port Vale, Northwich Victoria, Leek, Mitchell St George's, Walsall Town Swifts, Newton Heath, Long Eaton Rangers, Derby Junction, Notts Rangers, Blackburn Olympic, Darwen, Halliwell, Lincoln City, Gainsborough Trinity, Derby Midland, and Crewe Alexandra.

THE TEAMS THAT WERE FORMED IN THE EARLY YEARS OF MERSEYSIDE FOOTBALL 1878–1888

AINTREE CHURCH

Formed in 1885/1886, Aintree Church played at Walton Rugby Club's old ground at Rice Lane, Walton, with their changing room in the Queen Anne Hotel. Their colours were Oxford Blue and Cardinal Red. In 1887/8, they beat Prescot 3–1 in the First Liverpool Junior Cup Final. They had started to establish themselves as one of the area's best teams.

BIRKENHEAD AFC

Formed in August 1879, just before the start of the 1879/80 season, Birkenhead Association played their first match in October 1879, a game between a Captain's XI and a Vice Captain's XI. They played friendlies against Wrexham and Bootle St John's, and in a match against Everton United Churches on Stanley Park in November 1879, they won 2–0. They also beat Everton 2–0, a match where the *Athletic News* noted that Everton played roughly. In March 1880, they played St Domingo, who were still using that name despite recent changes. In the 1881 Cheshire Challenge Cup (Now Cheshire Senior Cup), they reached the final but forfeited the replay to Northwich Victoria after a 1–1 draw. By 1885, as reported by the *Birkenhead News*, the club had 'died a natural death' at the start of the 1885/86 season.

BIRKENHEAD ARGYLE

Formed around 1881, likely from a cricket club of the same name, Birkenhead Argyle quickly became one of the strongest teams on the Wirral Peninsula. When Birkenhead Association folded in 1885, Argyle took over their old ground at Heathcock's Field. The club disappeared sometime in late 1888.

BIRKENHEAD ROVERS

Formed in September 1884, Birkenhead Rovers initially played friendly matches and had their ground on Borough Road next to the tram terminus. Due to growing numbers, the club formed a second team in 1885. However, by 1887 they had disbanded. The *Birkenhead News* marked their closure with a poetic epitaph titled 'Epitaph to a Deceased Club':

'They tried to rise in the game of football, they tried very hard but went to the wall,

They tried the Wirral Cup to gain, with might and main, but all in vain;

They tried two teams at once to run, but found in this more work than fun;

They tried at last to merely exist, but from future annals their name will be missed.'

BOOTLE

Formed in 1879, Bootle was originally known as St John's Bootle and was founded by Rev. Alfred Keely, a Nottingham-born clergyman and Cambridge graduate. Ordained in Chester in 1877, he became vicar of St John's, Bootle, in 1879. Likely influenced by Cambridge's role in codifying the first rules of Association football in 1848, Keely sought to establish the game in a rugby-dominated area. He located a pitch at Bibby's Lane (formerly Bootle Marsh) and formed a team that played their first match against Birkenhead in December 1879, winning 3–1. At a meeting in July 1880, under Keely's presidency, the club adopted the name Bootle Football Club.

They beat Everton twice in February 1880 (2–0 and 4–0) and their second team provided the opposition for Southport's first match in November 1881. Bootle became the first Merseyside team to play in the FA Cup, beating Blackburn Law 2–1 in November 1881. In 1883, they won the first Liverpool Challenge Cup (now the Liverpool Senior Cup), beating Liverpool Ramblers 3–1 at the Liverpool College ground in Fairfield. They reached the final again in 1886 but lost 1–0 to Everton. In 1887, Bootle made history by signing Scottish international Andrew Watson, widely regarded as the first Black international footballer.

BROMBOROUGH POOL

Formed in 1884, Bromborough Pool was the works team of Messrs. Price and Co., a candle manufacturing firm. In their first season, they won the

Liverpool FA Medal Competition. They became the inaugural winners of the Wirral Senior Cup in 1885/86, defeating Claughton 3–1. They lost the title in 1886/87 to Birkenhead Argyle but reclaimed it in 1887/88 by beating Seacombe.

BURSCOUGH (1880)

Formed in 1880, Burscough played their first match against Croston in December of that year, winning 3–0 at home. They played on a recreational field owned by James Walker. Their first competitive game came in the Liverpool and District Amateur Cup in November 1884, where they beat Tranmere (possibly one of Tranmere's final matches). Burscough continued to play friendlies and cup matches until the advent of league football.

CAMBRIAN

Formed in September 1884 by a group of gentlemen connected with the Fitzclarence Street Welsh Church, Cambrian's first known match was a 6–2 defeat to Everton at Stanley Park. By April 1885, the club had played 20 matches, winning 13, drawing 3, and losing 4. They had been offered a ground in the Everton area by a Welsh supporter and had formed a second team, which lost only two games all season. The club made a name for itself in Wales after touring there in December 1884 and Easter 1885. Although they were again offered a ground in April 1885, in Balmoral Road, the £50 required for repairs proved a barrier. Reports of the club fade after early 1886, suggesting it folded around that time.

CHESTER

Formed in 1885 at a meeting at the Crown Vaults, Lower Bridge Street, Chester FC was born from the amalgamation of Chester Rovers (formed in 1880) and a team made up of King's School alumni, the Old King's Scholars. They played on the Chester Rovers pitch at Faulkner Street, Hoole. Their first game was a 1–0 win against Earlestown on 12 September 1885, followed by a sobering 10–0 loss to Oswestry. *The Sporting Life* newspaper referred to the team as 'Chester City' – almost a century before the name would become official. In the 1887–88 season, Chester were beaten 9–0 by Crewe Alexandra in their first Cheshire Senior Cup Final, held at Alexandra Cricket Ground, Crewe, in front of 4,000 spectators.

CHESTER ROVERS

Formed in 1880 by a cricket team of the same name, Chester Rovers initially played on the Roodee before moving to Faulkner Street in Hoole. Most of the Chester Football Association team that took part in a charity match in 1884 came from this club, and its players formed the foundation of the newly formed Chester FC in 1885. Chester Rovers faded soon after.

EARLESTOWN

Formed around 1880, Earlestown initially played at the back of the Swan Hotel on Newton Common. They wore white shirts with a black Maltese cross. Nicknamed the Waggoners – due to the local wagon works – Earlestown faced Everton in the 1884 Liverpool and District Cup Final (Now Liverpool Senior Cup), losing 1–0 at Bootle's ground in front of over 2,000 spectators. They also played in the first official match at Anfield in September 1884. In 1885, they defeated Everton 1–0 in the Liverpool and District Cup Final, despite a controversial disallowed goal for Everton. A crowd of 2,000 attended the opening of their new ground, The Mesnes, on Good Friday 1885, where they drew 1–1 with Darwen. The Mesnes featured a 7 ft high wooden perimeter fence and separate entrances for officials and spectators. Earlestown later won the 1886/87 Wigan District Challenge Cup, beating Haydock 3–1. In May 1887 what may have been an Earlestown Youth side lost 1–0 to Southport Youth side in what was called the Liverpool and District Junior Cup Final held at Anfield.

EARLESTOWN WANDERERS

Formed around 1883, Wanderers lost the Earlestown and District Junior Cup Final 4–2 to Newton St Peter's in the 1883–84 season. They also played on Newton Common.

EVERTON

In 1879, players from St Domingo's and Everton United Churches came together, prompting the club's name change to Everton in November of that year. Their first recorded match was on 23 December 1879, beating St Peter's of Everton 6–0. In 1883/84, they moved from Stanley Park to a field at Priory Road, owned by William Cruitt, where they won the Liverpool and District Cup by beating Earlestown 1–0. That arrangement lasted only a season before Everton moved to Anfield for the 1884/85 season, their first match there also being against Earlestown.

In 1885-86, Everton won the Liverpool and District Cup again by beating Bootle 1–0 and then defeated Oakfield Rovers 3–0 in the 1886/87 final. In 1887/88, they were found guilty of falsely registering seven professionals as amateurs in an FA Cup match against Bolton Wanderers. As a result, the Liverpool FA, led by Robert Lythgoe, removed the District Cup from Everton's Sandon Hotel trophy cabinet. Despite controversy, by the 1888–89 season, Everton joined eleven other clubs in forming the Football League. Between 1891 and 1914 they won the Liverpool Senior Cup on fifteen occasions and the Liverpool Senior Cup in 1894 and 1897.

EVERTON UNITED CHURCHES

Formed around 1879, this team played one of their earliest matches on 15 November 1879 against Birkenhead at Stanley Park, losing 2–0. It's believed players from Everton United Churches merged with St Domingo's to form Everton FC that same month. The club continued briefly before fading in the early 1880s.

GARSTON

In May 1887, a Garston team was formed by Mr T. Evans to promote Association football in the area. Comprising players from Everton, St Benedict's, Stanley, and the Gymnasium clubs, they played their first recorded match against Bootle, losing 1–0. Garston soon began appearing regularly in match fixtures.

HAYDOCK TEMPERANCE / HAYDOCK ASSOCIATION

Formed around 1879 as Haydock Temperance Football Club, their main rival in the first season was Garswood Recreation. A notable match ended in a 1–0 win for Haydock (and six corners), bringing joy to fans after six previous encounters between the clubs had ended in draws. In August 1885, the club changed its name to Haydock Association Football Club. They played on a ground behind the Waggon and Horses Hotel in Haydock and lost the 1886/87 Wigan District Challenge Cup final 3–1 to Earlestown.

HOYLAKE

Formed in 1887, Hoylake lost their first match 3–1 to West Kirby. Their ground was at the Royal Hotel in Hoylake.

KIRKDALE

Formed around 1884 (possibly earlier), Kirkdale may have played both rugby and association football. They initially used Stanley Park as their home ground before relocating to Goodison Road.

LIVERPOOL AFC

Formed in late 1879 or early 1880, they initially played at Newsham Park, later moving to Sandown Lane, Wavertree. The club faded by the mid-1880s, and it would be some time before another club used only the city's name.

LIVERPOOL CASUALS (1876)

Formed briefly in 1876 to play against Manchester University in what may have been the area's first published football match. The team consisted of Liverpool University students. The captain was J.W. Twist; other players included G.F. Bateson, H.G. Bateson, J.E. Gilbert, A. Hassall, H. Miller, W.S. Patterson, J.E. Stock, J.H. Stock, T.K. Twist, and A.H. Walker. No goalkeeper was mentioned. This team likely had no connection with the Liverpool Casuals formed in 1893.

LIVERPOOL GYMNASIUM

Founded in 1882 as a rugby club, based at Myrtle Street in Liverpool.

LIVERPOOL RAMBLERS

Formed at a meeting of Old Etonians and Old Harrovians in February 1882 at the offices of James Bateson Sons and Co. Students returning from public schools initially played friendlies. Their first ground was behind the Aigburth Hotel, and players changed at the nearby cricket ground. The team wore orange and blue – the colours of one of Eton's houses.

By June 1882, they were members of the Lancashire FA. In the inaugural Liverpool and District Challenge Cup final now the Senior Cup on 14 April 1883, the Ramblers lost 3–1 to Bootle at the College Grounds, Fairfield. In December 1887, they became the first Merseyside team to tour Ireland, losing 6–4 to Dublin University.

LIVERPOOL STANLEY

Often called 'Stanley,' the club, at one stage backed by Sir Alexander Bicket a well know figure in the shipping world, formed around 1882 and quickly became one of Liverpool's leading sides. They reached the first round of the 1887/88 FA Cup, losing 5–1 to Halliwell at their Walton Stiles ground in front of 2,000 spectators.

LIVERPOOL BLUES / LIVERPOOL POLICE

In 1886, as the Liverpool Police expanded – including the addition of a Mounted Division – they established an Athletic Club. Shortly beforehand, a police football team named the Liverpool Blues played Stanley on 7 December 1885

OAKFIELD ROVERS

Formed around 1883, Oakfield Rovers were described in 1885 by the *Liverpool Mercury* as a club of young players showing much promise. They validated this assessment by winning the 1885/86 Amateur Medal Competition final 2–0 against St Benedict's. However, the result was overturned after a successful appeal by St Benedict's to the Liverpool & District Amateur Football Association. Rovers reached the

Liverpool and District Cup final (later the Liverpool Senior Cup) in 1886/87, losing 3–0 to Everton. In 1887, they moved to a new ground at Orrell Park.

ORMSKIRK (1883)

Formed in 1883, Ormskirk played one of their first matches away at Burscough in October of that year, losing 6–1. They used the local cricket pitch for their games.

PRESCOT

Formed in 1884 when Prescot Cricket Club decided to play football during the winter on a sloping field next to their pitch on Warrington Road. Their first match was a 3–0 loss to St Thomas' second team from St Helens. Prescot reached the Liverpool Junior Cup Final in May 1888 but lost 3–1 to Aintree Church.

RUNCORN AFC``

Formed in 1886, Runcorn lost their first match in September of that year, 4–0 at home to Barnton Rovers.

SKELMERSDALE UNITED

Originally formed in 1882 as Skelmersdale Young Rovers by teachers from the Skelmersdale Wesleyan Day School. The name changed to Skelmersdale Wesleyans before local religious objections led to the adoption of Skelmersdale United. They played friendlies and local cup matches until league football arrived.

SOUTHPORT (1881)

Southport's first match as an Association side was on 12 November 1881 against Bootle's second team. They mostly played friendlies but entered the FA Cup in 1882, losing to Liverpool Ramblers. They won the first two Southport Charity Cups, beating Southport Crescent 5–0 (1884–85) and Southport Wanderers 4–0 (1885–86). In June 1886, the club amalgamated with Southport Wanderers. In May 1887, they lost 1–0 to Earlestown in the first Liverpool and District Junior Cup Final at Anfield. Later that year, they merged with Southport Recreation to form Southport Central.

SOUTHPORT CENTRAL
Formed in 1888 through the amalgamation of Southport FC and Southport Recreation. Their first match was against the Police Athletic Football Club and ended in a heavy 7–0 defeat. Southport Central was officially founded at a meeting held on 22 June 1888 at Victoria Galleries, marking the start of the club's modern history.

SOUTHPORT HIGH PARK
Formed around 1884 and based at Devonshire Road. While mostly playing friendlies, they also played notable cup matches against Everton (1884–85 Liverpool Senior Cup Quarter-Final) and Blackburn Olympic (1886–87). High Park declined to join the Southport Central amalgamation, giving rise to one of Southport's first football rivalries.

SOUTHPORT RECREATION
Originally founded as Christ Church Football Club, the team changed its name to Southport Recreation in 1886. For the 1886–87 season, they used a tent in club colours near their pitch. In 1888, they merged with Southport FC to form Southport Central.

SOUTHPORT WANDERERS
Formed in 1884, Southport Wanderers lost one of their earliest matches 20–0 to Halliwell. They played mostly friendlies. merged with Southport Recreation to form Southport Central in 1888.

ST. DOMINGO
Formed in 1878 by members of a cricket team connected to the St Domingo Methodist Church in Everton. Likely playing informal matches on Stanley Park at first, the club joined with Everton United Churches and others in 1879 to form Everton Football Club. The St Domingo name and cricket

team continued to exist, mostly playing friendlies, into the mid-1880s and was revived in later decades.

ST. HELENS AFC

Formed around 1886/87. Although reports mention the St Helens Cricket and Football Club forming an Association team in 1885, it seems the football club was properly established a year or two later. They played mostly friendly matches.

ST. PETER'S (EVERTON)

Formed around 1879, they were Everton's first recorded opponents under their new name, playing in December 1879. Mostly a side that played friendlies, they entered the first Liverpool Senior Cup in 1883, then called the Liverpool Challenge Cup. They played on Stanley Park and occasionally at Walton Stiles and were also known as St Peter's Athletic Club and Liverpool St Peter's.

TOXTETH WANDERERS

Formed around 1881, they joined the Liverpool and District FA in 1883 and played in the inaugural Liverpool and District Challenge Cup (later the Liverpool Senior Cup) in January 1883, losing 8–1 to Liverpool Ramblers.

TRANMERE ROVERS (1881)

Formed in 1881 by the Tranmere Rovers Cricket Club. Their first game was a 3–1 win over Anfield in October 1881. In March 1882, the name was changed to Tranmere at a cricket club meeting. The team faded from existence by the mid-1880s. A Tranmere Old Boys side was later formed, likely comprising former players.

TRANMERE ROVERS

Formed in 1884 by players from Belmont and Lyndhurst Wanderers cricket clubs. Initially named Belmont Football Club, they played their first recorded match in November 1884, winning 4–0 against Brunswick Rovers 2nd XI at Borough Road, Birkenhead. The Tranmere Rovers name was adopted in September 1885 during a meeting at the 'Santy' cocoa rooms behind Birkenhead Market. Their first match under the new name was a 1–1 draw with Birkenhead Argyle at Heathcock's Field.

WALLASEY VILLAGE

Formed in 1884, the club's ground was located at the local Working Men's Institute. They played mostly friendlies and local cup matches in their early years.

WARRINGTON ASSOCIATION

Founded at a meeting held in September 1884 at the Temperance Rooms on Sankey Street, Warrington's first Association football club was formed with their pitch located in Latchford. Their opening match, possibly against Northwich Victoria, ended in a heavy 12–0 defeat. Their second match was a 5–0 loss to Chester St Oswald's.

WEST KIRBY

Formed around 1886, West Kirby mainly played friendlies and charity cup matches. The *Birkenhead News* reported on a notable moonlight football match in November 1886, which West Kirby won 5–2 against Riversdale. The paper remarked it was the first time it had heard of a football club existing in West Kirby.

WHISTON

Formed in 1885, Whiston played their first match on 1 February 1885, drawing 1–1 with Sankey Sugar Works. They played on a pitch opposite the Green Dragon Pub on Warrington Road. In April 1887, Whiston reached the final of the Liverpool Amateur FA Medal Competition but lost 4–2 to Bootle Wanderers at Anfield.

WIGAN ASSOCIATION (1883)

Founded in 1883 by the Wigan Cricket Club after a meeting at the Royal Hotel on Standishgate. Adverts were placed in local newspapers to recruit players. Initially, matches were played on the cricket ground until a move to Greenough Street. In August 1884, the club amalgamated with the rugby-playing Wigan Parish Church Club. In 1888, the club cancelled its entire fixture list due to being unable to secure a ground and fell into decline, disappearing a few years later.

WHERE THEY PLAYED

Football on Merseyside in the late 1870s and early 1880s was rudimentary. Matches began on Liverpool's public parks such as Stanley Park and Newsham Park, where teams would send their fastest players to race in and claim the best patch of grass once the park gates were opened. Thomas Keates, in his 1928 history of Everton, recalled, 'There was neither dressing room nor shelter for the players or spectators, and no 'gate'. From the Park Lodge in Mill Lane, they carried the goal posts, fixed them in sockets, and whitened the lines.'

Will Eyton, a regular contributor to the *Liverpool Echo*'s 'Old Times and Timers' column, noted in 1935: 'Harry Williams was buried at Anfield Cemetery this week. He was one of the original six forwards playing for the Everton club in 1878 in Stanley Park, and dressing in the small sweet shop under the terrace in Walton Lane. They paid a subscription of 2s 6d per season.'

When Chester began playing at Faulkner Street in Hoole in 1885, players had to change at the Ermine Hotel – a fair distance from the pitch, which was initially roped off before being upgraded with wire.

A 1930 issue of the *Liverpool Football Echo* featured a letter from a fan in California recalling Bootle's early enclosure: 'I remember one season, when we played the Druids from Ruabon, Everton and Queen's Park Strollers from Glasgow, on three successive Saturdays. The players and members turned out each Friday evening to enclose the ground with the aid of poles and canvas to try and get a 'gate'.'

Securing an audience ('gate') was difficult. In October 1880, *Athletic News* published a letter from a reader new to Liverpool: 'I only came to Liverpool, from one of the large centres of the Association game, in the middle of last football season, and was much surprised to find the game so very little known here.' He had located three clubs: Liverpool (Newsham Park), Everton (Stanley Park), and Bootle (Bibby's Lane). Matches were advertised only via Messrs. Richardson & Co's fixture list in Lord Street. Messrs. Richardson & Co. were a cutler's that had provided a trophy for local cricket teams to play for in a Charity tournament. They advertised a list of local football matches at their shop at 36 Lord Street, Liverpool.

At Chester's Faulkner Street ground, spectators would watch from neighbouring houses to avoid paying. In 1885, Liverpool Parks officials proposed banning football in public parks. The *Echo* printed the letter, prompting a wave of complaints. One, from 'Left Half of Lower Breck Road,' defended Stanley Park: 'Stanley Park for many years has been the ground on which many of our principal clubs have been born .... The Everton, Cambrian and Stanley clubs grew here.' The committee relented and allocated football-specific areas: Sefton Park (40 acres), Newsham Park (30), Stanley Park (22), and all of Sheil Park.

Even after securing pitches, teams faced obstacles. When Earlestown acquired The Mesnes in Newton-le-Willows in 1885, they erected fencing that partially encroached on a public footpath. A local legal challenge ensued but was dismissed in court.

By 1888, football enclosures on Merseyside had developed enough that the Football Association selected Anfield to host a semi-final between Preston North End and Crewe Alexandra. Everton had by then installed a grandstand seating 200–300 spectators. However, public concerns remained. A letter from 'a ratepayer' to the *Liverpool Mercury* in 1888 complained about Stanley Park: 'From Mill Lane northwards to Walton Lane the grass has now wholly disappeared.... The numerous clubs digging holes for the insertion of sockets and claiming almost an absolute right to the ground, rudely ordering off any person who happens to intrude.'

AIGBURTH CRICKET GROUND

Opened in 1881 by Liverpool Cricket Club and owned by the Liverpool and South West Lancashire Cricket Ground Co. Ltd., the ground hosted the

England v Ireland international football match in February 1883. England won 7–0. Admission: one shilling.

ANFIELD, LIVERPOOL

Opened in 1884 by Everton FC. Previously, the club played on Stanley Park (1879–1883) and Priory Road. Initially staff and players alike fixed boards and railings around the Anfield pitch. A small stand was erected on the East side of the pitch, for officials, club members, affluent fans and the press. Other fans would stand on grassy sods to watch the game.

By 1885–86, both Everton and visiting teams still changed at the Sandon Pub across the road. A correspondent to *Athletic News* requested that Everton provide a proper pavilion due to the presence of alcohol at the pub. In 1887, the ground received upgrades: boarded goal railings, a roof on the grandstand and reserved side, and a gallery at the Anfield Road end. Capacity: 12,000.

CATTLE MARKET INN, STANLEY, OLD SWAN ROAD

A multi-use sports site since the 1840s, including wrestling, bowling, polo, baseball, and cricket. The first women's football match on Merseyside took place here in June 1881.

FAIRFIELD ATHLETIC GROUNDS

Established by Liverpool College Athletics Club in 1885, the grounds hosted an invitational football tournament in June 1886 featuring local teams. Everton defeated Bootle after extra time in the final.

FAULKNER STREET, HOOLE

Chester Rovers used this ground from 1884. Initially basic with rope and hoardings, it later featured a covered stand with tiered seating.

MESNES, NEWTON-LE-WILLOWS

Originally common land used since 1816. Earlestown's first match there, a 1–1 draw with Darwen, was played on Good Friday, April 1885, in front of 2,000 spectators. The pitch measured 120x80 yards and was enclosed with a 7 ft wooden fence.

POLICE ATHLETIC GROUNDS, SHIEL ROAD

Purchased in 1886 by the Liverpool Police Athletic Club at the corner of Shiel Road and Kensington. The first match, Liverpool Police v Royal Liver, ended in a 4–4 draw.

PRIORY ROAD, ANFIELD

Everton's home for the 1883–84 season. The ground had railings, some seats, a small grandstand and a dressing room. Sources differ on its exact location: possibly accessed from Arkles Lane or across from it near Stanley Park's southeast corner. The pitch had a noticeable slope. By the end of the only season at Priory Road, Everton had enclosed the pitch, added some seats, a small stand and a dressing area.

THE ROODEE, CHESTER

Primarily a horse racing venue since 1539, with a historic Shrove Tuesday football match played in 1533. A grandstand was added in 1817. Football began there around 1881.

SPORTS GROUND, SUSSEX ROAD, SOUTHPORT

Opened in 1882 by the Southport Athletic Society at a cost of £400. Southport Central played their first season here. The Grandstand was 195ft long and could seat around 2,000.

STANLEY PARK, WALTON

Acquired in 1866, designed by Birkenhead Park's Mr Kemp. Opened in May 1870. Football was played here by the mid-1870s. Everton's first pitch was in the park's southeast corner, opposite John Houlding's Stanley House.

TRANMERE'S FIRST GROUNDS: STEELE'S FIELD AND RAVENSHAW'S FIELD

Steele's Field (1884–1887) was criticised for poor drainage and slope. In 1887, Tranmere Rovers moved to Ravenshaw's Field, previously used by Tranmere Rugby Club. The ground was fenced, fitted with a cinder path, and had new dressing rooms.

WALTON STILES, WALTON

Opened by Stanley FC in 1885 on the site of Skirving's plant nursery. Aston Villa were one of the visitors that opened the ground in April 1885 the score was 3–3. Darwen had played the opening match the day before. While its exact location is debated, it was near Goodison Road and Spellow Lane. In 1886, Liverpool Stanley enclosed the pitch with boarding and railings. The 1886 Liverpool Senior Cup final was held here. An *Athletic News* report from December 1887 remarked on the area's transformation from a scenic walk to a rugged playground.

WOODSIDE ENCLOSURE, BIRKENHEAD

Originally Heathcock's Field, located opposite the *Birkenhead News* offices. Used by Birkenhead Association and Birkenhead Argyle. Everton played a charity match here in 1884. In 1888, it was taken over by the 1st Cheshire Engineer Volunteers and became a formal football venue.

CHAPTER 2

1888 - 1915

IN JUNE 1888, THE FIRST FIXTURES FOR THE NEW FOOTBALL LEAGUE WERE drawn up. Everton were given two home games to start their first League campaign. The final match was scheduled at home to Preston North End in mid-January, but unarranged fixtures against Wolverhampton Wanderers and West Bromwich Albion extended Everton's first League season to mid-March. One early effect of the new Football League came in October1888 with a change to the FA Cup format, with the early rounds now becoming known as qualifying rounds and League clubs believed they would enter at what was now called the First Round Proper. Everton however had been drawn to play Ulster FC but decided to scratch from the competition to concentrate on League football.

The Football Combination was slower to publish its fixtures. In mid-September 1888, *Athletic News* lamented the delay: 'Can anyone tell me which are and which are not Combination matches? It seems to me that the very object for which the Combination was formed is totally defeated by the neglect to send to the press a complete list of fixtures similar to those of the Football League.' No winner was determined for the Combination at the end of the season.

With the fixtures drawn, Everton's first League game at Anfield on 8 September 1888 saw them beat Accrington 2–1 in front of 12,000 spectators. Everton had been accepted into the Football League largely on the strength of their home attendance figures. They finished their first League season in eighth place but topped the attendance table with an average of 7,400 spectators.

Bootle's first Combination match was a 4–1 away win against Crewe Alexandra. However, as Combination fixtures were not obligatory, the league was derided by the press as ineffective. In November 1888, the Football League introduced a standard points system: two points for a win, one for a draw and none for a defeat, with tied teams separated by goal average (goals scored divided by goals conceded).

At the end of the 1888/89 season, Bootle applied to join the Football League. Under League rules, the bottom four clubs – Burnley, Derby, Notts County and Stoke – were subject to re-election and new applicants could also stand. At the election on 3 May 1889, Bootle competed with Birmingham St. George's, Wednesday, Sunderland and Newton Heath. None of the new applicants were successful; Bootle received only two votes.

A week later, the unsuccessful clubs met at the Douglas Hotel in Manchester. They abandoned the failing Football Combination and formed a new league – initially the Northern Counties League. By June 1889, the renamed Football Alliance finalised its rules at a meeting at the Midland Hotel in Derby. Bootle were founder members alongside Birmingham St. George's, Crewe Alexandra, Darwen, Grimsby Town, Long Eaton Rangers, Newton Heath, Nottingham Forest, Sheffield Wednesday, Small Heath, Sunderland Albion and Walsall Town Swifts. Bootle's first game in the new Alliance was an away defeat to The Wednesday (now Sheffield Wednesday). Bootle finished as runners-up to Sheffield Wednesday.

In May 1889, the Lancashire Junior League was formed at the Raven Hotel in Wallgate, Wigan. It featured twelve teams, including Churchtown and Southport High Park from the local area. Soon after, the more senior Lancashire League was formed, with Southport Central joining Blackpool, Blackburn Park Road, Bury, Fleetwood Rangers, Heywood FC, Heywood Central, Higher Walton, Hyde, FC Nelson, Oswaldtwistle Rovers and Rossendale as founder members.

The West Lancashire League became part of this structure, with teams including Aigburth Vale, Aintree Church, Bootle Athletic, Bootle Wanderers, Bromborough Pool, Liverpool Police Athletic, Prescot,

Stanley, St. Helens, Tranmere Rovers, West Manchester and Whiston, plus Ashton-in-Makerfield. Stanley were crowned champions and Aintree Church were runners-up.

In April 1890, the Liverpool and District Minor Cup Final – likely the region's first youth cup final – saw Lansdowne defeat Coburg 5-1. The cup and medals were presented by John Houlding. The competition had been organised by the newly formed Liverpool and District Minor Football Association. Thirty-two teams entered the tournament, including: Aigburth Vale Juniors, Aintree Juniors, Ashfield, Balliol Athletic, Belford Rovers, Bootle Commercial, Bootle Albion, Bromborough Pool Juniors, Christ Church Bootle, Dresdale, Everton Rovers, Free Wanderers, Garston Copper Works Reserves, Liverpool Primrose Rovers, Melrose, Melville, Newby Swifts, New Ferry Guild, Orrell Rovers, Prescot, St. Phillips, St. Polycarp's, Speke Junction Juniors, Southport Albion, Temple Rovers, Sutton Victoria, Tranmere Rangers Reserves, Warbreak College, Wentworth, West Seacombe and finalists Coburg and Lansdowne.

In 1890, the Football League introduced a standard minimum admission charge of 6d for League matches. Before this, admission fees had ranged from 3d to 6d across the country. Bootle set their prices at 4d for Alliance matches and 6d for games against Football League opponents.

Another Midlands/North West league – the (new) Combination – was formed at meetings in May and June 1890 at the Brunswick Hotel in Manchester. This was distinct from the earlier Football Combination of 1888. Chester joined founder members Ardwick, Burton Swifts, Denton, Derby St. Luke's, Gorton Villa, Hyde, Leek, Macclesfield, Northwich Victoria, Stafford County and Witton Blackburn. Ardwick did not begin the season and were replaced by Wrexham. The league ended its first season (1890/91) with nine clubs after Derby St. Luke's, Stafford County and Witton Blackburn withdrew.

By August 1890, the Lancashire Junior League had been renamed the Lancashire Alliance, with Southport High Park and Churchtown as local founder members.

Liverpool finally got its own league in 1890. The organisers had hoped to call it the West Lancashire League, but as the name was already in use, the matter was settled by arbitration. In August 1890, it was officially named the Liverpool and District League. The teams included Aigburth Vale, Aintree Church, Bromborough Pool, Bootle Athletic, Bootle Wanderers, Everton Athletic, Kirkdale, Prescot, Tranmere Rovers and Whiston, along with Ashton-in-Makerfield.

At the same time, an Amateur League was also created, featuring Walton Village, Garston Copper Works, 5th Irish, Edge Hill, Skelmersdale Rec., Fazakerley Signal Works Rec., 1st Cheshire Engineers, Waterloo, Walton Breck, Hoylake, L & NW and Skelmersdale United. Edge Hill were crowned the first champions.

Goal nets were invented by Liverpool civil engineer John Alexander Brodie in 1889 and trialled on Stanley Park, in a match between the Old Etonians and Old Harrovians at the Liverpool Ramblers Club in October 1890. It is also possible they were first trialled in Bolton in 1890, with their first competitive use occurring in a match between Bolton Wanderers and Nottingham Forest on New Year's Day 1891. The nets were also used in the North v South (England trials) match in Nottingham on 12 January 1891, a game watched by senior figures from the Football League. The North won 3–0, with Everton's Fred Geary scoring the opening goal after 15 minutes.

That 1890/91 season, Everton won the Football League title for the first time, having finished runners-up the season before. On Boxing Day 1890, they reclaimed top spot after beating Accrington 3–2 at Anfield and would not relinquish it for the rest of the season. Weather disruptions meant Everton played no league matches in February and it wasn't until 14 March that they secured the title. Travelling to Turf Moor to play Burnley, they knew a draw would be enough to clinch the championship. Despite losing 3–2, Everton were crowned champions after Wolves lost 6–2 to Aston Villa and Preston North End were beaten 3–0 by Sunderland. Everton fans had travelled on special £5 offers and would receive a commemorative medal if the team won the title.

In 1891, the laws of football were updated to resemble the modern game. Referees became the sole arbiters of matches, with umpires becoming linesmen. The penalty kick was introduced – a free kick at goal taken from any point 12 yards out, with no defenders between the ball and the goalkeeper, who was permitted to advance six yards from his goal. Pitches were now required to be between 100 and 200 yards long and 50 to 100 yards wide. The 12-yard and six-yard areas were marked with lines and a 10-yard centre circle was introduced. Home teams were also required to provide white kits for away teams in the event of a colour clash and all clubs had to register their kit colours before the season. The official football season now ran from the beginning of September to the end of April.

May 1891 saw Bootle Athletic crowned champions of the inaugural Liverpool and District League. However, by June 1891, Ashton-in-Makerfield and Tranmere Rovers had left the league – joining Liverpool Police Athletic, who had withdrawn earlier in the season. In February 1891, Everton's directors decided to purchase a set of goal nets after successfully using them in a friendly against Bolton Wanderers at Goodison. Goal nets were available for purchase locally at Mr Barclay's shop at 33 Everton Terrace, priced at £3 15s 6d.

In May 1891, Halliwell Football Club proposed a new Lancashire Combination league to rival the Lancashire League. A meeting at the Spread Eagle Hotel in Manchester was held, with clubs such as North Meols and Skelmersdale United attending. Everton were also invited to apply. The first season (1891/92) featured North Meols, Skelmersdale United and Stanley among nine founder members. Blackburn Rovers Reserves were crowned the first champions, while Halliwell, the league's initiators, dropped out after failing to fulfil fixtures. North Meols finished sixth, Skelmersdale seventh and Stanley eighth.

On 19 September 1891, a Football League meeting at the Royal Hotel in Manchester resolved that all League clubs must use goal nets by 1 November 1891.

Four local clubs – New Brighton Tower, North Meols, Prescot and Tranmere Rovers – played in the FA Cup for the first time in the 1891/92 season. New Brighton won 6–0 away at Middlewich. Tranmere Rovers lost 5–1 at home to Northwich Victoria, North Meols lost 6–0 away to Heywood and Prescot were beaten 7–1 at home by Crewe Alexandra.

To accommodate growing interest in competitions, the Lancashire FA introduced the Lancashire Amateur Cup in 1892, with Aintree Church, Birkdale South End and Liverpool Casuals among the area's first entrants. Aintree Church became the inaugural champions. The same season saw the launch of the Liverpool Shield (now the Intermediate Cup), won by Liverpool Caledonians.

In January 1892, growing tensions arose at Everton between the club's members and President John Houlding. The previous September, Houlding had proposed – and had rejected – a plan to set up a limited company to purchase land from Mr Orrell and himself to secure Anfield. The members preferred to negotiate a rent with Orrell, but Houlding refused. Instead, he set up the Everton Football Club and Athletic Grounds Company with a capital of £15,000. In February, a new ground was proposed at Mere Green in Walton on Goodison Road. George Mahon, leading the dissenting group, famously responded to a taunt – 'You can't find one' – by saying, 'I've got one in my pocket.' A split became inevitable, with the majority leaving to form a new Everton ground at Mere Green.

The FA issued a resolution recognising only the majority of Everton's members. Houlding was forced to choose a new name for his club. In April 1892, following legal actions and Football Association intervention, Everton formally resolved its dispute with Houlding, who founded Liverpool Football Club.

Also in April 1892, the Football League agreed to form a Second Division. At a meeting in Sunderland the following month, clubs were elected to each division. While the League absorbed many Football Alliance clubs, new applicants like Liverpool Caledonians and Liverpool FC were rejected, with the latter joining the Lancashire League instead.

The League also passed a rule prohibiting its members from playing clubs within four miles of their ground unless those clubs were in the League. In May 1892, the FA banned players and officials from betting on football matches.

In June 1892, the Wirral and District League was formed at the Crooked Billet pub in Lower Tranmere. Founding clubs included Hoylake, West Kirby, Melrose, Ellesmere Port, Seacombe St Paul's, West Seacombe, LNW Locomotives, Port Sunlight, New Ferry Guild and Tranmere Rovers Reserves. Ellesmere Port became the league's first champions.

For the 1892/93 season, the Liverpool Senior Cup was limited to eight teams: Liverpool, Aigburth Vale, Aintree Church, Bootle, Chester, Earlestown, Everton and Southport Central.

Liverpool's first game in the Lancashire League was an 8–0 home win against Higher Walton at the start of September 1892, played in front of 200 spectators. That same month, Liverpool played their first Lancashire Senior Challenge Cup tie, defeating Southport Central 2–0 at Anfield before 4,000 spectators. Liverpool's first FA Cup match came in October 1892, a 4–0 away win at Nantwich.

During this first season in which both Everton and Liverpool were active, season ticket pricing differed slightly between the clubs. Liverpool priced their season tickets at 7s 6d for the uncovered stands, 15s for the covered stand and 21s for the reserved stand. Everton priced their season tickets at 10s 6d for the uncovered stands, matching Liverpool for the other two areas.

On Friday 17 February 1893, Liverpool Schoolboys played their first match at Anfield. The team was selected from the twenty-four clubs that made up the Elementary Schools Football Association and played Churchtown Schoolboys. Schools football in Liverpool introduced the Edwards-Moss Challenge Cup for Schools to play for. The first winners being Aigburth National School.

At the end of the 1892/93 season, Everton reached their first FA Cup Final, held in late March 1893 at Fallowfield, Manchester. Everton were favourites going into the match against Wolverhampton Wanderers. Admission prices ranged from 3s for the uncovered stands to 10s 6d for covered reserved seats. A third-class return rail ticket from Liverpool Exchange to Manchester cost 2s 6d. Though the ground had a 40,000 capacity, estimates suggest that as many as 60,000 attended.

Prior to the final, a schoolboys' match took place, during which parts of the crowd broke down barriers and surged to the touchline. Spectators who attempted to improve their view were met with hostility; one man was reportedly struck by a thrown stake. The encroachment affected play, particularly for the Everton wingers who struggled with the limited space. After a goalless first half, a goalkeeping error by Williams handed the match to Wolverhampton. Everton lodged a protest after wrongly believing that Wolves had done the same, but eventually withdrew it and the cup was awarded to Wolverhampton Wanderers.

To formalise promotion and relegation between divisions, the Football League introduced 'Test Matches' at the end of the 1892/93 season. These matches, precursors to modern play-offs, saw the winners typically offered First Division membership.

Liverpool, having won the Lancashire League, entered the Second Division for the 1893/94 season. They began with a 2–0 away win at Middlesbrough in September 1893. For Bootle, however, the 1892/93 season proved their last in the Football League. Despite finishing eighth in the Second Division, their average attendance of 1,775 paled in comparison to Everton's 13,100. Proximity to Everton made survival untenable. Bootle's player wages alone amounted to £1,520 for the season. Although Derby County attempted to introduce a maximum wage in September 1893, the proposal failed. The issue would return in future years.

The Liverpool & District League expanded ahead of the 1893/94 season, introducing a Second Division. This division was occasionally called the Liverpool Junior League, while the First Division was sometimes referred to as the Liverpool Senior League. Teams at the meeting included Aigburth Vale Reserves, Aintree Church Reserves, Birkdale South-End, Bootle Athletic Reserves, Coburg, Kirkdale, Liverpool Recreation, L& NW Recreation, Southport Old Boys, Walton Breck, Whiston Reserves and White Star Wanderers Reserves.

Also in 1893, the Wirral Junior League was established with the following clubs: L& NW Loco Swifts, Egremont Rovers, Melrose Third,

St. John's, Alderney, St. Michael's, Silverdale, Post Office Reserves, Seacombe Swifts, New Brighton Boys' Brigade, Seacombe Victoria and St. Paul's Recreation Reserves. Melrose Third finished as inaugural champions.

The FA Amateur Cup was launched in 1893, with R.E. Lythgoe of Liverpool involved in both purchasing the trophy and serving on its organising subcommittee.

In December 1893, a meeting in Bolton established the County Palatine League. Everton and Liverpool joined other Lancashire clubs including Preston North End, Burnley, Blackburn Rovers, Darwen, Bolton Wanderers, Newton Heath, Accrington and Bury. Designed to fill blank weekends caused by FA Cup ties, the league was split into Northern and Eastern sections. Everton, who had proposed the league, placed Liverpool in the opposite section, following objections to their participation. Nonetheless, Liverpool were admitted after Bolton and Newton Heath threatened to withdraw without them. Bury were crowned the first champions after beating Burnley in a playoff.

Everton withdrew from the County Palatine League the following season and Accrington were also asked to leave. Only eight clubs continued and the league faded out soon after.

Everton became the region's first club to win the Lancashire Senior Challenge Cup in 1893/94, beating Bolton Wanderers 2–1 in the final. That same season, Everton and Liverpool both competed in the Football League for the first time. Everton's First Division matches drew an average crowd of 13,100, while Liverpool, in the Second Division, averaged 5,075.

At the end of April 1894, Liverpool defeated Newton Heath 2–0 in a test match and were invited to join the First Division for the 1894/95 season. Aintree Church won the Lancashire Amateur Cup that year.

Also in 1894, the Chester and District FA was formed along with the Chester and District Junior Football League. Its inaugural members were Buckley Swifts, Buckley Victoria, Chester Rovers, Hoole Rovers, L& NW Novices, Queen Street PSA, Rossett, Saltney Victoria, Saughall, St. John's, St. Mary's and St. Oswald's Athletic.

On 3 November 1894, Everton's 4–4 away draw at Small Heath made headlines. A goal credited to Alex Latta had, by his own admission, missed the target. Small Heath appealed, but the FA upheld the result, speculating that the ball passed through a hole in the net. The FA ruled that referees must inspect goal nets before each match. As the *Preston Herald* noted on 21 November 1894: 'Which smacks something of the famous verdict of 'Not guilty, but don't do it again."

In June 1895, women's football returned to Merseyside with a match involving the British Ladies' Football Club (BLFC), a London-based club fronted by the intriguingly named Nettie Honeyball. The club, made up of two touring teams – North and South – was managed by Honeyball's brother. The North's goalkeeper, known as Mrs Graham, was Helen Matthews, a Scot living in Bootle. She and her sister worked as sports journalists for local Lancashire newspapers under the pseudonym Lothian Lasses. Their brother had been a reserve for Preston North End and later played for Liverpool South End.

The match was held at the Athletic Grounds in Stanley before around 1,000 spectators. By October 1895, the BLFC had split, with Matthews forming her own team, Mrs Graham's XI. Both teams eventually folded – Honeyball's venture collapsed during a tour of Exeter when finances dried up, leaving players dependent on a local poor box for fare back to Liverpool, while Matthews' outfit dissolved within two years.

That year also saw Edward Arthur Morton, founder of the Old Xaverians, propose a new amateur league to provide competitive matches. Many clubs lacked fixed grounds, prompting the adoption of the Italian term I Zingari (meaning 'Gypsies') as the league's name. Founding members included Allerton Park, Birkdale, Blundellsands, the 2nd Volunteer Battalion King's Liverpool Regiment, Formby Rangers, Old Xaverians, Liverpool University College, Wallasey Village, Walton and Woolton. The league mandated full amateurism – clubs could only provide shirts and players covered all other expenses. Initially no league table was published, but newspaper pressure led the secretary to supply standings.

Professional football wasn't the only sport making inroads to people's hearts and minds. On 29 August 1895, twenty-one Rugby Football Union clubs from Lancashire and Yorkshire met at the George Hotel in Huddersfield to form the Northern Rugby Football Union (later the Rugby League). Among them were Runcorn, St Helens, Warrington, Widnes and Wigan. The league began play on 7 September.

At the start of September 1895, royal assent was granted to expand Liverpool's city boundaries to include Walton, Wavertree, Toxteth Park and West Derby, ending a fifteen-year campaign.

The 1895/96 season saw the merger of the struggling Wirral and District League and Liverpool and District League into the Liverpool, Wirral and District League. The Wirral clubs also contested their own competition within the league, winning the Pyke Cup, a trophy donated by local jeweller William Pyke in 1893. By 1900, the Pyke Cup had become a knockout tournament.

In June 1897, the St Helens and District Football League was formed. Founding members included St Helens Amateurs, St Helens St Paul's, Thatto Heath Athletic, Thatto Heath Reserve, Windle Start, Prescot Juniors, Holt Temperance, Peasley Cross, Peasley Cross Temperance and Parr Amateurs. Prescot Juniors (later Prescot Reserves) won the inaugural title. The trophy was donated by Lever Brothers.

Across the Mersey, July 1896 saw the formation of the New Brighton Tower and Recreation Co. Ltd., which purchased 20 acres of Rock Point Estate with plans to erect a 550-foot tower and develop surrounding attractions including a football ground and cycle track. By early 1897, the company formed a football club – New Brighton Tower FC – with ambitions of joining the Football League.

In August 1897, the club's application to join the FA was initially deferred pending inquiry but was later approved. The FA required membership in both the Cheshire FA and Liverpool & District FA. After an initial setback regarding contract validity, the club quickly reissued player contracts. The team was heavily backed and quickly assembled a competitive squad.

In April 1897, Everton reached their second FA Cup Final, facing Aston Villa at Crystal Palace before 65,000 fans. Again tipped as favourites, Everton fell short. Villa opened the scoring after 20 minutes; Everton equalised through Bell and briefly led before Villa made it 2–2 from a corner. Devey's headed goal before half-time secured Villa's 3–2 win. Despite their disappointment, Everton did claim the Lancashire Senior Challenge Cup that season, beating Manchester City 2–0.

That year also saw the formation of the Birkenhead and Liverpool District Thursday Amateur League, with Liverpool's John McKenna serving as first president. The league would undergo many changes in the years to follow. In August 1897, the Cheshire FA discontinued the Cheshire Junior Cup and launched the Cheshire Amateur Cup.

Local and amateur leagues continued to proliferate. For the 1897/98 season, a Second Division of the I Zingari League was established. Founding clubs included Allerton Park Reserves, Blundellsands Reserves, Formby Rangers Reserves, Liverpool Leek, Marine, Old Xaverians Reserves, St Agnes Reserves and Trinity Bible Class. Trinity Bible Class emerged as the division's first champions. In October 1897, Southport reconstituted a previously lapsed local league. The first division included Banks Reserves, Blowick United, Burscough Reserves, Chapel Street, Forest Rovers, High Park Reserves, L& Y Locos, Longton, Marshside Blues, New Lane, North Meols, Olympic and Southbank. A second division featured Blowick United Reserves, Laurel Rovers, North Meols Reserves, St Paul's, Southbank Reserves, Southport United, Trafalgar, Trinity Old Boys and Working Lads.

Two days before Christmas Day 1897, representatives of twenty League clubs, including Everton, met in Liverpool to discuss forming a players' union. The meeting was chaired by Everton forward John Bell, with trustees including Liverpool's Lord Mayor John Houlding and Preston North End Chairman Mr. Ord. Former Everton player Cameron was appointed Secretary and Treasurer. The union proposed rules to establish a widows and orphans fund, a permanent disablement fund and to serve as an intermediary in contract disputes. Named the National Football Players'

Union, it was based in Liverpool. However, the FA refused to recognise it unless two specific rules were amended. By summer 1898, with Bell and Cameron both having left Everton and moved out of Liverpool and other members losing interest, the union began to falter. Though it managed to survive until 1901, it never gained serious recognition from the Football Association or Football League and ultimately dissolved.

In May 1898, the Football League adopted the Fletcher system for scheduling fixtures, a method used until 1919. Teams were assigned numbers and paired off using a fixture matrix; clubs then met to agree dates and resolve scheduling conflicts. Under this system, Liverpool opened the 1898/99 season at home to Sheffield Wednesday, while Everton travelled to Sheffield United – both matches played on 3 September 1898. The first derby of the season took place at Goodison Park on 24 September.

That year also saw the end of the Test Match system for promotion and relegation. Instead, the top two Second Division teams were automatically promoted, replacing the bottom two from the First Division.

Another Merseyside team in New Brighton Tower joined the Football League Second Division for the 1898/99 season and finished fifth. That season, Aston Villa surpassed Everton in average attendance for the first time, drawing 20,675 compared to Everton's 14,525 and Liverpool's 13,975. New Brighton Tower averaged 3,350.

Elsewhere on the Wirral, Rock Ferry – seen as Tranmere Rovers' rising rival – folded in February 1899 despite being Combination runners-up in 1896/97. Their sudden collapse led to upheaval at Tranmere. Players urged club president James McGaul to move the team to Rock Ferry's vacated Bedford Park ground. When he refused, all but one of Tranmere's players departed and formed a new club, Birkenhead FC, in July 1899. Tranmere withdrew from the Combination a week before the season began and joined the Lancashire Alliance. McGaul scrambled to assemble a new squad for the 1899/1900 campaign.

By the end of 1899, another amateur-focused league – the Lancashire Amateur League – was launched, with inaugural members including Old

Xaverians, Blackburn Etrurians, Bolton Amateurs, Melling, Liverpool Leek, Owens College and Liverpool University College. The Old Xaverians, associated with league founder Edward Arthur Morton, were among its key members.

In the same year, the Wirral League and Wirral Junior League merged, forming a two-tier competition: the Senior Division and Junior Division. Meanwhile, in Spain, Barcelona Football Club was formed. The club's blue and red colours were suggested by Frederic Arthur Witty, a former pupil of Merchant Taylors' School in Crosby.

By the turn of the century, the Liverpool FA boasted 166 affiliated teams, each averaging fifteen players. Local leagues included: I Zingari League, Bootle and District Amateur League, Lancashire Amateur League, Prince's Park and District League, Anfield Junior League, Aigburth and District Combination, Liverpool and District Combination, North Liverpool and District League, West Derby and District League, Kirkdale and District Junior League, Liverpool and District Amateur Alliance, Wirral and District League, Southport and District Amateur League, Oakfield Junior League and the Warrington and District League.

Despite football's growth, Liverpool's social conditions remained bleak. In September 1900, the *Leeds Times* reported on trams costing a penny to most destinations and 5d from Aigburth to Fazakerley. Yet the article described ragged children, drunken women and poorly dressed men amid a proliferation of dramshops and pawnshops. Civic buildings impressed, but poverty remained widespread. In contrast, Southport, viewed as a Liverpool suburb, offered clean air and elegant parks like Hesketh Park and its marine lake.

Liverpool ended the 1899/1900 season with four consecutive wins, finishing tenth. Their form carried into 1900/01, starting with a 3–0 win over Blackburn Rovers at Anfield before 20,000 fans. They then defeated Stoke 2–1 and thrashed West Bromwich Albion 5–0. A 1–1 draw in the derby at Goodison Park saw them drop from second to fourth. With a quarter of the season remaining, Nottingham Forest led the table, followed by Sunderland, Bury and Newcastle United. Liverpool, then in eighth, defeated Sunderland 1–0 at Roker Park for the first time. Bury emerged as Forest's main challenger.

On 4 March 1901, Sunderland beat Bury 4–1 to go level on points with Nottingham Forest. Liverpool sat seventh, six points adrift. But Liverpool dropped just three points in a ten-match unbeaten run to set up a dramatic final day. They needed a draw against bottom club West Bromwich Albion to clinch the title and secured it with a goal from Johnny Walker. It was Liverpool's first league championship.

That season, New Brighton Tower FC finished fourth in the Second Division but disbanded shortly afterwards. In 1901, the Liverpool Senior Cup added two new clubs: Hudson's and Wrexham. The ten participants were Birkenhead, Everton, Hudson's, Liverpool, Melrose, Southport Central, Tranmere Rovers, Warrington, White Star Wanderers and Wrexham.

In 1901, the Football League introduced a maximum wage of £4 per week. Liverpool's John McKenna opposed the measure. Meanwhile, in March 1902, newspapers reported proposals to formalise the penalty area. The FA's International Committee approved a new layout that June: an 18-yard box, 44 yards wide, replacing the goal-line penalty arc. The six-yard goal area was also codified, forming a box 20 yards wide to protect goalkeepers from charging.

Also in 1902, the FA banned its members from playing against or renting grounds to women's teams. The move, aimed at distancing the association from the commercial exploits of defunct teams like the BLFC, followed rumours of a revival in women's football. The FA also extended its betting ban to include spectators and club grounds.

In 1902, Liverpool's city boundaries expanded once more to include Aigburth, Cressington and Grassendale. A year later, in 1903, the city's railway made a significant leap with the electrification of the line between Liverpool Central and Hamilton Square in Birkenhead, offering trains every three minutes and an eleven-minute journey time.

During the 1902/03 season, Chester entered the Welsh Cup in the third round but lost 2–0 at home to Wrexham. That same year saw major changes in regional competitions. The Lancashire League folded and its remaining clubs helped form a new Second Division of the Lancashire Combination. In an effort to avoid offending clubs from the defunct league, the divisions were named Division A and Division B. As *Athletic News* put it on 1 June 1903: 'Under a system which would not give offence to some clubs, particularly those of the Lancashire League. A second division was rather obnoxious and yet there must be one premier body.' Six clubs from Division A would be relegated each season without option, replaced by six from Division B.

From 1903 onward, the Liverpool FA decided that the Liverpool Senior Cup would be contested solely between Everton and Liverpool. Liverpool were relegated at the end of the 1903/04 season, while Southport lost the Lancashire Senior Cup. Earlestown won the Lancashire Junior Cup (also known as the Lancashire Challenge Trophy).

A new iteration of the Liverpool and District League launched in 1904 with clubs including Sutton Commercial, Garston Gasworks, Garston Church, Diamond Match Works, Prescot Wire Works, Garston North End, Bootle St. James's and Shaws' Ironworks. Garston Gasworks were the first champions, but this version of the league lasted only until 1906.

In June 1904, at a meeting held at the Alexandra Hotel in Liverpool, I Zingari League clubs met to create a new competition for their reserve teams. The clubs present included Balmoral, Bohemians, Bromborough Pool, Clifton Park, Farnworth Old Boys, Kirkdale, Marlborough Old Boys, Marine, Melville, Prenton, Valkyrie, Waterloo and Westminster. The resulting competition, the I Zingari Combination, was won in its first season by Kirkdale.

In the wider world of football FIFA was formed in May 1904 at a meeting in Switzerland of the Football Associations of Belgium, Denmark, France, the Netherlands, Spain represented by Real Madrid, Sweden and Switzerland. Germany accepted membership by telegraph while Austria and Italy gave an undertaking to join at another date. The English FA could not send a representative. However, two years later the English FA had joined FIFA.

That season also saw the formation of a national schoolboys' football competition – the English Schools Shield, now the ESFA Champions Cup.

Liverpool and Birkenhead school teams joined schools from Bury, Bolton, Darwen and Lancaster in the first group. Fourteen more schools completed the other groups. London Schools were crowned the inaugural champions. Meanwhile, Southport Central defeated Everton 2–1 to win the Lancashire Senior Cup.

The 1905/06 season proved historic for both major Merseyside clubs. Liverpool won their second league title; Everton won the FA Cup for the first time.

Liverpool had been promoted from the Second Division at the end of the 1904/05 season, finishing two points ahead of Bolton Wanderers. They began their First Division campaign poorly, losing their first three matches and sitting bottom of the table. Their form turned with a 2–1 away win at Sunderland, followed by a 2–0 home victory against Birmingham. From 21 October, when they beat Nottingham Forest 4–1 at Anfield, Liverpool went on an unbeaten run that carried them to the top of the table on 16 December following a 2–1 win at Sheffield United. Despite a 2–1 loss at Stoke on Boxing Day, they remained a point ahead of Aston Villa.

Liverpool maintained their position through February and March, eventually opening a five-point gap over Preston North End after beating Wolverhampton Wanderers 2–0 away. Despite a late-season defeat to Bolton Wanderers, Preston also lost to Sunderland, confirming Liverpool as champions with matches to spare.

In the FA Cup, Everton began their campaign with a 3–1 home win over West Bromwich Albion. They followed that with victories over Chesterfield (3–0), Bradford (1–0) and Sheffield Wednesday (4–3), all at Goodison Park. In the semi-final, Everton defeated Liverpool 2–0 at Villa Park with goals from Walter Abbott and Harold Hardman. The final, held at Crystal Palace in front of 75,609 spectators, saw Everton face Newcastle United. A disallowed goal by Alex 'Sandy' Young early in the second half did not deter the Blues. In the 77th minute, Young latched onto a cross from Jack Sharp to score the only goal of the match and secure Everton's first FA Cup triumph. Tickets, available to the public as early as January, ranged from 2s 6d to 5s, with companies like OXO offering travel packages with coupons.

The same season also marked the inauguration of the Liverpool Amateur Cup, won by Liverpool Balmoral.

In June 1906, the Cheshire FA approved the renaming of the Wirral League to the West Cheshire League. The new First Division featured thirteen teams: Harrowby, African Royal, Garston North End, Garston Gasworks, New Brighton Tower, Prescot Wireworks, Birkenhead North End, Wallasey Village, Saltney Carriage Works, Egremont Social, Ellesmere Port, Wirral Railway and Ogdens Athletic. The Second Division included eleven clubs: Heswall, West Kirby, Bebington St. Andrews, Hoylake, Lingdale, Wallasey Council, Rock Ferry Athletic, Birkenhead Locomotives, Little Sutton, Liscard Albion and Wallasey Village Reserves.

The Wirral Combination also formed that summer, with founder clubs including Birkenhead United Templars, Elmerswood, Birkenhead Parish Church, Wallasey Amateurs, Birkenhead St. Mary's, Birkenhead Municipal, Bebington St. Andrew's Reserves, Shaftesbury Vics, Birkenhead YMCA, Gilbrook Mission, Wallasey Village Reserves, Wallasey Council Reserves, Bebington Vics Reserves and Rock Ferry St. Paul's.

Another competition, the South Lancashire Amateur Combination, launched for the 1906/07 season with twenty-five clubs across two divisions. Allerton United were the first champions.

That same season, Tranmere Rovers entered the Welsh Cup in the second round, received a bye and were defeated 2–0 by Rhyl in the third round. Earlestown won the Lancashire Junior Cup (Lancashire Challenge Trophy) again.

The Liverpool and District League was revived again for the 1907/08 season, with member clubs including Birkdale, Castner-Kellner, Dominion Stevedores, Halton Villa, Helsby Athletic, Kirkdale, Liverpool Rovers, Liverpool Stanley, Orford Barracks, Prescot Athletic, Skelmersdale Royal, Sutton Commercial and Warrington Albion.

Chester won the Welsh Cup for the first time at the end of the 1907/08 season, defeating Connah's Quay 3–1. Chester would go on to be runners-up in the next two Welsh Cup finals. Birkenhead entered the Welsh Cup for the first time in 1908.

The same season saw the conclusion of the Liverpool Shield competition and the foundation of the Bootle District League. This new league launched with two divisions. The First Division included Bootle Corporation, Bootle St. Matthews, Caradoc Bible Class, Diamond Match Works, Hand-in-Hand, Hawthorne Olympic, Johnson's Dyeworks, Linacre Bible Class, Linacre Gasworks, St. Mary's (Bootle), Sandfield, Sandhurst and Seaforth PSA. The Second Division included Balliol Road PSA, Bootle Celtic, Bedford Old Boys, Bootle St. James, Bootle Victoria, Claythey Athletic, Cyprus, Globe Wireworks, Gonville, Hawthorne, St. Matthew's Reserves, St. Sylvester's and Seaforth PSA Reserves. Diamond Match Works were crowned the inaugural champions.

First played in 1906/07, the Lancashire Junior Shield (also known as the Lancashire Amateur Shield) saw Skelmersdale United become the first local club to win it in the 1907/08 season.

The 1907/08 season saw disappointment for St Helens Town, Southport Central whose applications to join a proposed Third Division of the Football League were rendered moot when the League opted against the expansion.

Northern Nomads joined eight other clubs to form the Amateur Alliance in 1908/09. Other members included Grimsby Rangers Amateurs, Hull Kingston Amateurs, Leeds St. Martin's, Leicester Nomads, Rotherham Amateurs, Sheffield Club, Sheffield Grasshoppers and South Nottingham. Northern Nomads won the league, clinching the title on the final day with two home victories: 2–1 against Leeds St. Martin's at 3:00 p.m. and 2–1 against Grimsby Rangers at 4:30 p.m.

In May 1909, following a commission prompted by the Cheshire FA and Wirral District FA, the FA ordered the Liverpool and District FA to change its name to the Liverpool County FA. The inquiry, which had begun two years earlier, focused on jurisdictional overlaps, particularly with clubs on the Wirral. Mr. Edward Case of the Wirral FA noted at the time that 'Liverpool at that time covered 16 miles on the Cheshire side of the Mersey.' As a result, the Liverpool County FA's jurisdiction was reduced by two miles in Lancashire and eight miles in Cheshire. Despite this, only one club was lost from its rolls.

Some Wirral clubs – including African Royal, Garston Gasworks, Garston North End, Widnes Wesley Guild and Prescot Wireworks – left the Wirral FA to join the newly reconstituted Liverpool County FA. Accusations of 'threats and inducements' were investigated and dismissed.

The Liverpool County Combination was created soon afterward, with inaugural members including African Royal, Buckley Engineers, Earlestown St. John's, Everton 'A', Garston Gasworks, Garston North End, Liverpool 'A', Old Xaverians, Prescot Wire Works, Skelmersdale United, St. Helens Recreation Reserves and Widnes Wesley Guild. Everton donated a silver challenge trophy in memory of their late chairman George Mahon. The Liverpool County Combination Cup's first draw was held in August 1909.

Garston Gasworks were the inaugural champions of the Liverpool County Combination in 1909/10, finishing nine points ahead of Prescot Wire Works. The following season, the Combination added a Second Division featuring Banks Road, Widnes County Reserves, Sliding, Linacre Gasworks, Prescot Swifts, Aughton Wanderers, South Liverpool Reserves, Welling, Calder & Mersey Athletic, Garston Gasworks Reserves and Frodsham. Banks Road were the first Second Division winners, finishing one point ahead of Widnes County Reserves. Skelmersdale United won the First Division.

The Central League was formed in 1911 following growing friction within the Lancashire Combination. League clubs, frustrated by the increasing power of non-league members, opted to secede. At a meeting in Blackpool's Winter Gardens, eleven League clubs, including Everton and Liverpool, decided to break away. In June, at a meeting in Manchester's Mosley Hotel, they reviewed twelve applications to join their new league. Southport Central, with thirteen votes, was the only local club accepted. Tranmere Rovers, St. Helens Recreation and South Liverpool were unsuccessful.

The I Zingari Challenge Cup was inaugurated in 1911/12 as a knockout competition for league members. That same season, the Second Division of the Liverpool County Combination was disbanded.

Birkenhead Schools reached the final of the English Schools Shield in 1911/12, but lost 3–1 to West Ham Schools after taking an early lead in the match at Leytonstone.

The 1911/12 season again saw disappointment for St Helens Town, Southport Central and this time South Liverpool whose applications to join a proposed Third Division of the Football League were rendered moot when the League opted against the expansion.

For 1912/13, the I Zingari League created the I Zingari Alliance as a feeder division. The inaugural clubs included Birkenhead Institute Old Boys, Civil Service, Elton, Liverpool Rifles, Liverpool St Andrew's, Liverpool Scottish (10th Battalion, King's Liverpool Regiment), North Western, Royal Liver, White Star Athletic and the 5th King's Liverpool Regiment. Liverpool Scottish were the first champions.

In 1913/14, Liverpool reached their first FA Cup Final. Their run included wins over Barnsley (after a replay), Gillingham, West Ham United (also after a replay), Queens Park Rangers and Aston Villa in the semi-final. The final, held at Crystal Palace, ended in a 1–0 defeat to Burnley.

The Liverpool Senior Cup was revised that season to include four teams: Everton, Liverpool, Tranmere Rovers and New Brighton.

The 1914/15 season opened brightly for Everton, with victories over Tottenham Hotspur and Newcastle United placing them briefly top of the table. By mid-season they had dropped to third but remained in title contention. Everton eventually claimed the league championship, although the competition was suspended at the end of the season due to the outbreak of the First World War.

By the time League football was suspended due to the outbreak of the First World War in 1915, nearly sixty local football leagues had been established across Merseyside and the surrounding region. Alongside the more prominent competitions such as the I Zingari League and I Zingari Alliance, a vast network of area-based leagues had emerged. These included the Birkenhead and District Minor Combination, Ormskirk and District Amateur League, South Lancashire League, Wavertree and

District League, West Cheshire League, Wirral Combination, Bootle League, Kirkdale Junior League, Widnes and District League, Wigan and District League, Birkenhead Alliance, Liverpool County Combination, Newsham Park League and the Liverpool Central Combination.

Many of these leagues were rooted in geographical identity, but by the early twentieth century, they increasingly reflected religious, institutional and commercial affiliations. Church-based leagues became especially prevalent, with examples such as the Liverpool Free Church League, Church of England League, Liverpool Sunday School Union League, Wirral Church League and the United Church Football League all organising regular competition among faith-affiliated teams.

Promotional leagues also became a growing feature of the local football landscape. One such example was the Suggs League, founded by Frank Sugg, a former Everton footballer and Lancashire cricketer who operated a sports outfitter in Liverpool. Sugg also established the Invinsa League in both Liverpool and Wirral, named after the footballs he manufactured and sold. Another ex-player, Jack Sharp, launched a league in conjunction with his own sports retail business. The Wirral Thursday League, meanwhile, was created by local shopkeepers to cater for midweek fixtures.

This shift towards niche, purpose-driven leagues – whether religious, commercial, or occupational – foreshadowed the exponential growth of amateur football structures in Merseyside after the First World War.

THE TEAMS THAT PLAYED BETWEEN 1889 AND 1915

AFRICAN ROYAL

Formed in 1904, African Royal began as the works team of African Oil Mills Ltd., a company that made its fortune importing palm oil from West Africa. They first played at Grafton Street in Toxteth and entered the Sefton Park & District League in 1904/05, winning the title at their first attempt. They progressed to the Liverpool & District Amateur League for the 1905/06 season and then joined the West Cheshire League in 1906/07, finishing as runners-up to Harrowby by just one point. That same season, they also won the Liverpool Shield, defeating Tranmere Rovers 1–0.

In 1907/08, they dominated the league, losing just one game and finishing eight points ahead of Garston Gasworks. They also shared the Pyke Cup with Harrowby. In 1908/09, African Royal retained the league title, edging Birkenhead North End by two points. They also won the Wirral Senior Cup in both those seasons. The following season, they became founder members of the Liverpool County Combination and finished ninth out of twelve teams. In December 1910, the club changed its name to South Liverpool.

AINTREE CHURCH

Aintree Church were founder members and runners-up to Stanley in the first season of the West Lancashire League in 1889/90. They also helped found the Liverpool and District League in 1890/91, finishing fifth and improved to second place the following year. In 1892/93, they won the Liverpool Shield, defeating Earlestown in a replay. They also claimed the inaugural Lancashire Amateur Cup in 1893/94, beating Lytham 3–0 and narrowly missed out on the Liverpool and District League title, finishing one point behind White Star Wanderers. They were runners-up in the Lancashire Amateur Cup again in 1894/95, losing to Liverpool Police and came third in the league. Following the dissolution of the Liverpool and Wirral District League at the end of the 1896/97 season, Aintree Church disbanded.

ASHTON-IN-MAKERFIELD

Ashton-in-Makerfield were founder members of the West Lancashire League in 1889/90, finishing mid-table in its inaugural season. In 1890/91, they finished one point behind Bootle Athletic in the Liverpool and District League. They joined the Lancashire Alliance for the 1891/92 season, finishing sixth and were runners-up to Earlestown in 1895/96. In 1896/97, they played in the Wigan Challenge Cup Final against Hindley but left the league at the end of the 1897/98 season.

BALMORAL

Formed around 1901 in Walton, Balmoral played at Cherry Lane. They joined the I Zingari Third Division in 1901/02, winning it by a single point over Melrose's third team. After a fourth-place finish in the Second Division in 1902/03, they won the division the following year, edging Melrose by two points. They struggled in the First Division in 1904/05, finishing fourth from bottom.

Balmoral won the inaugural Liverpool Amateur Cup in 1905/06. Between 1907 and 1909, they made three Easter tours to Belgium, competing in the Beerschot Toernooi (see European chapter). They were I Zingari League runners-up in 1907/08 and champions in 1909/10, finishing seven points clear of Bromborough Pool. In 1910/11, they were runners-up again, just one point behind Marine. In 1909, they hosted Dutch side Quick FC at Goodison Park. They lost 3–2 to Orrell in the 1913/14 Liverpool Amateur Cup Final.

BIRKENHEAD

Birkenhead FC was formed in 1899 by former Tranmere Rovers players following a dispute with club officials. They joined The Combination in 1899/1900, finishing fifth. They won the Wirral Senior Cup in 1901/02 and 1902/03, defeating Melrose 4–0 and 2–0 respectively. In 1903/04, they won the Combination and again claimed the Wirral Senior Cup, finishing five points clear of Chester. In 1905/06, they were runners-up to Port Sunlight in the same competition.

The club disbanded in December 1909 and withdrew from The Combination after failing to complete its fixture list. *The Athletic News* (27

December 1909) cited frequent relocations due to building developments as a major factor. It stressed, however, that football interest on the Wirral was not waning – Tranmere Rovers, it noted, now stood alone in The Combination.

BIRKENHEAD NORTH END

Founded in 1900, Birkenhead North End won their first match 12–0 against Excelsior. They joined the Wirral League for the 1900/01 season, finishing runners-up in the Second Division. They repeated this in 1901/02 and won the division in 1902/03.

In their debut First Division season (1903/04), they finished fourth and lost the Wirral Junior Cup Final 4–0 to Valkyrie. In 1908/09, they finished second in the West Cheshire League, two points behind African Royal. They lost the 1909/10 Wirral Senior Cup Final 1–0 to Burnell's Ironworks but won the cup the following year by beating Hoylake. The club left the West Cheshire League after the 1911/12 season and folded shortly thereafter.

BOOTLE

Bootle's first Football Combination match was a 4–1 away win at Crewe Alexandra in September 1888, overcoming a first-half deficit. Their Alliance League debut came at Sheffield Wednesday's Olive Grove ground in front of 3,000 fans. A train delay postponed kickoff to 3:55 p.m. and Bootle lost 2–1. Bootle finished as runners-up to Sheffield Wednesday.

In September 1892, Bootle's Football League debut ended in a heavy 7–0 defeat away at Ardwick. However, they won their first home match at Hawthorne Road 2–0 against Sheffield United before 4,000 spectators. They finished in eighth place in their only Football League season.

Despite joining the Second Division with optimism, the club's finances were perilous. At a May 1892 shareholders' meeting, the club revealed debts and proposed forming a limited liability company. Though they completed the 1892/93 season in eighth, another meeting in August 1893 confirmed only £23 of a required £150 had been raised. Just days later, the club was formally wound up. Five decades would pass before a club of the same name was resurrected.

BOOTLE ALBION

Formed around 1887, Bootle Albion began as a youth side. They lost the 1890/91 Liverpool Minor Cup Final 4–0 to Bootle Commercial. In 1901/02, they finished second from bottom in their only season in the Wirral League Third Division.

They joined the Waterloo and District Combination in 1908/09 and won the title in their first season. Moving to the South Lancashire Amateur Combination Second Division in 1909/10, they finished second. They won the First Division title in 1910/11 and also joined the I Zingari League Third Division, finishing third. In 1911/12 they joined the I Zingari League Second Division finishing seventh.

BOOTLE ATHLETIC

A founder member of the West Lancashire League in 1889/90, Bootle Athletic finished ninth in its inaugural season. They won the first Liverpool and District League title in 1890/91, edging Ashton-in-Makerfield by one point. In 1893/94, they lost the Liverpool Shield Final to White Star Wanderers. Athletic continued in the Liverpool and District League until 1894, after which they appear to have folded.

BOOTLE WANDERERS

Bootle Wanderers were founder members of the West Lancashire League in 1889/90, finishing fifth. They also participated in the inaugural Liverpool and District League in 1890/91 but ended the season bottom of the table. The club became defunct in early 1893 and it is likely that it reformed as White Star Wanderers, as the newly named club initially used Wanderers' former ground.

BROMBOROUGH POOL

Bromborough Pool were founder members of the West Lancashire League in 1889/90, finishing second from bottom. That same season they won the Wirral Senior Cup, defeating Tranmere Rovers 3–1. In 1890/91, they joined the newly renamed Liverpool and District League, finishing ninth. In 1893/94, their reserves were runners-up in the Wirral Junior Cup (now the Wirral Amateur Cup), losing 4–1 to Cleaveland Athletic. The following season they finished mid-table in the Wirral & District League and were runners-up in the Wirral Senior Cup, losing 1–0 to L& NW Locos.

They joined the I Zingari League Second Division in 1900/01, with their reserve side joining and winning the Third Division at the first attempt. In 1902/03, they were runners-up in the Second Division and they lost the Wirral Amateur Cup Final 1–0 to Rake Lane PSA. The first team were runners-up in the I Zingari League First Division in 1906/07, one point behind Widnes Wesley Guild. In 1907/08, they won the First Division by five points ahead of Liverpool Balmoral and finished runners-up in the Liverpool Amateur Cup, losing to Old Xaverians.

They were runners-up in the league again in 1908/09, finishing three points behind Valkyrie and losing the Liverpool Amateur Cup Final 3–2 to Merton. In 1909/10, they again finished runners-up – this time seven points behind Liverpool Balmoral – but won the Wirral Amateur Cup with a 1–0 win over Lingdale. In 1910/11, they won the Liverpool Amateur Cup, beating Liverpool University 1–0 and followed that with victory in the inaugural I Zingari Challenge Cup in 1911/12, defeating Beresford Old Boys 2–1. In 1912/13 they claimed the I Zingari Charity Cup and in 1913/14 they were runners-up in both the I Zingari Challenge Cup (losing to Marlborough Old Boys) and the Wirral Amateur Cup (losing to Hoylake Trinity). They beat Cranford in the Cheshire Amateur Cup Final 1–0 in 1913/14.

BURNELL'S IRONWORKS & MERSEY IRONWORKS
Both clubs were formed in 1907. Burnell's Ironworks likely replaced the defunct Ellesmere Port FC. Burnell's won the West Cheshire League Second Division in 1908/09, three points ahead of Bebington St Andrew's. They lifted the Wirral Senior Cup in 1909/10, beating Birkenhead North End and were runners-up to Hoylake in the West Cheshire League First Division in 1910/11. Both clubs dropped out of the league after the 1911/12 season and amalgamated to form a new Ellesmere Port Football Club.

BURSCOUGH (1880)

Burscough entered the Liverpool and District Amateur Combination (later known as the West Lancashire Amateur Combination) in 1895/96. They opened with a 14–0 home win against Liverpool Celtic. After just one season, they joined the Liverpool and District Amateur Alliance in 1896/97 and the following year moved again to the Liverpool and District Amateur League. Struggling for results, the club disbanded after the 1898/99 season.

BURSCOUGH RANGERS

Reformed in 1905, Burscough Rangers played a season of friendlies before joining the Southport and District League Second Division in 1906/07. They opened with a 6–0 win over Birkdale Working Lads and finished third, earning promotion to the First Division. In 1908 they moved from Vicarage Field to Mart Lane, opening the new ground with a 14–0 win over Southport Territorials.

In 1912/13, they joined the Lancashire Football Alliance and finished runners-up, four points behind Golborne United, but beat the same team 4–2 to win the Wigan Challenge Cup. In 1913/14, they claimed the league title, three points ahead of Golborne, but lost to them 1–0 in the Wigan Cup Final. The following season, 1914/15, they joined the Liverpool County Combination, finishing as contentious runners-up to Skelmersdale United, after a key match against them was played without a referee, and also won the Liverpool Challenge Cup.

CADBY HALL

Formed in 1902 as the works team of Lyons Tea Company, Cadby Hall played at Penny Lane and entered the South Lancashire Amateur Combination. They finished as runners-up in 1909/10. In 1910/11 they played in the I Zingari Combination, finishing third. They joined the I Zingari League in 1912/13, finishing runners-up in the Third Division, six points behind Aughton Wanderers. Promoted to the Second Division for 1913/14, they finished fifth.

CHESTER

In 1889/90, Chester beat Northwich Victoria 5–0 to win their first trophy, the Yerburgh Charity Cup. The cup had been donated by Chester MP R.A. Yerburgh, also the club's vice-president. Chester were among the twelve founder members of The Combination league in 1890/91, opening the season with a 1–0 win over Wrexham and finishing third, though three teams had dropped out before the season ended.

Until 1892, Chester had a local rival in St Oswald's, who refused to merge with them and remained amateur. When St Oswald's folded in January 1892, Chester became the city's sole representative. In 1893, Chester entered the Liverpool Senior Cup for the first time but were well beaten by the newly formed Liverpool FC.

Between 1893 and 1895, Chester reached three consecutive Cheshire Senior Cup finals, losing the first two (to Crewe Alexandra and Macclesfield in replays) but finally winning in 1895 with a 2–1 victory over Macclesfield in front of 3,000 fans. Their return to Chester was met by a crowd of 1,000 and a celebratory wagonette parade.

In 1895/96, they reached the Liverpool Senior Cup final after Liverpool defaulted their semi-final, but lost 4–0 to Everton's Combination side. The club's finances became precarious as attendances dropped and wages went unpaid. In 1896/97 they won the Cheshire senior cup v Northwich Vics. In July 1897, players refused to start the new season without changes to the committee. A new board was installed in August and the players agreed to stay. However, further complications arose over rent demands and required changes at Faulkner Street. They relocated to the old Royal Showgrounds at Hoole, but storm damage left only the press box standing.

In 1898/99, Chester could not secure a ground and were expelled from The Combination. They spent two years in limbo until they secured a new home at Whipcord Lane, opening with a match against Everton before 1,000 spectators. They rejoined The Combination in 1901/02 but finished bottom. In 1903/04 and 1904/05 they finished as runners-up and added the Cheshire Senior Cup in 1904 and were runners up the following season.

Further League near-misses followed in 1905/06 and 1906/07, both to Whitchurch. Accusations of match-fixing were unproven. In 1907/08, Chester again finished runners-up, this time to Tranmere Rovers on goal average, but won both the Cheshire Senior Cup and the Welsh Cup, beating Connah's Quay 3–1 in front of 8,000 fans.

In 1908/09, Chester finally won The Combination title, losing only twice and going nineteen games unbeaten. They also won the Chester Senior Cup but lost the Welsh Cup Final to Wrexham. In 1909/10, they finished third in their final Combination season and lost a third Welsh Cup Final in a row to Wrexham.

They joined the Lancashire Combination Second Division in 1910/11, finishing third and gaining promotion. They lost that season's Cheshire Senior Cup Final to Macclesfield. In 1911/12, Chester finished sixth in the First Division.

By 1914/15, the impact of the First World War hit hard. Though top of the league by January 1915, the club faced financial crisis. Players were still being paid peacetime wages and the club couldn't meet the cost. Despite attempts to switch to amateur status and transfer out professionals, the situation was unsustainable. After a 6–0 defeat to Eccles and dismal gate receipts, this iteration of Chester folded in March 1915.

CHURCHTOWN

Churchtown were founder members of the Lancashire Junior League, finishing seventh in the inaugural 1889/90 season. They joined the newly formed Lancashire Football Alliance for the 1890/91 season and ended the campaign in eleventh place. At the close of that season, they amalgamated with Southport High Park to form North Meols Football Club.

CLEVELAND ATHLETIC

Formed in 1893, Cleveland Athletic joined the Second Division of the Wirral League for the 1893/94 season. They won the division in their debut season, finishing two points ahead of Bromborough Pool Reserves and defeated the same side 4–1 in the final of the Wirral Amateur Cup (then called the

Wirral Junior Cup). They retained the Wirral Amateur Cup (then called the Wirral Junior Cup) in 1894/95 with a 4–0 win over Gordon Villa, though they finished second in the league behind LNW Locomotive Reserves. The club disbanded during the 1895/96 season but later reformed, appearing in the Wirral Minor League in 1899/1900, before disbanding again around 1904.

COLLEGIATE OLD BOYS
Originally formed in 1906, Collegiate Old Boys played at the Police Football Ground in Fairfield. After the City Council took control of the school in 1908, the club formally adopted the name Collegiate Old Boys. They joined the I Zingari Third Division, finishing as runners-up to Seafield after a deciding match. In 1909/10, they also competed in the Liverpool and District Amateur Combination and began ground-sharing with Marlborough Old Boys at Deysbrook Lane. At the start of the First World War, the club moved to Hornspit Lane and later to Clubmoor Cricket Ground.

EARLE
Earle FC was formed in 1915 as an under-18 side. Their ground on Lance Lane and Woolton Road opened in 1925. They joined and won the UBC League in their founding year and captured the South Liverpool Amateur Alliance title in 1916/17.

EARLESTOWN
Earlestown were Liverpool Senior Cup runners-up in 1883/84 to Everton 1–0 and again in the 1888/89 Liverpool Senior Cup Final, losing 5–3 to Bootle. They were also runners-up in the 1892/93 Liverpool Shield Final after a replay defeat to Aintree Church. After a third-place finish in the Liverpool and District League, they left in 1894 to join the Lancashire Alliance. They won the Alliance in 1895/96, seven points clear of Ashton-in-Makerfield and again in 1898/99 by two points from Haydock. Earlestown reached the Wigan Challenge Cup Final several times, winning it in 1900/01.

They joined the Lancashire League in 1899/1900 and remained until its dissolution in 1903. Earlestown then became founder members of the Lancashire Combination Second Division, finishing runners-up to Southport Central in 1903/04 and winning the Lancashire Junior Cup. They experienced promotion and relegation over the next few seasons and won another Lancashire Junior Cup in 1906/07. However, by 1911 the club folded. As the *Liverpool Evening Express* noted on 7 October 1911, 'After fighting grimly against great odds for nearly three years, Earlestown have at last been compelled to acknowledge defeat.'

EARLESTOWN ROVERS (ST. JOHN'S)

Originally known as Earlestown St. John's, the club formed around 1908 and began in the Warrington and District League. They joined the Liverpool County Combination in 1909/10, finishing tenth and reaching the inaugural George Mahon Cup Final, where they lost 2–1 to Garston Gas Works. By the 1912/13 season, they had become Earlestown Rovers and defeated Garston Gas Works 3–1 in the same competition. They remained in the Liverpool County Combination until the First World War.

EARLESTOWN WANDERERS

Wanderers appear to have faded from existence after 1888, with the last record of their activities dating to 1892.

EDGE-HILL

Formed in September 1888 by the Edge-Hill Cricket Club, they were founder members of the Liverpool Amateur League in 1890/91. Their ground was located on Picton Road in Wavertree. Edge-Hill were effectively crowned champions by March, having lost only one match. They joined the Liverpool and District League for the 1891/92 season.

ELLESMERE PORT (1890)

Founded in January 1890 by the Ellesmere Port Cricket Club, the football side soon joined the Liverpool Junior Cup and were beaten 8–0 by Edge Hill. They were founder members of the Wirral League in 1892/93, winning it in their debut season. Winning the League again in 1895/96 after being runners up the season before. After fluctuating success in the league, they briefly folded in 1896 but reformed and won the Second Division titles in 1897/98 and 1898/99. They also had Wirral junior cup wins in 1898/99 and 1899/00 and won the Liverpool Junior Cup 1900/01.

Their honours include a Pyke Cup victory in 1903/04 and a league title the same season. However, they were expelled from the league shortly after and returned to the West Cheshire League in 1906/07, finishing eleventh. They disbanded soon after.

ELLESMERE PORT (1912)
This club was formed in 1912 through the amalgamation of Burnell's Ironworks and Mersey Ironworks teams. They competed in the West Cheshire League from the 1912/13 season until the outbreak of the First World War.

EVERTON
Everton nearly pipped the unbeaten Preston North End ('The Invincibles') to the title in 1889/90, finishing second. The following season, 1890/91, they won the league, securing the title at Turf Moor despite a final-day defeat, with rival clubs also losing. Everton fans had travelled in large numbers, drawn by promises of medals if the title was secured.

They reached their first FA Cup Final in 1893 but lost to Wolverhampton Wanderers amid chaotic crowd scenes. In 1897, they lost a second final to Aston Villa. Despite this, Everton enjoyed local success, winning the Lancashire Senior Cup in both 1894 and 1897.

Everton's reserve side, often called 'Everton Combination,' won the Combination League seven times between 1891 and 1899. They briefly joined the Lancashire Combination but soon returned to their dominant run in the Combination.

In 1905/06, Everton finally won the FA Cup, beating Newcastle United 1–0 at Crystal Palace thanks to a goal by Sandy Young. Evertonians travelled en masse, with special trains and promotions (including an OXO-sponsored carriage) bringing 20,000 fans to London.

They returned to the final the following season but lost 2–1 to The Wednesday. In 1909/10 they claimed another Lancashire Senior Cup. In 1914/15, Everton won their second First Division title. Despite dropping down the table early in the season, a strong run in March and April saw them edge out Oldham Athletic by a single point. The league then shut down for the duration of the war.

Everton were also League runners-up in 1894/95 (5 points behind Sunderland), 1901/02 (three points behind Sunderland), 1904/05 (One point behind Newcastle United), 1908/09 (Seven points behind Newcastle United) and 1911/12 (Three points behind Blackburn Rovers). They were also runners up in the Lancashire Senior Cup in 1902/03 and 1904/05. Everton Reserves also won the Central League 1913/14.

FLORENCE ALBION

The Florence Institute for Boys was built in 1889 on Mill Street in Dingle. A team called Florence Institute appeared around 1892, with a Florence Albion cricket team also appearing in local newspapers the following year. The earliest football mention of Florence Albion dates to 1894. By the 1902/03 season, they were playing in the Wavertree and District Junior League. In 1906/07, they joined the Park and District Junior League and by 1908/09 were competing in the Edge Hill and District Alliance Second Division, which they won. They moved to the West Cheshire League Second Division in 1909/10 but finished bottom in what would be their only season there. They joined the I Zingari League Third Division in 1910/11 and won it by three points ahead of Claughton St. Mark's.

FORMBY AND RANGERS

Formed around 1892, Formby and Rangers initially played in the Liverpool Junior League (also known as the Liverpool District League Second Division) during the 1892/93 season. They joined the Liverpool Combination in 1893/94 and became founder members of the I Zingari League in 1895/96, finishing sixth. They dropped into the Second Division for the 1898/99 season, finishing runners-up to Melrose Reserves. The club moved to the

Liverpool Amateur League for 1898/99 and won the title at the end of 1899/1900. Due to financial issues related to travel, they left the league late in the 1900/01 season. They opted not to join a league for 1902/03 but later entered the Southport and District Second Division. Trouble continued and in March 1903, the club was reported to the Lancashire FA for repeated no-shows. On 9 September 1903, at a meeting held in Formby's Three Tuns-lane New Hall, the executive committee voted to disband the club.

GARSTON COPPER WORKS

Formed around 1888, Garston Copper Works were founder members of the first Liverpool Amateur League in 1890/91. They later played in the Liverpool and District Combination during 1892/93 and joined the joint Liverpool, Wirral and District League in 1896/97, winning the league by six points ahead of White Star Wanderers. They returned to the Combination in 1897/98, finishing ninth. A poor season followed in 1898/99 and the club left the league at the end of that campaign.

GARSTON GASWORKS

Formed around 1900, Garston Gasworks played at Bank's Road. They joined the Liverpool Amateur Alliance League and won it in the 1900/01 season. They lost the 1901/02 Liverpool Junior Cup Final to local rivals Garston North End but won it the following year, beating Valkyrie 3–1 at Prenton Park. They joined the Wirral League in 1905/06, winning the title by 12 points and also winning the Pyke Cup with a 6–0 victory over West Kirby. Remaining in the renamed West Cheshire League in 1906/07, they added the Wirral Senior Cup to their list of honours, beating Prescot Wire Works. They reached the final again in 1907/08 but lost to African Royal. And were league runners up to the same team that season.

In 1908/09, they were runners-up in the Wirral Junior Cup (now the Amateur Cup), losing to Bebington St. Andrews. In 1909/10, they became founder members of the Liverpool County Combination, winning the league by nine points and also securing the first George Mahon Cup by beating Earlestown St. John's (Rovers) 2–1. They repeated their league title success in 1912/13 and were runners-up in the George Mahon Cup. In 1913/14, they returned to the West Cheshire League, won it by three points from Wirral Railway and claimed the Pyke Cup with a 1–0 win over Tranmere Rovers Reserves. The Gasworks did not compete in the final pre-war season of 1914/15.

GARSTON NORTH END

Founded around 1895, Garston North End played in the Sefton Park and District League in 1896/97. In 1901/02, they won the Liverpool Junior Cup, beating Garston Gasworks 2–1. The following year, they won the Liverpool Alliance League and built a new pavilion for fans. In 1904/05, they won the Liverpool Junior Cup again, defeating Lively Polly. The club disbanded for a season due to Garston Cricket Club withdrawing use of their pitch. They returned in 1906/07 in the West Cheshire League, finishing third. After leaving in 1908/09, they became founder members of the Liverpool County Combination in 1909/10, finishing fifth. In 1911/12, they won the league by one point over Skelmersdale United and also beat them 3–0 in the George Mahon Cup Final. Garston North End remained in the Combination until the outbreak of the First World War.

GARSTON ROYAL

Founded in 1910 as Byron Street Recs, the club later adopted the name Garston Royal, with 'Royal' referring to the colour of their shirts. Founded by George Simpson, who became club secretary, they played in the Anfield and District League in 1910/11, moved to the Edge Hill and District Alliance in 1911/12 and by 1913/14 were in the Liverpool and District League.

HARROWBY

Formed in 1900 by a group of local youths from Harrowby Road in Egremont, Harrowby began in the Princes Park and District League. They joined the I Zingari First Division in 1902/03, remaining until 1903/04 and finishing no higher than fourth. In 1904/05, they joined the West Cheshire League First Division, finishing fifth and winning the Liverpool Shield by beating Birkenhead. They were runners-up in 1905/06 and champions in 1906/07. They won the 1907/08 Cheshire Amateur Cup Final, beating Northern Nomads 2–1 and shared the Pyke Cup with African Royal. In 1908/09, they were runners-up in the Wirral Senior Cup and winners of the Pyke Cup. In 1909/10, they won the Pyke Cup again but lost the Cheshire Amateur Cup Final to Northern Nomads. Their colours in 1910 were salmon pink. That year, they lost their ground at Wallasey Road and relocated to the Tower Grounds, previously used by New Brighton Tower FC. They were league runners up in 1909/10 and in 1911/12 Harrowby had a highly successful season, winning the Cheshire Amateur Cup (3–0 vs Lostock Gralam), the Wirral Senior Cup (1–0 vs Wallasey Rovers) and the Pyke Cup (4–2 vs Birkenhead North End). They won the league again in 1912/13 and were runners-up in the Cheshire Amateur Cup to Marple Amateurs. In the final league season before World War One, they were top after nineteen games.

HAYDOCK

Haydock joined the Lancashire Alliance for the 1891/92 season, finishing eleventh. They won the league in 1893/94 by three points from Chorley and retained it the following season, again winning by three points, this time over Hindley. A third title came in 1897/98, ahead of St. Helens Recs., although they lost 1–0 to them in the Wigan Challenge Cup. After finishing as runners-up to Earlestown in 1898/99, Haydock left the Alliance and joined the Lancashire League, finishing runners-up. In 1899/1900 they again lost to St. Helens Recs. in the Wigan Challenge Cup, this time 2–1. They remained in the Lancashire League until the end of the 1901/02 season.

HUDSON'S (SOAP)

Hudson's entered the Liverpool and District Combination League in 1893. They won the league in 1895/96 and again in 1898/99, finishing two points ahead of Seacombe Swifts and also won the Liverpool Junior Cup in 1895/96. In 1900/01 they joined the Combination, finishing seventh in their first season.

JOHNSON'S DYEWORKS

Formed around 1898 and wearing blue shirts, Johnson's Dyeworks joined the Bootle and District Amateur League for the 1898/99 season. They moved to the North Liverpool and District League in 1900/01 and then to the Liverpool and District Alliance by 1901/02. In 1903/04, they took over the ground and pavilion formerly used by White Star Wanderers. In 1907/08, they joined the newly formed Bootle District League and remained until the end of the 1909/10 season.

KIRKDALE

A founding member of the Liverpool and District League in 1890/91, Kirkdale finished sixth in the inaugural season and won the Liverpool Junior Cup, defeating Saltney 1–0. The following season, they won the league. By 1894/95, they had joined the Liverpool District Combination and won the Junior Cup again in 1896/97, beating Whiston Wanderers 4–1. In 1899/1900, Kirkdale moved to the I Zingari League and won the title in their debut season. They finished as runners-up in 1901/02 and 1902/03, before winning again in 1905/06. They joined the Liverpool District League in 1907/08 and then moved to the West Cheshire League Second Division for 1910/11, finishing fifth in what would be their final season.

L. & N.W. LOCO (BIRKENHEAD LOCOS)

Formed around September 1891, they joined the Wirral League for the 1892/93 season, finishing fourth. They won the league in 1893/94 and the Wirral Senior Cup, repeating the cup victory in 1894/95 and were runners up to and won the Liverpool Junior Cup. In 1895/96 they completed a hat-trick of Senior Cup wins and reached the final again in 1896/97 but lost to Melrose. The club then became known as Birkenhead Locos and joined the Lancashire Alliance in 1898/99, finishing bottom of the table. After losing their ground, they disbanded but reformed in 1906/07, finishing eighth in the West Cheshire League Second Division. In 1909/10 they were runners-up to Eastham in the Wirral Combination before disbanding again.

LIVERPOOL

Founded in 1892 following a boardroom split at Everton, John Houlding remained at Anfield and established Liverpool Football Club. With John McKenna's help, a team was assembled, largely of Scottish players. Liverpool's first match, a friendly against Rotherham Town, was followed by entry into the Lancashire League in 1892/93, which they won. Their debut FA Cup match was a 4–0 win over Nantwich and their reserve team also won the Liverpool & District League.

Liverpool joined the Football League Second Division in 1893/94, replacing Bootle. They won their opening match 2–0 at Middlesbrough Ironopolis and dominated the season, finishing as champions. A Test Match victory over Newton Heath secured promotion. Their 1894/95 First Division campaign saw them relegated, but they bounced back in 1895/96, winning the Second Division again and succeeding in the revised Test Match league format.

They were League runners up in 1898/99 and Liverpool's rise continued with a strong finish to the 1899/1900 season. In 1900/01, they began with three straight wins and eventually secured their first league title on the final day, beating West Bromwich Albion thanks to a goal from Johnny Walker.

Relegated in 1903/04, Liverpool once again won the Second Division in 1904/05. In 1905/06, after a slow start, they climbed from bottom to top of the table by December and held off Preston North End to claim their second league title. They were League runners up in 1909/10. They also lost to Blackburn Rovers in the 1907 and 1909 Lancashire Senior Cup finals.

Liverpool reached their first FA Cup Final in 1913/14, finishing runners-up to Burnley at Crystal Palace, losing 1–0.

LIVERPOOL CALEDONIANS

Formed around 1891, Liverpool Caledonians emerged from the city's Scottish community. The idea had been floated as early as 1884, likely in response to the Welsh community's Cambrian club. In March 1891, an advert in the *Athletic News* invited interested parties to attend a meeting at the Star and Garter Hotel. Chaired by Robert Kirkland, the meeting led to the club's foundation.

In August 1891, the *Liverpool Mercury* reported the club's preparations for a debut match at their new ground, Woodcroft Park. Their first match, however, came on 28 September 1891 against Everton, who won 1–0. The team's inaugural season was promising: they played 37 matches, won 22, scored 117 goals and conceded 48. The club had capital of £5,000 and a strong Scottish lineup. They won the inaugural Liverpool Shield, defeating Southport Central 2–1 at Woodcroft Park before 4,000 spectators.

However, financial troubles struck in late 1892. A failed investment deal and unpaid share capital of £600 led to liquidation proceedings in December. By January 1893, Old Boys Rugby Club had purchased Woodcroft Park.

Despite these setbacks, the club resurfaced in the early 1900s. Between 1901 and 1904, they competed in the West Cheshire League, winning the Pyke Cup in 1901/02. They joined the I Zingari League in 1904/05, earning promotion from the Second Division. They reached the Wirral Junior Cup Final that same season, losing to Liscard CEMS. They remained in the I Zingari First Division until departing the league in 1911.

LIVERPOOL CASUALS

The Casuals formed in 1892/93 after Oakfield FC merged with Coburg FC. In their first season, they won the Liverpool Junior Cup, defeating Saltney Borderers. Secretary Tom H. Jackson, later of Northern Nomads, guided the club.

They joined the I Zingari League in 1896/97 and won it by a point over Melrose. That same season, they captured the Lancashire Amateur Cup, beating Liverpool Ramblers 5–1. The Casuals retained the I Zingari title in 1897/98, edging Old Xaverians by one point. In 1901/02, they again won the Lancashire Amateur Cup, defeating Blackburn Etrurians 1–0. They joined the Lancashire Amateur League in 1902/03 and won the Second Division, remaining in the league until 1904.

LIVERPOOL LEEK

Founded in 1889 in the Everton area, Liverpool Leek secured a ground near Clarendon Road, Cabbage Hall. They joined the I Zingari League in 1897/98, finishing sixth. After leaving in 1899, they became founder members of the Lancashire Amateur League. They remained until resigning in 1909, at which point the club disbanded.

LIVERPOOL RAMBLERS
The Ramblers reached the Lancashire Amateur Cup Final in 1896/97 and 1897/98, losing to Blackburn Etrurians and the Casuals respectively.

LIVERPOOL ROVERS
Rovers joined the Sefton Park and District League in 1905/06. They won the Liverpool Junior Cup in 1906/07 by beating Dingle Recs and joined the Liverpool and District League for 1907/08.

LIVERPOOL SCOTTISH
Formed in 1903 as part of the 10th Battalion King's (Liverpool) Regiment, the club joined the West Lancashire Territorial Force League in 1910. They entered the I Zingari Second Division in 1911/12, finishing fourth and fifth the following season. Their second team won the inaugural I Zingari Alliance title in 1912/13 and again in 1913/14. The first team also won the I Zingari Second Division in 1913/14, finishing 13 points ahead of Catholic Institute Old Boys.

LIVERPOOL SOUTH END
Based at Beresford Road, South End joined the Liverpool and District League in 1893, finishing fourth. In 1894/95, they won the league, beating White Star Wanderers 4–2 before 4,000 spectators. They joined the Lancashire League for 1895/96 and finished fifth. In 1895, *Liverpool Mercury* published a letter from an Everton shareholder alleging that Everton sought to boycott South End.

In February 1897, the club withdrew from the Lancashire League after struggling to field full teams and suffering heavy defeats, including 15–0 against Chorley. The club dissolved shortly after.

LIVERPOOL STANLEY

Stanley won the inaugural West Lancashire League in 1889/90, three points ahead of Aintree Church. Their ground hosted many local finals. They played in the Liverpool and District League until 1908/09.

LIVERPOOL UNIVERSITY

A founder member of the I Zingari League in 1895/96, the university team played again in 1897/99 before joining the Lancashire Amateur League in 1899/1900. They remained until 1904/05.

MARINE

Marine joined the I Zingari Second Division in 1897/98, finishing runners-up. After three strong seasons, they won the division in 1901/02, earning promotion. They won the First Division in 1902/03 after a play-off win over Kirkdale. They repeated as champions in 1903/04, edging Valkyrie by one point.

Marine were runners-up in 1905/06 to Kirkdale. In 1909/10, they won the Liverpool Amateur Cup, defeating Marlborough Old Boys 3–0. They won the league again in 1910/11 by one point over Balmoral. In 1912/13, they were runners-up in the I Zingari Challenge Cup and in the final pre-war season (1913/14), they finished sixth and lost the Lancashire Amateur Cup Final to Ogden's Athletic.

MELLING

Melling were founder members of the Lancashire Amateur League and won back-to-back titles in 1900/01 and 1901/02, both times finishing ahead of Old Xaverians.

MELROSE

Melrose were founder members of the Wirral League in 1892/93, finishing fifth in their inaugural season. They played one season (1893/94) in the Liverpool District Combination before rejoining the Wirral League for 1894/95, finishing eighth. In 1895/96, they were runners-up in the Wirral Senior Cup, losing 3–0 to L& NW Locos.

Melrose joined the I Zingari League at the start of the 1896/97 season, finishing as runners-up by a single point behind Liverpool Casuals. That season they avenged their earlier loss to L& NW Locos by beating them 4-2 to win the Wirral Senior Cup. They claimed the I Zingari League title in 1898/99, finishing eight points ahead of Stanley Victoria, while their reserves won the Second Division by ten points ahead of Formby Rangers, and the Liverpool Junior Cup. In 1899/1900, the first team finished second to Kirkdale by three points, while the reserves retained their Second Division title by one point ahead of Marlborough Old Boys.

In 1900/01, Melrose won the I Zingari League again, this time by three points over Aintree. Their reserves secured a third consecutive Second Division title by a narrow margin over St. Michael's. In 1901/02, the club were runners-up in both the Liverpool Shield (losing 2-0 to Tranmere Rovers) and the Wirral Senior Cup (losing 4-0 to Birkenhead). They again lost the Wirral Senior Cup final to Birkenhead in 1902/03 by a 2-0 scoreline.

The club's reserves were also frequent finalists in the Wirral Junior Cup (now the Wirral Amateur Cup), finishing runners-up in 1892/93, 1895/96, 1896/97 and 1899/1900, before finally winning the cup in 1900/01 with a 3-1 victory over Clarendon. They were runners-up again the following year, losing 2-1 to Clarendon. In total, the reserves won the I Zingari League Second Division in three consecutive seasons: 1898/99, 1899/1900 and 1900/01.

Melrose left the I Zingari League Third Division after finishing as runners-up to Waterloo Melville in 1903/04. That same season they won the Wirral Senior Cup, beating Port Sunlight 1-0. They rejoined the I Zingari League Third Division for the 1906/07 season and won it by two points ahead of Birkenhead St. Andrews. Promoted to the Second Division, they finished third in 1907/08 and earned promotion to the First Division, where they finished sixth in 1908/09. The 1909/10 season saw them finish third from bottom, after which they left the league.

An application to join the West Cheshire League for 1910/11 appears to have failed and the club subsequently disbanded.

LIVERPOOL POLICE / MERSEYSIDE POLICE

Liverpool Police joined the newly formed West Lancashire League in 1889/90, finishing mid-table. In 1894/95, they entered the Lancashire Amateur Cup and won it at the first attempt, beating Aintree Church in the final. The club competed in the Liverpool, Wirral and District League in 1895/96, again finishing mid-table. They joined the I Zingari League for the 1896/97 season. In 1898, they claimed their second Lancashire Amateur Cup title, defeating Old Xaverians 3–1.

After leaving the I Zingari League at the end of the 1899/1900 season, the team played briefly in the Lancashire Amateur League before joining the Liverpool Wednesday League, which they would go on to win.

NEW BRIGHTON TOWER

New Brighton Tower joined the Lancashire League in 1897/98. Despite early scepticism, they topped the league with four straight wins and ultimately claimed the title, finishing five points ahead of Nelson. They lost the Liverpool Senior Cup Final to Everton 3–0 that season.

Elected to the Football League Second Division for 1898/99, their first scheduled game against Darwen was postponed due to a dispute over Alf Milward's transfer from Everton. Their debut match, instead, was against Gainsborough Trinity on 13 September 1898, which they won 3–2. They finished fifth in their first Football League season and again lost the Liverpool Senior Cup Final to Everton, this time 8/1. They won the Cheshire Senior Cup in 1897/98 but they also forfeited the Cheshire Senior Cup Final against Crewe Alexandra by failing to appear the following season.

Tower won the Wirral Senior Cup three seasons in a row between 1898/01, defeating Seacombe Swifts in the first two finals and Wirral Railways in the third. In the 1899/1900 season, they again lost the Liverpool Senior Cup Final to Everton (2–0) and were beaten in the Cheshire Senior Cup Final replay by Crewe Alexandra.

In 1900/01, their final full Football League season, Tower finished fourth. Their reserves played in the Lancashire Combination, finishing seventh. By September 1901, the club board announced it could not fulfil its Second Division fixtures. A public meeting failed to secure new investment and the club folded.

NEWTON-LE-WILLOWS

Newton-le-Willows were formed around 1893 and joined the West Lancashire League for the 1893/94 season, playing their first match against the 5th Irish. They moved to the Warrington and District Amateur League in 1894/95, finishing third and then to the West Lancashire and District League for 1895/96. Their reserves remained in the Warrington league.

From 1898 to 1903, they competed in the Liverpool and District Combination, finishing bottom in 1900/01 and losing the Wigan Challenge Cup final 3–1 to Earlestown. They joined the Lancashire Combination Second Division in 1903/04, finishing tenth. In 1905/06, they narrowly avoided relegation thanks to Wigan Town being denied entry.

Their final season in the Combination was 1907/08, finishing last. They rejoined the Lancashire Alliance in 1909/10. By the end of 1911, the club was renamed Golborne and continued in the Lancashire Alliance until the outbreak of the First World War.

NORTH MEOLS

North Meols FC was formed in June 1891 through the merger of Southport High Park FC and Churchtown FC. Southport High Park had been runners-up in the 1890/91 Lancashire Alliance. North Meols joined the Lancashire Combination, finishing sixth in both the 1891/92 and 1892/93 seasons. They then spent two seasons in the Lancashire Alliance, finishing sixth and twelfth, respectively. Though they appeared to fold in 1895, they resurfaced to compete in the reconstituted Southport League in 1897.

NORTHERN NOMADS

Founded in Blackburn in 1902, Northern Nomads quickly based themselves in Liverpool, largely due to their secretary Tom Jackson, a Liverpool solicitor. They wore black shirts and white shorts and initially used Everton's ground for home fixtures. In 1908, they were runners-up to Harrowby in the Cheshire Amateur Cup and toured Denmark later that year.

In 1908/09, they joined the newly formed Amateur Alliance and won the league in their only season. On the final day, needing three points to win the title, they beat Grimsby Rangers and Leeds Amateurs (both 2–1) in matches played back-to-back.

They won the Cheshire Amateur Cup in 1909/10 and later that year travelled to Brussels, winning a tournament featuring clubs from Belgium, the Netherlands, Germany and Austria-Hungary. Between 1911 and 1913, they toured the Netherlands and wider Low Countries and in April 1914, they toured Hungary. In 1913/14, they finished runners-up in the FA Amateur Cup Final, losing 1–0 to Bishop Auckland at Elland Road.

OAKFIELD ROVERS
Oakfield Rovers merged with Coburg Football Club in 1892 to form Liverpool Casuals.

OGDEN'S ATHLETIC
Ogden's Athletic was established in 1906 by the Ogden's branch of the Imperial Tobacco Company. They played at Clubmoor Cricket Ground and began their football journey in the West Cheshire League during the 1906/07 season, finishing bottom of the thirteen-team division. They won the Lancashire Amateur Cup in 1912/13, defeating Orrell 3–0 and retained it in 1913/14 with a 1–0 victory over Marine. Ogden's remained in the West Cheshire League until the outbreak of World War One.

OLD XAVERIANS
Formed by cricketers from the Old Xaverians' Athletic Association, the football club was established in September 1893. Their first match was a friendly against Old Amplefordians of Stoneyhurst College, played at Newsham Cricket Club in Newsham Park. They were founder members of the I Zingari League in 1895/96, finishing fifth. In 1897/98, they were

runners-up in the league to Liverpool Casuals by one point and also lost the Lancashire Amateur Cup final to Liverpool Police Athletic.

At the start of the 1899/1900 season, they joined the newly formed Lancashire Amateur League – created by Arthur Morton – and won the title in its inaugural year. They continued to field a team in the I Zingari League until leaving it at the end of that season. In 1899/00 they won the Lancashire Amateur League and in 1900/01, they finished as runners-up. And again in 1901/02.

In 1902, Old Xaverians toured the Netherlands. They beat Amsterdam 7-0 and received a 'right royal reception' before and after the game. They then lost 3-1 to Handt Braeft Stant and drew 3-3 with an Eastern Holland XI. As they left the ground in their carriages, the team was attacked by locals throwing stones and even a lump of timber, which the police had to intervene to stop.

They retained the Lancashire Amateur League title in 1902/03, finishing six points ahead of Burnley Belvedere. In 1903/04, they were runners-up to Blackburn Crosshill and runners-up again in 1904/05. The 1906/07 season brought another league title, this time ahead of Southport YMCA. In 1907/08, they again claimed the league title, finished ahead of Aughton Wanderers, won the Liverpool Amateur Cup by beating Bromborough Pool 2-1 and were runners-up in the Lancashire Amateur Cup to Preston Winckley.

In 1908, Old Xaverians were invited to Belgium over Easter for the inaugural Dupuich Cup tournament (see European chapter). In 1909/10, they were runners-up in the Lancashire Amateur Cup to Wigan Amateurs. In 1911/12, they rejoined the I Zingari League, finishing fourth in the First Division and won the Liverpool Amateur Cup again, defeating Orrell 2-0.

In 1913, Old Xaverians toured Spain, defeating Deportivo 3-2 in Bilbao and a Basque XI 1-0 in San Sebastián.

ORMSKIRK

Formed in 1909, Ormskirk joined the Liverpool County Combination in 1911/12 and finished fifth. They remained in the league until the end of the 1913/14 season, after which the club disbanded.

ORRELL

Established in 1894 as a schoolboy club under the name Orrell Rangers, the team played local schools in its first year. By 1895, under secretary Mr. Cox, they arranged friendlies against more competitive sides and joined the Aigburth and District Combination in 1897, dropping the 'Rangers' name. They won the league in 1899/1900 and joined the I Zingari League Second Division the following season. A vacancy in the First Division led them to accept promotion, finishing fourth in their debut season.

After some inconsistent seasons, Orrell were runners-up to Helsby Athletic in 1904/05. Their next notable season came in 1911/12 when they finished second behind St. Cleopas and lost the Liverpool Amateur Cup final 2-0 to Old Xaverians. Orrell won the I Zingari League in 1912/13 by one point over Marlborough Old Boys but lost 3-0 to Ogden's in the Lancashire Amateur Cup Final. They retained the league title in 1913/14, edging St. Cleopas by a single point and also won the Liverpool Amateur Cup, defeating Balmoral 3-2.

PORT SUNLIGHT

Port Sunlight joined the Wirral League in 1892/93, finishing ninth. They won the league in 1894/95 by six points and were runners-up the following season. After a brief absence, they returned in 1902/03, losing 1-0 to Melrose in the Wirral Senior Cup.

In 1904/05, they moved to the Combination League and then joined the Lancashire Combination Second Division for the 1905/06 season, finishing fifth. That same season, they won the Wirral Senior Cup by defeating Birkenhead 2-0. In 1907, the club was given permission by the Liverpool FA to change its name to Wirral United. However, just months later, the team resigned from the Lancashire Combination having joined in 1907, unable to pay rent on either the Pool Bank or Wirral Park grounds.

By 1910, Port Sunlight were competing in the Wirral Combination Minor Division and in 1913 became founder members of the Wirral Association Football League. They won the Wirral Junior Cup in 1913/14 by defeating Laird Street Athletic.

PRESCOT / PRESCOT ATHLETIC

Prescot joined the West Lancashire League in 1889/90, finishing eighth. In that season's Liverpool Junior Cup final, the club's first team beat its reserve side, the Swifts, 7–2. In 1890/91, the newly formed Liverpool & District League began, with Prescot finishing fourth.

After a brief spell in the reformed Liverpool & District League in 1894/95, Prescot joined the Lancashire Alliance and reached the Liverpool Shield final, losing 5–0 to White Star Wanderers. In 1895/96, they defeated Tranmere Rovers 2–0 in the Liverpool Shield Final.

Over the next few years, they alternated between the Lancashire Alliance and the Lancashire Combination, resigning from the Combination in November 1897 and rejoining the Alliance to take over Hindley's fixtures. They won the Alliance in 1899/1900, narrowly beating Parr.

Prescot left the Alliance after 1900/01 to join the Lancashire League, but a dispute with Prescot Cricket Club over access to their shared ground forced the football club to fold in 1902. The club was revived in 1906 as Prescot Athletic and moved to the Hope Street ground, debuting against Haydock Athletic. They joined the St Helens and District League, finishing runners-up, then moved to the Liverpool and District League in 1907/08.

In 1910/11, they entered the Liverpool County Combination, winning their first match 1–0 against Buckley Engineers. They finished fourth in both 1910/11 and 1911/12, tenth in 1912/13 and fifth in 1913/14.

PRESCOT WIRE WORKS

Founded in 1903, Prescot Wire Works joined the St Helens and District League for the 1903/04 season. In 1905/06, they won the Liverpool and District League and the Liverpool Junior Cup. They joined the newly named West Cheshire League in 1906/07, finishing sixth and losing the Wirral Senior Cup final to Garston Gasworks.

In 1909/10, they became founding members of the Liverpool County Combination, finishing as runners-up to Garston Gasworks. They repeated the runner-up finish in 1910/11 and again in 1912/13, narrowly missing the title by two points. In 1914/15, they rejoined the West Cheshire League.

ROCK FERRY

Formed in 1896, Rock Ferry joined the Combination League in 1896/97 and finished second behind Everton's Combination side. They moved to the Lancashire League the following season but disbanded in February 1899 after internal disputes. A key incident occurred when most players refused to play at Halliwell Rovers due to the hard ground. Their argument led club president Luke Lees to withdraw support and the club dissolved. The loss of their Bedford Park ground contributed to a split at Tranmere Rovers.

SEACOMBE SWIFTS

Founded around 1894, Seacombe Swifts won the Wirral Junior League (Third Division) in their first season. They won the Second Division in 1895/96 and were runners-up the following season. They beat Melrose Reserves to win the Wirral Junior Cup (now Amateur Cup) in 1896/97.

Swifts joined the Liverpool District Combination for 1897/98 and finished as runners-up to Hudson's in 1898/99. They lost two consecutive Wirral Senior Cup Finals to New Brighton Tower in 1898/99 and 1899/1900. They spent one season in the Lancashire Alliance, finishing third. A brief mention in the *Birkenhead News* in 1903 suggests the club had disbanded by that time.

ST. HELENS (ASSOCIATION)

The club was still playing friendlies in 1892 when it lost its ground to a railway project. They relocated and played Sutton Victoria on 3 September 1892, winning 1–0. There are no further records after this date.

ST HELENS RECREATION (RECS.)

Originally formed in 1878 as a Rugby Union team, St Helens Recs switched to the Northern Union in 1896 and briefly played Rugby

League before adopting the Association game in 1898. They joined the Lancashire Combination in 1899/1900 and finished 16th but won the Wigan Challenge Cup for a third time. In 1900/01, they rose to fifth place.

After the Lancashire League folded in 1902/03, Recs joined the Lancashire Combination Second Division, finishing 11th in 1903/04. In 1905/06, they won the Second Division and replaced St Helens Town in the First Division.

In 1911/12, they finished second behind Rochdale – their best performance to date. After an eighth-place finish in 1912/13, Recs reverted to Rugby League in June 1913 and resigned from the Lancashire Combination.

ST HELENS TOWN

Founded in 1901 to rival St Helens Recs, the club played at the Park Road Primrose Ground and debuted against Liverpool's A team on 5 September 1901, losing 3–0. The first derby against Recs came in February 1902 before a crowd of over 5,000.

Town joined the Lancashire League in 1901/02 and finished sixth. They moved to the Lancashire Combination Second Division in 1903/04, finishing fifth. They were promoted to the top division but finished bottom in 1905/06 and were replaced by Recs.

Town were promoted again in 1908/09 and again relegated in 1909/10, but returned for the 1911/12 season due to league restructuring. They finished 13th, then 14th in 1912/13. Their final season in 1913/14 ended with relegation and they rejoined the Liverpool County Combination for the shortened 1914/15 season before folding.

SKELMERSDALE MISSION

Formed around 1892, Skelmersdale Mission played in the Liverpool Minor League before joining the Skelmersdale District League in 1894/95. They competed in the Ormskirk and District League by 1902/03, winning the title in 1908/09 and 1909/10.

Mission lost the 1910/11 Liverpool Junior Cup final to Banks Road but won it in 1911/12, defeating Stirling 3–2. That same season, they joined the St Helens and District League. In 1913/14, they joined the Lancashire Alliance, finishing fourth in a six-team league.

SKELMERSDALE UNITED

Skelmersdale United joined the Liverpool Amateur League in 1890/91, initially playing matches opposite the Horseshoe on Liverpool Road and at the Skelmersdale Arms on Sandy Lane. They became one of the first Merseyside clubs to join the Lancashire Combination, finishing second from bottom in the 1891/92 season and retaining the same position in the expanded eleven-team league the following year.

United moved to the Lancashire Alliance for the 1895/96 season but remained in the lower reaches of the table, with ninth in 1898/99 being their highest position during this period. After a brief absence, they returned in 1900/01 and performed significantly better, finishing runners-up to Parr by just one point. The following season, 1901/02, they won the Lancashire Alliance by four points from Southport Central Reserves, secured the Southport Charity Cup and were runners-up in both the Liverpool Senior Cup (losing 1–0 to Liverpool) and the Liverpool Shield (beaten 1–0 by Birkenhead).

After one more season in the Alliance, United returned to the Lancashire Combination for 1903/04 in the newly created Second Division. Between then and 1906/07, they never finished higher than twelfth, ending the 1906/07 campaign bottom of the table. They rejoined the Lancashire Alliance in 1907/08 and won the Lancashire Junior Challenge Shield, beating Portsmouth Rovers 2–1 at Accrington. Their final Alliance season in 1908/09 ended in third place.

United were founder members of the Liverpool County Combination in 1909/10, finishing seventh in their debut season. The following year, they topped the league, remaining unbeaten into February and winning the title by six points from Prescot Wire Works. In 1911/12, they were runners-up to Garston North End in both the league and the George Mahon Cup (losing 3–0), but won the Liverpool Challenge Cup, defeating Widnes County

1–0. In 1913/14, they again won the league by seven points from Wallasey Borough and claimed another Liverpool Challenge Cup, beating Southport Park Villa 1–0 in front of 5,000 fans at Anfield. In 1914/15, Skelmersdale United won the Liverpool County Combination and the Lancashire Junior Cup, beating Rossendale United.

SOUTH LIVERPOOL (1894 and 1910)

The original South Liverpool FC was founded in 1894, the same year as Marine and played at Wavertree Playground before moving to Shorefields on Beresford Road. They joined the Combination in 1898/99 and finished 11th out of 15 teams. The following season, they moved to the Lancashire League and finished 13th of 16 teams.

In December 1910, African Royal changed its name to South Liverpool, intending to provide a club in the city's south end to rival Everton and Liverpool. The newly renamed team, for the 1910/11 season, finishing fifth and their reserve team came seventh in Division Two. That season, South Liverpool won the Liverpool Challenge Cup, beating Dominion 2–0 in a replay at Anfield.

Following the formation of a new Lancashire Combination Second Division in 1911, South Liverpool were elected to join. They finished fifth in 1911/12 and became a limited company in 1912 with aspirations of Football League status. The 1912/13 season was a high point: on Easter Monday, 24 March 1913, they beat Skelmersdale United 3–0 in the Liverpool Challenge Cup final at Goodison before thrashing Nelson 10–0 in a league match the same afternoon. They won the Second Division title and were promoted.

In 1913, the club lost its Grafton Street ground to Elder Dempster Shipping and relocated to Dingle Park for their first season in the Lancashire Combination First Division. They were not elected to the Football League in 1914.

SOUTHPORT (CENTRAL)

By August 1889, Southport Central had purchased an enclosure on Scarisbrick New Road and opened the ground with a match against Preston

North End. They joined the Lancashire League that same season, defeating Rossendale 3–1 in their debut match. In December 1889, they hosted the region's first 'illuminated' football match under Wells patent limelight.

Southport finished sixth in their inaugural campaign and retained sixth and fifth places in the next two seasons. They lost the inaugural Liverpool Shield Final in 1892 to Liverpool Caledonians (2–1). In 1895/96, they placed fourth but came close to folding due to financial troubles. Despite fears of dissolution in May 1896, they survived and continued playing.

Southport Central won the final Lancashire League title in 1902/03 and were admitted to the Lancashire Combination Division B. They won the division in 1903/04 by a single point over Earlestown and came third in their first top-flight campaign in 1904/05. That year, they also won the Lancashire Senior Cup, beating Everton 2–1.

In 1911/12, Southport Central joined the newly formed Central League and remained there until the outbreak of the First World War.

SOUTHPORT HIGH PARK

Southport High Park were founder members of the Lancashire Junior League, finishing ninth. They joined the inaugural Lancashire Alliance season in 1890/91 and finished runners-up. After leaving the league, they returned in 1899/1900 and finished sixth before leaving again at the end of the season.

SOUTHPORT Y.M.C.A.

Southport YMCA after joining in 1905, finished the 1909/10 Lancashire Amateur League level on points with Wigan Amateurs but with a superior goal average. In a show of sportsmanship, they proposed a play-off, which they lost 3–0, forfeiting the league title.

TRANMERE ROVERS

Tranmere Rovers played their first West Lancashire League match on 21 September 1889, defeating Bromborough Pool 6–0 at the Borough Road Enclosure. That season, they changed their kit from Belmont FC's blue to orange and maroon halved shirts with navy-blue shorts. They finished third and claimed their first honour by winning the Wirral Senior Cup, defeating Primrose Rovers 3–0 in April 1889.

In 1889/90, they were runners-up in the Wirral Senior Cup and won the trophy again in 1890/91, beating their own reserve side 3–1. Tranmere entered the FA Cup in 1891/92, losing 5–1 at home to Northwich Victoria.

In 1892/93, Rovers joined the Lancashire Combination, but finished bottom and left the league the following season. They returned to the Wirral and District League in 1894/95 finishing as runners-up and remained as the league evolved into the Liverpool, Wirral and District League. They lost the Liverpool Shield final in 1895/96, beaten 2–0 by Prescot, but won the Pyke Cup the following season.

Rovers rejoined The Combination in 1897/98, finishing second from bottom but winning the Wirral Senior Cup with a 7–0 victory over Hoylake. In 1898/99, they placed third behind Everton and Liverpool's reserve sides and won the Liverpool Shield, defeating Hudson's 2–1 in the final at Rock Ferry. However, internal tensions over player expenses and the prospect of moving to Bedford Park led to a mass player exodus to the newly formed Birkenhead FC.

In 1899/1900, with a rebuilt squad, Rovers joined the Lancashire Alliance and finished sixth. They returned to The Combination in 1900/01, finishing eighth, one place ahead of Birkenhead. In 1904/05, they won the Wirral Senior Cup, defeating Bebington Victoria, while the reserves finished runners-up in the Wirral Amateur Cup the following season. Rovers lost the 1906/07 Liverpool Shield Final to African Royal (1–0), but in 1907/08 won The Combination on goal average ahead of Chester. Tranmere were crowned Liverpool Challenge Cup winners 1908/09.

Rovers left The Combination after 1909/10 and joined the Lancashire Combination Second Division, finishing 13th in 1910/11, the same year they became a limited company. In 1911/12, they placed third and opened Prenton Park on 9 March 1912. Promoted to the First Division for 1912/13, they finished sixth and in 1913/14 won the league title, seven points ahead of Barrow. They also lifted the Wirral Senior Cup, beating Wirral Railway. In 1914/15, Tranmere lost the Cheshire Senior Cup Final 1–0 to Stockport

County. Rovers also won the Liverpool Shield in 1898/99, 1900/01, 1901/02, 1904/05 and 1905/06.

TRINITY BIBLE CLASS

Trinity Bible Class FC was founded in 1893 in Bootle. A founder member of the I Zingari League Second Division in 1897/98, they won the division in their debut season, finishing seven points ahead of Marine.

VALKYRIE

Valkyrie FC was established in 1901, emerging from a team formerly known as Ivanhoe. They joined the I Zingari League Second Division in 1901/02, finishing fourth. Their home ground was the Liverpool Cricket Club's Riversdale Ground in Aigburth.

In 1902/03, Valkyrie won the Second Division and reached the Liverpool Junior Cup Final, losing 3-1 to Garston Gasworks at Prenton Park. In 1903/04, they won both the Liverpool Junior Cup (beating Garston Church) and the Wirral Amateur Cup (beating Birkenhead North End 4-0). Their reserve team won the I Zingari Combination in 1905/06.

In 1908/09, Valkyrie, known as the 'Yachtsmen,' won the I Zingari First Division by three points from Bromborough Pool. However, in 1911/12, the club was expelled from the league for fielding an ineligible player in a Challenge Cup match. They joined the Liverpool County Combination, where the 1912/13 season proved difficult – they finished bottom, with just two wins.

WALLASEY VILLAGE

Wallasey Village FC were founder members of the I Zingari League in 1895/96, finishing third in their debut season and fourth the following year. The original club appears to have folded soon after.

A reconstituted Wallasey Village side emerged in 1901/02, joining the Wirral League Second Division (later the West Cheshire League), finishing first by two points over Birkenhead North End. They won the

Birkenhead News Challenge Cup that season and they won the Second Division in 1903/04 ahead of Rock Ferry St. Pauls.

In 1906/07, they lost 6–1 to Egremont Social in the Pyke Cup Final.

In 1910, they lost their ground and shared with Harrowby before moving to Oarside Farm in 1910/11, finishing bottom of the First Division and suffering relegation. They were promoted again for 1912/13 but finished 11th in the top flight and left the league at season's end.

WARRINGTON ASSOCIATION

The original Warrington Association Football Club disbanded in 1893 due to financial difficulties. A phoenix club of the same name was established in August 1899 but met a similar fate, folding in January 1902. Despite its short lifespan, the club managed to win the local Warrington and District Cup.

WEST KIRBY

West Kirby was a founder member of the Wirral Football League in 1892/93, finishing in sixth place. That same season, they won the Wirral Junior Cup (later the Wirral Amateur Cup), defeating Melrose Reserves 4–1. They were relegated at the end of the 1894/95 season after finishing bottom of the First Division. The club rejoined the First Division at the start of the 1900/01 season, finishing runners-up by three points to Wheatlands. The following year, they were runners-up in the Pyke Cup Final, losing to Liverpool Caledonians. In 1902/03, West Kirby won the league title by four points from Wirral Railway. They were Pyke Cup runners-up again in 1904, losing 2–0 to Ellesmere Port Town, but won the trophy the following year, beating Connah's Quay 3–0. In the 1905/06 final, they were heavily defeated by Garston Gasworks, 6–0. When the league became the West Cheshire League in 1906/07, West Kirby finished as Second Division runners-up to Heswall by four points. This proved to be their final season, as the club soon disbanded.

WHEATLANDS

Wheatlands was formed in October 1897, initially playing friendlies before joining the Wirral Junior League Second Division. In 1898/99, they finished as runners-up to New Ferry St. Mark's. They joined the newly formed Wirral League (later the West Cheshire League) in 1899/1900. Following the amalgamation of the league's two divisions in 1900/01, Wheatlands won the unified competition by three points from West Kirby, becoming the first recipients of the Pyke Cup, which was awarded to the league champions. They retained the title in 1901/02, edging out Clarendons by one point. However, by the summer of 1903, financial difficulties stemming from low support led to the club disbanding.

WHITE STAR WANDERERS

White Star Wanderers were formed after Bootle Wanderers (or possibly Bootle Athletic) became defunct in early 1893. The new club took over Bootle Wanderers' ground and was reportedly backed by the powerful White Star Line shipping company. The team, composed of former Bootle Reserves and Bootle Wanderers players, won both the Liverpool Shield and the Liverpool & District League title in the 1893/94 season. They joined the Combination in 1897/98, finishing eighth. After a one-season absence in 1899/1900, they returned to the Combination in 1900/01, finishing sixth, but left again after the 1901/02 season. In November 1902, the Athletic newspaper reported their colours as red with a white star. The club's decline began shortly after, when a Liverpool Shield match against Old Xaverians was postponed due to neither side showing up. White Star, as the home team, was ordered by the Liverpool FA to pay the referee's fee. The club refused, resulting in suspension. By April 1903, they had withdrawn from the Combination, their record was expunged and the club disbanded. They also won the Liverpool Shield 1893/94, 1894/95 and 1896/97.

WHISTON

Whiston was a founder member of the West Lancashire League in 1889/90, finishing fourth. In 1890/91, they came third as the league was renamed the Liverpool and District League. They won the Wigan Challenge Cup in 1891/92, beating Park Lane Wanderers 3–2. Whiston joined the Liverpool and Wirral District League in 1895/96, finishing ninth, before moving to the

Lancashire Alliance in 1896/97, where they finished eleventh. After three seasons near the bottom of the Alliance, they left at the end of 1898/99. They joined the Liverpool District Combination in 1899/1900 but finished last; this would be the club's final season.

WIDNES WESLEY GUILD

Founded in 1903, Widnes Wesley Guild played at Victoria Road, Widnes. They joined the Liverpool and District Free Church League in 1904/05, winning it at the first attempt. The club joined the I Zingari League in 1905/06, again winning the Second Division in their debut season. The 1906/07 campaign was highly successful – they won the I Zingari First Division by one point ahead of Bromborough Pool, the Liverpool Amateur Cup (beating Marine 1–0) and the Widnes Charity Cup. After that season, they moved to the West Cheshire League and finished fourth in 1907/08, also winning the Liverpool Shield and Widnes Charity Cup. In 1908/09, their second team won the Liverpool Junior Cup, beating Inglewood 1–0.

They remained in the West Cheshire League until 1909/10, when they became one of the founder members of the Liverpool County Combination, finishing sixth in their debut season and winning the Liverpool Challenge Cup, beating Garston Gasworks 1–0. In 1910, at their end-of-season meeting, the club changed its name to Widnes County, believing the original name to be 'detrimental to their interests.' They remained in the Liverpool County Combination until the outbreak of the First World War.

WIGAN AMATEURS

Wigan Amateurs joined the Lancashire Amateur League in 1905/06. Their only major success came in 1909/10 when they won the Lancashire Amateur Cup, defeating Old Xaverians 2–1 in the final at Blackpool after winning the trophy for the first time at the end of the preceding season.

WIGAN COUNTY

Wigan County was formed in 1897 by the Wigan Trotting and Athletic Company. They joined the Lancashire League for the 1897/98 season, finishing eighth. The club attempted to join the Football League for the 1898/99 season but received only seven votes and were not elected. They left the Lancashire League after the 1899/1900 season and soon disbanded.

WIGAN TOWN

Formed in late 1905, Wigan Town held trial games before Christmas and entered the Combination in January 1906. They finished bottom that season, having taken over the records of Middlewich. After finishing third in 1906/07, their membership of the Lancashire Combination Second Division was annulled and Newton-le-Willows, who had finished third from bottom, retained their place. Wigan Town rejoined the Lancashire Combination for the 1907/08 season, finishing second from bottom and then folded.

WIGAN UNITED

Wigan United was formed in 1900 and joined the Lancashire League. They finished tenth in their first season (1900/01) and improved to third in 1901/02. The club remained in the Lancashire League until it folded at the end of the 1902/03 season. Wigan United also folded around this time, following the expiration of their lease on Springfield Park midway through the season.

WHERE THEY PLAYED

By 1888, football enclosures on Merseyside had developed sufficiently for the Football Association to select Anfield to host an FA Cup semi-final between Preston North End and Crewe Alexandra. Everton, who were using Anfield at the time, had erected a stand capable of holding 200 to 300 spectators. However, not everyone welcomed the rapid spread of football. A letter published in the *Liverpool Mercury* in 1888 from 'A Ratepayer' expressed outrage at the degradation of public parkland, particularly Stanley Park: 'From Mill Lane northwards to Walton Lane the grass has now wholly disappeared... The numerous clubs digging holes for the insertion of sockets and claiming almost an absolute right to the ground, rudely ordering off any person who happens to intrude on the space claimed by them.'

Transport to the grounds in the 1890s was largely on foot. A 1925 article in the *Liverpool Echo* recalled that supporters walked from the docks via Sandhills and Lambeth Road and from the south via Sheil Road. Other key routes included Breck Road, St. Domingo Road and Everton Valley. Tram stops included Walton and Breckfield Road, with additional access via Robson Street. More affluent fans could hire taxis from Castle Street, the Pierhead, or St George's Crescent, while others used privately hired buses or wagonettes.

When Goodison Park hosted the 1894 FA Cup Final between Notts County and Bolton Wanderers, the *Liverpool Mercury* described the various means by which spectators reached the ground: 'It was a great day for the trams, the buses and the cars of all descriptions that were requisitioned for the use of the crowd. It's a pretty stiff walk, especially when a man is in a hurry, from the centre of the city to Goodison Park and everybody seemed to want to ride.' Although trains to Walton or Spellow Lane were an option, most spectators relied on road transport, even milk floats, which were commandeered for the occasion.

In 1895, Everton became embroiled in a scandal when gate receipts at Goodison were discovered to be suspiciously low. With average attendances of around 16,000, the shortfall was eventually traced to tampered turnstiles. Fifteen employees were charged and eleven received prison sentences ranging from one to three months. Everton subsequently upgraded their turnstiles and introduced gate books to prevent future fraud.

One of football's most iconic structures, the Kop, owes its name to a battle fought over 8,000 miles from Liverpool. During the Second Anglo-Boer War, British forces including many Liverpudlians serving in the King's (Liverpool) Regiment were besieged – Other British forces including the South Lancashire Regiment attempted to relieve the besieged town of Ladysmith in January 1900. The key to this effort was an assault on Spion Kop, a steep hill held by the Boers. Though the hill was initially taken, British troops found themselves exposed to fire from surrounding heights, suffering heavy casualties before ultimately retreating. In 1904, Woolwich Arsenal's Manor Ground was the first to use the term 'Kop' for a terrace and when Archibald Leitch redesigned Liverpool's Anfield in 1906, its new earth embankment was dubbed the Kop in memory of the fallen.

A national tragedy shaped football stadium design in the early 20th century. In 1902, during an England v Scotland international at Ibrox Park in Glasgow, a wooden terrace collapsed, killing 25 and injuring over 500. The disaster was blamed on substandard construction. In response, Archibald Leitch introduced the now-standard steel 'crush barrier' in 1906 and terraces thereafter were constructed from reinforced concrete or compacted earth.

By 1914, access to playing spaces had become a serious concern. Frank Sugg, a former Everton footballer and Lancashire cricketer, created the Invisa League for local boys' teams. He lamented that thousands of boys aged 14 to 18 were unable to play on Saturdays due to a shortage of grounds. Of the 72 clubs that had applied to join his league, 30 had dropped out for lack of pitches. He appealed to Liverpool City Council to open more parks to football and to purchase additional land for sporting use closer to the city.

ANFIELD, LIVERPOOL

By 1889, Anfield had a capacity of around 12,000 and included a dedicated player entrance. The Anfield Road end featured wooden benches (bleachers) for approximately 4,000 spectators. At the south end (prior to the construction of the Kop) stood a small stand, while the Kemlyn Road side had a narrow-covered area backing onto terraced houses. Opposite, on the Lothair Road side (now the Millennium Stand), a small pavilion also abutted housing. In 1891, *The Illustrated Sporting and Dramatic News* described Anfield as admirably arranged for the populace, with seating at both ends and covered stands on both sides. Spectators could sit on wooden tiers and umbrellas were banned due to obstructed views. It is also believed that a flagpole that still stands at Anfield was bought around this time from the sale of a mast from the SS Great Eastern.

In October 1928, an Everton supporter recalled early visits to Anfield in a letter to the *Liverpool Echo*, remembering matches attended with only a slim rail separating the crowd from the pitch and a modest stand he likened to 'a glorified hen roost.'

The Anfield Road end was rebuilt in 1902 with brick and timber. In 1905/06, architect Archibald Leitch redesigned Anfield: the ground was enclosed, the pitch raised by five feet and new entrances installed. A perimeter paddock was introduced and three sides of the ground received roofed stands. The most dramatic addition was the large terrace of 132 steps on the Walton Breck Road side, which would become known as the Spion Kop. The Main Stand featured reinforced concrete and could seat 3,000 with standing space in front. By 1907, the club had purchased the ground outright with help from the Royal Liver Friendly Society, securing a 20-year repayment term.

ASH LANE, SOUTHPORT

Southport Central moved to Ash Lane in summer 1905 after vacating Scarisbrick New Road. Volunteers transported equipment to the new site, with the entire relocation costing £200. The inaugural match at Ash Lane was between Central committee members and the volunteers who had prepared the ground.

BEDFORD ROAD, ROCK FERRY

Opened in September 1895 by L&NW Loco FC, the ground occupied land purchased by Luke Lees Jnr., proprietor of the Bedford Hotel. A converted stable served as the dressing room. Upon opening, the pitch surface was uneven and hazardous. The Birkenhead News described it as needing considerable attention and suggested a different pitch orientation would have provided better play conditions.

CAMMELL LAIRD ATHLETIC GROUND, BIRKENHEAD

Constructed in just seven weeks in 1909, the Cammell Laird ground featured terracing for 10,000 spectators, built with 2,000 tons of clinker and 25,000 feet of timber. The pitch measured 105 by 70 yards and was enclosed by railings. Facilities included a pavilion with dressing rooms, baths, wash basins, referee and committee rooms, a bar and a veranda. High wire netting behind the goals prevented balls from leaving the enclosure. Entry was managed through multiple pay boxes.

CATTLE MARKET INN, STANLEY OLD SWAN ROAD
The Cattle Market Inn was sold in 1900 following earlier sale of the surrounding land and athletic field.

FAULKNER STREET, HOOLE
In 1898, encroaching housing development forced the club to relocate from Faulkner Street to nearby Panton Road, known as the 'Old Showground.' Makeshift stands, including a press box, were erected, but repeated storm damage to hoardings made the site untenable.

GOODISON PARK, WALTON
Everton opened Goodison Park in 1892 after leaving Anfield. Mere Green Field, part of Skirving's Nursery, was leased for £50 per year. Work began on Good Friday, clearing four-and-a-half feet of cinders to level the pitch, which was then turfed with grass from Aintree. Initial facilities included timber baths and a referee's room. A covered Goodison Road stand and open stands behind each goal could accommodate 10,000 each. Improvements in 1897 included a new Bullens Road stand and roofed Goodison Road stand.

In 1907, a new double-decker stand was added at the Park End, holding 15,000 fans. In 1909, further renovations introduced a Main Stand on the Goodison Road side, with double-decker seating, improved amenities and integrated spectator and press areas. All terracing was concreted with stepped access.

GRAFTON STREET, LIVERPOOL
Described by the *Birkenhead News* in 1907 as an unlikely football venue, the Grafton Street enclosure was hidden among industrial ruins and known for its bleak surroundings. Despite this, it had a miniature

grandstand, a chimney-stack press box and 60-foot-high walls sheltering the pitch. Improvements in 1907 included newly laid turf and turnstiles.

HAWTHORNE ROAD, BOOTLE
Approved in 1889, the ground featured an open stand for 2,500, a covered stand for 800 and additional seating for 700. It was later used by Bootle Athletic after Bootle FC's demise.

HOLMEFIELD ROAD, AIGBURTH
Opened in 1903 by Garston North End, the ground was set in woodland with a new pavilion. It was accessible by tram and a short walk from Garston.

MESNES, NEWTON-LE-WILLOWS
Used until 1911, the ground had separate entrances for members and the public and included a spectator stand.

MOOR LANE, CROSBY
Home of Northern Cricket Club from 1906 after vacating Waterloo Park. A new pavilion was built at a cost of £750.

NEW BRIGHTON TOWER ATHLETIC GROUND
Opened in 1897 as part of a larger entertainment complex. The oval stadium featured a main stand with a restaurant, a refreshment bar and roofed seating. The football pitch was encircled by a cycle and running track.

POOL BANK, PORT SUNLIGHT
Opened in 1903 by Port Sunlight FC, built at a cost of £600. With a 10,000-spectator capacity, the pitch was railed off and immaculately maintained. It had turnstiles and basic dressing facilities, but no covered stand.

RAVENSHAW'S FIELD AND PRENTON PARK, TRANMERE
Purchased for £5 from Tranmere Hall Estate, Ravenshaw's Field was enclosed, equipped with dressing rooms and renamed Prenton Park.

Improvements in 1902 included a 250-seater stand and extended tram service. By 1912, a second, larger Prenton Park had been developed with upgraded stands, a cinder track and a new Kop. In 1914, a stand from Ellesmere Port's Oval was added.

ROSSETT PARK, COLLEGE ROAD, CROSBY

Marine relocated to Rossett Park in 1903 from Waterloo Park. The area had initially been Marsh land that had held circuses in its time. The Park was named after a local Welsh builder William Rossett Rogers. The inaugural match was against Liverpool Reserves.

SANDFIELD PLACE, BOOTLE

In 1897, White Star Wanderers transported a large hut from Canada Dock to Sandfield Place for use as dressing rooms.

SCARISBRICK NEW ROAD, SOUTHPORT

Opened in 1889 by Southport Central at a cost of £300. It featured a grandstand that had been left to them after the Southport Horticultural Society Show and player tents. The railings around the ground came from the timbers of the SS Great Eastern. The inaugural match, a 5–1 loss to Preston North End, was attended by 3,000 spectators.

SPRINGFIELD PARK, WIGAN

Opened in 1897 by Wigan Trotting and Athletics Grounds Ltd. It included a trotting track, cycle track, football and cricket grounds and a pavilion. Wigan County FC debuted there in September 1897.

TRAMWAYS ATHLETIC GROUNDS, GREEN LANE, LIVERPOOL

Opened in 1903 by the Tramway Employees' Social, Athletic and Thrift Society, this 14-acre complex included cricket, football, cycling, tennis and bowling facilities.

HOPE STREET, PRESCOT

Opened in 1906 by Prescot Athletic, the ground featured a grandstand and cinder cycle track. The pitch was re-laid in 1907.

VICTORIA ATHLETIC AND PLEASURE GROUNDS, ORMSKIRK

Opened in 1894 by the Countess of Derby on land donated by James Eastham. It included multiple sports facilities and pavilions. Dug up during WWI, it was no longer used for football thereafter.

WALTON HALL PARK, WALTON

Acquired by Liverpool City Council in 1913/14, the 120-acre site was intended as a public park, but development was delayed by cost and the outbreak of war.

WHIPCORD LANE AND SEALAND ROAD, CHESTER

Chester's Whipcord Lane ground, opened in 1901, was inadequately sized and lacked facilities. Sealand Road was opened by Chester in 1906 with seating for 1,000 and standing for 2,000. By 1908, additional seating and amenities were added.

WOODCROFT PARK, WAVERTREE

Opened in 1891 by Liverpool Caledonians. By 1892, the ground featured two stands (one covered for 1,000; another open for 2,000) and a cinder track. Following the club's liquidation, it was sold to Old Boys Rugby Club in early 1893.

WOODSIDE ENCLOSURE, BIRKENHEAD

Closed in 1904 following a final match between Birkenhead and Chirk, which Birkenhead won 3–0.

CHAPTER 3

INTERWAR YEARS

DURING THE REMAINDER OF THE WAR, WITH THE MEN'S GAME SUSPENDED, women's football returned – predominantly to raise money for wounded soldiers returning from the front. The women's matches gained popularity mainly from 1916 onwards. With the exception of occasional charity matches, women's football had largely disappeared due to the 1902 ban. The cessation of the men's Football League in April 1915 created a new opportunity. As businesses lost their male workforce – particularly in munitions factories – women were employed to fill the gap. During their spare time, many of these women formed football teams, playing matches before growing crowds to raise funds for the war effort and for newly formed charities supporting injured soldiers and victims of war.

One such team, Dick, Kerr's Ladies, formed at a munitions works near Preston, would go on to become perhaps the most famous women's team of all time. Merseyside saw its own counterpart in the Aintree Ladies Football Team, which played in various locations around Merseyside and Wrexham. By March 1918, the *Liverpool Echo* reported that they had performed in front of a cumulative crowd of 30,000. It was at Goodison Park that Dick, Kerr's Ladies set a world record for a women's match, when a crowd of approximately 53,000 watched them play against St. Helens Ladies on Boxing Day 1918.

Men's football did continue in the Lancashire Section of the Football League. In the men's game, the 1917/18 season saw the formation of two new amateur leagues: the Liverpool Football League, which received a league trophy from Everton and the St Helens and District Junior League. The secretary of the Liverpool Football League at the time was Will Sawyer; a cup named in his honour is still contested today. That same season, the Liverpool Schools team defeated West Ham Schools 1–0 to win the English Schools Shield for the first time.

For the Anniversary of World War One, the *Liverpool Echo*, produced a database that showed the war claimed the lives of over 13,000 people from Merseyside. Local Football inevitably had casualties Among them were twelve current or former Everton, Liverpool and Tranmere Rovers players – Wilfred Bartrop, James Brannick, Frederick Collinson, Joseph Dines, Thomas Gracie, David Murray, Thomas Norse, Robert Randles, Leigh Roose, Donald Sloan, Wilfred Toman and Jack Tosswill.

In March 1919, the Football League voted to expand from 40 to 44 clubs, increasing each division to 22 teams. Arsenal were elected to the First Division. A ballot was held to select additional clubs for the Second Division, but Southport missed out. In April 1919, the Cheshire County League was formed at the Moseley Hotel in Manchester. Chester, Runcorn and Tranmere Rovers were among the 13 founding members. Runcorn finished as champions in the inaugural season, Chester sixth. Tranmere's reserve team resigned after eight matches to take the place of for their first team, which had left the Lancashire Combination to replace Leeds City in the Central League.

The Cheshire League introduced a new trophy, the Edward Case Cup, named after the league's chairman, to be awarded to the highest-placed non-league side. The Cheshire County Medal competition was also launched, contested by the four senior Cheshire clubs – Tranmere Rovers, Stockport County, Crewe Alexandra and Stalybridge – since their reserve sides participated in the Cheshire Senior Cup.

The Lancashire Combination resumed for the 1919/20 season with 18 clubs. Tranmere Rovers Reserves finished fourth, South Liverpool 11th and

Prescot 17th. In the Central League, Tranmere's first team ended the season in fourth place, above the reserve sides of Everton and Liverpool and a struggling Southport. Liverpool won the first two post-war Lancashire Senior Challenge Cups in 1918/19 and 1919/20.

Locally, 1919 saw the founding of the Central Amateur League, the Wesleyan League and the Birkenhead League. The inaugural members of the Birkenhead League included St Catherine's, Grange Road PM, Shaftesbury 2nd, Tranmere Athletic, South End Juniors, Brunswick Wesleyans, Oxton Congregational, Conway Athletic, 12th Birkenhead Boys Scouts (later replaced by Beachcroft's) and Birkenhead Juniors. New Ferry, who joined the league in November 1919, were its first champions and also won the league's initial knockout competition.

The Football League resumed in the 1919/20 season with 22 clubs in the First Division. Liverpool finished fourth after 42 matches, while Everton came 16th. That season saw the introduction of a new fixture scheduling system which had been devised by Charles Sutcliffe, who would often carry out his work while sat on a bench near the band stand on Southport's Lord Street. Though still a ballot system, it used a complex arrangement of chequered boards, charts and a proprietary regional matrix known only to Sutcliffe and later his family. This system was used for fixture scheduling from 1919 until 1967, except for a brief interruption.

The Liverpool League introduced two new challenge cups in 1919/20. The Houston Cup, named after local MP R.P. Houston, replaced the Mutch Cup, previously awarded in 1917/18 and won by Comets. Harland and Wolff had claimed the 1918/19 Liverpool League Cup by defeating Port Sunlight. The Second Division received the Sir Reynolds Cup (later the Lord Colwyn Cup). Southport won the Lancashire Junior Cup/Lancashire Challenge Trophy in 1919/20.

In May 1920, a group of Southern clubs met with 27 Northern clubs in Manchester to discuss the creation of a Third Division. Southport's E. Clayton was part of the delegation that subsequently met with Football League representatives. The Third Division was introduced in July 1920, though its initial members were mainly drawn from the Southern League.

Northern clubs were advised to prepare for a new Northern Section, which would be formalised in February 1921.

Clubs were to be selected from the Birmingham, Central, Lancashire, Midland and North Eastern Leagues. Tranmere Rovers were one of the clubs chosen from the Central League. Ultimately, four teams were elected to join, including Southport, who received 25 votes. Wigan Borough, a newly formed club, also secured a place. South Liverpool was unsuccessful, earning just one vote. To secure their inclusion, both Tranmere and Southport improved their grounds and issued shares. Southport became a Limited Liability Company in April 1921 and raised £4,000 through a share issue.

The Liverpool Shipping Football League began in July 1920 at a meeting held at the Cunard Buildings. Matches commenced in September, with most games played on a ground in West Derby secured for use by up to six teams. Ten clubs participated in the inaugural season: White Star, Lamports, Elders, CPOS, Furness, Cunard, Booth, Neptune, Ebani and Walford. White Star won the first championship (the Lewis Championship), while Cunard claimed the league's Challenge Cup, the GH Melly Cup. Walford failed to complete the season. 1920 also saw the introduction of the Elementary Schools Football Cup.

In general football regulation, 1920/21 saw the introduction of a rule change: players could no longer be offside from a throw-in. That season also saw the establishment of the Bootle JOC League. 'JOC' stood for Juvenile Organisation Committees, developed by the Home Office in 1916 to combat juvenile crime in urban areas. Bootle received certification in March 1918, but the football element of the initiative did not launch until 1921 due to a lack of available playing fields. Waterloo JOC also formed a league. That summer, the Liverpool County FA introduced a medal competition involving Everton, Garston Gasworks, Liverpool, Marine, Orrell, South Liverpool, Skelmersdale United and Tranmere Rovers. In the final at Goodison Park, Marine beat Everton 2–0. During the match, it was announced that the Liverpool Schools team had defeated West Ham Schools 3–2 to win the English Schools Shield for the second time.

The 1921/22 season saw Liverpool win their third League Championship, despite beginning the campaign with a 3–0 defeat to Sunderland and initially sitting at the bottom of the First Division. Consecutive wins over Manchester City and Sunderland at Anfield lifted them into mid-table and by mid-October, a 4–0 win over Preston North End placed them second. After a 1–1 draw at Goodison on 5 November, Liverpool climbed to first place with a 4–0 win over Middlesbrough on 19 November – a position they would retain for the remainder of the season, finishing six points clear of Tottenham Hotspur.

That same season, the Liverpool Shipping League introduced a new trophy – the Concanon Challenge Cup – for its Second Division. The cup was donated by Colonel H. Concanon TD CBE.

In December 1921, the Football Association reintroduced its ban on women's teams playing on FA-affiliated grounds, echoing a similar 1902 restriction. The decision was prompted by concerns about how matches were being arranged and how funds were allocated – specifically, that much of the money intended for charity was not reaching its targets. In response, representatives from 57 women's clubs met in Liverpool and resolved to form the English Ladies' Football Association.

In the postwar years, new competitions emerged. Southport launched the Colonel White Cup and a Victory Cup, while in Liverpool, the Colonel Hall Walker Cup (later the Lord Wavertree Cup) and another Victory Cup were reintroduced. The Liverpool League's Third Division began contesting the Sawyer Cup, named for one of the league's founders.

Lancashire competitions remained prominent. Marine won the 1921/22 Lancashire Amateur Cup. In the Lancashire Junior Cup (also known as the Lancashire Challenge Trophy), New Brighton emerged as winners. In August 1922, leading Lancashire clubs formed the Northern Mid-Week League – originally called the Lancashire Mid-Week League – to give reserve teams regular match practice. As a result, the Lancashire Alliance went on hiatus for two seasons and did not feature any Merseyside teams upon its return.

Liverpool won the League Championship again in 1922/23, marking their second successive title and fourth overall. They reached top spot on 16 September and maintained it throughout the campaign. A 1–0 victory over Newcastle United at St James' Park in December launched a 13-match unbeaten run – 11 wins and two draws – culminating in a four-point lead over Sunderland. A 1–1 draw at home to Huddersfield Town in April, combined with Sunderland's loss at Burnley, secured Liverpool's title, eventually finishing six points ahead of Huddersfield.

April 1923 saw the opening of the Empire Stadium – better known as Wembley Stadium – in London. That year also marked the founding of Littlewoods Pools by three Liverpool messenger boys: John Moores, Colin Askham and Bill Hughes. Inspired by a Birmingham man's concept of pooled football betting, the trio each invested £50, purchased a printing press and rented an office in Church Street. They printed 4,000 coupons for distribution at Old Trafford, but only 35 were returned, generating £4 7s 6d in stakes. The first dividend paid out £2 12s. Moores later bought out his partners and built a fortune from the venture.

For the 1923/24 season, both the Third Division North and South were expanded by two teams. New Brighton was elected to the Third Division North. Wallasey United, formed earlier that year, failed to gain entry to either the Third Division or the Lancashire Combination. They instead joined the Cheshire County League, finishing 15th. A second team competed in the West Cheshire League. Without a home ground, the club soon folded. For the 1923/24 season the Liverpool Old Boys League was also formed, with first champions being Collegiate Old Boys.

On 12 January 1924, Tranmere Rovers lost 5–1 away to Rotherham County in a match notable for marking the League debut of 16-year-old William Ralph Dean. He had scored within four minutes in his senior debut during a Liverpool Senior Cup semi-final against New Brighton days earlier. Selected to face Rotherham, Dean was named alongside Stan Sayer as 'the best of the visitors' forwards' by the *Athletic News*. Liverpool won the Lancashire Senior Cup that season. Liverpool Police also completed a hattrick of Lancashire Amateur Cup wins.

Marine won the Lancashire Amateur Cup in 1925/26. That same season, Liverpool Schools lost 3–2 to Grimsby Schools in their third English Schools Shield final appearance.

In 1925/26, Vernon's Pools was established in Bootle by Edmund Sangster and his son Vernon with a £200 investment, building on Edmund's earlier pools operation in Preston.

The offside rule was amended in 1925/26 to require only two defenders between an attacker and the goal line, down from three. 1925/26 also saw Liverpool Schools team win the Lancashire County Schools Cup beating Blackburn Schools team 7–0. The followings season Liverpool Schools lost 2–0 to Manchester Schools team but they regained the Cup in 1927/28 beating Manchester Schools 2–0. That same 1927/28 season saw Liverpool Schools beat Bootle Schools 1–0 in the first Merseyside Schools Final.

The 1926/27 season featured a notable transfer: Dick Forshaw, a Widnes-born inside-right who had scored 123 goals in 288 games for Liverpool, joined Everton. He had won league titles with Liverpool in 1921/22 and 1922/23. He then added another championship with Everton in 1927/28, making him the only player to win titles with both Merseyside giants. He left for Wolverhampton Wanderers in 1929, having scored eight goals in 42 appearances for Everton.

That season also saw the creation of the Business Houses League in Liverpool, modelled after the London Business Houses Amateur Sports Association, which had been successfully running in the capital for thirty years and covered every sport. Founding teams in Liverpool included Bramtoco, Diamond Athletic, Harrison Line, Hartley's, Parr Bros, Silcock's, Tillotson's, Union Association Recreation, Walker's Athletic and Watson's Athletic.

Everton claimed their third league title in 1927/28. Forshaw linked up with Dixie Dean, who scored a record 60 goals that season. Everton topped the table by the end of December but briefly ceded the lead to Huddersfield in March. They regained top spot in April with a 4–1 win over Blackburn, lost it again and finally reclaimed it with a 3–0 victory over Newcastle. When Huddersfield lost to Aston Villa, Everton secured the title before their final game against Arsenal. Dean, needing a hat-trick to break George Camsell's record of 59 league goals, scored twice early and added a third –

his sixtieth – seven minutes from time, heading in from a corner. That record still stands. Everton finished two points ahead of Huddersfield. During that season, Britain withdrew from FIFA, due to a dispute over payments to amateur players.

Inaugurated in 1929 to honour Robert Lythgoe, founder of the Liverpool FA, the Lythgoe Memorial Cup raised funds for a benevolent fund supporting footballers forced to retire through injury. The inaugural competition featured Marine, Howson's, Bootle Celtic and Whiston, with Marine defeating Howson's in the final held at their College Road ground.

The West Cheshire League shut down during the 1929/30 season, prompting several clubs to seek new competitions. Ellesmere Port Town and Shell Mex joined the Liverpool County Combination, while Ellesmere Port Cement, Little Sutton and Hoylake moved to the Liverpool League. Proposals to restart the league followed swiftly and the Cheshire FA authorised the formation of a new competition under the name of the Cheshire Combination. The Pyke Cup continued during the league's hiatus, contested by Shell Mex, West Kirby, Neston Brickworks and Hoylake.

Relegated from the First Division at the end of 1929/30, Everton began the 1930/31 Second Division campaign with a 3–2 win at Plymouth Argyle. They won their first five games and remained at or near the top of the table all season. A mid-season run of 14 consecutive League and Cup victories – a club record – helped secure the title, confirmed by a 3–2 win over Burnley at Goodison with three games remaining. Everton finished seven points clear of second-placed West Bromwich Albion.

That season also saw the formation of the North Wales Football Combination. Nine clubs joined, including Ellesmere Port Town and eight Welsh sides: Bangor City, Bethesda Victoria, Caernarvon Athletic, Colwyn Bay United, Holyhead Town, Llandudno, Rhyl and Llanfairfechan. Ellesmere Port Town lost heavily to champions Colwyn Bay in their debut match and left the league after finishing sixth, due to merger difficulties with the Welsh League. Concurrently, the Bootle District League folded due to insufficient entries.

Marine won the 1930/31 Lancashire Amateur Cup, beating Cadby Hall 4–2, while Liverpool claimed the Lancashire Senior Challenge Cup.

On 1 June 1931, the Football League held its re-election meeting for the Third Division North. Chester and Nelson tied with 27 votes each. In a second vote, Chester prevailed 28–20 and joined the League for the first time. In 1931 the Liverpool Schools Football Association was formed.

Everton returned to the First Division in 1931/32 with a 3–2 home win over Birmingham City, helped by a Jimmy Dunn hat-trick. By late October, they reached the top of the table following a 3–2 win at Aston Villa and stayed there for the remainder of the season. A 1–0 win over Bolton at Goodison, with a goal from Dixie Dean, sealed the title in April. Everton finished five points clear of Arsenal.

Marine also had a notable season, finishing runners-up in the FA Amateur Cup. They defeated Maidenhead United (4–1), Leyton (3–0) and Yorkshire Amateurs (2–1) to reach the final at Upton Park, where they lost 7–1 to Dulwich Hamlet. They retained the Lancashire Amateur Cup with a 4–2 win over the Casuals.

The Cheshire Bowl replaced the Cheshire Medals in 1932. In its first final, Chester beat Crewe Alexandra 3–1.

In 1932/33, Everton won the FA Cup, defeating Manchester City 3–0 in the final – the first in which players wore squad numbers (Everton 1–11, City 12–22). Everton's route to Wembley included wins over Leicester City, Bury, Leeds United, Luton Town and West Ham United. Goals in the final came from Dixie Dean, Jimmy Dunn and Jimmy Stein. Standing tickets at Wembley cost 2s 6d, while seats ranged from 5s to one guinea.

That season, Chester won the Welsh Cup, beating Wrexham 2–0. Marine again secured the Lancashire Amateur Cup, while Liverpool won the Lancashire Senior Challenge Cup. Liverpool also joined the Northern Mid-Week League in 1933, winning Section A in 1933/34. A final against Blackpool ended 1–1 at Anfield; Blackpool won the replay 2–0. Liverpool did not win the title again before WWII. Southport joined the league in 1936.

In the early 1930s, three major infrastructure projects transformed the region. Speke Airport officially opened in July 1933, situated on part of the Speke Hall estate. In 1934, the East Lancashire Road was completed, linking Liverpool with Salford. That same year, the Queensway Tunnel between Liverpool and Birkenhead opened. Built at a cost of over £7 million (the equivalent of £650 million in 2025), the tunnel employed more than 1,000 workers across eight years and involved the excavation of over one million tons of rock.

The West Cheshire League was revived in 1934 with 13 teams: Hoylake, West Kirby, Dee Rangers (Neston), Heswall, Brougham Athletic, Shaftesbury Old Boys, Bebington, Bromborough Port, Little Sutton, Ellesmere Port, Shell Mex, Phoenix Social (Ellesmere Port) and Bowater's. The Pyke Cup also resumed. That year, the Cheshire County League introduced the Edward Case Trophy for the highest-placed non-league team. Case, founding Chair of the League in 1919, held the post until his death in 1953.

The Lancashire Alliance faded out after the 1934/35 season. In the same campaign, Everton won the Lancashire Senior Challenge Cup and Tranmere Rovers lifted the Welsh Cup for the only time, beating Chester in the final. They had lost the previous year's final 3–0 to Bristol City.

In 1935, the Liverpool Senior Cup adopted a new format, inviting Marine, Prescot Cables and South Liverpool to join the competition alongside Everton and Liverpool Reserves, New Brighton, Tranmere Rovers and Southport.

At the start of the 1935/36 season, Marine and South Liverpool joined the Lancashire Combination. Wigan Athletic won the Lancashire Junior Cup that season, while Chester lost 2–0 to Crewe Alexandra in the Welsh Cup final.

The so-called Pools War of 1936 had its origins two years earlier, in June 1934, when Watson Hartley, an accountant from Nelson working in Liverpool, proposed a scheme whereby a portion of the football pools companies' profits would supplement Football League funds. Initially rebuffed by the League's management committee, Hartley's proposal gained traction as pools revenue surged from £9 million in 1934 to £20 million in 1935. His key argument was that, as copyright holders of the fixture list, the Football League could and should charge all commercial users – including calendar publishers, sports media and the pools operators – for its use.

While the League considered its response, John McKenna was approached by Liverpool solicitor E. Holland Hughes, representing the pools promoters. A January 1936 meeting between League and pools representatives followed. During this, John Moores informally proposed a £100,000 annual payment from the pools companies for use of the fixture list. Although the League never formally demanded this amount, they subsequently warned that failure to present a satisfactory offer could result in legal action for copyright infringement.

Talks deteriorated into stalemate, prompting the League to devise a bold strategy: scrap the published fixtures and issue revised, secret fixture lists at the last minute, thereby disrupting the pools industry. At a 20 February 1936 meeting at Manchester's Midland Hotel, 85 League clubs approved the plan under strict secrecy.

Two days later, on 22 February, the pools companies convened at Liverpool's Adelphi Hotel, publicly accusing the League of making unreasonable financial demands. The League countered by insisting it had merely discussed, not demanded, a sum. The revised fixtures went into effect: clubs were informed of away fixtures by telephone on Thursday and home fixtures on Friday. For example, Everton, initially scheduled to host Blackburn Rovers, now faced Manchester City. Liverpool were redirected from a match at Huddersfield to Aston Villa. Similar changes occurred across the region: Tranmere played at Accrington instead of Stockport, Chester faced Carlisle instead of Mansfield and Southport played Walsall in place of Hartlepools United.

Confusion and dissatisfaction grew. Headlines such as 'The Big Hush' appeared in the press, while the pools companies urged punters to consult Friday's papers for guidance. Weather disruptions complicated efforts to assess the strategy's impact on attendance. Nonetheless, by early March, a coalition of First and Second Division clubs demanded a return to regular fixtures. That weekend's games again followed secret scheduling, but low gates – Liverpool's home match against Portsmouth attracted their smallest crowd of the season – undermined support for the plan. On the following Monday, the League abandoned the tactic. The Pools War was over.

Meanwhile, Chester enjoyed success in the Football League Third Division North Cup, introduced in 1933/34. They won it in 1935/36 and 1936/37, defeating Darlington and Southport respectively. Southport triumphed in 1937/38 with a 4–1 win over Bradford City. The game continued to evolve. In 1937, the penalty area was redesigned with the addition of the now-familiar 10-yard arc or 'D'.

The region's schools continued to make a mark. Liverpool Schools won the English Schools Shield for the third time in 1936/37, beating Blyth 1–0. Bootle Schools reached the final for the first time in 1937/38 but were beaten 12–0 by Manchester. 1936/37 also saw Liverpool Schools beat Manchester Schools 2–1 to win the Lancashire Schools Cup but lost to Manchester Schools 7–0 in the final the following season.

South Liverpool lifted the Lancashire Junior Cup in 1937/38 and followed up with another win in the Welsh Cup, beating Cardiff City 2–1 at Wrexham's Racecourse Ground. Tranmere Rovers finished the season as Third Division North Champions.

In 1938/39, Everton secured their fifth First Division title. They started the season with six consecutive victories, including a 2–0 away win at Blackpool and led the table until late October when Derby County overtook them. By January, Everton were five points adrift but with a game in hand. They regained top spot in early February after a 3–0 win at Anfield, overtaking Derby on goal difference. With three matches remaining, they led second-placed Wolverhampton Wanderers by six points. A 2–1 defeat at Charlton was inconsequential, as Wolves could only draw at Bolton. Everton finished four points clear to claim the championship.

That season also saw South Liverpool win both the Welsh Cup and the Lancashire Junior Cup, capping a successful period for the club.

THE FOOTBALL TEAMS FORMED AND ALREADY PLAYING ON MERSEYSIDE BETWEEN 1919 AND 1945

AINTREE S.S. (SORTING SIDINGS)
Following the First World War, Aintree S.S. competed in the L& NW League before moving to the Liverpool and District League for the 1923/24 season. They enjoyed early success, winning the Liverpool Junior Cup in 1924/25 with victory over Woolton Juniors. After switching to the Liverpool League in 1925/26, they continued to compete until claiming the Liverpool Amateur Cup in 1932/33, beating Jabisco 3-0. The club left the Liverpool League at the end of the 1935/36 season to join the Bootle JOC League Premier Division, but returned to the Liverpool League shortly before the outbreak of the Second World War.

BALMORAL
Balmoral rejoined the I Zingari League after the First World War, finishing second from bottom in the First Division in 1919/20. A similar result followed in 1922/23, after which the club withdrew from the league and appears to have disbanded.

BOOTLE ALBION
Bootle Albion re-entered the I Zingari League First Division for the 1919/20 campaign and finished a creditable fourth, they were also the runners-up in the I Zingari Cup to Marine. However, their fortunes declined steadily and they ended the 1924/25 season at the foot of the table. The club seemingly folded shortly thereafter.

BOOTLE CELTIC
Formed in 1925 by disaffected players from Bootle St. James Football Club, Celtic won the Bootle League in the 1925/26 season before moving on to play in the Liverpool County Combination. They won the George Mahon Cup in 1927/28, beating Whiston. They finished as runners-up in 1929/30,

three points behind the Liverpool 'A' side. They left the league after finishing sixth in the 1930/31 season and returned to Bootle to play in the Bootle JOC League for the 1931/32 season.

BOOTLE ST. JAMES

Formed in 1919 as St. James CYMS, they joined the CYMS League for the 1919/20 season and won it at the first attempt before moving to the Bootle League for the start of the 1920/21 season, winning it in their first season. Although they kept a team in the CYMS League and won it again in 1921/22, they also maintained a team that finished in the top half of the Bootle League that season. The following season, 1922/23, they won the Liverpool Junior Cup. They won both the Bootle League and Bootle Cup in 1923/24 and claimed the Bootle League for the last time in 1926/27.

They joined the Liverpool County Combination for the start of the 1928/29 season, finishing bottom of the ten-team league. They left the league at the end of the 1930/31 season after finishing second from bottom in the fourteen-team league. They joined the Bootle JOC League for the start of the 1931/32 season and won the Bootle JOC Everton Cup in the 1939/40 season.

BROMBOROUGH POOL

Bromborough Pool resumed playing in the I Zingari League following the First World War. They won the Wirral Senior Cup in 1922/23 by defeating Harrowby 1-0 and remained in the First Division until their relegation in 1928/29. They bounced back by winning the Second Division in 1930/31, ten points clear of Southport Trinity. Further honours followed, including the I Zingari Challenge Cup in 1933/34 (5-0 vs The Casuals) and the Pyke Cup in 1937/38 (6-1 vs Stanlow Social). The club experienced further relegation in 1936/37 and remained in the Second Division until the outbreak of war. They were also Wirral Senior Cup runners-up in 1934/35 (to Shell Mex) and in 1936/37 (to Hoylake).

BURSCOUGH RANGERS

Rangers resumed play after the war in the Ormskirk and District Amateur League in 1919/20 before rejoining the Liverpool County Combination the following season, finishing as runners-up to Whiston Parish Church and winning the George Mahon Cup. They claimed the league title in 1921/22 and Hall Walker Cup winners that season and were consistent contenders throughout the 1920s. Notable achievements include back-to-back Combination titles in 1925/26 and 1926/27 and victories in the George Mahon Cup (1925/26) and Liverpool Challenge Cup (1926/27). In 1927, they joined the Lancashire Combination but struggled with low attendances and mounting financial issues, eventually resigning early in the 1933/34 season. A brief stint in the West Lancashire League ended in 1935 and the club folded. Their Victoria Park ground was subsequently taken over by Northern Nomads. They were runners-up in the Liverpool Challenge Cup in 1920/21 and 1924/25.

CADBY HALL

Cadby Hall re-entered the I Zingari League in 1920/21, starting in the Third Division and earning successive promotions. They finished fourth in their debut First Division season (1923/24) and emerged as one of the competition's dominant teams over the following decade. Cadby Hall won multiple league titles (1925/26, 1927/28, 1928/29, 1935/36), along with the Liverpool Amateur Cup 1925/26 and 1935/36, I Zingari Challenge Cup 1924/25 and 1929/30 and two Lancashire Amateur Cups 1927/28 and 1929/30. As well as being runners-up in the I Zingari Cup and Liverpool Amateur Cup. Their reserve side was also successful, claiming multiple Combination honours. Though their dominance waned slightly in the mid-1930s, they remained competitive up to the eve of the Second World War.

CHESHIRE LINES

Founded in 1927, Cheshire Lines joined the Shipping League and quickly made their mark, finishing as runners-up in 1932/33 and 1933/34. They then secured back-to-back league titles in 1934/35 and 1935/36, along with two Melly Challenge Cup wins.

CHESTER / CHESTER CITY

After the war, the club had to rebuild from scratch. They secured Sealand Road on a yearly basis and, by the 1919/20 season, were founder members of the newly formed Cheshire County League, finishing sixth. The following season (1920/21), they finished tenth and changed their playing colours from green and white (worn since 1901) to black and white stripes.

In 1921/22, Chester won the league title. By January, they were sixth and ten points behind leaders Congleton Town, but with seven games in hand due to FA Cup commitments. A 3–2 home win against Congleton helped close the gap. A strong run of form in their final nine games saw Chester overtake Congleton, clinching the title with a 3–1 victory over Witton Albion. They also beat Sandbach Ramblers 3–2, marking their ninth successive win.

In 1923/24, Chester shared the Cheshire Challenge Cup with Stockport County. The reserve side finished runners-up in the West Cheshire League in 1924/25, also winning the Cheshire Amateur Cup (3–1 vs Barnton Victoria Reserves) and the Wirral Senior Cup (vs Ellesmere Port Cement Reserves).

In 1925/26, Chester won the title again. By New Year, they had won eight consecutive matches and closed the gap on leaders Port Vale Reserves to six points. A win over Port Vale Reserves at Sealand Road reduced the deficit to four. Four further wins brought their streak to thirteen. At Easter, they moved into first place, clinching the title with a 2–2 draw against Ashton National with two games remaining. Chester finished five points ahead of Port Vale Reserves. Their reserves lost 4–2 in the Pyke Cup Final.

The winning habit continued in 1926/27, as Chester retained the Cheshire County League title, going unbeaten in their final nine games and finishing three points clear of Ashton National. They capped the season with a 3–0 win over Stockport County in the Cheshire Senior Medals Final.

In 1928/29, Chester were runners-up in the Cheshire Senior Cup, losing 2–0 to Northwich Victoria. In their final Cheshire County League season (1930/31), they again finished runners-up, three points behind Port Vale Reserves and lost to the same club in the Cheshire League Challenge Cup

Final. However, they did win the Cheshire Senior Cup, thrashing Crewe Alexandra 6–1.

In July 1931, Chester were elected to the Football League Third Division North at the League's AGM. The club's directors personally canvassed First and Second Division clubs. The first vote tied them with Nelson at 27 votes each. In a second ballot, Chester received 28 votes to Nelson's 20, securing League membership.

Ground improvements were made for their first League season (1931/32) and 12,000 fans attended the opening fixture at Sealand Road on 29 August 1931, where Chester beat a financially troubled Wigan Borough 4–0. However, Wigan withdrew from the league two months later and their results were expunged. Chester's first official League point came in a 1–1 draw against Wrexham on 2 September 1931.

Chester ended their debut League season in third place, won the Cheshire Senior Cup (6–1 vs Crewe Alexandra) and lost the final Cheshire Senior Medals Final to Tranmere Rovers.

In 1932/33, they beat Wrexham 2–0 to win the Welsh Cup and became inaugural winners of the renamed Cheshire Bowl with a 2–1 win over Crewe Alexandra.

In 1933/34, they lost the Cheshire Bowl Final to Stockport County in a replay. In 1934/35, after winning a coin toss for choice of venue, they lost the Welsh Cup Final 1–0 to Tranmere Rovers but beat Stockport 4–2 in the Cheshire Bowl Final.

In 1935/36, Chester were Welsh Cup runners-up again, losing 2–0 to Crewe, but won the Third Division North Cup with a 2–1 win over Darlington. The 1936/37 season brought further silverware: Chester finished third in the league, won the Third Division North Cup (3–1 vs Southport) and the Cheshire Bowl (1–0 vs Tranmere).

In 1938/39, they lost the Cheshire Bowl Final 2–1 to Crewe. During World War Two, Chester won the Cheshire Bowl three times: in 1940/41 (4–2 vs Stockport), 1943/44 (6–1 vs Stockport) and again in 1944/45 with two-legged wins (3–0 and 4–2).

COLLEGIATE OLD BOYS

At the start of World War I, the club moved to Hornspit Lane, then to the Clubmoor Cricket Ground. They joined the I Zingari League Second Division in 1919/20, finishing second from bottom. At the start of the 1923/24 season, they were promoted to the First Division but lost the Lancashire Amateur Cup Final to Liverpool Police.

In 1931/32 they were League runners-up and in 1933/34, they secured their first major honour, winning the Lancashire Amateur Cup with a 4–0 victory over Manchester University and League runners-up. They remained in the First Division until World War Two and won the I Zingari Challenge Cup in 1938/39, defeating Cadby Hall 3–0.

COSTAINS

Formed in 1927, Costains was the team of a well-known building firm. They joined the Liverpool League in 1927/28. They were runners-up in the RP Houston Cup Final in 1929/30 (lost to Formby) and won the Sawyer Cup in 1930/31. In 1932/33, they lost 5–0 to Marine Reserves in the Houston Cup Final. The club disbanded before the 1934/35 season.

DEE-JAY UNITED (LATER DEE-JAYS)

Formed around 1928 by Messrs David Jones Provisions Merchants of Red Cross Street, Liverpool. They began in the Liverpool League Third Division in 1928/29 and entered the Shipping League Third Division in 1929/30. They played in the Welsh Amateur Cup in 1930.

Rejoining the Liverpool League in 1937/38, they won the Liverpool Amateur Cup, beating Earlestown Bohemians 2–1 and also won the RP Houston Cup in 1938/39, defeating Belvidere 3–2.

EARLE

After the war, Earle joined the I Zingari League, winning the Third Division in 1919/20, eight points clear of Sudley. They were Second Division runners-up in 1920/21 and champions in 1921/22, five points ahead of Cadby Hall, earning promotion.

In 1922/23, they finished as First Division runners-up to Marine in both the League and Challenge Cup. Between 1920 and 1923, Earle went unbeaten in 55 league games.

In 1923/24, they again lost a play-off for the title to Marine. The 1926/27 season saw them win the I Zingari Challenge Cup (vs Orrell), the Lancashire Amateur Cup (2–1 vs Marine) and the Combination (reserves).

They claimed their first I Zingari League title in 1930/31, finishing six points ahead of Thorndale but lost in the I Zingari Challenge Cup Liverpool Casuals. In 1932/33, they shared the I Zingari Challenge Cup with Formby. In 1933/34, their reserves won the I Zingari Combination.

In 1934/35, they won the league again (two points clear of Maghull) but lost the Lancashire Amateur Cup Final to Formby. They were runners-up to Cadby Hall in 1935/36, won the I Zingari Challenge Cup (2–0 vs Maghull) and the reserves again took the Combination.

In 1936/37, they won the League by five points from Formby, claimed the Challenge Cup (6–2 vs Bromborough Pool) and won the Liverpool Amateur Cup by beating Collegiate Old Boys.

They retained the I Zingari Challenge Cup in 1937/38 (3–0 vs Port Sunlight) and were League runners-up. They won the final pre-war League title in 1938/39, eleven points ahead of Maghull. That season, they were Liverpool Amateur Cup runners-up (2–1 loss to Earlestown Bohemians), a team they had beaten earlier in the Barnes Cup Final.

EARLESTOWN CYMS / EARLESTOWN BOHEMIANS

Formed around 1916 as Earlestown CYMS, the club initially joined the St Helens & District League before moving to the Warrington & District League. In 1934, they changed their name to Earlestown Bohemians and joined the Liverpool County Combination for the 1934/35 season. They also moved grounds after previously sharing the Sankey Sugar Works pitch.

Their first match was away to Liverpool 'A' at Cadby Hall, where they came back from 3–0 down to draw 3–3. Their first home game – and first win – came against Skelmersdale United in front of a large crowd.

They were George Mahon Cup runners-up in both 1935/36 (losing 3–0 to Everton 'A') and 1936/37 (losing to Prescot Cables) and League runners-up. In 1937/38, they won the George Mahon Cup by beating Prescot BI 3–1 and also lifted the Lythgoe Cup after defeating Dee Jays. However, they lost 2–1 to Dee Jays in the Liverpool Amateur Cup Final. In 1938/39, they won the Liverpool Amateur Cup by beating Earle 2–1 at Holly Park and were runners-up to Earle in the Barnes Cup Final.

EARLESTOWN WHITE STAR
Formed around 1930, Earlestown White Star were associated with the White Star Ship Owners group. They initially competed in the Warrington Amateur Football League and won the Liverpool Junior Cup in 1930/31, defeating Garston Protestant Reformers.

They resigned from the Warrington Amateur League at the end of the 1931/32 season but rejoined for 1932/33. That same season, they lost the Liverpool Junior Cup Final 6–1 to Haydock Athletic.

They joined the Liverpool County Combination for the 1934/35 season and lost their opening match 2–0 at home to Marine. They ended that campaign in seventh place, winning ten of their thirty fixtures. The following season (1935/36), they finished bottom of a nine-team league. In March 1937, they were beaten 6–1 by South Liverpool Reserves in the Liverpool Challenge Cup Final at Anfield.

In their final season before World War Two (1938/39), season tickets cost five shillings (2s 6d for the unemployed). They finished third from bottom in the Liverpool County Combination.

ELLESMERE PORT CEMENT
In 1921, a new club was formed in Ellesmere Port under the name Ellesmere Port Cement. Their first match was against Whitchurch and they went on to compete in the Chester & District League. They joined the Cheshire County League in 1921/22, finishing fourteenth.

In 1923/24, they entered the West Cheshire League and won the Wirral Senior Cup beating Bebington. That season, their reserve side won the Cheshire Amateur Cup by beating Barnton 2–1. The following season (1924/25), Ellesmere Port Cement won the West Cheshire League. Their reserves were runners-up to Chester Reserves in the Wirral Senior Cup. However, the first team withdrew from the Cheshire County League after finishing second from bottom.

In 1925/26, they won the West Cheshire League again and were runners-up to Wirral Railway in the Wirral Senior Cup. The 1926/27 season saw them finish second in the league and lose the Pyke Cup Final to Victoria Lodge and won the Cheshire Amateur Cup. They returned to the Pyke Cup Final in 1927/28, beating Neston Brickworks and also reached the Cheshire Amateur Cup Final, losing 2–1 to rivals Ellesmere Port Town. They were also runners-up to Ellesmere Port Town in the West Cheshire League.

In 1929/30, they won the Liverpool League by two points ahead of Garston Gasworks. The club disbanded in 1932.

ELLESMERE PORT (1912)

After World War One, Ellesmere Port rejoined the West Cheshire League and were runners-up in both the Wirral Senior Cup (to Harrowby) and the Pyke Cup Final (to West Kirby) in 1919/20.

In 1920/21, they won the West Cheshire League title and the Pyke Cup, beating Ellesmere Port Cement and also claimed the Wirral Senior Cup by defeating West Kirby. They retained the league title in 1921/22 but were beaten by West Kirby in the Wirral Senior Cup Final.

Ahead of the 1923/24 season, the club secured a new ground at the Whitby Road Recreation Ground and joined the Liverpool County Combination, finishing in seventh place. This appears to have been the final season for the original Ellesmere Port Football Club, which seems to have continued under the name Ellesmere Port Town Football Club.

ELLESMERE PORT TOWN

A new Ellesmere Port Town Football Club was formed in 1924. They were elected to the Cheshire County League for the 1924/25 season, beginning with a 1–0 away defeat to Macclesfield. Unfortunately, they finished bottom of the league. In 1926/27, they again came last, conceding 196 goals and it proved to be their final season in the competition.

By August 1927, this version of the club had folded at a public meeting. However, a week later, a separate meeting agreed to form a new Ellesmere Port Football Club. In September, the York Road ground tenancy of the former club was transferred to the newly formed Ellesmere Port Town.

They entered the West Cheshire League and won it at the first attempt in 1927/28. Chasing down Ellesmere Port Cement required playing four games in eight days and winning all of them. They finished the season four points ahead of their rivals.

In 1928/29, Ellesmere Port Town won the Pyke Cup, defeating Runcorn 4–3. In July 1929, they joined the newly formed Wirral Combination and became its inaugural champions in the 1929/30 season. That same season, they were runners-up in both the Wirral Senior Cup (to Planters) and the Wirral Combination Challenge Cup (to Neston Brickworks).

At the start of the 1931/32 season, Town joined the Liverpool League. After a 4–1 defeat away to West Kirby in their opening match, they applied to rejoin the Cheshire County League in November 1931. Although unsuccessful, they resigned from the Liverpool League at the end of the season.

They moved to the Liverpool County Combination for the 1932/33 season, finishing in eighth place and spent the next two seasons (1933/34 and 1934/35) in that league. In 1934/35, they rejoined the newly revived West Cheshire League, finishing runners-up to Shell Mex. They remained in the West Cheshire League until its suspension due to World War Two.

During the war, in 1940, Ellesmere Port Town reached the Pyke Cup Final, beating Bromborough Pool 5–3 and won the Wirral Senior Cup with victory over Tranmere Rovers.

EVERTON

After the First World War, Everton's first season back in the First Division (1919/20) saw them finish in sixteenth place. In 1921/22, while Liverpool won the league, Everton narrowly avoided relegation by four points. In 1922/23, the club improved to fifth place.

The 1924/25 season was more notable for the debut of Dixie Dean than the team's seventeenth-place finish. Dean, signed from Tranmere Rovers, made his League debut in a 3–1 defeat away at Arsenal in March 1925. He scored his first Everton goal on his home debut a few days later in a 2–0 win against Aston Villa at Goodison Park.

At the end of the 1926/27 season, Everton finished third from bottom, again avoiding relegation by four points. Remarkably, the following season (1927/28), Everton won the First Division for the third time in their history, propelled by Dean's record-breaking haul of 60 league goals.

By the end of October, Everton had gone top with a 3–1 away win at Portsmouth. Dean had scored 30 goals in 19 games by December and Everton remained top, ahead of Cardiff City and Huddersfield Town. In January, they stayed top with Dean reaching 39 goals. Although Huddersfield closed the gap in early February, Everton retained their lead. In early March, Everton slipped to second behind Huddersfield, who had games in hand, but reclaimed the top spot by the end of the month with two wins and a draw. Another brief setback in mid-April saw Huddersfield go ahead again, but Everton responded with four straight wins to top the table once more.

Going into the final game, Everton were three points clear of Huddersfield, who had two games in hand. The title was secured when Aston Villa beat Huddersfield in early May, ensuring they could not overtake Everton. All eyes then turned to Dixie Dean, who had 57 goals and needed three more in the final game against Arsenal to break George Camsell's record of 59. Dean scored his first with a shot in the first half, converted a penalty for his second and completed his historic hat-trick with a header from a corner, reaching 60 goals – a record that still stands. Everton won the league by two points.

However, their success was short-lived. Everton were relegated at the end of the 1929/30 season, finishing bottom of the First Division. They bounced back immediately by winning the Second Division title

AND THEN THERE WAS FOOTBALL

in 1930/31, finishing seven points clear of runners-up West Bromwich Albion. Everton went top at the end of September 1930 and never relinquished the lead. They reached the FA Cup semi-final but lost 1–0 to WBA at Old Trafford.

In 1931/32, Everton won the First Division title again, completing an immediate return to the top flight as champions. They took first place in October and held it throughout the season. By January, they led West Brom by two points. In late February, they were three points ahead of Arsenal, who had games in hand. By early April, they led Huddersfield and Sheffield Wednesday by five points with a game in hand. With four matches remaining, Everton needed three points to seal the title. A 1–0 win over Bolton Wanderers at Goodison Park secured it, as Arsenal could no longer catch them. A final point came in a goalless draw at Newcastle United. Everton finished two points clear of Arsenal.

In 1932/33, Everton completed a remarkable three-year spell by winning the FA Cup, beating Manchester City 3–0 at Wembley in the first final to feature numbered shirts. Their cup run included victories over Leicester City (3–2 away), Bury (3–1 at home), Leeds United (2–0 at home), Luton Town (6–0 at home in the quarter-final) and West Ham United (2–1 at Molineux in the semi-final).

In 1937/38, Everton won the Liverpool Senior Cup and the Central Leeague. Dixie Dean played his final game for the club on 9 March 1938, in the same competition, against South Liverpool. The following season (1938/39), Everton were league champions once again. After surrendering top spot to Derby County at the end of October, they returned to the summit in early February 1939 following a 3–0 win over Liverpool at Anfield and held it for the rest of the campaign. The title was clinched with three games to spare. Although Everton lost 2–1 away to Charlton Athletic, Wolverhampton Wanderers – six points behind – were only able to draw 0–0 away to Bolton Wanderers, meaning Everton were crowned champions. They finished five points clear of Wolves.

Everton won the Liverpool Senior Cup eleven times between 1919 and 1940 and the Lancashire Senior Cup in 1940.

127

FLORENCE ALBION

Following the First World War, Florence Albion were members of the Liverpool Central Amateur League. They joined the Liverpool League in 1933/34 and remained in the lower divisions until the outbreak of the Second World War.

FORMBY

Formby Football Club was founded at a meeting on Three Tuns Lane on 23 September 1919. They joined a newly formed extension to the Southport & District League and played their first match on 25 October 1919, losing 5–2 to Bescar Lane. A week later, they recorded their first win, beating High Park Maple Crescent 3–2. Initially playing at Formby Cricket Ground on Green Lane, they moved to farmer James Eccles's field on Church Road in April 1920 and then to the Brows Lane Enclosure later that year.

They joined the main Southport League in 1921/22. By the 1923/24 season, Formby had finished runners-up in the Liverpool & District League and the following season (1924/25) they won it. In 1925, the club raised funds to build a new stand and pavilion at Brows Lane.

Formby rejoined the Liverpool League for the 1925/26 season. In 1927/28, they lost the Houston Cup Final to Ainsdale. They went on to win the Liverpool Amateur Cup in 1929/30 by beating Harrowby and they won the Houston Cup that same season by beating Costain's after a replay.

In 1931/32, Formby joined the I Zingari League Second Division and finished runners-up, seven points behind Port Sunlight. In 1932/33, they won the division after a play-off victory over Maghull and shared the I Zingari Challenge Cup with Earle.

Their first season in the I Zingari First Division (1933/34) saw them finish in eighth place. In 1934/35, they won the Lancashire Amateur Cup by beating Earle. In 1936/37, they finished second in the league, five points behind Earle.

Formby left the I Zingari League at the end of the 1937/38 season. For the 1938/39 campaign, they joined the Liverpool County Combination, finishing bottom of the table.

FURNESS WITHY

Formed around 1919, Furness Withy joined the Liverpool & District League and won the title in the 1920/21 season, finishing one point ahead of Harland & Wolff. That same season, they also won the Liverpool Junior Cup, beating Orford St John's 3–0.

For the 1921/22 season, they moved to a new ground at Hollyfield Road, Orrell Park and retained the league title. They also won the Liverpool Challenge Cup with a 1–0 victory over Garston Gasworks. In 1922/23, now playing at Walton Hall Avenue, they won the league again – this time by five points from Howson's. The following year, 1923/24, they moved to Hawthorne Road in Bootle and secured their fourth successive Liverpool & District League title. That season they also won the Mersey Cup (2–1 vs Blundellsands), the Allen Cup (5–2 vs Howson's) and the Bootle Hospital Cup (6–0 vs Seaforth Albion).

For the 1925/26 season, they joined the Liverpool League and won the RP Houston Cup by beating Garston Royal. In 1926/27, they were beaten in the same cup by Seaforth Albion. By 1930, there is no further mention of Furness Withy in league records, suggesting the club had disbanded.

GARSTON GASWORKS (RECREATION)

After World War One, Garston Gasworks – nicknamed 'The Tanks' – were runners-up to Harrowby in the West Cheshire League in 1919/20. The following season, they lost the Liverpool Challenge Cup Final 1–0 to Furness Withy. They won the Pyke Cup in 1921/22 but left the West Cheshire League at the end of 1922/23 and joined the Liverpool League for 1923/24.

They won the Third Division of the Liverpool League in 1926/27, also claiming the Sawyer Cup by beating Furness Withy Reserves. They followed up with the Second Division title in 1927/28 and completed a hat-trick of promotions by winning the First Division in 1928/29, finishing ahead of Blundellsands. That season, they were also runners-up to Blundellsands in the RP Houston Cup.

In 1931/32, they won the RP Houston Cup by defeating Little Sutton 4–1 and claimed the Liverpool Amateur Cup with a 4–1 win over

Seaforth Albion. They remained in the Liverpool League until the outbreak of the Second World War.

GARSTON PROTESTANT REFORMERS

Founded in 1921, the club joined the Liverpool League for the 1921/22 season. They won the Liverpool Junior Cup in 1927/28 and were runners-up the following year, losing to Derby Crescent. In 1930/31, they were beaten in the Liverpool Junior Cup Final by Earlestown White Star. In 1933/34, they lost 1–0 to Marine in the Liverpool Amateur Cup Final. The club disbanded in 1935.

GARSTON ROYAL

Garston Royal won the Liverpool Central Combination in 1920/21 and joined the Liverpool League in 1922/23. That season, they lost the RP Houston Cup Final 2–0 to Howson's. In 1923/24, they won the Liverpool League by a single point ahead of Prescot Newtown. They were RP Houston Cup runners-up again in 1925/26, this time to Furness Withy.

In 1926/27, they spent a single season in the Liverpool County Combination, finishing second from bottom. They then joined the Bootle League for 1927/28 and returned to the Liverpool League in 1930/31. In 1932/33, they won the Liverpool League Second Division. The club disbanded in 1937 with George Simpson still serving as manager.

GARSTON WOODCUTTERS

Formed in 1932, Garston Woodcutters joined the Liverpool League Second Division in 1933/34. Their first match was a 5–1 defeat away to West Derby Recs. They shared a ground with Garston Royal at Byron Park.

The 1934/35 season was a successful one: they were runners-up in the Liverpool League, won the RP Houston Cup by beating BI Social 2–1 and shared the Liverpool Amateur Cup with Maghull. In 1935/36, they retained the RP Houston Cup.

In 1936/37, they completed the double – winning the Liverpool League by two points over Marine and the RP Houston Cup with a 4–3 win over

Aigburth Parish Church. The following season, 1937/38, they won the league again, four points ahead of Everton Amateurs and shared the RP Houston Cup with Marine.

HARLANDIC

Harlandic was formed shortly after World War One as part of the revived Harland & Wolff Football Section under the Employees' Recreation and Athletics Association. They played at Pirrie Park on Walton Hall Avenue and joined the Liverpool & District League in 1920/21. They finished as runners-up to Formby in 1924/25, their final season in the league and won the Liverpool Amateur Cup.

In 1925/26, Harlandic won the Liverpool Challenge Cup, defeating Prescot 5–0 and placed third in their only season in the Liverpool County Combination. They joined the Business Houses League First Division in 1927/28 and won the league in their first season. They won it again in 1929/30 and remained in the league until the end of the 1932/33 season, after which they joined the Bootle JOC League.

HARROWBY

Following World War One, Harrowby moved into the Tower ground vacated by New Brighton Tower. They were runners-up to Tranmere Rovers in the 1918/19 Wirral Senior Cup and then won both the West Cheshire League and Wirral Senior Cup in 1919/20.

In 1922/23, they lost the Wirral Senior Cup Final 1–0 to Bromborough Pool. By 1923/24, they had rejoined the I Zingari League Second Division, leaving it again after the 1924/25 season. They won the I Zingari Second Division 1925/26 After one year's absence, they returned in 1926/27, now in the First Division and finished as runners-up to Cadby Hall by two points.

In 1927/28, they won the Wirral Senior Cup for a second time, beating Shell Mex and were runners up in the First Division. In 1929/30, they lost the I Zingari Challenge Cup Final to Cadby Hall 3–1. Harrowby were relegated to the Second Division at the end of 1934/35 but returned to the First Division in 1936/37 after finishing top. They placed eighth in their first season back and second from bottom in 1938/39, the final season before the war.

HAYDOCK ATHLETIC

Formed around 1930, Haydock Athletic began in the St Helens Combination before moving to the Warrington & District League. In 1931/32, they won the Liverpool Junior Cup with a 6–1 win over Earlestown White Star.

They disbanded at the end of the 1934/35 season for two years but reformed to join the Liverpool County Combination in 1937/38. They also moved into a new ground named Vistar Park in Haydock.

HESWALL

In 1919/20, Heswall won the Wirral Junior Cup, beating Rock Ferry Pres. In 1922/23, they were runners-up in the Wirral Amateur Cup, losing to Port Sunlight. After a spell in the newly formed Birkenhead Association Football League, they rejoined the West Cheshire League in 1922/23, entering the Second Division and finishing sixth.

Promoted to the First Division in 1923/24, they remained in the league until leaving after the 1927/28 season. They rejoined the revived Wirral Combination in 1929/30. In 1931/32, they won the Wirral Amateur Cup, defeating Upton 3–1.

In 1932/33, Heswall were runners-up in the Wirral Senior Cup (lost to Shell Mex), won the Wirral Amateur Cup (vs Thornton Hough) and claimed the Pyke Cup (vs West Kirby). In 1933/34, they won the Amateur Cup again, this time beating Rock Ferry Social.

They won the West Cheshire League for the first time in 1935/36, beginning a three-year run of league titles. That season, they were also Wirral Senior Cup runners-up (lost to Rock Ferry Social) and Wirral Amateur Cup winners. They repeated as league champions in 1936/37 (again beating Rock Ferry Social for the Amateur Cup) and in 1937/38, finishing one point ahead of Stanlow Social.

In 1938/39, they won both the Wirral Senior Cup (vs Brookville) and the Pyke Cup (5–3 vs Buckley Town).

JABISCO

Formed in 1920, Jabisco was the works team of the Jacob's biscuit factory in Long Lane, Aintree. They joined the Central Amateur League in 1923 and later moved to the Shipping League.

They won the Second Division of the Shipping League in 1928/29 and lifted the Concanon Cup in 1927/28. Jabisco were league champions in both 1929/30 and 1933/34 and won the Melly Cup in 1930/31 and 1931/32. In 1932/33, they lost the Liverpool Amateur Cup Final to Aintree SS.

JOHNSON'S DYEWORKS

After the First World War, Johnson's Dyeworks joined the Bootle Football League, finishing mid-table in the 1919/20 season, which appears to have been their final campaign in that competition. The club seems to have disbanded shortly afterwards but was later reformed by workers and re-entered competitive football in 1928/29, joining the Third Division of the Business Houses League.

KIRKDALE

Kirkdale competed in the Liverpool League after World War One. They won the RP Houston Cup in 1919/20 and were runners-up in 1920/21, losing to Huyton Quarry. They reclaimed the cup in 1921/22, alongside winning the league title. They won the Houston Cup again in 1924/25, beating Fairries Football Club.

The club remained in the Liverpool League until 1934, when they disbanded due to difficulties securing a ground and lack of funding.

LIVERPOOL

The Football League resumed in 1919/20, now expanded to twenty-two clubs and forty-two games per season. Liverpool finished fourth in this first post-war season.

In 1921/22, Liverpool won their third League Championship. The season began poorly with a 3–0 defeat at Sunderland, leaving the Reds bottom of the First Division. However, back-to-back home wins (3–2 vs Manchester City and 2–1 in the reverse fixture against Sunderland) helped them climb into the top ten. By mid-October, a 4–0 win over Preston North End lifted them to second place. A 1–1 draw in the Merseyside derby at Goodison Park on 5 November temporarily dropped them to third, but a 4–0 win over Middlesbrough on 19 November put them top of the table – a position they would retain for the rest of the season, eventually finishing six points ahead of Tottenham Hotspur.

In 1922, Liverpool also joined the Northern Midweek League, established to provide more fixtures for reserve players.

The 1922/23 season saw Liverpool retain their First Division title. They reached the top of the table on 16 September and held it throughout the season. A 1–0 win over Newcastle United at St James' Park on 9 December sparked a thirteen-game unbeaten run in the league, including eleven victories. Even so, by early March, their lead over Sunderland was just four points. The title was clinched at Anfield with a 1–1 draw against Huddersfield Town, as Sunderland had lost 2–0 to Burnley, leaving Liverpool five points clear with only four matches remaining. They eventually won the league by six points.

Liverpool forward Dick Forshaw, who had played a key role in these consecutive title wins, was transferred to Everton in March 1927. He later won the 1927/28 First Division title with Everton, becoming the only player to have won the championship with both Merseyside clubs.

Liverpool's fortunes declined during the remainder of the decade. From 1923/24 through 1929/30, their highest league finish was fourth place (1924/25) and they did not progress far in the FA Cup.

In the 1930s, Liverpool continued to struggle, rarely finishing above mid-table and reaching the FA Cup quarter-finals only once – a 2–0 home defeat to Chelsea in 1932. However, the 1935/36 season was notable for the debut of Matt Busby, who joined from Manchester City and made his first appearance for Liverpool on 14 March 1936 away at Huddersfield Town.

LIVERPOOL POLICE (MERSEYSIDE POLICE)

Liverpool Police left the Liverpool & District League after the 1921/22 season and joined the I Zingari League Second Division in 1922/23, finishing runners-up to Cadby Hall by two points. That season, they won the first of three consecutive Lancashire Amateur Cups, beating Marine.

In 1923/24, they placed third in their debut season in the I Zingari First Division and retained the Lancashire Amateur Cup, defeating Collegiate Old Boys. The following season, they completed a hat-trick of Lancashire Amateur Cup wins, this time beating Orrell.

In 1925/26, they won the I Zingari Challenge Cup, beating Thorndale. In 1926/27, they claimed the I Zingari League title for the first time, finishing four points clear of Thorndale.

They were relegated in 1933/34 after finishing bottom of the First Division but were runners-up to Oakmere in the Second Division in 1935/36. In 1936/37, they again finished second – this time to Harrowby – regaining First Division status. Liverpool Police remained in the I Zingari League until the outbreak of the Second World War.

MAGHULL

Maghull FC was formed in 1921 and initially played at Boyer Fields. They joined the I Zingari Alliance for the 1922/23 season. In 1924/25, they won both the I Zingari Alliance League and the Alliance Cup. Promoted to the I Zingari League for the 1925/26 season, they finished as runners-up in Division Three.

The club moved to Pimbley Playing Fields in 1928. They won the I Zingari League Division Two in both 1928/29 and 1933/34. After promotion to the top division, Maghull finished as runners-up in their first season (1934/35). That year, they also won the I Zingari Challenge Cup and shared the Liverpool Amateur Cup with Garston Woodcutters. They lost in the (1935/36) I Zingari Challenge Cup to Earle.

In 1937/38, Maghull reached the final of the Lancashire Amateur Cup but were beaten by Fulwood FC of Preston.

MARINE

After the First World War, Marine resumed competition in the I Zingari League and won the title in the first season back (1919/20), defeating Marlboro Old Boys in a play-off after both sides finished level on points. They also won the I Zingari League Cup and the Liverpool Amateur Cup, beating Orrell 3–0. The reserves claimed the I Zingari Combination Cup, while the first team were runners-up in the Lancashire Amateur Cup, losing 3–0 to Manchester University at Anfield.

In late 1920, the Rossett Park Land Company Ltd. was established to purchase 5.5 acres of land at College Road, Crosby – later known as Rossett Park. Marine secured a long-term lease for the football ground, with the remaining land designated for wider sporting use.

At the end of the 1920/21 season, Marine won the I Zingari League Division One title again, finishing four points ahead of Birkenhead Institute Old Boys. They also retained the League Cup, beating North Western and won the Liverpool County Medal Cup. The reserves completed a double, winning both the I Zingari Combination and the Combination Cup. However, Marine lost the Lancashire Amateur Cup Final 2–0 to Liverpool University and the Liverpool Amateur Cup Final 3–2 to Orrell.

In 1921/22, Marine were runners-up in the I Zingari League, finishing three points behind Orrell, but won the Lancashire Amateur Cup by defeating Liverpool Police 2–0. The reserves again won the I Zingari Combination. Hightown beat them in the I Zingari Challenge Cup.

The 1922/23 season saw Marine reclaim the I Zingari League title, finishing two points clear of Earle and they also retained the League Cup. That season they won the Liverpool Amateur Cup, beating Hightown 1–0 at Goodison Park, but lost the Lancashire Amateur Cup Final 1–0 to Liverpool Police.

In 1923/24, Marine won the I Zingari League for the third time in four years, again needing a play-off to defeat Earle. They also retained the League Cup, beating Orrell and won the Liverpool Amateur Cup by defeating Harlandic.

Marine joined the Liverpool County Combination at the start of the 1925/26 season, finishing fifth. They won the Lancashire Amateur Cup that season with a commanding 6–0 win over Blundellsands.

In 1926/27, Marine were runners-up in the George Mahon Cup, losing 3–2 to Prescot Cables, but won the Liverpool Amateur Cup, beating Cadby Hall 4–3. However, they were runners-up in the Lancashire Amateur Cup, losing 2–1 to Earle.

In 1927/28, Marine won the Liverpool County Combination, finishing three points ahead of Whiston. They retained the Liverpool Amateur Cup by again beating Cadby Hall, this time 4–3 in a replay after the first match ended 4–4.

In 1928/29, Marine were runners-up in the County Combination, two points behind Whiston. They won the Liverpool Amateur Cup for the third year in a row, defeating Howsons 4–0.

The 1929/30 season saw Marine as joint runners-up in the County Combination behind Liverpool 'A'. In 1930/31, they won the league by seven points from Everton 'A'. That season they also won the George Mahon Cup (3–2 vs Peasley Cross), the Lancashire Amateur Cup (4–2 vs Cadby Hall) and the Liverpool Amateur Cup (4–2 vs The Casuals).

In 1931/32, Marine reached the FA Amateur Cup Final but lost 7–1 to Dulwich Hamlet at West Ham United's Boleyn Ground on 16 April 1932. The pitch was in poor condition and after a tight first half, Dulwich scored six times in twenty minutes after the break. Marine also won the Lancashire Amateur Cup (4–2 vs The Casuals) and were runners-up in the George Mahon Cup, losing 3–2 to Liverpool Cables.

In 1932/33, Marine again lifted the Lancashire Amateur Cup, beating Cadby Hall 2–0.

The 1933/34 season brought another Liverpool County Combination title, finishing three points ahead of Everton 'A', as well as a Liverpool Amateur Cup win over Garston Protestant Reformers (1–0) and a 3–1 victory over Everton in the RE Lythgoe Memorial Cup Final.

In 1934/35, Marine retained the County Combination title, finishing one point ahead of Everton 'A' and won the RE Lythgoe Cup again, this time beating Liverpool Reserves.

In 1935/36, Marine joined the Lancashire Combination, finishing fourteenth in their first season. That same season, Marine, Prescot Cables and South Liverpool were invited to join Everton and Liverpool Reserves, New Brighton, Tranmere Rovers and Southport in contesting the Liverpool Senior Cup.

Throughout the 1930s, Marine hosted an annual medal competition at Rossett Park.

During World War Two, Marine remained active, winning the 1942/43 Liverpool Challenge Cup by beating an RAF XI 3–2 at Goodison Park and the George Mahon Cup by defeating Randle 1–0 at Anfield. In 1943/44, they won the George Mahon Cup again, beating Liverpool 3–2 on aggregate and claimed the Liverpool County Combination title. In 1944/45, they won the Liverpool Challenge Cup (15–5 aggregate vs Napiers) and another George Mahon Cup (4–0 vs Randle).

MIRANDA

Formed in Bootle around 1919, Miranda initially played in the Bootle & District League before moving to the Liverpool Alliance League, where they were runners-up in 1930/31. They then joined the Bootle JOC League for the 1933/34 season.

At the end of that season, Miranda won the Liverpool Junior Cup, defeating Litherland Amateurs 3–2 and were runners-up to Bootle Labour in the Premier Division.

In 1934/35, they won the first of four consecutive Bootle JOC League titles. They repeated the feat in 1935/36 and also lifted the Liverpool Challenge Cup by beating Skelmersdale United 2–1. In 1936/37, they won a third league title and completed a fourth consecutive league triumph in 1937/38, also beating Belvidere 1–0 in the Liverpool Challenge Cup Final. That same season, they added the JOC Everton Cup to their collection.

At the end of the 1938/39 season, Miranda were beaten in the Liverpool Challenge Cup Final by Skelmersdale United. They also shared the Lythgoe Cup with Earle.

NEW BRIGHTON

By August 1921, South Liverpool had collapsed. The club had lost their New Dingle ground and were effectively defunct. A consortium from New Brighton, led by Dr Tom Martlew, proposed to reconstitute South Liverpool as a new professional club named New Brighton, taking over the club's fixtures and gaining a head start on their own project. An outlay of over £1,500 cleared South Liverpool's debts and funded share purchases, while a further issue raised money to build a ground near Liscard High School.

New Brighton took South Liverpool's place in the Lancashire Combination for the 1921/22 season. After rejecting other ground options – including the Tower Ground and a site at Oakside Farm – they settled at Sandhey's Park, later known as Rake Lane. Their first match, away to Hurst, ended in a 3–1 win and they beat Rochdale 2–1 in their first home league fixture. They finished third in the Lancashire Combination and also lifted the Lancashire Junior Cup, beating Chorley 2–1 in a replay and the Lancashire Combination Cup, beating Lancaster Town. They also won the Liverpool Challenge Cup, defeating North Liverpool 2–1.

In May 1923, New Brighton were elected to the Football League Third Division North, receiving 45 votes. In their first league match, they drew 1–1 with Bradford Park Avenue after conceding in the opening minute. They finished their debut season in 18th place but won the Cheshire Senior Cup (1–0 vs Tranmere Rovers) and a second consecutive Liverpool Challenge Cup (vs Port Sunlight). They lost the George Mahon Cup Final to Prescot.

In 1924/25, New Brighton finished third in the League and claimed a third consecutive Liverpool Challenge Cup, beating Fairries 5–0.

In 1925/26 and 1926/27, they reached successive Liverpool Senior Cup Finals, losing 1–0 to Everton and 8–2 to Liverpool respectively.

In 1931/32, they finished 20th but avoided relegation after Wigan Borough resigned and their record was expunged. Financial concerns mounted, with debts of £12,000 and unpaid player wages. A fundraising appeal and proposed move to Gorsey Lane were shelved following local opposition.

In 1932/33, New Brighton finished 21st, level on points with York City but behind on goal average. They were successfully re-elected to the League with 47 votes. That year they won the Liverpool Senior Cup for the first time, beating Southport 6–1 at Rake Lane and also won the Liverpool Challenge Cup.

In 1933/34, they were runners-up in the Liverpool Senior Cup, losing 4–1 to Tranmere Rovers. In 1934/35, they beat Tranmere 2–0 to reclaim the trophy.

In 1935/36, they again had to seek re-election, finishing nine points from safety and seven behind second-bottom Southport. They secured 13 votes – two fewer than Southport – but enough to retain League status.

New Brighton remained in the Football League until its suspension for World War Two. Their wartime football ended in February 1942 and bomb damage that summer led to football ceasing at their ground, which was requisitioned for housing by the local council.

NEWTON
Formed in 1933, Wirral-based Newton FC began life in the Birkenhead League, remaining mostly in the lower divisions. They played their home matches at Cross Lane, Newton.

NEWTON-LE-WILLOWS
Newton-le-Willows joined the Lancashire Alliance League for the 1920/21 season, finishing sixth. In 1921/22 – the final season of the old Lancashire Alliance – they finished runners-up to Orrell YMCA. With the Alliance folding, they moved into the newly renamed Lancashire Central League in 1922/23, finishing again in sixth place.

At the end of that season, club officials met to determine the club's future. Unable to afford the rent for a new ground and choosing not to rejoin the Lancashire Central League, they decided not to operate for the 1923/24 season. It appears the club disbanded permanently at that point.

ODYSSEY
Odyssey FC was formed around 1920 by Alfred Holt & Co. Shipping Company. They joined the Second Division of the I Zingari League in

1919/20, finishing third and were promoted to the First Division, where they placed third in 1920/21.

After finishing bottom of the First Division in 1923/24, they were relegated. They remained in the Second Division until 1932/33, when they again finished bottom and subsequently disbanded. The club briefly reformed and rejoined the I Zingari League for the 1939/40 season, which was ultimately cancelled due to the war.

OLD XAVERIANS

After the war they returned to the I Zingari League. They were runners-up to Marine in the Lancashire Amateur Cup in 1921/22 and were relegated from the I Zingari First Division in 1925/26. They changed ground to Druid's Cross, Woolton using an old bus as a dressing room and in 1931 used a Nissan Hut as a dressing room. They remained in the I Zingari Second Division until WW2.

ORRELL

Orrell rejoined the I Zingari League at the start of the 1919/20 season, finishing third and reaching the Liverpool Amateur Cup Final, where they lost 3–0 to Marine. That same year they participated in the Pasternooi Tournament in Belgium.

In 1920/21, they won the Liverpool Amateur Cup by beating Marine 3–2 and again took part in the Belgian tournament. Mid-season, they moved from Park Lane to a new sports facility in Orrell Park.

In 1921/22, they won the I Zingari League by three points over Marine. They captured the title again in 1924/25, defeating Cadby Hall in a play-off. In 1925/26, they were runners-up, finishing one point behind Cadby Hall. Orrell also won the league in 1929/30 (by one point from The Casuals) and again in 1933/34 (by one point from Collegiate Old Boys). They were also I Zingari Challenge Cup runners-up four times in this period to Marine, Cadby Hall, Earle and Hightown.

They remained in the I Zingari League until the outbreak of the Second World War. Their reserve side also enjoyed success, winning the I Zingari Combination in 1909/10, 1912/13, 1925/26, 1927/28 and 1936/37.

PORT SUNLIGHT (ATHLETIC)

After World War One, Port Sunlight joined the West Cheshire League, finishing bottom in 1919/20. In 1922/23, they were runners-up to Poulton Rovers and won the Wirral Amateur Cup, defeating Heswall.

In 1923/24, the club fielded two teams – one in the West Cheshire League and another in the Liverpool County Combination. They placed mid-table in the former and near the bottom in the latter. In 1924/25, they focused solely on the County Combination and won the title, finishing ahead of Everton 'A'. By the end of the 1925/26 season, they had left the County Combination.

They next appeared in the I Zingari League Third Division in 1930/31, winning it by five points from Richmond Old Boys. Promoted, they won the Second Division in 1931/32, finishing seven points clear of Formby.

In 1937/38, they won the I Zingari League First Division by a ten-point margin over Earle but were runner-up to Earle in the I Zingari Challenge Cup. They remained in the league until the outbreak of World War Two.

POULTON VICTORIA

Formed in 1935, Poulton Victoria began in the Wallasey Combination League during the 1935/36 season before moving to the Birkenhead League. They disbanded during World War Two.

PRESCOT B.I. SOCIAL

Formed around 1931 as BI Social, the club later became Prescot BI Social and was the works team of the Cable Works in Prescot. They joined the Liverpool Business Houses League in 1932/33, winning the league and the Business Houses Cup by beating Bibby's Social.

They moved to the Liverpool League in 1933/34, where they lost the RP Houston Cup Final 3–1 to West Kirby. In 1934/35, they won the Liverpool League and the Liverpool Challenge Cup (7–3 vs Liverpool Cables), but lost the RP Houston Cup Final to Garston Woodcutters.

In 1935/36, they retained the Liverpool League title. In 1936/37, they joined the Liverpool County Combination, finishing seventh and then placed third in both 1937/38 and 1938/39 before football was suspended for the war.

PRESCOT CABLES

Formerly known as Prescot Athletic, the club competed in the Liverpool Section of the Lancashire Combination in 1918/19, finishing as runners-up. In 1919/20, following the departure of several Cheshire teams, Prescot stayed in the Lancashire Combination and finished seventeenth out of eighteen. That same season, they also rejoined the Liverpool County Combination, placing fifth and competing in the inaugural Liverpool County FA Medal competition.

In 1920/21, they focused solely on the Liverpool County Combination, again finishing fifth. They won the George Mahon Cup in 1923/24 (beating New Brighton Reserves after a replay) and again in 1926/27 (3–2 vs Marine), but lost the 1925/26 Liverpool Challenge Cup Final to Harlandic (5–0).

By 1927/28, Prescot had spent seven seasons in the County Combination. In February 1928, they were invited to complete Fleetwood's remaining fixtures in the Lancashire Combination while still fulfilling their own County Combination commitments. On the same day as their first Lancashire Combination match (a 3–1 loss to Southport Reserves), they also played Bootle Celtic in the George Mahon Cup Semi-Final, losing 4–0 with a scratch team.

That season, they finished third in the County Combination and sixteenth in the Lancashire Combination, but won the Liverpool Challenge Cup, defeating Liverpool 'A' at Goodison Park.

In 1928/29, now renamed Prescot Cables following a generous donation from BICC, including a new 1,000-seat stand, they won the Liverpool Challenge Cup again, beating Whiston at Anfield. In 1929/30, they claimed the same cup for a third consecutive time, again beating Whiston (1–0 at Goodison) and were runners-up in the Lancashire Combination League Cup (lost 2–0 to Darwen).

In 1930/31, they were runners-up in the Lancashire Combination, finishing three points behind Darwen and beat Whiston in the Lythgoe Cup Final.

They were runners-up again in 1931/32 (seven points behind Darwen) and in 1932/33 (nine points behind Chorley). In May 1933, they were elected to the Cheshire County League for 1933/34 after receiving 12 votes. They marked their debut with a 5–3 home win over Nantwich and finished fifth overall. That season, their reserves won the Lord Wavertree Cup, beating Skelmersdale United.

In 1936/37, Prescot Cables returned to the Lancashire Combination, finishing eighteenth. The reserve side beat South Liverpool 1–0 in the George Mahon Cup Final at Hope Street.

In October 1937, Prescot entered discussions with Liverpool about becoming a nursery club. Talks continued into January 1938 and included the possibility of renaming the club Prescot Athletic. However, in August, they discovered a drawback: the FA barred nursery teams from competing in the FA Cup. As a result, Sandhurst FC were awarded a walkover.

In 1938/39, they finished nineteenth in the Lancashire Combination and were League Cup runners-up, losing 3–1 to South Liverpool.

ROCKVILLE

Formed in 1918 as St John's Juniors, the club changed its name to Rockville after the First World War. It competed in the Wallasey Junior League and I Zingari Alliance before switching to friendly fixtures after 1926. This arrangement continued until after the Second World War.

RUNCORN

Established in 1918 by the Highfield and Camden Tanneries as part of their Recreation Club, Runcorn joined the Lancashire Combination for the 1918/19 season, finishing in fifth place. They also won the Lancashire Junior Cup, defeating Blackpool RAMC 2–0 in a replay at Anfield.

In 1919/20, the club opted not to continue in the Lancashire Combination and applied – unsuccessfully – for membership of the Central League.

Instead, they became founding members of the Cheshire County League and also entered a reserve side into the West Cheshire League. Their Cheshire League campaign began with a home defeat to Monks Hall, but the loss – and subsequent press criticism – spurred them on. They won the league at the first attempt, finishing eleven points clear of Mossley, with 17 wins from 20 matches. The reserves ended mid-table in the West Cheshire League.

In 1920/21, Runcorn were favourites to retain the league title, but distractions from the FA Cup and Cheshire Cup meant they finished third. In 1921/22, the first team came bottom of the Cheshire County League, although the reserves finished fourth in the West Cheshire League.

Runcorn lifted the Cheshire Senior Cup for the first time in 1924/25, beating Crewe Alexandra 1–0 and followed it up in 1925/26 by winning the Pyke Cup, defeating Chester Reserves 4–2. In 1926/27, their reserve side joined the Liverpool County Combination, opening with a match against St Helens Town.

They lost the Pyke Cup final 5–3 to Ellesmere Port Town in 1928/29. However, they won the Cheshire Senior Cup again in 1935/36 by beating Macclesfield 2–1. That same season, they finished sixth and started the 1936/37 campaign in good shape, opening with a 2–0 win over Crewe Alexandra. By the end of September, they were second in the table and by early December, they had reached the summit, although Northwich Victoria remained level on points.

By mid-April, Runcorn were on the brink of the title after thrashing Ashton National 7–1. Eight points clear of Stockport County Reserves with four games to play, they secured the championship in the next fixture, beating Manchester North End 5–1 at Canal Street. The *Runcorn Weekly News* reported their triumph on 23 April 1937. They won the Cheshire County League by nine points and added the Cheshire Challenge Trophy, defeating Winsford United 3–0 in the final.

In 1937/38, Runcorn finished as runners-up to Tranmere Rovers Reserves by three points but beat Tranmere 5–4 after extra time to win the Cheshire Bowl. They were subsequently barred from defending the trophy as an amateur club.

In 1938/39, with three matches remaining, Runcorn were two points clear at the top. A win over Northwich Victoria and Tranmere's defeat to Winsford United widened the gap. Runcorn then beat Winsford again to seal their second Cheshire County League title in three years. In 1939/40, they topped the Western Section of the wartime Cheshire League and beat Droylsden 5–3 on aggregate in a playoff to become county champions once more.

SEAFORTH ALBION

Formed in 1920 by local sportsmen, Seaforth Albion joined the Seaforth and Litherland JOC League in 1920/21 and won it at the first attempt. They moved to the Second Division of the Bootle League in 1921/22 and again won promotion immediately. In 1922/23, they finished runners-up in the First Division and joined the Liverpool League the following season.

In 1926/27, they won the Houston Cup and completed a league and cup double by finishing ahead of Furness Withy. They remained in the Liverpool League until at least 1929/30. In 1931/32, they were runners-up in the Liverpool Amateur Cup, losing to Garston Gas Works and by 1934/35, they had moved into the Bootle JOC League.

SEAFORTH FELLOWSHIP

Founded during the First World War by an Army chaplain named Phillimore, Seaforth Fellowship joined the Bootle Football League for the 1919/20 season and won the league title in 1921/22. By 1923/24, they were competing in the Liverpool League, finishing fourth and also reached the Bootle Hospital Cup Final, where they lost 6–0 to Furness Withy.

ST HELENS TOWN

After the First World War, St Helens Town returned briefly to the Liverpool County Combination in 1925/26, finishing eighth. They remained in the league for two further seasons, placing eleventh in 1926/27 and seventh in 1927/28 – their final season of this period.

SKELMERSDALE MISSION

Skelmersdale Mission returned to the Lancashire Alliance from 1919/22 before joining the St Helens & District Combination for 1922/23. They later re-joined the Lancashire Alliance and finished as runners-up in 1924/25, six points behind Hindley Green Celtic. For the 1925/26 season, they switched to the Southport & District League. They were due to enter the Ormskirk & District League in 1926/27, but the competition was cancelled due to a lack of local colliery teams. The last mention of the club came in their 5–1 victory over Ormskirk Old Boys in the Stanley Cup Final, after which they appear to have disbanded.

SKELMERSDALE UNITED

In 1919/20, Skelmersdale United won the Liverpool County Combination, finishing one point ahead of Frodsham Athletic. They also won the Liverpool Challenge Cup, beating Sutton Colliery Manor at Goodison Park.

In 1920/21, they joined the Lancashire Combination and repeated their Liverpool Challenge Cup success, beating Burscough Rangers. However, after three seasons in the Lancashire Combination, they finished bottom in 1923/24 and returned to the Liverpool County Combination for 1924/25. That season, they also lifted the George Mahon Cup, defeating Burscough 1–0 after extra time in a replay.

Remaining consistently in the upper half of the County Combination table, they won the George Mahon Cup again in 1934/35, defeating Marine 3–2 and were runners-up in the league in 1935/36, just two points behind Everton 'A'.

In 1938/39, the final full league season before the Second World War, they won the Liverpool County Combination by two points from Everton 'A' and also secured the Liverpool Challenge Cup with a 3–2 win over Miranda. They repeated the feat in 1939/40, beating Liverpool 3–1 in the Challenge Cup and defeating Miranda again to win the George Mahon Cup. In 1940/41, they beat Liverpool 'A' in a play-off to win another County Combination title.

SOUTHPORT

Despite having played throughout World War One, Central needed financial support, which arrived in the form of sponsorship from the local Vulcan Motor Company. In August 1918, Central applied to the Football League to change their name to Southport Vulcan. Initially, the request was rejected and the club was advised to adopt either Southport or Southport Athletic. However, two weeks later, the League granted permission for the club to use the name Vulcan temporarily. This may have been the first instance of a Football League side including a sponsor's name.

Vulcan's first match was a 3–0 win at Ash Lane against Blackburn Rovers. By the 1919/20 season, the Vulcan Motor Company had relinquished control and the club became Southport Football Club. Around the same time, the Southport Education Committee took over the lease of the Ash Lane ground, allowing the club to use it on alternate Saturdays. Southport won the Lancashire Junior Cup by beating Lancaster Town 1–0. In April 1921, the club became a limited liability company and issued £4,000 worth of shares.

In 1921/22, Southport joined the Third Division North, possibly due to Clayton's role in forming the original third division. Their first Football League match came on 27 August 1921 at home to Durham City. A crowd of 7,000 – likely drawn by the fine weather – watched a 1–1 draw. Southport finished ninth. In 1923/24, they placed seventh and the reserves joined the Lancashire Combination, finishing runners-up and winning the Lancashire Combination Cup by defeating Morecambe 2–0.

In 1930/31, Southport won the Liverpool Senior Cup, beating Tranmere Rovers 3–1 after extra time at Prenton Park. The following season, they retained the trophy by defeating Liverpool 2–1 at Haig Avenue. However, by the end of 1935/36, Southport required re-election to the Football League. The reserves joined the Northern Midweek League for 1936/37.

In 1937/38, Southport won the Third Division North Cup by beating Bradford City 4–1 but lost the Lancashire Senior Cup Final 1–0 to Manchester United. During the war, they won the Liverpool Senior Cup in 1943/44, defeating Everton 2–1.

SOUTH LIVERPOOL

After World War One, South Liverpool returned to the reformed Lancashire Combination for the 1919/20 season. In February 1920, they learned they would lose their Dingle Park stadium to the Mersey Docks & Harbour Board. In 1920/21, they played mainly at Green Lane, Old Swan, while using various other venues across the city. By January 1921, they were struggling to secure a home ground. The *Liverpool Echo* suggested sharing Harrowby's ground or amalgamating as Wallasey Borough. Facing no realistic prospect of securing suitable accommodation in south Liverpool, the directors planned to fold the club. They applied to join the Football League but received only one vote.

However, a group of Wirral businessmen offered to relocate the club to Wallasey. On 28 June 1921, South Liverpool officially became New Brighton FC and secured Sandheys Park on Rake Lane as their new ground. Contemporary documents confirm that African Royal, South Liverpool and New Brighton were all iterations of the same club.

In 1935, South Liverpool was revived. At a packed meeting in Vale House, Aigburth Vale, in February, it was unanimously agreed to relaunch the club. They secured a ten-year lease at Holly Farm, Garston and established a public liability company, offering shares at 2s 6d. They aspired to join the Football League but initially applied to the Lancashire Combination or Cheshire League, ultimately entering the Lancashire Combination for 1935/36. They opened with a 3–1 win at Marine and reached the top of the league after four games, finishing the season in fourth. They were runners-up in the Lancashire Junior Cup, losing a replay 3–0 to Wigan Athletic at Anfield.

In 1936/37, South Liverpool beat Accrington Stanley Reserves by one point to win their first Lancashire Combination title, securing it with a 7–3 win at Leyland Motors. Their reserves won the Liverpool Challenge Cup, defeating Earlestown White Star 6–1 at Anfield and also won the Lancashire Junior Cup with a 7–0 win over Fleetwood at Deepdale. They reached the Lythgoe Cup Final against Earle. Having enjoyed a triple-winning season, South Liverpool applied for election to the Third

Division North but received just four votes, losing out to Shrewsbury and Wigan Athletic.

In 1937/38, South again topped the Lancashire Combination by October and remained competitive throughout. Their board invested in ground improvements, hoping to accommodate 10,000–15,000 spectators for a future Football League bid. In April, they secured the Lancashire Junior Cup for the second consecutive year with a 4–1 win over Lancaster City in front of 6,000 fans at Deepdale. The title was clinched at the end of April with a victory over Bacup.

In 1938/39, they claimed their third consecutive Lancashire Combination title, narrowly beating Bangor City. They also won the Lancashire Junior Cup with a 3–0 victory over Wigan Athletic at Anfield and lifted the Welsh Cup by defeating Cardiff City 2–1 at Wrexham.

THE CASUALS

Casuals were either reformed or newly formed after World War One, joining the I Zingari League Second Division in 1921/22 and finishing seventh. They won the division in 1927/28, nine points ahead of Windsor Athletic and placed third in their debut First Division season (1928/29). They were runners-up to Orrell in 1929/30 and lost the Lancashire Amateur Cup Final 3–1 to Cadby Hall.

Although they lost to Marine in the Liverpool Amateur Cup Final, they won the I Zingari Challenge Cup in 1930/31 (1–0 v Cadby Hall) and again in 1931/32 (5–3 v Harrowby). Casuals won the league title in 1932/33 by one point from West Derby Union. They lost 5–0 to Bromborough Pool in the 1933/34 Challenge Cup Final. In 1935/36, they were relegated to the Second Division and did not regain promotion before World War Two.

TRANMERE ROVERS

At the start of the 1919/20 season, Tranmere Rovers replaced Leeds City in the Central League. Their first match came on 25 October at Burnden Park against Bolton Wanderers Reserves. The reserve side joined the Lancashire Combination and finished fourth. In 1920/21, the first team placed seventh in their final Central League season. Their reserves withdrew from the Lancashire Combination and instead competed in the Cheshire County League, finishing fourteenth. They also won the Cheshire Senior Medals Final 3–1 against Stockport County.

Tranmere joined the newly formed Third Division North in 1921/22. Their debut match was a 4–1 home win over Crewe Alexandra before a crowd of 8,000. They finished eighteenth. In 1922/23, they were runners-up in the Cheshire Senior Medals Final, losing 1–0 to Stockport County. In 1923/24, they were runners-up in the Liverpool Senior Cup and lost the Cheshire Senior Cup Final to New Brighton. In the same season, 16-year-old Birkenhead native William Ralph Dean made his Football League debut for the club on 12 January 1924 against Rotherham United.

Dean scored his last goal for Tranmere in March 1925 before transferring to Everton. Rovers finished second bottom that season but were re-elected to the League with 32 votes. In 1925/26, they won the Cheshire Senior Cup by beating Winsford United 3–1 but again lost to Stockport County in the Medals Final (4–1). In 1926/27, they won the Senior Cup again, beating Winsford 4–1. Over the next three Medals Finals, they won once (4–2 v Stockport in 1927/28) but lost twice (3–2 in 1928/29 and 5–2 in 1929/30).

In 1931/32, Tranmere beat Chester 2–0 in the final Medals Final. In 1933/34, they reached their first Welsh Cup Final but lost 3–0 to Bristol City in a replay. They won the 1934/35 final by defeating Chester 1–0 after a coin toss decided the venue. In 1937/38, Tranmere won the Third Division North title and were promoted to the Second Division. Promotion was sealed with a 1–0 win at Lincoln City's Sincil Bank, with Eden scoring a penalty.

They finished the season unbeaten, clinching the title against Doncaster Rovers. The reserves also won the Cheshire County League, though they lost 5–4 after extra time to Runcorn in the Cheshire Bowl Final. Tranmere were relegated after just one season in the Second Division (1938/39). During the war, they were runners-up to Ellesmere Port Town in the 1940 Wirral Senior Cup and in 1941, Tranmere B beat Tranmere A in the final.

VALKYRIE

Post-WWI, Valkyrie joined the Liverpool and District League in 1925/26, moved to the I Zingari Alliance in 1926/27 and then entered the Liverpool Football League Second Division from 1927/28 until 1929/30, when the club appears to have disbanded.

WEST KIRBY

West Kirby won the West Cheshire League Section A and the Pyke Cup in 1919/20. In 1920/21, they were Wirral Senior Cup runners-up, but they lifted the trophy in 1921/22 and finished as Cheshire Amateur Cup runners-up. They won the Pyke Cup again in 1924/25 and were joint holders of the Wirral Amateur Cup.

They won the Wirral Amateur Cup again in 1926/27 and were runners-up in the Wirral Senior Cup to Shell Mex. Joining the Liverpool League in 1929/30, they finished mid-table. They won the Wirral Senior Cup the next season and took back-to-back Liverpool League titles in 1932/33 and 1933/34. In 1933/34, they were also runners-up in the Wirral Senior Cup. In 1934/35, they were runners-up in the Wirral Amateur Cup. In February 1936, they lost their ground to building works. A move to Carr Lane, Hoylake, proved unviable due to a lack of spectator facilities and the club was disbanded.

WHISTON PARISH CHURCH (WHISTON)

Whiston Parish Church formed a football team soon after World War One. They joined the Liverpool County Combination for the start of the 1919/20 season and finished in eighth place. The following season, 1920/21, they went on to win the title, finishing three points ahead of Burscough Rangers. They also fielded a side in the Lancashire Alliance League in the same 1920/21 season, finishing in ninth place in what proved to be their final campaign in that competition.

They finished as runners-up in the County Combination at the end of the 1925/26 season, ten points behind Burscough Rangers. For the following season, 1926/27, they changed their name to simply Whiston

Football Club and finished in eighth place. They were runners-up again in 1927/28, three points behind Marine and also won the George Mahon Cup. In 1928/29, they won the County Combination for a second time, finishing two points ahead of Marine, but lost 3–1 to Prescot Cables in the Liverpool Challenge Cup final. They were again runners-up in the Liverpool Challenge Cup the following season, losing 1–0 to Prescot Cables. They were also Lord Wavertree Cup winners in 1928 and 1929.

In 1931/32, they finished just one point behind Everton 'A' in the league and were runners-up to Prescot Cables in the Robert Lythgoe Cup. However, they claimed the league title in 1932/33, finishing one point ahead of Everton 'A'. The 1933/34 season proved to be their last, with Whiston finishing in sixth place.

WIGAN ATHLETIC

Following the demise of Wigan Borough, who had resigned from the Football League in October 1931, the desire to maintain an association football presence in Wigan remained strong. In February 1932, a meeting held at the Queens Hall by the Mayor of Wigan led to the formation of a committee to establish a new club. A further meeting in May formally created Wigan Athletic. Shares were issued at ten shillings each and Springfield Park was to be purchased from its then owners. The committee also entered discussions with the creditors of the old Wigan Borough club.

Wigan Athletic applied to join the Football League Third Division North but received only one vote. They then applied to join the Cheshire County League and, despite objections from the Lancashire FA, were admitted at the end of July. Their first match took place in August 1932, with 5,000 spectators witnessing a 2–0 home defeat to Port Vale Reserves. They finished fifth in their debut season.

Between 1933/34 and 1935/36, Wigan won the Cheshire County League title three times in succession. In 1933/34, they secured the championship by five points ahead of Macclesfield. The following season, they won on goal average after finishing level on points with Altrincham and Stalybridge Celtic. Their third successive title in 1935/36 was more comfortable, finishing thirteen points clear of Altrincham, but lost in the Lancashire Senior Cup Final. Wigan remained in the league until the outbreak of World War Two.

WIGAN BOROUGH

Formed in 1920 following the collapse of Wigan United, Wigan Borough took over their Lancashire Combination fixtures for the 1920/21 season, playing at Springfield Park. They finished second from bottom that season. In 1921/22, Borough joined the newly formed Football League Third Division North. Their first match was a 2–1 away win against Nelson and they ended the season in seventeenth place.

The club's highest Football League finish came in 1928/29 when they ended the campaign in fourth place. They won the Manchester Senior Cup in 1929/30. By the 1931/32 season, the club had fallen into severe financial difficulties. After receiving an ultimatum from the FA to pay off their debts, the club was unable to continue and folded after just ten games. Their record for the season was expunged.

WHERE THEY PLAYED

In May 1936, the Secretary of Larkhill AFC wrote a letter of complaint to the *Echo* on behalf of amateur football about the many grounds used by both Everton and Liverpool 'A' teams over the years. In it he said Collegiate Old Boys had moved from Cadby Hall due to Liverpool 'A' taking it and they also acquired Coney Green and Pirrie Park among others. Everton 'A' shared Marine's ground with Northern Nomads having to move out. Everton 'A' also fancied other grounds. 'God only knows where they haven't been' he complained. He also said that no amateur club could offer the same money as Everton and Liverpool could and that the two teams should share a ground for their A teams to use and banish the nightmare of any amateur club that may have a decent ground taken by both 'A' sides. The *Echo* partly agreed that they should have a joint ground for their A sides but also mentioned the many housing developments that had restricted use or taken away football grounds.

ANFIELD, LIVERPOOL

In 1926, the Kop was revamped, with a new roof design pushing the stand back. Windows were added to the rear and the Oakfield Road stand was joined to it, providing seating for an additional 592 spectators. By 1927, the Anfield Road End was also extended. By early 1928, Anfield was nearly fully covered, with the Kop able to accommodate 22,000 fans.

BELLEFIELD, WEST DERBY

Opened in 1920 by White Star Football Club (Cunard Shipping Company), Bellefield was originally built in the 1820s. It was bought by Edward Bates who owned a ship chartering business and he and his family are shown living there on the 1851 census. In the 1880s the Bates family left Bellefield but it remained in the family. The Bates family shipping business merged with Cunard Shipping Company in 1913. In 1920 the Bellefield estate was bought by Cunard with the agreement of Percy Bates and they developed it into a sports ground. Colonel Concannon OBE formally opened the new enclosure in November 1920. Situated near Sandfield Park, it included football, hockey, tennis, cricket and bowling facilities. In 1935, it was bought by builder William Tyson and leased to the Co-op for staff recreation.

BOOTLE STADIUM, BOOTLE

Opened in June 1933 on a 14-acre former waste tip near Aintree Road, Bootle Stadium cost £20,000. It featured a banked asphalt running track, two winter-use football pitches and dressing rooms with hot and cold showers. It had a capacity of 10,000.

CANAL STREET, RUNCORN

Purchased in 1918 by the Highfield and Camden Tanneries after the dissolution of Runcorn Rugby Football Club, Canal Street was first used by the new Runcorn Football Club for Lancashire Combination fixtures beginning in October 1918.

GOODISON PARK, WALTON

In 1925, a Boys' Pen was built at the corner of Gwladys Street and Bullens Road. A year later, a new double-decker stand was constructed along Bullens Road by Francis Morton and Co. Ltd. The 483-foot-long, 43-foot-high stand used 700 tons of steel and featured tip-up seats. It added 11,000 seats and expanded the Paddock standing area, bringing total capacity to about 70,000, with 41,000 under cover.

In 1936, Archibald Leitch designed a new stand at the Gwladys Street End (then called the Aintree End). Nearby houses were demolished and the new stand connected with Bullens Road, offering 4,000 seats on the upper tier and standing room for 10,000 below. Everton had planned to build a new stand since 1914 but a war and one stubborn resident, William Fraser, delayed the building until 1937.

Goodison was bombed during the Second World War.

GROVE MOUNT, PENNY LANE

In 1920, the Lyons Tea Company gave nine acres of land at Cadby Hall, Penny Lane, for use as playing fields by workers and locals. Cadby Hall's football team used it until folding during the Second World War.

HAIG AVENUE, SOUTHPORT

In July 1921, the area of Ash Lane in Southport was renamed Haig Avenue after Sir Douglas Haig, who had commanded British forces during the First World War. Southport FC added a full-length covered enclosure opposite the main stand in 1921, following their election to the Football League. Further improvements came in 1931/32, including an extension to the enclosure and new terracing, aided by an FA Cup run and the club's jubilee celebrations.

HALTON STADIUM

In 1932, Widnes's football and cricket grounds on Lowerhouse Lane were earmarked for town planning and housing. Local support saved the football ground, with improvements funded by weekly contributions from working men. It was renamed Naughton Park in memory of club secretary Tom Naughton. The cricket ground was not retained and the club relocated to Farnworth.

HARLAND AND WOLFF SPORTS GROUND, PIRRIE PARK, WALTON HALL AVENUE

Opened in 1923 by Harland and Wolff Shipbuilders, the sports ground spanned over ten acres and included facilities for baseball, cricket, hockey, tennis and bowls. It featured a large pavilion with dressing rooms, baths, an assembly room and refreshment areas.

HOLLY PARK, GARSTON

In 1935, the reincarnated South Liverpool FC secured a 10-year lease on Holly Farm. By June 1936 and again in 1937, the club added terracing and extended covered areas, including improvements to the Kop end.

HOPE STREET, PRESCOT

In 1928, British Insulated Cables (BICC) funded a new 1,000-capacity stand at Hope Street. It was 100 feet long and 26 feet wide, with 700 seats, dressing rooms, store rooms, two baths and electric lighting. The cost was between £350 and £400.

KIRKLANDS STADIUM, ROCK FERRY

Purchased in 1918 by Cammell Laird and opened in 1920, Kirklands was developed as a 30-acre social club in St. Peter's Road. It included football pitches, two cricket fields, two bowling greens and six tennis courts. The main building had a library, lecture and meeting rooms, a billiards room and a ladies' tea room. Cammell Laird had over 2,000 members in its sports section.

MOOR LANE, CROSBY

In time for the 1935/36 season, Liverpool Ramblers built a new pavilion at Moor Lane and added a second playing pitch.

MOSSLEY HILL ATHLETIC CLUB, MOSSLEY HILL

Emma Holt, a philanthropist and women's rights campaigner born into a shipping line family, took over Sudley House in Mossley Hill after her parents' death. In September 1927, she donated 26 acres of land from her estate for use as a recreation ground. This land was used by Mossley Hill Athletic Club and Mossley Hill Football Club.

NEW BRIGHTON TOWER ATHLETIC GROUND

After the collapse of New Brighton Tower FC, the ground continued to host various sporting events, including stock car racing. It is claimed that up to 100,000 people attended a cycle race there in the 1920s. The tower itself was dismantled in 1919 and during the war, the pitch and stands were repurposed for military vehicle storage.

ORRELL PARK SPORTS CLUB, ORRELL PARK

Opened in 1920 and used by Orrell Football Club from that year's end, the club featured six and a half acres of land, a clubhouse and facilities for cricket, tennis, bowls and football.

ORRELL PLEASURE GROUNDS, BOOTLE

Located at Dunningsbridge Road/Southport Road, this site hosted twenty-three pitches used by the Bootle JOC League on match days. Originally featuring three timber buildings for accommodation, improvements in 1936 saw a £3,000 extension added to the pavilion. The expanded facility included 42 dressing room cubicles, a refreshment bar, meeting room, lavatories and separate accommodation for female players and spectators. A six-foot-wide veranda spanned the entire length of the pavilion.

PEASLEY CROSS LANE, ST HELENS

Opened in 1926 by local colliers, this ground was developed from a flooded waste site. It became home to Peasley Cross Athletic. A 1929 *Liverpool Echo* report described the bleak surrounding industrial landscape. In 1931, the ground hosted its first FA Cup match. It closed during the Second World War.

PIMBLEY RECREATION FIELD, MAGHULL

Opened in June 1927 after John Pimbley of Kensington Farm donated six acres for sports use. He also contributed nearly £2,000 toward the development of facilities. Maghull FC began using the ground regularly from 1928, starting with a win over Windsor Athletic.

PORT SUNLIGHT RECREATION GROUND, THE OVAL, BEBINGTON

Founded in 1888, the recreation ground was revitalised in 1919 when Lever Brothers acquired it. It spanned 76 acres and included cattle sheds, a 4,000-seat grandstand and later improvements like a running track. Port Sunlight FC relocated there in 1925, gaining full use of the Oval, including player baths.

PRENTON PARK, TRANMERE

In 1920, a new stand was built along Borough Road and Tranmere secured Prenton Park's freehold ahead of joining the Football League. Funding came via a share issue and land sales. By 1921, the site covered eleven acres with a capacity of 18,000. In 1931, the Cowshed was built for £1,000. In 1936, new dressing rooms were added behind the Kop. Tranmere had previously used a hut known as Salem Cottage in the corner of the ground as dressing rooms.

ROKER PARK, EARLESTOWN

Opened in 1934 by Earlestown Bohemians FC on a site formerly used by Earlestown Central. The Bohemians fenced the ground and constructed a pavilion with dressing rooms and cold water.

ROSSETT PARK, COLLEGE ROAD, CROSBY

Marine raised money during 1919 to improve the dressing rooms at Rossett Park. By October they had raised enough to dismantle an army hut in Aintree and rebuild it at the ground for use as changing rooms and cinder banking was used from 1920. A company formed in 1921 purchased Rossett

Park. In 1935, Marine FC built a new 1,500-capacity covered stand and expanded their Spion Kop end. A new tearoom and plunge bath were also added.

SANDHEY'S PARK, RAKE LANE, NEW BRIGHTON
Opened in 1921 by New Brighton FC, who purchased 17,500 square metres of waste land. The ground included a 1,000-seat stand, terracing, a covered enclosure and social facilities at Osborne Mount. Bombing forced closure in 1942 and the site was later used for prefabs in 1944.

THE STADIUM, SEALAND ROAD, CHESTER
By 1931, the Sealand Road end was covered and the main stand expanded to 4,500. A public address system was installed and in 1932 the ground was purchased. In 1934, major upgrades included concrete perimeter walls, new terraces and painted iron railings. The venue was transformed compared to its Cheshire County League days.

VICTORIA PARK, MART LANE, BURSCOUGH
Burscough Rangers returned here in 1921. In 1926, Everton donated parts of their Bullens Road stand to help build a 400-seat grandstand, which was assembled by local volunteers.

VICTORIA PARK, EARLESTOWN
Opened in 1933 by Earlestown White Star FC, the ground was accessed via a footbridge over a railway. A 38-foot pavilion was built, including a shower bath. Season tickets cost 3/6 or 2/6 for the unemployed. In 1934, the club requested a new footpath from the council.

VISTA PARK, HAYDOCK
Revamped in 1937 by the newly reformed Haydock Athletic. A 40-foot-wide stand with dressing rooms and a referee's room was added, along with plans for two slipper baths and a seated paddock.

WALTON HALL PARK, WALTON

In the late 1920s, when the park was being developed as an ornamental space, it hosted seventy-five football teams, twenty cricket teams, six hockey teams, four rounders teams and two baseball teams. A lake and general improvements were completed in the 1930s.

WEMBLEY STADIUM (EMPIRE STADIUM), LONDON

In February 1923, a live test with 1,200 McAlpine employees evaluated safety. Activities included cheering, mass movement, swaying and stampeding. Results confirmed the stadium's readiness. The pitch consisted of 76,250 turf sections on a 10½-inch ash and clinker base.

28 April 1923 saw the FA Cup Final held at Wembley for the first time – the stadium's inaugural football match. The game featured Bolton Wanderers and West Ham United, with Bolton winning 2–0 in front of over 126,000 spectators. However, the crowd scenes became more memorable than the match itself. The turnout was so immense that the Bolton team disembarked their coach a mile from the ground and walked to the stadium. At 2:15pm, fans forced their way into Wembley, climbing fences to escape the crush and spilling onto the pitch. Spectators lined the touchlines and it took mounted police to clear the field. One grey horse, 'Billie' (which appeared white on newsreels), gave the final its nickname: 'The White Horse Final'.

A choir sang 'Abide with Me' as order was restored – an act widely believed to have led to the hymn being played before every FA Cup Final since 1927. The match kicked off 45 minutes late. The House of Commons later launched an inquiry, recommending pre-purchased tickets for future finals, improved turnstiles, more entrances and railings and dividing terraces into self-contained sections.

LOCAL TEAMS WHO PLAYED AT WEMBLEY DURING THIS TIME: Everton FA Cup Final, 1933.

CHAPTER 4

THE POST-WAR YEARS

BACK IN 1939/40, LIVERPOOL HAD FINISHED THE SOMEWHAT AD HOC
Football League season as runners-up, Everton were (3rd), New Brighton
(7th), Chester (9th) and Tranmere Rovers (12th). 1940/41 had become a
regional football league and decided on goals difference. Everton were
(5th), New Brighton (13th), Liverpool (16th), Chester (18th), Tranmere
Rovers (29th), Southport (30th) and so the league followed the same system
in the following seasons with teams playing different amounts of games
and seasons being decided on goal difference.

The 1945/46 Football League season returned to a 22-club division but
still under the wartime format, with Everton and Liverpool placed in the
North League. Everton finished as runners-up behind Sheffield United,
while Liverpool ended the season in eleventh place.

The Liverpool County Combination restarted in earnest that season
after being played under wartime's truncated football system since 1939/40
till 1944/45. Skelmersdale United won it in 1939/40, Liverpool A 1941/42,
Liverpool Reserves 1942/43, Marine 1943/44 and Liverpool Reserves 1944/45
and the George Mahon Cup was often run on league lines with the winners
being decided in a final. Skelmersdale United won in 1939/40 with Burscough
Vics. 1940/41, Liverpool A 1941/42 and Marine 1942/43, 1943/44 and 1944/45.

The 1945/46 Liverpool County Combination First Division featuring:
Everton A, Fazakerley, Formby, Kirkby, Liverpool A, Marine, Napiers, Earle,

Southport Reserves, Skelmersdale United, Earlestown, Newton YMCA, Haydock C&B and South Liverpool. The Second Division included A.T.M. Castner Kellner, IFI Widnes, Liverpool Co-op, Marlborough, Varsity, Earle Reserves and Old Cathinians. In the final edition of the Football League Third Division North Cup, Chester were runners-up, losing 5–4 on aggregate to Rotherham United.

Likewise, the Liverpool Football League continued during the war and restarted after it. Orrell won the 1939/40 First Division with Earle winning the Houston Cup. However, the teams taking part changed radically season by season and therefore the regulars in the competition regularly dropped in and out.

In the final edition of the Football League Third Division North Cup, Chester were runners-up, losing 5–4 on aggregate to Rotherham United.

When the Football League officially resumed for the 1946/47 season, the *Liverpool Echo* promised to return its football coverage to pre-war levels but asked readers to place orders to avoid wasting newsprint. Liverpool Corporation Passenger Transport introduced an early version of the soccer bus service, with buses running from Leyfield Road to Goodison Park or Anfield for 4d. The FA set a maximum player wage of £12 per week. In June 1946, the Football League clubs agreed to a minimum ticket price of 1s 3d–3d less than during wartime football, but 3d more than in 1939. The average weekly wage at the time was £4 6s 1d. – a

The first competitive post-war Football League matches were held on Saturday, 31 August 1946. Everton lost 2–0 to Brentford at Goodison in front of more than 55,000 spectators. Liverpool won 1–0 away at Sheffield United. In the Third Division North, Chester drew 4–4 at York City, New Brighton lost 3–2 at Wrexham, Southport lost 4–2 at Darlington and Tranmere Rovers lost 4–1 at home to Rotherham United.

Liverpool won their fifth League title that season. They reached the top of the table in November following a 4–1 away victory over Derby County, with all four goals scored by Jack Balmer. A severe winter disrupted the season and in March the Football League and FA agreed to extend the campaign to 14 June 1947, following the Government's suspension of midweek sport. Power cuts caused by the weather led to temporary unemployment peaking at 800,000.

By February, Liverpool sat fifth, five points behind leaders Blackpool but with four games in hand. Three other teams were also in contention. Liverpool's 2-1 away wins over Arsenal and Wolves in their final two matches secured top spot and had finished their season. They needed to wait a fortnight before Stoke City played their final game – away at Sheffield United on 14 June – They needed to win to overtake Liverpool on goal average. As the Stoke City game unfolded, Liverpool were playing Everton in the Liverpool Senior Cup Final at Anfield. News that Stoke City had lost was announced over the loudspeaker ten minutes before full time, confirming Liverpool as champions. They went on to win the Senior Cup moments later. In addition, they won the Lancashire Senior Cup.

Attendances surged across the region in 1946/47, with most clubs enjoying better figures than before the war: Chester averaged 6,466 (up from 5,963 in 1938–39), Everton 40,854 (up from 35,040), Liverpool 45,732 (up from 31,422), New Brighton 5,927 (up from 4,510), Southport 4,708 (down from 5,862) and Tranmere Rovers 8,076 (down from 9,938).

That season, Chester won their third Welsh Cup by defeating Merthyr Tydfil 5-1 in a replay at Wrexham, following a goalless draw at Ninian Park. The I Zingari Combination introduced a Challenge Cup as a knockout competition for member clubs in 1947/48. That year's Lancashire Amateur Cup winners were Earle. The following decade they would lose three successive Welsh Cup finals between 1953 and 1955.

Liverpool's youth teams reached two finals in 1947/48: the English Schools Shield, which they shared with Stockport after a 2-2 draw and the FA County Youth Cup, where they lost 5-3 on aggregate to Essex. The following year, Liverpool County FA Youth won the competition 4-3 on aggregate against Middlesex. Maghull won the Lancashire Amateur Cup in 1948/49, beating Manchester University 1-0 at Goodison Park.

The Liverpool County FA introduced the Liverpool Senior Non-League Cup in 1949/50 as an amateur counterpart to the Liverpool Senior Cup. Bootle won the inaugural final against South Liverpool over two legs. The

Northern Midweek League resumed in 1949 with Southport again involved, but it faded in the early 1950s.

In 1950/51, Everton were relegated to the Second Division. That season, Liverpool Schools defeated Brierley Hill and Sedgley Schools 5–3 on aggregate to win the English Schools Shield. Collegiate Old Boys won the Lancashire Amateur Cup in both 1950/51 and 1951/52. In 1951, white footballs were introduced and the maximum player wage increased to £14. The national average wage was about £6 per week.

Queen Elizabeth II ascended to the throne on 6 February 1952 following the death of King George VI. In the 1950s, Britain was still recovering from World War II. On the Wirral, this included slum clearance and prefabricated housing projects. Cammell Laird added a dry dock in 1953. Rationing ended in 1954, by which time eggs cost 3d–4d, bread 5d per pound, beef 2s 4d per pound, ham 5s 6d and tea 4s 8d.

In 1953/54, Everton were promoted back to the First Division, Everton went to Oldham Athletic for the final game of the season knowing a win would see them regain First Division status. They won the game 4–0 and finished on the same points as Division winners Leicester City with Everton but were two goals short of gaining top spot. Liverpool passed them by and were relegated to the second tier. That season Aigburth Peoples Hall won the Lancashire Amateur Cup and Wigan Athletic retained the Lancashire Junior Cup. In 1954, orange footballs were introduced for winter use. That same year, Liverpool County FA Youth won the FA County Youth Cup. Chester lost the 1954/55 Welsh Cup Final.

The inaugural seasons of the European Cup and Inter-Cities Fairs Cup – the latter originally intended to promote trade fairs – were held in 1955/56. That season, Liverpool won the Lancashire Senior Cup, Wigan won the Lancashire Junior Cup, Collegiate Old Boys won the Lancashire Amateur Cup and Liverpool Schools beat Brighton and Hove Schools 7–2 on aggregate to win the English Schools Shield. Chester won the Lancashire Senior Challenge Cup in 1956/57.

Floodlit football arrived on Merseyside in 1957/58. Everton hosted Liverpool under lights and Tranmere played their first floodlit match against

Rochdale at Prenton Park before 16,700 fans. Southport, who had hosted a pioneering floodlit game in 1889, did not experience another until 1962.

The idea of a Fourth Division had long been discussed. In 1957, a vote narrowly fell short of the required two-thirds majority. At the 1958 League AGM, a four-up, four-down system was agreed. The top half of both Third Division North and South formed the new Third Division, while the bottom halves became the Fourth Division. Tranmere Rovers, who finished 11th in 1957/58, joined the new Third Division, while Chester (21st) and Southport (23rd) became founder members of the Fourth Division.

In 1958, the maximum and minimum player wages were set at £20 and £8 respectively. At the Football League AGM the new nationwide Fourth Division was agreed, replacing the old regional Third Division North and South, and a four-up, four-down system was agreed. That season, Maghull won the Lancashire Amateur Cup. Chester lost the 1958 Welsh Cup Final 2–1 to Wrexham in a replay at the Racecourse Ground.

In the 1958/59 Lancashire Cup competitions, Liverpool won the Senior Cup by beating Everton 1–0, while Aigburth Peoples Hall beat Blackpool Rangers 4–1 in the Amateur Cup. In 1959/60, Florence Albion beat Aigburth 3–2 to win the Amateur Cup and Wigan Athletic won the Lancashire Challenge Trophy, defeating Chorley 2–1.

Around this time the Littlewoods Pools millionaire John Moores increased his shareholding in Everton to take control of the club. The purchase, together with shares in Liverpool held by John and his brother Cecil, set both clubs onto a path of success. Cecil's son, David, later took over the reins at Liverpool, leading them to domestic and European success.

Two new cup competitions were inaugurated in the 1960/61 season. In Europe, the European Cup Winners' Cup began and in the English Football League, the Football League Cup was launched. Participation in the latter was voluntary for Football League clubs. Chester, Everton, Liverpool, Southport and Tranmere Rovers all took part in its inaugural season, while six clubs–including Arsenal and Tottenham Hotspur–declined to participate.

Chester's first tie in the competition ended in a 1–0 defeat in a replay against Leyton Orient. Everton beat Accrington Stanley 3–1 at Goodison

Park, Liverpool won their opening tie 5–2 away at Luton Town, but were beaten 2–1 by Southampton at Anfield in the next round. Southport lost 2–0 away to Plymouth Argyle, while Tranmere Rovers, having received a bye in the first round, beat Port Vale away in round two. Everton eliminated Tranmere in the fourth round with a 4–0 win at Prenton Park. Everton losing 2–1 away to Shrewsbury Town in the Quarter finals. At the end of the season, both Everton and Liverpool withdrew from the competition, citing European football commitments.

The fight to abolish the maximum wage in football had been ongoing for several years, but matters came to a head in 1960 when Jimmy Hill, chairman of the Professional Footballers' Association (PFA), threatened strike action if two key demands were not met: the abolition of both the maximum wage and the 'retain and transfer' system. When the League rejected most of the players' demands, Hill and his committee stood firm. The pressure intensified as leading players such as Jimmy Greaves and Brian Clough were being courted by Italian clubs, raising concerns that others might follow. After months of negotiation, the maximum wage was finally abolished in January 1961.

However, the 'retain and transfer' system was only partially reformed. The amendments included four key points:

1. A player could not be transferred during his contract unless by mutual consent.
2. A player had to be informed by 19 May whether the club intended to offer a new contract.
3. If a player rejected a new contract, he was to be placed on the transfer list and paid his club wages until 31 July.
4. If he had not been transferred by 31 July, he would be offered a monthly contract. If still not transferred by 31 August, the case would be referred to the League's Management Committee.

These reforms were reluctantly accepted, to Hill's displeasure.

In the 1960/61 and 1961/62 seasons, the Liverpool Schools team reached the finals of the English Schools Shield but were beaten on both occasions.

In 1961, they lost 2–1 over two legs to Barnsley Schools and in 1962, were defeated 3–2 on aggregate by Stoke.

In 1961/62, Liverpool were promoted to the First Division as champions of the Second Division. Having dominated the Division from the start of the season, with and unbeaten eleven match run that included six initial back-to-back wins, they finished the season eight points ahead of second placed Leighton Orient.

The 1962/63 season saw Everton crowned champions of the Football League. They began with four consecutive wins: 3–1 away at Burnley, 3–1 at home to Manchester United, 4–1 at home to Sheffield Wednesday and 1–0 away at Manchester United. These results helped them reach the top of the table. However, the season was severely disrupted by a prolonged spell of extreme weather – 'The Big Freeze' – and Everton did not play a league match between 22 December and 12 February. Upon resumption, they dropped to third after a 3–1 defeat away to Leicester City, who had played more games during the break.

As the season progressed, Tottenham Hotspur and Everton made up their games in hand. Everton regained top spot with six matches remaining, holding their position and securing the title with a 4–1 win over Fulham at Goodison Park in front of 60,578 fans in the final game of the season.

In 1963, two years after partial reforms were introduced, the 'retain and transfer' system again came under legal scrutiny. Since 1893, the system had allowed clubs to retain a player's registration against his will. In 1959, George Eastham refused to sign a new contract with Newcastle United. The club retained his registration, but the dispute eventually led to his transfer to Arsenal and culminated in a High Court case in 1963. The judge ruled that the system's retain clause constituted 'an undue restraint of trade' under common law. As a result, the Football League abolished the retain rule, meaning players could no longer be forced to remain at clubs against their will – although they could still be transferred without their consent. This revised system would remain in place for another 30 years.

Sunday football on Merseyside followed a similar trajectory to the rest of England. The FA had long opposed Sunday football, in part due to the Sunday Observance Acts. By 1939, the FA had begun to examine the issue, prompted by the proliferation of Sunday matches –particularly in London – since the 1920s. World War II delayed any resolution. In the early 1950s, a National Sunday Football Association was formed and Merseyside clubs joined it, establishing the Liverpool Sunday Football Association. By 1960, the FA was looking to absorb the Sunday Football Association into its structure. Ike Robinson (Secretary of the Liverpool County FA) and Gordon Brown (Secretary of the Liverpool Sunday FA) were both adamant that only one governing body should oversee the game.

In 1964, the FA formally sanctioned Sunday football under its jurisdiction, taking control across Merseyside and the wider country. While informal Sunday leagues in Liverpool had existed since 1954, the Liverpool Sunday League was officially recognised in 1964. The Wallasey Sunday League began in 1963, followed by the Birkenhead Sunday League in 1964. The Liverpool Sunday Premier Cup was also launched in the 1963/64 season. Everton won the Lancashire Senior Cup that season.

Three local towns – Runcorn, Skelmersdale and Warrington – were designated as New Towns, either fully or in part, to accommodate population overspill from Liverpool and Manchester caused by wartime bomb damage and slum clearance. These developments arose from the New Towns Act of 1946. Runcorn and Skelmersdale were designated during the second wave of New Town developments (1961-64), while Warrington, particularly the Birchwood area, was designated in the third wave in 1968. Runcorn was planned to accommodate 90,000 residents, while Skelmersdale was intended as an overspill for north Liverpool. Warrington served as an overspill for both Liverpool and Manchester.

In 1963/64, Liverpool won the title, their first under Bill Shankly's management, four points ahead of Manchester United, after they led the First Division from April onwards.

In August 1964, the BBC aired its first episode of Match of the Day, featuring Liverpool's 3–2 home win over Arsenal at Anfield. That season,

Liverpool went on to win the FA Cup for the first time. In the third round, they won 2–1 away at West Bromwich Albion. In the fourth round, Stockport County held them 1–1 at Anfield before Liverpool won the replay 2–0. They then beat Bolton 1–0 away in the fifth round. A goalless draw at Leicester in the quarter-finals was followed by a 1–0 win in the replay. In the semi-final, Liverpool defeated Chelsea 2–0 at Villa Park and in the final at Wembley, they overcame Leeds United 2–1.

Aigburth People's Hall won the Lancashire Amateur Cup that season.

The first National Sunday Cup competition, held in 1964/65, was open only to County Associations. Sixteen entered, with fifteen submitting representative teams. The trophy, a superb example of Persian craftsmanship, had been presented to the FA by the Shah of Iran as a gift to mark its centenary in 1963. Its unique design made it a distinctive feature of the competition.

At the end of the 1965/66 season, Liverpool won the League title for the seventh time. Having already secured the FA Cup, they set about adding the League championship. Two convincing home victories in mid-November – 5–0 against Northampton Town and 5–2 against Blackburn Rovers – saw Liverpool rise to the top of the table. Their main rivals were Burnley, whom they defeated 2–1 at Anfield on 27 November. From that point on, Liverpool held top spot for the rest of the campaign, eventually finishing six points clear of Leeds United and Burnley.

That same season, Everton won the FA Cup. In the third round, they beat Sunderland 3–0 at Goodison Park. A fourth-round trip to non-league Bedford Town ended in another 3–0 win. The fifth round brought a third 3–0 victory, this time at home against Coventry City.

In the quarter-finals, Everton faced Manchester City. After a 0–0 draw at Maine Road and another goalless draw in the replay at Goodison three days later, a second replay was held at Molineux. Everton won 2–0 to reach the semi-final. There, at Burnden Park, they defeated Manchester United 1–0, reaching the final without conceding a single goal in the competition.

In the final at Wembley, Everton fell two goals behind to Sheffield Wednesday but mounted a remarkable comeback to win 3–2, with two goals from Mike Trebilcock and a winning goal from Derek Temple.

Chester, meanwhile, were eliminated from the Welsh Cup after losing to Swansea Town over two legs and a subsequent play-off. In the Lancashire Junior Cup / Lancashire Challenge Trophy, Wigan Athletic were crowned winners.

The 1965/66 season also saw the introduction of substitutes in Football League matches. Everton's first use of a substitute came when John Hurst replaced Fred Pickering in an away game at Stoke City. Liverpool's first substitute was Geoff Strong, who came on for Chris Lawler at Anfield against West Ham United. For Chester, Tommy Singleton replaced Starkey at home against Stockport County. Southport's first substitute was Dick Marshall, who replaced Watt at home against Doncaster Rovers. At Tranmere Rovers, John Lornie came on for Steve 'Mandy' Hill in a match at Prenton Park against Chester.

The FIFA World Cup was held in England during the summer of 1966. Goodison Park hosted five matches and was one of two grounds, along with Old Trafford, selected for Group 3 fixtures, featuring Brazil, Bulgaria, Hungary and Portugal.

The first match at Goodison saw Brazil beat Bulgaria 2–0 on 12 July in front of 47,308 spectators. On 15 July, Brazil lost 3–1 to Hungary before 51,387 fans. In their final group match on 19 July, Brazil were again defeated 3–1, this time by Portugal, with 58,479 in attendance. On 23 July, Portugal beat North Korea 5–3 in a dramatic quarter-final, watched by 40,248. The Goodison semi-final saw West Germany defeat the Soviet Union 2–1 in front of 38,273 spectators.

The 1966/67 season brought success for Southport, who finished as runners-up in the Fourth Division and secured promotion to the Third Division. Tranmere Rovers, who finished fourth, were promoted alongside them. A crucial fixture came late in the season when Tranmere hosted Southport at Prenton Park. Tranmere could afford a defeat, but Southport needed a win. Two Tranmere errors – an own goal by Stan Storton and a header from Eric Redrobe – gave Southport the advantage. Although Tranmere got a goal back, Southport won 2–1 and moved closer to promotion.

On 6 May, George Andrews scored in the 79th minute against Southend United at Haig Avenue to seal Southport's promotion to the Third Division for the first time and confirm second place. Tranmere confirmed their own promotion on 12 May with a 3–1 home win over Rochdale.

That season, Southport and Chester joined eight other northern lower-league sides as founder members of the Northern Floodlit League, which launched in November 1966. Each season was split into a league campaign followed by a Challenge Cup competition.

In the FA Amateur Cup, Skelmersdale United reached the final but were beaten by Enfield. The original match at Wembley ended 0–0 and Enfield won the replay 3–0 at Maine Road.

The Liverpool Schools side won the English Schools Shield in 1966/67, defeating East London 1–0 over two legs. Burscough won the Lancashire Junior Cup / Lancashire Challenge Trophy that same season.

In 1967 BBC Radio Merseyside was launched, and its sports department went onto commentate on the area's local matches, both home and away, at Wembley and overseas.

Everton first featured on Match of the Day at Goodison Park in August 1967, beating Manchester United 3–1. Manager Harry Catterick had previously banned television cameras from Goodison, arguing it would reveal tactics and form to rival teams. That season, Everton reached the FA Cup final but were runners-up to West Bromwich Albion. Their cup run began with a 1–0 win away to Southport, followed by a 2–0 win away at Carlisle United. Tranmere Rovers were beaten 2–0 at Goodison in the fifth round and a 1–0 victory over Leeds United at Old Trafford took Everton to the final. There, they lost 1–0 to West Brom.

Wigan Athletic once again won the Lancashire Junior Cup / Lancashire Challenge Trophy in 1967/68.

That season also saw the formation of the Formby and District Sunday League, which would later become the Crosby and District Sunday League. The first winners were Crosby Dynamo. The league was formed in 1965 by Gerry McLean, Bill Birch and Ian Kelly and was based at the Formby Gild Hall. Original teams included Crosby Dynamo, Real Inira and Crow's

Nest. The local church, Our Lady's in Formby, also provided a team and introduced the Canon Francis Cup to mark the parish priest's jubilee. Crow's Nest won the first cup, followed by Allandale United and Crosby Dynamo. When the league restarted as the Crosby and District Sunday League in 1967, Don Williams was credited with its formation; the league trophy was later named in his honour.

The Northern Premier League (NPL) was formed in 1968. The idea had originally been raised in 1961 by Wigan Athletic, who proposed a North West Counties League involving ten clubs from the Cheshire League and Lancashire Combination. However, the Lancashire Combination rejected the proposal. In protest, Wigan left the Combination and re-joined the Cheshire League. The idea was revisited in 1966 and a committee made up of officials from six leagues – including the Lancashire Combination, Cheshire County League and Midland League – was formed to develop a new structure. The NPL launched in 1968/69, with clubs such as Runcorn, South Liverpool and Wigan Athletic invited as founder members.

Promotion was agreed for the champions of the Cheshire County League, Lancashire Combination and West Midlands (Regional) League, who would replace the bottom three clubs of the NPL each season. Skelmersdale United, who had won the Cheshire County League in 1968/69, were denied entry because they were an amateur side. They eventually joined the NPL in 1971/72, when the league expanded to 24 clubs and Skelmersdale had turned professional.

In 1968, Southport won the Northern Floodlit League Challenge Cup and the Liverpool Schools team beat Swindon Schools 3–1 over two legs to win the English Schools Shield.

Also in 1968, a European amateur competition was inaugurated, contested by the winners of the FA Amateur Cup and the Coppa Italia Dilettanti. It was named after Italian FIFA official Ottorino Barassi, who had famously hidden the Jules Rimet Trophy from the Nazis during World War Two.

At the end of the 1969/70 season, Everton were crowned League champions. They began the season with four consecutive victories putting them in first place. Although they lost top spot after a 2–1 defeat at Derby County in early September, they regained it with a 2–0 home win against West Ham United on 13 September. After briefly slipping again in January, Everton reclaimed top spot following a 1–0 win away to Tottenham Hotspur in mid-March. They held the position for the remainder of the season, securing the title with a 2–0 win over West Bromwich Albion at Goodison Park on 1 April. They finished three points clear of Leeds United.

In schools' football, the Liverpool Schools side again beat East London 1–0 over two legs to retain the English Schools Shield for a second successive year.

In 1970, Tranmere Rovers joined the Northern Floodlit League after the club's board concluded it would be more financially viable than remaining in the Cheshire League. The decision was driven by a need to reduce the playing staff and play fewer fixtures.

Two further competitions were inaugurated in 1970: the Texaco Cup and the Anglo-Italian Cup. In addition, the FA Trophy was contested for the first time.

By the late 1960s, women's football was beginning to grow again. In Manchester, Foden's Ladies had emerged as the leading women's team, taking over from the famous Dick, Kerr's Ladies. An unofficial Women's World Cup had taken place and in 1970 the Women's FA Cup was held for the first time. However, it would be another decade before the Merseyside region produced its first winners.

Nevertheless, the first women's football league was formed locally in 1971: the Merseyside and Wirral Women's Football League. Its founder members included: Cadbury, Chester, Girobank, Paarden, Plessey (Stoneycroft), Raffles, Squibb (Moreton) and Southport.

At the same time, a new North West Women's Regional Football League was also established, with Foden's Ladies among its founding members. The league would soon expand to four divisions, reflecting the growing popularity of the women's game.

In the FA Amateur Cup, Skelmersdale United had previously lost the 1966/67 final, drawing 0–0 at Wembley with Enfield before losing the replay 3–0 at Maine Road, Manchester. However, in the 1970/71 season, they returned to Wembley and won the competition.

In the second round, Skelmersdale beat Sutton Coldfield Town 3–0 at home. In the third round, after drawing 1–1 away to Tow Law Town, they won the replay 1–0. In the quarter-final, they recorded an emphatic 3–0 away win against Wycombe Wanderers and then beat Leatherhead 2–0 in the semi-final at Bolton's Burnden Park. In the final at Wembley, Skelmersdale United defeated Dagenham 4–1, earning the right to represent England in the Coppa Ottorino Barassi against Italian club Montebelluna over two legs (see European chapter).

That same season, Liverpool were FA Cup runners-up. They beat Everton 2–1 in the semi-final, but were defeated 2–1 by Arsenal in the final at Wembley, with Arsenal completing a league and cup double.

Merseyside's schools' teams, having won the last two English Schools Shield titles of the 1960s, continued their success in 1970/71. This time, it was the Huyton Schools team who lifted the trophy, beating Stoke Schools 5–1 over two legs.

TEAMS FORMED OR ACTIVE BETWEEN 1945 AND 1972

AIGBURTH PEOPLES HALL

Aigburth Peoples Hall was named following the resumption of football after the Second World War. They played on land at Sudley Recreation Ground in Mossley Hill, donated by the Emma Holt Foundation. Joining the I Zingari League in 1945/46, they won their first trophy the following season, clinching the Second Division title by 12 points ahead of Southport Trinity. They also won the Liverpool Junior Cup that year, defeating Birkdale Central Albion.

The 1947/48 season was a double-winning campaign, as they secured the I Zingari First Division title by eight points ahead of Collegiate Old Boys, whom they also beat in the I Zingari Challenge Cup final. In 1948/49, they retained the Challenge Cup against Collegiate Old Boys but finished runners-up to them in the league.

Another double followed in 1949/50, again winning the league and beating Collegiate in the Challenge Cup. The following year, Collegiate gained some revenge by winning the Challenge Cup final.

In 1951/52, Aigburth Peoples Hall won the Liverpool Amateur Cup against Collegiate and again triumphed over them in the Challenge Cup, though they were league runners-up. In 1952/53, they narrowly won the league title by a point from Collegiate and also retained the Challenge Cup.

In 1953/54, they added another Liverpool Amateur Cup (beating Earle), won the I Zingari League by four points from Liverpool Technical Students and defeated Middleton Amateurs 4–0 to lift the Lancashire Amateur Cup. Another league title came in 1957/58, five points ahead of Florence Albion and they won the Lancashire Amateur Cup in 1958/59 by beating Blackpool Rangers. However, they were runners-up in both the I Zingari League (to Florence Albion) and the Challenge Cup (losing 3–2 to Rockville of Wallasey).

Three more league titles followed: in 1959/60 (one point ahead of Florence Albion), 1960/61 (five points ahead of Crosby) and 1963/64 (two points ahead of Liverpool University). They also suffered cup final defeats in this period–losing the Lancashire Amateur Cup final to Florence Albion and the Liverpool Amateur Cup final to Unit Construction in 1959/60 and were League runners-up in 1961/62.

Other achievements included winning the I Zingari Challenge Cup in 1962/63 (beating NALGO), though they were runners-up in the Liverpool Amateur Cup to Maghull. In 1964/65, they won the Lancashire Amateur Cup again, this time defeating Manchester University at Old Trafford. In 1970/71, the club was relegated from the I Zingari First Division.

AINTREE S.S. (SORTING SIDINGS)
Aintree S.S. joined the Second Division of the Liverpool County Combination in 1948/49, finishing sixth in their first season. They won the Second Division title in 1954/55 by three points ahead of Everton's 'B' team, and the Lord Wavertree Cup the same season.

In 1955/56, they finished third in the First Division. They won the Liverpool Amateur Cup in 1957/58, defeating Maghull in the final. In 1960/61, they added a reserve side to the Second Division. They also shared the George Mahon Cup in 1965/66. The senior side was relegated from the First Division in 1967/68.

AINTREE VILLA
Formed in 1954, Aintree Villa began life in the Bootle JOC League before joining the I Zingari Alliance in 1955/56. After twice winning the Alliance, they joined the I Zingari League Third Division in 1958/59 and won it at the first attempt, finishing nine points clear of Croxteth United.

In 1959/60, they won the Second Division by a single point over Melling. In 1960/61, they spent one season in the First Division before relegation. They returned in 1964/65 after again winning the Second Division, seven points ahead of Old Holts and also won the Liverpool Junior Cup, beating Coronation.

Their first I Zingari First Division title came in 1966/67, one point ahead of Odyssey. That year, their pavilion at Aintree Racecourse was destroyed by vandals. They retained the league title in 1967/68 on goal average from Quarry Bank Old Boys and won it again in 1968/69. In the same season, they shared the I Zingari Challenge Cup with Molyneux after a replay failed to produce a winner.

Villa were runners-up in the 1969/70 Lancashire Amateur Cup, losing to Manchester YMCA. They regained the I Zingari League title in 1970/71 by two points from Florence Albion and won the Challenge Cup by beating St Andrews United.

ASHVILLE

The modern Ashville FC was formed in 1949 as a youth side in Wallasey, playing in the Wallasey Youth League. After winning successive Third, Second and First Division titles in the Wirral Combination, they joined the West Cheshire League in 1955.

In 1955/56, they won the Second Division by ten points from Cammell Laird and claimed the West Cheshire Bowl. In 1956/57, they finished ninth in the First Division, won the Wirral Amateur Cup (beating Shell) and retained the West Cheshire Bowl.

In 1960/61, they were runners-up to Runcorn Reserves in the Pyke Cup (losing 2–1) and were also runners-up in both the Wirral Senior Cup (to Stork) and the Benevolent Cup. In 1961/62, they won the Wirral Senior Cup by defeating Bromborough Pool 2–0. That same year, they opened a new ground, Villa Park, to mark the achievement. They affiliated with the Cheshire FA in 1963.

In 1967/68, Ashville won the West Cheshire League First Division, finishing two points clear of Christleton and their reserves were runners-up in the Second Division to Bromborough.

BOOTLE

Bootle FC was briefly revived after the Second World War. Plans had existed to reform the club in the 1930s, but a new side was only formally established after a 1947 meeting of local councillors.

In 1948, a new Bootle side–sometimes referred to as Bootle Athletic–was formed and joined the Lancashire Combination after initially considering the West Cheshire and Cheshire County Leagues. Their home ground was Bootle Stadium (also known as the Peace Stadium) on Maguire Avenue, which had a capacity of 30,000.

Their first match in the Lancashire Combination Second Division came on 21 August 1948, drawing with Barnoldswick & District. Bootle topped the division that season, one point ahead of Horwich RMI and were promoted to the First Division for 1949/50, where they finished 16th. They also won the inaugural Liverpool Non-League Senior Cup, beating South Liverpool 4–1 on aggregate.

In 1951, the club moved to Seaforth Stadium (10,000 capacity), intending to install floodlights. Managed by former Everton player Alex Stevenson, they retained the Liverpool Non-League Senior Cup in 1951/52 and had won it the season before as well. Bootle finished 10th in 1951/52 and 12th in 1952/53. The club folded mid-season in 1953 after repeated warnings from the *Liverpool Echo* that poor support might force closure.

B.R.N.E.S.C. (British Rail North End Social Club)
B.R.N.E.S.C. played in the Business Houses League following the Second World War. In 1959/60, they finished runners-up in the Second Division and by 1961/62, they were competing in the First Division.

BROMBOROUGH POOL
After the war, Bromborough Pool rejoined the West Cheshire League, with the senior team in the First Division and reserves in the Second. In 1945/46, they were runners-up in the Wirral Senior Cup, losing to Ellesmere Port Town.

They finished ninth in the 1947/48 season but were relegated in 1950/51. In 1952/53, they were Pyke Cup runners-up, losing to Moreton. They returned to the First Division in 1953/54, finishing ninth, but were again relegated in 1954/55.

In 1960/61, they won the Second Division by seven points over Newton Reserves and claimed the West Cheshire Bowl with a 5–3 win over Port Sunlight. They were runners-up in the Wirral Amateur Cup that season, losing 2–1 to Lawrence's CYMS.

In 1961/62, they lost the Wirral Senior Cup final to Ashville (2–0). The club was again relegated from the First Division in 1968/69.

BRUNSWICK BOYS

The origins of Brunswick Boys FC trace back to a group of British prisoners of war held in Oflag 79, near Braunschweig, Germany. In February 1944, two American bombers accidentally dropped bombs on the camp, worsening already harsh conditions. At the next morning's muster, Major Percy Flood proposed that they establish a boys' club in Britain after the war, inspired by the suffering of children back home.

Brunswick Boys Club was established in 1947 in Liverpool by former prisoners H.C. Mounsey, P. Radcliffe Evans, J.M. Marshall and J. Tegid. It opened in 1948 on Bedford Road South, Toxteth. In 1951, teams from Liverpool, Fulham and Glasgow boys' clubs competed for the Percy Flood Cup in Heswall. London won the tournament.

After their original premises succumbed to dry rot, the club moved to Princes Avenue and then to Marsh Lane, Bootle, in 1964. The club's football team started in the Liverpool Boys Association League in the early 1950s and later competed in the Bootle JOC.

BURSCOUGH

Formed in 1945/46 at a meeting held in the cellars of the Stanley Institute, Burscough Football Club was established using assets from two defunct local clubs–Burscough Vics and Lathom Juniors. Their application to join the First Division of the Liverpool County Combination was accepted and their first game came in August 1946 against Prescot BI, which they lost 5–2. They went on to finish third that season.

The 1947/48 season was a highly successful one. Burscough won three trophies: the Lancashire Junior Cup (beating Fleetwood 2–1 at Broomfield Road, Blackpool), the George Mahon Cup (defeating Earlestown 2–0 at Holly Park) and the Liverpool Challenge Cup (beating Skelmersdale United 4–1 at Haig Avenue).

In 1949/50, they won the Liverpool County Combination by one point ahead of Skelmersdale United. That same season, they also lifted the Lancashire Junior Cup again, beating Nelson 2–1 at Ewood Park, Blackburn. The following year, they retained the Liverpool Challenge Cup, defeating St Helens Town 3–1.

In 1953/54, Burscough joined the Second Division of the Lancashire Combination and won the title, finishing six points ahead of Blackpool 'B'. Their reserve team also won the Second Division of the Liverpool County Combination and the senior team were runners-up to South Liverpool in the Liverpool Senior Non-League Cup Final.

In their debut season in the Lancashire Combination First Division (1954/55), Burscough finished fourth. The reserves won the Liverpool Challenge Cup, defeating Fleetwood Hesketh 3–2.

In 1955/56, they won the Lancashire Combination First Division, two points clear of Horwich RMI and also won the Liverpool Senior Non-League Cup by beating New Brighton 1–0. They were runners-up in the Lancashire Combination Cup in 1957/58, losing 2–0 to New Brighton.

In 1966/67, Burscough again lifted the Lancashire Junior Cup, defeating South Liverpool 1–0. The reserves won the Second Division of the Liverpool County Combination in 1967/68, along with the Lord Wavertree Cup.

In 1968/69, Burscough were runners-up to Marine in the Lancashire Combination Cup, losing 6/5 over two legs. The following season (1969/70), they won the Lancashire Combination title, finishing three points ahead of Prestwich Heys.

In 1970/71, Burscough joined the Cheshire County League, finishing as runners-up to Rossendale United, seven points adrift.

CAMMELL LAIRD (1907)

Cammell Laird joined the Second Division of the West Cheshire League in 1948/49, finishing tenth in their debut season. They were runners-up in the Wirral Senior Cup in 1950/51, losing to Newton. They were later relegated from the First Division but they were also Second Division runners-up in 1954/55 and again in 1955/56. In 1957/58, they finally won the Second Division title, finishing one point ahead of Newton Reserves. That season they were also runners-up to Port Sunlight in the Wirral Amateur Cup and won the West Cheshire Bowl.

In 1958/59, they retained the Second Division title, finishing two points clear of Heswall and were promoted to the First Division. They were also runners-up in the Wirral Junior Cup, losing to Birkenhead St Anne's.

In 1962/63, they were runners-up in the Wirral Amateur Cup, losing to Our Lady's. They won the West Cheshire League First Division in 1968/69 by seven points from Newton. In 1969/70, they won the Wirral Amateur Cup (beating Shell), the Pyke Cup (beating Christleton 3–2) and the Cheshire Bowl.

In 1970/71, they retained the West Cheshire League title by a single point over Poulton Victoria.

CANADA (DOCK)

Canada Dock FC was formed in 1966 by John Slocombe and dock workers from the Canada Dock in Liverpool. They joined the Business Houses League for the 1965/66 season and won both the league's Senior Cup and the Liverpool Sunday Junior Cup in their first campaign. They retained the Senior Cup in 1966/67 and also won the Liverpool Sunday Premier Cup.

In 1967/68, they left the Business Houses League to join the Kirkby Newton Combination Premier Division, where they won the league's Challenge Cup in 1967/68, 1968/69 and 1969/70, while also claiming two league championships and two Senior Cup titles.

In 1970/71, they joined the Liverpool & District Sunday League, winning the Third Division in dominant fashion and earning promotion to the First Division. Canada continued to win titles but was expelled on occasions from Sunday League football in the 70s and 80s.

CHESHIRE LINES

Cheshire Lines joined the Second Division of the Liverpool County Combination in 1968/69. Their first match was a goalless draw away to Formby Reserves.

CHESTER / CHESTER CITY

Chester's first post-war trophy came in 1945/46 when they won the Cheshire Bowl by beating Crewe Alexandra 3–1. They also reached the final of the final Third Division North Cup that same season, losing 5–4 on aggregate to Rotherham United.

In the first full post-war league season (1946/47), Chester finished third in the Third Division North–one of the club's highest finishes for the next seven seasons. They also won the Welsh Cup that year, beating Merthyr Tydfil 5–1 in a replay following a goalless draw.

In 1947/48, they were runners-up in the Cheshire Bowl, losing 1–0 to Tranmere Rovers. In 1952/53, they were runners-up in the Lancashire Senior Cup (losing 5–1 to Manchester City), the Welsh Cup (losing 2–1 to Rhyl) and the Cheshire Bowl.

In 1953/54, Chester hit the bottom of the league, winning only one away game and finishing two points above Halifax Town in 23rd. They faced re-election to the Football League but survived with 48 votes. That season, they won the Cheshire Bowl (beating Tranmere Rovers 3–2 over two legs) but lost 2–0 to Flint Town United in the Welsh Cup Final.

Things worsened in 1954/55. Chester failed to win any of their last 11 league matches and again finished bottom, one point behind Grimsby Town. Once again, they survived re-election with 47 votes. That year also saw another Welsh Cup final defeat, this time 4–3 to Barry Town and a Cheshire Bowl final loss to Tranmere Rovers (3–2).

In 1956/57, they won the Lancashire Senior Cup by beating Burnley 1–0. In 1957/58, they finished 21st in the Third Division North and were placed into the newly formed Fourth Division for the 1958/59 season. They also lost the 1958 Welsh Cup Final to Wrexham (2–1).

Their first Fourth Division game was a 2–0 defeat away at Torquay United. In the 1960s, they won the Cheshire Bowl in 1964/65 (beating Tranmere Rovers 2–0) but lost the 1965/66 Welsh Cup Final to Swansea Town (2–1). In 1969/70, they were beaten 5–0 over two legs by Cardiff City in the final. They suffered League re election in both 1960/61 and 1961/62.

In 1970/71, they lost the Cheshire Premier Cup final 1–0 to Stockport County.

CHESTER LADIES

Formed circa 1969, Chester Ladies played in the Merseyside and Wirral Ladies Football League. In 1970/71, they reached the final of the Con Rogan Cup but lost 3–2 to Giro Ladies.

COLLEGIATE OLD BOYS

Following the war, Collegiate Old Boys joined the I Zingari League First Division for the 1946/47 season. In 1947/48, they finished runners-up, eight points behind Aigburth Peoples Hall. They won the league in 1948/49, finishing five points ahead of Aigburth Peoples Hall, but were runners-up to them in the I Zingari Challenge Cup.

In 1949/50, they won the Liverpool Amateur Cup, beating Earle, but again finished second to Aigburth Peoples Hall in the league and lost to them in the Challenge Cup final. The 1950/51 season brought a treble: Collegiate were I Zingari League champions (eight points clear of Maghull), won the Lancashire Amateur Cup and again lifted the Liverpool Amateur Cup (beating Earle) and finally beat Aigburth Peoples Hall in the Challenge Cup final.

In 1951/52, they retained the I Zingari League and won the Lancashire Amateur Cup once more but lost the Challenge Cup final to Aigburth. In 1952/53, they were league runners-up, two points behind Aigburth Peoples Hall.

In 1954/55, they won the Liverpool Amateur Cup (beating Liverpool Police) and were I Zingari League runners-up to Maghull by six points. They repeated as runners-up in 1955/56, this time four points behind Maghull, but won the Lancashire Amateur Cup, beating Alsop Old Boys. They were defeated by Florence Albion in the Challenge Cup finals of both 1954/55 and 1955/56.

In 1956/57, they regained the I Zingari League title, finishing one point ahead of Florence Albion and also won the Liverpool Amateur Cup, defeating Maghull. In 1968/69, they were First Division runners-up, three points behind Aintree Villa.

CROSBY DYNAMO

A Crosby Dynamo youth team played in the Formby and District Youth League in 1950. However, the club that would become associated with Formby FC was founded by Ray Leary and competed in the Formby and District Sunday League, which began in 1965.

Crosby Dynamo won the Formby, Crosby and District Sunday League in 1967/68 and also claimed the Canon Francis Cup that season. They retained the league title in 1968/69 and won the Canon Francis Cup again in 1970/71.

DINGLE RAIL

Originally formed in 1967 as Empress, Dingle Rail joined the Liverpool Sunday League in the Eleventh Division in the 1967/68 season. They gained promotion every season and won the Ninth Division along the way.

DUNLOP

Formed in 1946, Dunlop initially fielded teams in the Liverpool Shipping League and the Business Houses League. Their first team joined the Liverpool County Combination Second Division in 1946/47 and remained until 1949/50, when they returned to the Business Houses League.

They re-joined the County Combination Second Division in 1953/54. In 1955/56, when the County Combination reverted to a 20-team structure, Dunlop finished fourth. In 1956/57, they won their first major trophy-the George Mahon Cup-beating Formby. They claimed the league title in 1957/58, four points ahead of Marine Reserves.

In 1958/59, they won the Lord Wavertree Cup final against Burscough. The following season, they lost the George Mahon Cup final to Guinness Exports. In 1964/65, they lifted the Liverpool Amateur Cup and their reserve team won the Second Division of the County Combination. The reserves also won the Second Division titles in 1966/67 and 1969/70 and the club won the George Mahon Cup in 1970/71.

EARLE

Following World War Two, Earle joined the First Division of the Liverpool County Combination, with their reserves entering the Second Division. They finished sixth in their debut season (1945/46) and shared the Liverpool Amateur Cup with Marine.

In 1946/47, they won the Liverpool Amateur Cup outright, defeating Liverpool Police at Anfield. In 1947/48, they also won the Lancashire Amateur Cup. The club finished bottom of the First Division in 1952/53 and again in 1953/54 and once more in 1959/60.

Despite their struggles in the league, they reached the 1967/68 Liverpool Challenge Cup final, where they lost 3-2 to Formby at Edinburgh Park.

EARLESTOWN

Formed in 1945, the new Earlestown club joined the Liverpool County Combination and finished ninth in their debut season (1945/46). They became league champions in 1947/48, finishing four points ahead of Formby.

At the end of the 1948/49 season, they moved to the Lancashire Combination Second Division, where they finished as runners-up in their first season (1949/50) and were promoted. They placed 17th in their first season in the First Division (1950/51) and were relegated after the 1951/52 season.

They returned to the First Division in 1958/59 after promotion and remained until they left the league following the 1962/63 season. The club then became briefly prominent again when former manager Wilf Mannion successfully sued the club for lost earnings.

EAST VILLA

Formed in 1959 by a group of players from the Muirhead Avenue East area, East Villa began in the Third Division North of the Liverpool League in 1960/61, having won the Sawyer Cup in 1959/60. They earned promotion to the Second Division after finishing runners-up in 1961/62.

They again finished as runners-up in 1964/65 and were promoted to the First Division in 1967/68. They joined the I Zingari Alliance Second Division for the 1968/69 season, finishing as runners-up. In 1969/70, they won the First Division at their first attempt.

ELLESMERE PORT TOWN

In 1945/46, soon after the war, Ellesmere Port Town won the Wirral Senior Cup Final, beating Bromborough Pool. They then won the George Mahon Cup in 1946/47. Their first team joined the Cheshire County League in 1948/49, while the reserves competed in the West Cheshire League for two seasons (1948/50).

They went on to win the Wirral Senior Cup Final in 1948/49 and 1949/50, both times beating Stork FC. The 1950s began with near misses: they were beaten in the Senior Cup final by Stork in 1951/52 and 1955/56 and by Moreton in 1953/54.

The reserves rejoined the West Lancashire League in 1955/56, finishing fourth. In 1956/57, the senior side won the Cheshire Senior Cup Final, beating Hyde United 3–2.

A golden era followed. In 1957/58, Ellesmere Port won the Cheshire County League title, finishing level on points with Hyde United and the reserves won the West Cheshire League. In 1958/59, they retained the league title by eight points over Bangor City and also won the Wirral Senior Cup (beating Port Sunlight), though they lost the Cheshire Senior Cup Final to Winsford United.

In 1959/60, they secured a third consecutive league title, finishing four points ahead of Hyde United. They were runners-up in 1960/61, five points behind Macclesfield Town, but reclaimed the title in 1961/62, three points ahead of the same team.

In 1963/64, they won the Wirral Senior Cup, defeating West Kirby. In 1968, the club moved from York Road to a newly built municipal sports ground featuring a football pitch and running track.

EVERTON

In the first Football League season after the Second World War (1946/47), Everton began with a 2–0 home defeat to Brentford and finished the season in 10th place. In 1948/49, the Everton 'A' side were runners-up to Formby in the Liverpool County Combination.

The 1950/51 season saw Everton relegated from the First Division for only the second time in their history. They dropped to 22nd position after a 4–0 defeat at Blackpool on 4 November – a place they would remain until a 2–1 away win at Huddersfield Town on 16 December. That victory sparked a five-match unbeaten run (four wins and a draw), lifting them to 16th by the end of the year. Everton stayed out of the relegation zone into the new year, but a 1–1 home draw against Wolves on 7 April saw them drop to 20th. They entered the final match away at Sheffield Wednesday needing only a draw to survive, but a heavy 6–0 defeat confirmed their relegation to the Second Division. That same season, the Everton 'A' side finished runners-up to Skelmersdale United in the Liverpool County Combination.

In 1951/52, Everton's first season back in the Second Division began with a 1–0 defeat at Southampton. They eventually finished seventh. The following season (1952/53), they dropped to 14th, but the 'A' team won the Liverpool County Combination.

In 1953/54, Everton secured promotion. They began their campaign with three away games, earning four points: a 3–3 draw at Nottingham Forest, a 1–1 draw at Luton Town and a 3–1 win at Hull City. A John Willie Parker hat-trick helped Everton to a 3–1 home win over Oldham Athletic, lifting them to second place by the end of August. They went on an 11-match unbeaten run starting 12 December and reached the top of the table on 13 March after a 3–0 win over Rotherham United at Goodison, featuring another Parker hat-trick.

Despite briefly falling back after losses to West Ham United (2–1 at home) and Leeds United (3–1 away), they remained in contention. On 29 April, they faced Oldham again in their final game, needing a win to secure second place and promotion. They triumphed 4–0 and were promoted as runners-up–just two goals shy of the title. Everton's reserve team also won the Central League that season while the 'A' Team again finished runners-up to Skelmersdale in the Liverpool County Combination.

In 1954/55, Everton returned to the top flight with a 5–2 away win against Sheffield Wednesday and finished the season 11th. The 'A' team won the Liverpool County Combination.

A new era began in April 1961 when Harry Catterick replaced Johnny Carey, who had infamously been sacked by chairman John Moores during a taxi ride. The decision was soon vindicated: in 1962/63, Everton won the First Division title. They opened the campaign with four straight wins: 3–1 away at Burnley, 3–1 at home to Manchester United, 4–1 at home to Sheffield Wednesday and 1–0 away at Manchester United.

The season was disrupted by the 'Big Freeze', with Everton not playing between late December and mid-February. They slipped to third behind Leicester City and Tottenham Hotspur, but regained top spot with a 1–0 home win over Spurs on 20 April, while Leicester could only draw 1–1 with Wolves. Everton sealed the title on the final day with a 4–1 win over Fulham at Goodison Park, finishing six points ahead of Spurs.

As 1962/63 champions, Everton became Merseyside's first European Cup representatives. In the 1963/64 European Cup, they faced Inter Milan in the preliminary round. A 0–0 draw at Goodison Park on 18 September was followed by a 1–0 defeat at the San Siro a week later, Jair scoring early in the second half to knock Everton out.

In 1965/66, Everton won the FA Cup. They beat Sunderland 3–0 at home in the third round, Bedford Town 3–0 away in the fourth and Coventry City 3–0 at Goodison in the fifth. After two replays in the quarter-final, they beat Manchester City 2–0 in the second replay at Molineux. A 1–0 semi-final win over Manchester United at Burnden Park set up a final against Sheffield Wednesday. Despite falling 2–0 behind, Everton came back with goals from Mike Trebilcock (2) and Derek Temple to win 3–2.

They returned to Wembley in 1967/68 but lost 1–0 to West Bromwich Albion in the final. That season the reserves again won the Central League.

In 1969/70, Everton won the League title again. They started with four wins in August: away at Arsenal (1–0) and Manchester United (2–0) and at home to Crystal Palace (2–1) and Manchester United (3–0). Although a 2–1 defeat at Derby County briefly cost them top spot, they reclaimed it with a 2–0 win over West Ham on 13 September.

They remained top until 17 January, when a 2–1 defeat at Southampton saw them overtaken by Leeds United. Everton regained the lead in mid-March with a 1–0 away win at Tottenham and didn't relinquish it again. The title was confirmed on 1 April with a 2–0 win against West Brom at Goodison Park. Everton finished nine points ahead of runners-up Leeds.

FLORENCE ALBION

After World War II, Florence Albion rejoined the Liverpool League and won the Houston Cup in 1949/50 by beating Mellors United. They soon moved into the I Zingari Alliance and in 1953/54 re-entered the I Zingari League Third Division, which they won by four points. That same season, they also won the Liverpool Intermediate Cup.

In 1954/55, they won the Second Division by eleven points from Odyssey and claimed their first of four I Zingari Challenge Cups, beating Collegiate Old Boys. The reserve team won the I Zingari Combination Second Division and retained the Liverpool Intermediate Cup.

In 1955/56, they finished fifth in the First Division and won a second, I Zingari Challenge Cup, once again defeating Collegiate Old Boys. In 1956/57, they were First Division runners-up by a point and won the I Zingari Challenge Cup, beating Essemay Old Boys. The following season, 1957/58, saw them again defeat Essemay Old Boys to win a fourth I Zingari Challenge Cup, though they again finished league runners-up, this time by five points.

In 1958/59, Florence Albion finally won the I Zingari First Division title, finishing ahead of Aigburth Peoples Hall and won the Liverpool Amateur Cup with a 2–1 win over Maghull. In 1959/60, they finished runners-up by a point but won another I Zingari Challenge Cup, beating Old Xaverians.

The First Division title returned in 1961/62, won by two points. Their reserve side won the I Zingari Combination title, though the senior team lost the I Zingari Challenge Cup final to Liverpool Police.

Florence Albion added further I Zingari Challenge Cup wins in 1966/67 (beating Liverpool University) and 1967/68 (defeating Stoneycroft). In 1969/70, they claimed another league title, another I Zingari Challenge Cup and another Liverpool Amateur Cup. In 1970/71, they finished runners-up in the league by two points.

FORMBY

After the Second World War, Formby returned to the Liverpool County Combination, finishing 14th in the 1945/46 season. In 1947/48, they finished as runners-up, four points behind the leaders and won the Liverpool Amateur Cup by beating Earle 3–0.

In 1948/49, Formby won the Liverpool County Combination title, finishing five points clear of Everton 'A' and retained the Liverpool Amateur Cup by defeating Haydock C & B. However, Haydock C\&B beat them the following season (1949/50) in the George Mahon Cup Final.

In 1951/52, Formby finished one point behind league winners Skelmersdale United and won the Liverpool Challenge Cup by defeating New Brighton 3–1. The following season, they were again runners-up, this time finishing seven points behind Everton 'A'.

Formby were runners-up in the George Mahon Cup in 1955/56 (losing to Unit Construction) and again in 1956/57 (to Dunlop, Speke) and 1957/58 (to Aintree SS). They were again runners-up in the George Mahon Cup in 1961/62, this time losing to Guinness Exports.

In 1963/64, they won the Liverpool Challenge Cup, beating South Liverpool 2–1. In 1964/65, they finished four points behind league winners Langton in the Liverpool County Combination and beat Langton 1–0 in the George Mahon Cup Final. However, they were runners-up to Langton in the Liverpool Challenge Cup.

Formby remained in the Liverpool County Combination until the end of the 1967/68 season, finishing that campaign by winning the Liverpool Challenge Cup, defeating Earle 3–2 at Edinburgh Park. They joined the Lancashire Combination in 1968/69, finishing 10th in their debut season. They stayed in the Lancashire Combination until the end of the 1970/71 season and were League Cup runners-up in that final season, losing 4–1 over two legs to Prestwich Heys.

GARSTON ROYAL

Following the war, Garston Royal were reconstituted and rejoined the Liverpool League. They won the Liverpool Intermediate Cup in 1961/62. Relegated to the Second Division at the end of the 1964/65 season, they resigned from the division in August 1966.

GARSWOOD UNITED

Formed in 1967 by a group of friends who began playing informal matches, Garswood United applied to join the St Helens Combination Fourth Division but were instead offered a vacancy in the First Division, which they accepted. In their first season (1967/68), they finished fourth.

They were runners-up in the Griffiths Cup in 1969/70. After being relegated to the Second Division at the end of the 1970/71 season, they responded by winning the Griffiths Cup and the Worral Cup in 1971/72 before leaving the St Helens Combination.

GUINNESS EXPORTS
Guinness Exports FC were formed in 1948, initially playing at Bootle Stadium. The club was associated with the nearby Guinness distribution centre and players and supporters used the Export Club social venue.

They started in the Fifth Division of the Liverpool Shipping League. By the mid-1950s, they had joined the Liverpool League and entered the Liverpool County Combination First Division in 1958/59, winning the title at their first attempt by beating Earle in the final match to finish above Burscough. They also played in the Lord Wavertree and Houston Cup Finals.

In 1959/60, they retained the title on goal difference over Unit Construction and also won the George Mahon Cup by beating Dunlop (Speke). In 1960/61, they finished runners-up to Rylands Recreation by three points but gained revenge in the George Mahon Cup Final.

In 1961/62, they regained the league title by one point over Langton and added a third George Mahon Cup title (beating Formby) and the Liverpool Junior Cup (beating Rainford North End). They were runners-up in the Liverpool Amateur Cup, losing 2–1 to Unit Construction, while their reserves won the Second Division.

In 1962/63, they won another league and George Mahon Cup double, again beating Langton in both. They also won the Liverpool Challenge Cup (defeating Marine) and their reserves again won the Second Division.

In 1963/64, they completed a clean sweep: the Liverpool County Combination title (seven points ahead of Unit Construction), George Mahon Cup (beating Dunlop, Speke), Liverpool Amateur Cup (1–0 v Essemay Old Boys) and Lord Wavertree Cup. Their reserves won the Second Division for the third successive season.

In 1964/65, Guinness Exports joined the Second Division of the Lancashire Combination, finishing fourth and earning promotion, while still playing in the Liverpool County Combination. In 1965/66, they won the Liverpool Challenge Cup, beating Unit Construction and were runners-up to Langton in the Liverpool Amateur Cup the following year.

After two mid-table finishes in the Lancashire Combination, they finished runners-up to Morecambe in 1967/68 and moved to the Cheshire League. They finished fourth and sixth respectively in their two seasons in the top division.

In 1969/70, they were runners-up to Marine in the Liverpool Senior Non-League Cup and beat Marine to win the Cheshire League Cup Final. In 1970, the club changed its name to Ormskirk Football Club.

HARROWBY

After World War II, Harrowby relocated to Saughall Massie and rejoined the West Cheshire League in 1948/49. Both their first team and reserves finished bottom of the First and Second Divisions, respectively. They spent much of the next decade near the bottom of the league.

In 1959/60, they were runners-up in the Second Division and were promoted the following season. In 1965/66, Harrowby won the West Cheshire League title by two points over Moreton. Their reserves were runners-up in the Second Division (three points behind Shell) and the club won the West Cheshire Bowl.

However, by 1968/69 they were relegated after finishing second from bottom. That same season, they were runners-up to Bebington Hawks in the Wirral Amateur Cup and won the West Cheshire Bowl. In 1969/70, they were runners-up to Christleton in the Wirral Senior Cup.

Although they topped the Second Division in 1969/70, they had to wait until repeating the feat in 1970/71 to secure promotion. They also won the West Cheshire Bowl again that year. However, their ground at Saughall Massie was earmarked for redevelopment into a housing estate in 1971.

HESWALL

Heswall joined the West Cheshire League Second Division in 1958/59 and finished runners-up by two points behind Cammell Laird. They were again runners-up in 1963/64 and finally won the Second Division in 1968/69, earning promotion.

They finished 13th in their first season (1969/70) in the First Division.

JABISCO

Jabisco won the Liverpool Shipping League in 1952/53, 1957/58, 1966/67 (by four points from Tillotsons) and 1967/68. They lost the Melly cup in 1952/53, 1954/55 and 1957/58 but won it 1959/60. They joined the Liverpool County Combination Second Division in 1968/69, finishing runners-up in their first season.

They finished 14th in the First Division in 1969/70 and remained in the lower reaches of the division in the following two seasons.

KIRKBY TOWN / KNOWSLEY UNITED

Formed in 1962/63 as Kirkby Town, the club played in yellow and blue. They joined the Lancashire Combination Second Division in 1963/64, finishing second from bottom in their first season.

They were promoted to the First Division in 1966/67 after winning the Second Division. They were runners-up in 1968/69 and finished fourth in 1969/70, earning promotion to the Northern Premier League for the 1970/71 season, where they finished second from bottom. They were also Liverpool Challenge Cup winners in 1968/69.

LANGTON

Formed in 1953, Langton played at the 'Docker's Wembley' at Edinburgh Park. They joined the Liverpool Shipping League Fifth Division in 1954 and, after successive promotions, won the Shipping League First Division in 1959/60. In 1960/61, they joined the Second Division of the Liverpool County Combination and came third in their first season, earning promotion to the First Division, and also winning the Lord Wavertree Cup.

They finished as runners-up in both the 1961/62 and 1962/63 seasons. Langton were crowned Liverpool County Combination champions in 1964/65, finishing four points ahead of Formby. They also reached the

George Mahon Cup final that season, losing 1–0 to Formby, but won the Liverpool Challenge Cup.

The following season, 1965/66, they retained the Liverpool County Combination title (a deciding game had to be played at the start of the following season) and also won the Liverpool Amateur Cup, beating Maghull 5–3. In 1966/67, they repeated their Amateur Cup success, this time defeating Guinness Exports 3–2. They were also runners-up in the Liverpool Challenge Cup to South Liverpool Reserves, but won the George Mahon Cup, beating Maghull.

Langton's success continued in 1967/68, as they again won the Liverpool County Combination title, along with the Liverpool Amateur Cup (beating Merseyside Police) and the George Mahon Cup. In 1968/69, they retained the County Combination title, with Guinness Exports Reserves finishing four points behind and again won both the Liverpool Amateur Cup (defeating Guinness Exports) and the George Mahon Cup (beating Earle 2–0).

In 1969/70, Langton won the Liverpool County Combination once more, this time finishing level on points with Lucas Sports but winning on goal average. They also triumphed in the George Mahon Cup with a 7–0 win over Dunlop. In 1970/71, they retained the league title, finishing five points ahead of Lucas Sports.

LEYFIELD

Formed in 1965, Leyfield joined the Liverpool League Third Division and were promoted to the Second Division at the end of the 1967/68 season.

LITHERLAND REMYCA

Originally formed as Bootle AB, the club changed its name to REMYCA United during the 1968/69 season. Its roots date back to 1959 with St. Thomas Football Club in Seaforth, later evolving into Bootle Church Lads Brigade. They used the Bootle YMCA as their ground.

REMYCA joined the I Zingari League–specifically the Alliance League Third Division–in 1968. They won promotion at the end of the 1970/71 season and progressed steadily through the Alliance ranks.

LIVERPOOL

Liverpool won the First Division title in 1946/47, starting their campaign with a 1–0 win away at Sheffield United. They hit top spot in November after a 4–1 victory over Derby County, powered by four goals from Jack Balmer. That season was disrupted by a severe winter and in March 1947 the Football League extended the season to 14 June, partly because the Government had banned midweek sport to conserve electricity.

Despite a backlog of fixtures, Liverpool finished strongly. Wins away at Arsenal and Wolves in their final two matches gave them a total of 57 points–enough to lead the table. Their title was only confirmed on 14 June, when Stoke City lost their final game at Sheffield United. News of Stoke's defeat was relayed over the loudspeakers at Anfield during Liverpool's Senior Cup Final against Everton. Ten minutes later, Liverpool secured that trophy too.

After winning the league, Liverpool's form declined, culminating in relegation from the First Division in 1953/54. A promising start with a 3–1 win over Portsmouth and draws against Manchester United and Newcastle was undone by a run of five consecutive defeats, beginning with a 2–0 loss to Bolton. A 5–1 defeat at Old Trafford on 19 December left them bottom at Christmas–a position they never recovered from. Despite a couple of late wins, including a 4–3 result against Sunderland, Liverpool were relegated following a 1–0 home defeat to Cardiff on 17 April.

Life in the Second Division began in 1954/55 with a 3–2 home win over Doncaster Rovers. Liverpool finished that season in mid-table and remained outside the top flight until December 1959, when Bill Shankly was appointed manager. He guided Liverpool to third place in 1959/60 and again in 1960/61, before securing promotion in 1961/62.

Liverpool began that promotion-winning season with a 2–0 win at Bristol Rovers and quickly embarked on a run of five wins, one draw and four more victories. After 11 unbeaten games, they reached top spot and never relinquished it. With new signings Ron Yeats and Ian St John bolstering the side, Liverpool clinched the title and promotion with five games to spare following a 2–0 home win over Southampton. They finished eight points ahead of Leyton Orient and were unbeaten at Anfield all season.

Back in the top flight in 1962/63, Liverpool's campaign was affected by the 'Big Freeze,' with no league matches played between 22 December and 12 February. They still managed to finish in eighth place. The following season, 1963/64, they won the league title. After reaching top spot briefly in November, a decisive 3–1 win over Tottenham at Anfield in late March helped them regain first place during a seven-match winning streak. A 5–0 thrashing of Arsenal at Anfield confirmed the title with three games to spare. They finished four points ahead of Manchester United.

In 1964/65, Liverpool finally lifted the FA Cup for the first time in their history. Wins over West Bromwich Albion (2–1), Stockport County (after a replay), Bolton Wanderers and Leicester City (also after a replay) led to a semi-final victory over Chelsea at Villa Park. In the final, they beat Leeds United 2–1 after extra time, with goals from Roger Hunt and Ian St John.

Liverpool won another league title in 1965/66, hitting top spot in mid-November following emphatic wins over Northampton (5–0) and Blackburn (5–2). They maintained their lead after beating title rivals Burnley 2–1 and eventually finished six points ahead of Leeds United and Burnley. That season also saw them reach the European Cup Winners' Cup Final (see Europe chapter).

Shankly set about making Melwood in West Derby into a proper training ground. Liverpool had bought the site in the early-1950s. It was named after two priests from St Francis Xavier's College, Fathers Meilling and Woodlock, who developed the area into local playing fields. The training ground was improved many times, especially in 1967. The club would use it until 2020.

In 1968/69, Liverpool finished league runners-up to Leeds United and in 1970/71 they were beaten 2–1 by Arsenal in the FA Cup Final.

Liverpool's reserves were also serial winners of the Central League, winning it in 1968/69, 1969/70 and 1970/71 – adding those titles to the one they won in 1956/57.

LIVERPOOL AND BOOTLE POLICE (MERSEYSIDE POLICE)

Following the Second World War, the club returned to the I Zingari League First Division, winning the 1946/47 title by six points from Maghull. They left the league at the end of the 1947/48 season to join the Liverpool County Combination. In their first Combination season (1948/49), they finished thirteenth and in their final season (1951/52), they ended bottom of the First Division.

They rejoined the I Zingari League in 1952/53, entering the Third Division and winning it by two points from St. Matthew's OSA. The following year, they claimed the Second Division title by four points from Melling.

In 1961/62, the club won the I Zingari Challenge Cup, beating Florence Albion in the final. A golden era followed in 1965/66, when they completed a domestic treble: winning the Lancashire Amateur Cup (defeating Padiham at Turf Moor), the I Zingari League (by three points from Quarry Bank Old Boys) and the I Zingari Challenge Cup. Their reserve team also won the I Zingari Combination First Division and the Combination Challenge Cup.

From the 1967/68 season onward, the club became known as Liverpool & Bootle Police, the forerunner to Merseyside Police FC.

LIVERPOOL NALGO (National Association of Local Government Officers)

Formed in 1957, Liverpool NALGO played at Alder Road, part of the Stoneycroft Sports Centre. They joined the I Zingari Alliance in 1957/58 and won the Alliance A2 Division in their debut season.

In 1960/61, they moved into the I Zingari League Third Division, finishing runners-up to St. Anne's and earning promotion to the Second Division. They finished fifth in 1961/62.

The 1962/63 season was badly disrupted by the Big Freeze. That season's league competition was cancelled, though Liverpool NALGO did reach the I Zingari Challenge Cup final, losing to Aigburth Peoples Hall.

In 1963/64, they were placed directly into the First Division, where they finished seventh. However, they were relegated after finishing second from bottom in 1964/65. They bounced back in 1965/66, finishing runners-up in the Second Division and regaining First Division status.

They were relegated again in 1967/68 but once more secured promotion in 1969/70, finishing two points behind champions St. Andrew's United.

LOBSTER

Formed in 1959, Lobster FC began life in the Kirkby Newtown Combination. In 1963/64, they joined the Liverpool Sunday League First Division and won it at the first attempt, earning promotion to the Premier Division for the 1964/65 season.

They enjoyed early success, winning the Sunday Premier Cup in 1965/66. However, they were relegated at the end of the 1969/70 season. They regained Premier Division status by securing promotion in the 1971/72 season.

LUCAS SPORTS

Formed in the 1959/60 season, Lucas Sports won the Liverpool Shipping League Second Division in their debut campaign, along with the Colcannon Cup. They entered the Lancashire Combination for the 1961/62 season, finishing bottom of the Second Division. At the same time, they also fielded a team in the Liverpool County Combination, and finished tenth in the Second Division.

From 1962/63 onward, the club concentrated solely on the Liverpool County Combination, finishing bottom in the Second Division that season. In 1964/65, they were runners-up to Dunlop (Speke), three points behind and gained promotion to the First Division.

In 1965/66, they won the First Division at the first attempt, finishing six points ahead of Maghull. In 1969/70, Lucas Sports finished runners-up to Langton in the First Division and won the Liverpool Challenge Cup with a 3–0 win over Dunlop (Speke). They were again runners-up to Langton in 1970/71 and were beaten 1–0 by Prescot B.I. in the Liverpool Challenge Cup Final.

MAGHULL

After the Second World War, Maghull rejoined the I Zingari League and finished runners-up in 1946/47. They also won the I Zingari Challenge Cup that season. They lifted the Lancashire Amateur Cup for the first time in 1948/49, beating Manchester University 1–0.

In 1950/51, they were runners-up in the I Zingari First Division, eight points behind Collegiate Old Boys. In 1954, they moved to their present ground at Old Hall, Hall Lane and promptly won back-to-back I Zingari League titles: in 1954/55 by six points and in 1955/56 by four, both ahead of Collegiate Old Boys.

They were runners-up in the Liverpool Amateur Cup in 1956/57, losing to Collegiate Old Boys, but won the Lancashire Amateur Cup in 1957/58. Their reserve team also won the I Zingari Combination that year. The first team were again Liverpool Amateur Cup runners-up in 1958/59, this time losing to Florence Albion.

In April 1960, Maghull were accepted into the Liverpool County Combination. Their first season (1960/61) saw them finish mid-table. In 1962/63, they were Lancashire Amateur Cup runners-up, beaten by East Chorlton, and won the Liverpool Amateur Cup.

In 1965/66, Maghull were runners-up in the County Combination, six points behind Lucas Sports. The following season, 1966/67, they won the Liverpool County Combination by seven points over Dunlop (Speke) but lost the George Mahon Cup Final to Langton. In 1967/68, they finished runners-up to Langton in both the Liverpool County Combination and George Mahon Cup.

MARINE

Marine finished runners-up in the Liverpool County Combination in 1945/46 and shared the Liverpool Amateur Cup with Earle after a 3–3 draw over two legs. In 1946/47, they rejoined the Lancashire Combination and finished runners-up to Bacup Borough by three points, but did win the Lancashire Combination Cup with a 2–1 victory over Bacup in the final. They were Liverpool Non-League Senior Cup runners-up to South Liverpool in 1949/50.

They were Liverpool Amateur Cup winners in 1952/53, beating Liverpool Police 3–1 at Anfield. In 1960/61, Marine were Lancashire Junior Cup runners-up, losing 2–0 to Chorley in a replay at Southport after a 1–1 draw at Ewood Park.

During the Big Freeze of 1962/63, Marine played only three matches between 22 December and 10 March, with no game at College Road for ten weeks. In 1963/64, they won the Lancashire Combination League Cup, defeating Netherfield 4–3 at Chorley.

In 1967/68, Marine were runners-up in the Lancashire Junior Cup, losing 2–0 to Wigan Athletic at Preston. In 1968/69, they won the Lancashire Combination League Cup, beating Burscough 6/5 on aggregate and lifted the Liverpool Senior Non-League Cup with a 1–0 win over Guinness Exports at White Moss Park, Skelmersdale.

In 1969/70, Marine joined the Cheshire League. Their debut match was a 2–1 win over Mossley. That season, they were Cheshire League Cup runners-up, losing 1–0 to Guinness Exports in a replay after a 1–1 draw. They also lost 3–1 to South Liverpool in the Liverpool Senior Non-League Cup Final.

In 1970/71, Marine won the Liverpool Amateur Cup, beating Rylands Recs 4–1 at Bibby Sports Ground.

MENTMORE (Later ROMA FC)

Formed in 1968, the club initially joined the Under-21 division of the Bootle JOC League. By the 1970/71 season, they were playing in the I Zingari Alliance.

MERSEY ROYAL

Re-formed in 1946, Mersey Royal joined the Birkenhead League. They finished runners-up in the Wirral Junior Cup for three consecutive seasons: losing to Shaftesbury Old Boys in 1951/52 and again to Shaftesbury Old Boys in 1953/54.

In 1965/66, they won the Wirral Amateur Cup (beating Higher Bebington) and the Wirral Junior Cup (beating Castrol). The following season, 1966/67, they topped the Birkenhead League and subsequently joined the Wirral Combination.

In 1969/70, they won the Wirral Combination First Division, with their reserve team winning the Second Division. They also secured the league's Challenge Cup.

MOND RANGERS (Later RUNCORN TOWN, formed 1968)

The club began life as CKD, the works team of the D section at the Castner Kellner chemical plant and initially joined the Runcorn Sunday League. In 1970, they changed their name to Mond Football Club, reflecting their parent company. They continued to play in the Runcorn Sunday League's First Division.

N.E.L.T.C. (North East Liverpool Technical College)

Formed in 1961 under the name N.E.T.C., they joined the I Zingari League for the 1971/72 season.

NEW BRIGHTON

After the war, New Brighton moved to the Tower Grounds in time for the 1946/47 season. In 1948/49, they faced Tranmere Rovers in the Liverpool Senior Cup Final, losing 3–1 and again played Tranmere in the following season's final, this time losing 5–0. In 1950/51, New Brighton lost their Football League status to Workington. They replaced their reserve team in the Lancashire Combination. Their first match in the Lancashire Combination was away at Ashton United in front of 1,000 spectators at the start of the 1951/52 season; the following week, 1,800 watched their home game against Clitheroe. Both matches were lost and the team finished thirteenth. The reserves left the Lancashire Combination for the West Cheshire League.

New Brighton spent the 1954/55 season playing at Castleway North in Leasowe, home of the Wallasey Girls' Hockey Club. In one home match that season, the official attendance was just 19 – a stark contrast to their recent Football League days. In 1956/57, they finished runners-up in the Lancashire Combination, missing out on top spot by three points to Prescot

Cables. However, they won a quartet of trophies: the Lancashire Junior Cup/Lancashire Challenge Trophy, the Liverpool Non-League Senior Cup (against Prescot Cables), the Liverpool Challenge Cup (over two legs against South Liverpool) and the Wirral Senior Cup (beating Tranmere Rovers).

In 1957/58, they again won the Liverpool Non-League Senior Cup, this time against Wigan Athletic and added the Lancashire Combination League Cup, beating Burscough 2–0. The reserves finished runners-up in the West Cheshire League, just two points behind Ellesmere Port Town Reserves and won the Pyke Cup, defeating Hoylake.

In 1958/59, New Brighton began with a 1–0 loss at Darwen but scored 23 goals in a five-match unbeaten run (four wins, one draw) to reach fourth place by mid-September. By late October, they had slipped to fifth, two points behind new leaders Morecambe. Mid-November saw them in sixth, three points behind Horwich RMI. A further two wins and a draw propelled them to third, just one point behind the leaders by early December. Three straight wins just before Christmas lifted them to second, again one point behind with a game in hand. Despite a win and a draw allowing Horwich to pull ahead by three points in early 1959, New Brighton re-established a three-point gap by mid-March.

The title race came down to New Brighton, Horwich RMI and Prescot Cables. With six games remaining, New Brighton led Prescot Cables by seven points, though Cables had four games in hand. A crucial win over Prescot sealed New Brighton's first Lancashire Combination title by a four-point margin. The reserves finished runners-up in the West Cheshire League, two points behind Stork.

In 1959/60, the first team won the Liverpool Non-League Senior Cup against Wigan Athletic at Anfield, while the reserves won the West Cheshire League by three points over Runcorn Reserves. In 1961/62, the first team again lifted the Non-League Senior Cup, once more defeating Wigan Athletic at Anfield and in 1963/64, won it for a third time, beating South Liverpool. New Brighton left the Lancashire Combination in 1965 to join the Cheshire County League. They finished eleventh in their debut season, 1965/66 and were runners-up to Poulton Victoria in the Wirral Senior Cup.

NEWTON

After the war, Newton won the Wirral Amateur Cup in 1946/47, beating Stork. They joined the West Cheshire League in 1947/48, finishing fifth. They lost the 1948/49 Wirral Amateur Cup final to Moreton but bounced back to win the league by three points from Shell in 1949/50. In 1950/51, they were runners-up to Port Sunlight by two points, but won the Wirral Senior Cup, defeating Cammell Laird. They lost the Wirral Amateur Cup Final that same season to Port Sunlight.

In 1951/52, Newton won the Pyke Cup, beating Shell and finished as league runners-up to Bromborough. In 1955/56, they won the Cheshire Amateur Cup and League in 1956/57. They won the West Cheshire Bowl in 1958/59 and regained the league title in 1960/61 by a single point over Stork. In 1961/62, they retained the title by seven points and added both the Pyke Cup (1–0 win over Stork) and the West Cheshire Bowl.

In 1962/63, they finished runners-up by a single point to Stork and lost to them again in the Wirral Senior Cup final. They won the Wirral Amateur Cup in 1963/64. Newton won the Pyke Cup once more in 1964/65, beating West Kirby and then won the Liverpool Junior Cup in 1965/66.

NORTHERN NOMADS

Having disbanded in 1939, the club was revived in late 1951 by a group of amateur players in Manchester and resumed competitive football in 1952. They joined the Mid-Cheshire League, winning the title in 1956/57 and then entered the Lancashire Combination for the 1957/58 season.

They remained in the Lancashire Combination until the end of the 1963/64 season, after which they switched to the Manchester League.

OLD XAVERIAN

In 1947/48, Old Xaverian re-joined the Second Division of the I Zingari League. They won the division in 1949/50 to earn promotion and finished sixth in their first First Division season. In 1961/62, the club moved from Druids Cross, Woolton, to Colebrooke Road, Dingle.

They were I Zingari League Challenge Cup runners-up in 1964/65. Relegated at the end of the 1966/67 season, they bounced back immediately, finishing second in the Second Division in 1967/68, five points behind Liverpool Telecoms. However, they were relegated again the following season (1968/69). In 1970/71, they regained First Division status, finishing second in the Second Division, two points behind Crosby and were again Challenge Cup runners-up.

POULTON VICTORIA

They re-formed in 1948 and played at the Cadbury Factory in Moreton. They re-joined the Birkenhead League in 1954, playing at Lingham Park. They would later play at Ashville's first ground at Wallacre Park. They joined the West Cheshire League in 1961/62 and were promoted at the end of their first season in the Second Division as runners-up.

They won the Wirral Senior Cup in 1965/66, beating New Brighton. The following season, 1966/67, they won the West Cheshire League for the first time, finishing eight points ahead of Cammell Laird. For the start of the 1967/68 season, their reserve side joined the Second Division.

They were again Wirral Senior Cup winners in 1970/71, beating Hoylake Athletic. That season, they also won the Cheshire Amateur Cup, beating Middlewich Athletic and were runners-up in the West Cheshire League to Cammell Laird.

PRESCOT B.I.

They returned to the Liverpool County Combination after World War Two. They generally remained a mid-table side but shared the George Mahon Cup in 1965/66. In 1970/71, they beat Lucas Sports 1–0 to win the Liverpool Challenge Cup.

PRESCOT CABLES/TOWN

After the war, they re-joined the Lancashire Combination, finishing tenth at the end of the 1945/46 season. In 1947/48, they won the Lancashire

Combination League Cup, beating Lancaster City 1-0. The following season, 1948/49, they won the Liverpool Challenge Cup.

In 1950/51, they finished second from bottom and were relegated to the Second Division. The 1951/52 season saw a turnaround, with Prescot winning the Second Division by three points from Nelson Reserves and earning promotion back to Division One. They also won the Liverpool Senior Non-League Cup, beating Skelmersdale United at Southport.

In 1952/53, Cables were runners-up in the Lancashire Combination, twelve points behind Wigan Athletic and won the Liverpool Senior Non-League Cup again, defeating Bootle Athletic in the final. The following season, 1953/54, they finished bottom of the Lancashire Combination (after Bootle Athletic had resigned from the league) and were relegated to the Second Division.

They stayed just one season in the Second Division/54/55–finishing as runners-up to Burnley 'A' by three points. In 1956/57, they won the Lancashire Combination by three points from New Brighton. In 1957/58, they were runners-up, two points behind Horwich RMI. They were runners-up again in 1958/59, four points behind New Brighton and also won the Liverpool Senior Non-League Cup.

In 1960/61, they again won the Liverpool Senior Non-League Cup, beating South Liverpool after a 0-0 first leg at Holly Park. In 1961/62, they won the Liverpool Challenge Cup, beating Burscough over two legs.

The 1963/64 season brought change. Cables dropped their reserve side and by season's end had decided to focus on amateur players, largely due to financial difficulties. A more significant change came before the 1964/65 season, when a public meeting at the Social Centre on Hope Street resulted in the club dropping the 'Cables' part of its name and becoming Prescot Town. The reserve side won the Lorc Wavertree Cup in 1966.

The name change did not bring success. They finished bottom of the 22-team league, four points behind Accrington Stanley, winning only four games and conceding 132 goals. In 1966/67, they were runners-up in the Lancashire Combination Second Division, seven points behind Kirkby Town having been relegated the season before.

By August 1970, Prescot Town faced severe financial problems. The club had borrowed £11,000 from Allied Breweries eight years earlier to build a new social club. A public appeal fund was set up, but the response was poor. In November 1970, the brewery demanded repayment and the matter went to court. Prescot were given six weeks to pay.

Seven weeks later, the debt remained unpaid. A shareholders' meeting resolved to wait for contact from Allied Breweries. Eventually, it was agreed the debt would be repaid at £30 per week, but this was still insufficient and another appeal was launched. Even former Prime Minister Harold Wilson, MP for Huyton, donated. The club managed to continue, but financial issues persisted.

ROCKVILLE

Rockville joined the I Zingari League after World War Two, finishing third in the Second Division at the end of the 1946/47 season. By 1951/52, they had three teams playing in the Zingari set-up and in 1954/55 they were Second Division champions.

In 1958/59, they won the I Zingari Challenge Cup, edging Aigburth PH 3–2 in the final at the Police Ground. The following season, 1959/60, they were beaten by St Dominics in the Liverpool Junior Cup. However, in 1960/61, they won that competition, beating Liverpool NALGO 3–1 at Holly Park, South Liverpool's ground. Rockville won I Zingari Second Division in 1960/61 but not promoted they remained in the Second Division until they were relegated at the end of the 1970/71 season.

RUNCORN

Runcorn finished ninth in the first post-war season of the Cheshire County League in 1945/46. By 1952, financial difficulties had caught up with the club. They had lost around £1,000 over the previous three years. The Highfield and Camden Tanning Company–who had helped form the club in 1918–usually covered losses and managed the club through a committee of employees and local members of the public. But with attendances falling to about half the league average, the company could no longer cover the deficit.

They proposed forming a new company with a share issue aimed at raising £5,000. In July, a joint meeting of the Football Club and Supporters' Club agreed to circulate a letter among local businesses, offering shares at £1 each. The tanning company agreed to continue financing the ground, but the club itself needed public support.

By January 1953, the share issue was struggling. In May, plans were announced to form a new company and recruit a manager. By July 1953, the company had been incorporated and asked those who pledged support to begin paying for their shares.

Runcorn remained in the Cheshire County League through these changes. In 1958/59, Runcorn Reserves joined the West Cheshire League. Over the next three seasons, the reserves finished as runners-up in 1959/60 and third in both 1958/59 and 1960/61. They also won the Pyke Cup in all three seasons: beating Stork 2-1 in 1958/59, Newton 3-0 in 1959/60 and Ashville 2-1 in 1960/61.

In 1961/62, the first team won the Cheshire Senior Cup, defeating Hyde United 2-1. The following season, 1962/63, they won the Cheshire County League by ten points from Buxton. They again reached the Cheshire Senior Cup Final but lost 3-1 to Hyde United. In 1964/65, they won the Cheshire Senior Cup once more, beating Tranmere Rovers 3-2.

By 1966, their Canal Street ground was under threat from redevelopment plans that ultimately did not proceed. In 1967/68, they won the Cheshire Senior Cup again, defeating Crewe Alexandra 1-0 over two legs (0-0, 1-0). In 1968/69, they became founder members of the Northern Premier League. Their first NPL match was a 3-0 home win over South Shields and they finished fifteenth in their inaugural season.

They were also runners-up in the first Northern Premier League Challenge Cup, losing 5-2 over two legs to Bangor City. In 1971, a combination of poor league form and financial issues led the chairman of the Supporters' Club to warn the club could go bust. Amid growing discontent among supporters and criticism in the local press, the board banned the *Runcorn Weekly News* from reporting on any off-field matters at the club.

RUNCORN ATHLETIC

Formed in 1947 as an ex-servicemen's team, Runcorn Athletic opened their new enclosure on the Manchester Ship Canal at Percival Lane in September 1947. They defeated Northgate Athletic from Chester 11–0 in the first round of the Chester and Runcorn Junior Cup.

Their first competitive season came in the Liverpool County Combination Second Division in 1947/48, where they finished fourth. By June 1948, they had joined the Mid-Cheshire League but retained a second team in the Liverpool County Combination.

In 1948/49, they were runners-up in the Mid-Cheshire League in their debut season and won the Lord Wavertree Cup. Their reserves also finished runners-up in the Liverpool County Combination Second Division and won the Lord Wavertree Cup by beating Everton 'B' 2–1 at Holly Park.

In 1950, they moved up to the Cheshire County League and shared the Canal Street ground with Runcorn Football Club, though they insisted they were not a nursery club.

They won the Mid-Cheshire League in 1955/56 and were runners-up in 1956/57. They then claimed back-to-back league titles in 1957/58 and 1958/59. During the latter season, they moved to the Boston Ground.

Four seasons later, they resigned midway through the 1962/63 season and became defunct. An advert appeared in the *Runcorn Weekly News* in March 1963 detailing the club's winding up. In August 1963, a deal was made to sell the Boston Ground to Runcorn Boys Club.

ST. DOMINICS

Formed in 1948, St. Dominics began playing at St. Dominics School, Lordens Road, Huyton. They entered competitive football in the Prescot & District League in 1948/49, winning the Stanley Cup that season.

They won the Second Division of the Prescot & District League in 1950 and were promoted to the First Division, which they won in 1956/57, having also claimed the Stanley Cup in 1954/55 and 1955/56. They won the league again in 1957/58 and also lifted the Liverpool Intermediate Cup.

In 1959, they joined the Liverpool League and won the First Division in both 1959/60 and 1960/61 and had won the Liverpool Junior Cup in 1959/60. They were runners-up in 1961/62 before winning two more league titles in 1962/63 and 1963/64. They also won the Lord Colwyn Cup and the Liverpool Intermediate Cup in the latter season.

In 1964/65, they were runners-up again and also finished as runners-up in the RP Houston Cup. They won the Liverpool Junior Cup in 1966/67, beating St. Philomena's 2–1 and also won the RP Houston Cup.

In 1967/68, they won the First Division again, along with another RP Houston Cup and were runners-up in the Sawyer Cup Final. Seeking stronger opposition, they joined the Liverpool County Combination Second Division in 1969/70 and were promoted in their first season. In 1970/71, they finished fourth in their debut season in the First Division.

ST. HELENS TOWN

In April 1947, Derbyshire Hill–a pre-war St. Helens Combination side and 1931–32 Liverpool Junior Cup winners–was renamed and St. Helens Town was revived. The club played at Sutton Cricket Ground on Hoghton Road and began the 1947/48 season in the Liverpool County Combination, finishing tenth.

In 1948/49, they improved to seventh and won the George Mahon Cup, beating Runcorn 2–1 at Prescot. In 1949/50, they joined the newly formed Second Division of the Lancashire Combination, finishing seventh.

The following season, 1950/51, they won the Second Division and were promoted to the First Division. However, 1951/52 proved to be a short stay in the top tier, as they were relegated after finishing second-bottom.

During the 1950s, they moved grounds twice–first to St. Helens Recs on City Road and then in 1953 back to Hoghton Road. After three mid-table seasons in the Second Division, they were promoted again as part of a restructure of the Lancashire Combination for the 1955/56 season. However, they finished bottom and were relegated after just one season.

They remained in the Second Division until earning promotion in 1964/65 by finishing third behind Chorley Reserves and Netherfield Reserves.

In 1968/69, despite many clubs departing for the new Northern Premier League or the Cheshire League, St. Helens Town stayed in the Lancashire Combination and finished sixth in the restructured 22-club league.

SEAFORTH FELLOWSHIP

Seaforth Fellowship remained in the Bootle JOC League after World War Two and won five consecutive Senior Division titles: 1946/47, 1947/48, 1948/49, 1949/50 and 1950/51.

They also won three consecutive Everton Cups in 1948/49, 1949/50 and 1950/51 and claimed the Harwood Benevolent Cup in 1946/47.

SKELMERSDALE UNITED

In the first post-war season, 1945/46, Skelmersdale United won the Liverpool County Combination, finishing one point ahead of Marine. They also defeated South Liverpool over two legs to win the Liverpool Challenge Cup.

In 1946/47, they were runners-up to Liverpool 'A' in the County Combination and retained the Liverpool Challenge Cup by beating Everton 'A' 2–1. They also won the George Mahon Cup, defeating Ellesmere Port over two legs to complete a treble.

In 1949/50, they were again runners-up in the Liverpool County Combination, one point behind Burscough. They won the league in 1950/51, beating Everton 'A' by one point and retained it in 1951/52 by the same margin. That year they also won the George Mahon Cup (beating Haydock) and were runners-up in the Senior Non-League Cup Final to Prescot Cables.

In 1953/54, they won the league again by a single point from Everton 'A' and the following season they shared the George Mahon Cup with Liverpool 'A'.

They joined the Lancashire Combination in 1955/56 and won Division Two at the first attempt, edging Droylsden by one point and scoring 110 goals.

Due to poor gates, the club chose to go amateur at the end of the 1961/62 season, hoping to boost community interest.

In 1966/67, they reached the FA Amateur Cup Final, drawing 0–0 with Enfield at Wembley before losing 3–0 in the replay at Maine Road. They were also runners-up to Wigan Athletic in the Liverpool Senior Non-League Cup.

In 1968/69, they joined the Cheshire County League and won it by six points from Stafford Rangers. The following season, 1969/70, they retained the title by 14 points from Mossley and also won the Lancashire Challenge Cup (beating Wigan Athletic 2–1) and the Lancashire Floodlit Cup.

They applied to join the Northern Premier League but were rejected due to their amateur status.

The 1970/71 season was one of their finest. They won the FA Amateur Cup at Wembley, beating Dagenham 4–1, retained the Lancashire Challenge Cup (again defeating Wigan Athletic) and were runners-up to Ormskirk in the Liverpool Senior Non-League Cup.

In January 1971, Skelmersdale United were granted membership of the Northern Premier League and agreed to turn professional at the end of the season. They also won a European trophy, the Copa Ottorina Barassi.

SOUTH LIVERPOOL

After competing in the Cheshire County wartime league, South Liverpool remained in the league for the first post-war season, 1945/46, finishing in seventh place.

In 1949/50, South Liverpool Reserves won the Liverpool Challenge Cup, beating Maghull at Goodison Park and were runners-up to Bootle in the Liverpool Senior Non-League Cup. They repeated the runners-up finish to Bootle in 1950/51, losing 2–1 in the final.

They left the Cheshire County League at the end of the 1951/52 season to rejoin the Lancashire Combination. In 1952/53, they entered the Second Division and finished as runners-up, earning promotion to the First Division.

In 1953/54, their first season in the top division, they finished seventh and won the Liverpool Senior Non-League Cup, beating Burscough 1–0.

In 1956/57, South Liverpool Reserves were runners-up in the Liverpool Challenge Cup, losing 4–3 on aggregate to New Brighton. The following season, 1957/58, they reversed the result, defeating New Brighton over two legs to win the same cup. The Reserves also won the Lord Wavertree Cup in 1957 and 1958.

The George Mahon Cup was won in 1958/59, with the Reserves beating Burscough at Anfield. In 1959/60, the senior team were relegated to the Second Division after finishing bottom of the First Division.

They regained First Division status in 1961/62 by finishing as runners-up in the Second Division.

In 1965/66, South Liverpool won the Lancashire Combination title, finishing four points ahead of Chorley. The following season, 1966/67, the Reserves won the Liverpool Challenge Cup, defeating Langton 1–0.

In 1967/68, the senior team won the Liverpool Senior Non-League Cup, beating Wigan Athletic. After sixteen seasons in the Lancashire Combination, they left in 1968/69 to become founding members of the Northern Premier League, finishing twelfth in their debut season.

In 1969/70, they won the Liverpool Senior Non-League Cup, defeating Marine 3–1 at College Road.

SOUTHPORT

Southport began their post-war campaign on 31 August 1946 with a 4–2 defeat at Darlington, setting the tone for a difficult season. The club had to rely on re-election to remain in the Football League.

They remained in the lower reaches of the Third Division North until a fifth-place finish in 1955/56. In 1957/58, a 23rd-place finish consigned them to the newly formed Fourth Division. That same season, they shared the Liverpool Senior Cup with Everton after a 0–0 draw.

In their inaugural Fourth Division campaign (1958/59), they lost 6–1 away to Watford on the opening day. A run of six consecutive defeats to close the season left them bottom of the league, once again requiring re-election.

In 1963/64, they shared the Liverpool Senior Cup with Liverpool, having won it the year before and previously in 1944. In 1966/67, Southport finished as runners-up in the Fourth Division and earned promotion to the Third Division.

A crucial match came late in the season at Prenton Park against Tranmere Rovers. Southport needed a win, while Tranmere could afford a loss. Capitalising on two Tranmere errors–an own goal by Storeton and a header from Redrobe–Southport led 2–0 before Tranmere pulled one back through Williams. The game ended 2–1 in Southport's favour.

On 6 May, George Andrews scored in the 79th minute against Southend United at Haig Avenue to secure promotion and runners-up honours–the club's first promotion to the Third Division in their history.

Two seasons later, in 1969/70, they finished bottom of the Third Division and were relegated. Their fate was dependent on other results, which did not go in their favour. Manager Billy Peat departed and Alex Parker, the former Everton full-back, took over.

Although relegated, the club benefited from a Football League decision allowing Friday night matches for one season, helping them avoid clashes with Everton, Liverpool and Tranmere and potentially improving attendances. They finished eighth in their first season back in the Fourth Division.

SOUTHPORT LADIES

Formed in 1969, Southport Ladies were founder members of the Merseyside and Wirral Ladies Football League in the 1971/72 season.

STORK

Stork were runners-up to Grayson's in the 1944/45 Wirral Senior Cup and joined the West Cheshire League in 1946/47, finishing third and winning the Wirral Senior Cup by defeating Port Sunlight.

In 1947/48, they won the league by one point from Hoylake Athletic and in 1948/49 they retained the title, this time finishing eight points clear–again of Hoylake Athletic. They were runners-up to Ellesmere Port Town in the Wirral Senior Cup.

In 1949/50, they lost the cup final to Ellesmere Port Town again. The club left the league for three seasons after the 1950/51 season, although they shared the Pyke Cup with Shell.

They joined the Liverpool County Combination in 1951/52, finishing fifth in the First Division and winning the Wirral Senior Cup by beating Ellesmere Port Town 4–1.

They finished eighth in 1952/53 and tenth in 1953/54 before returning to the West Cheshire League in 1954/55. That season, they were runners-up to Everton 'C' by three points and lost the Wirral Senior Cup to Moreton.

In 1955/56, they won both the Pyke Cup (beating Ellesmere Port Town) and the Wirral Senior Cup. In 1956/57, they won the league by ten points from Newton, with their reserves finishing second in the Second Division, five points behind Newton Reserves.

In 1957/58, they defeated Tranmere Rovers to win the Wirral Senior Cup. In 1958/59, they won their fourth league title, finishing two points ahead of New Brighton Reserves.

In 1959/60, they lost the Wirral Senior Cup to Port Sunlight. In 1960/61, they were runners-up in the league to Newton by one point and beat Ashville to win the Wirral Senior Cup.

In 1961/62, they were league runners-up to Newton, seven points behind. In 1962/63, they won the league again, edging Newton by one point and also won the Wirral Senior Cup, again defeating Newton.

They won the Wirral Amateur Cup in 1944/45, 1945/46, 1947/48 and 1953/54 and runners up 1946/47. Pyke Cup winners 1949/50, 1956/57 and 1962/63.

TRANMERE ROVERS

In 1946/47, Tranmere returned to the Third Division North, opening the season at home to Rotherham after having been relegated prior to the war. To circumvent minimum charge rules, the club offered season tickets at 26s 3d (equivalent to 1s 3d across 21 games), while matchday prices were set at 1s 6d.

They won the Cheshire Bowl in 1947/48 (beating Chester 1–0) and again in 1949/50 (beating Crewe Alexandra 2–0). In 1953/54, they lost the final to Chester over two legs, drawing 1–1 and losing 2–1. Tranmere's A team won the Pyke Cup, beating Port Sunlight.

They were Cheshire Bowl winners again in 1954/55, beating Chester 3–2, but lost the following two finals to Stockport County (1–0 in 1955/56 and 2–0 in 1956/57). They were runners-up in the Wirral Senior Cup to New Brighton in 1956/57.

In 1957/58, Tranmere won the Cheshire Senior Cup, beating Stockport County 6–2 on aggregate and also won the Cheshire Bowl, defeating Crewe Alexandra 5–0. They were runners-up in the Wirral Senior Cup to Stork.

They finished seventh in the league that season, securing their place in the new Third Division for 1958/59. They won the Cheshire Bowl again in 1959/60, sharing it with Stockport County after a two-legged final (2–0 win at home, 2–0 defeat away).

In 1960/61, they were relegated to the Fourth Division. A poor start saw them in the bottom three by October and bottom four by December. Manager Peter Farrell departed and Walter Galbraith, formerly of New Brighton, took over in January. Relegation was confirmed after a 4–1 defeat at Notts County, a match in which only goalkeeper Harry Leyland's heroics prevented a worse outcome.

That match marked the end of Tommy Eglington's career. The former Everton winger had joined Rovers in 1957, shortly before his former teammate took over as player-manager.

In 1962/63, they lost the Cheshire Bowl final 1–0 to Stockport County, but won the trophy in 1963/64, defeating the same opponents 3–0.

In 1964/65, they lost the Cheshire Senior Cup final to Runcorn (3–2) and the Cheshire Bowl final to Chester (2–0). In 1965/66, they lost 4–1 to Crewe Alexandra in the Cheshire Bowl final.

In 1966/67, Tranmere finished fourth in the Fourth Division and were promoted. Promotion was secured on 12 May with a 3–1 win over Rochdale at Prenton Park. They also beat Crewe 2–1 in the Cheshire Bowl final.

In 1968/69, Tranmere won the inaugural Cheshire Premier Cup (formerly the Cheshire Bowl), beating Stockport County 4–1 in the final.

UNIASCO

Formed in 1964, Uniasco were playing in the Bootle JOC League by 1966/67. They joined the Liverpool League at the start of the 1967/68 season.

UNIT CONSTRUCTION

Formed in 1946, Unit Construction first played in the Liverpool Shipping League before joining the Liverpool County Combination in the 1955/56 season, finishing fifth. They won the Liverpool Junior Cup in 1953/54 and shared the Lord Wavertree Cup in 1956. They won the Combination title the following season (1956/57), finishing five points ahead of South Liverpool Reserves.

They were runners-up to Guinness Exports in 1959/60 but won the Liverpool Amateur Cup, beating Aigburth People's Hall. They won the cup again in 1961/62, defeating Guinness Exports 2–1.

Unit were runners-up once more to Guinness Exports in the Liverpool County Combination in 1963/64, finishing nine points behind. In 1964/65, they moved to Bootle Stadium after leaving their ground in Speke.

In 1965/66, they lost the Liverpool Challenge Cup final to Guinness Exports. Unit remained in the County Combination until the end of the 1968/69 season.

The League management insisted they field a stronger side, but after a string of heavy defeats in the first five games of the 1969/70 season, the League expunged their results and expelled the club. Struggling to field enough players from the parent company, the club subsequently folded.

VAUXHALL MOTORS

Formed in 1963, Vauxhall Motors initially played in the local Ellesmere Port League. They joined Division Two of the West Cheshire League in 1965/66, finishing fourteenth.

In the following two seasons (1966/67 and 1967/68), the club came close to promotion, finishing fourth on both occasions. They secured promotion in 1968/69, finishing third behind Heswall and Harrowby Reserves.

In their debut First Division season (1969/70), they finished tenth out of sixteen clubs. During the 1970s, now playing at the company-owned Hooton Park, the club remained in the First Division, typically finishing mid-table.

WARRINGTON TOWN

Originally founded as Stockton Heath, the club competed in the Mid-Cheshire League during the 1950s and won the title in 1960/61. They changed their name to Warrington Town in 1961 and remained in the Mid-Cheshire League.

They won the Runcorn Challenge Cup in 1965/66, 1966/67 and 1968/69. The club had played at Cantilever Park since 1956.

WATERLOO DOCK

Formed in 1963, Waterloo Dock joined the Liverpool Business Houses League Second Division in the 1963/64 season. Within four years, they had gained promotion, finishing as runners-up in 1965/66 and champions in 1966/67.

They won the Premier Division at the first attempt in 1967/68 and added the Business Houses Senior Cup. After being promoted to the Premier Division in 1968/69, they finished runners-up and then won the league in 1969/70, again winning the Business Houses Senior Cup.

In 1970/71, they joined the Liverpool County Combination Second Division and won it at the first attempt also winning the Liverpool Junior Cup – marking the beginning of a long period of trophy success.

WEST KIRBY

West Kirby rejoined the West Cheshire League after the War, winning it in 1963/64 and 1964/65. The Pyke Cup in 1963/64 and 1966/67 and Wirral Senior Cup in 1967/68 were also won.

WIGAN ATHLETIC

Wigan rejoined the Cheshire County League for the 1945/46 season but finished bottom in 1946/47 and were not re-elected. They then joined the Lancashire Combination, winning the title in 1946/47, two points ahead of Nelson.

They were runners-up to Nelson in 1949/50. That same season, the reserves joined the Second Division and the club were Northern Floodlit League runners-up.

In 1950/51, Wigan again won the Lancashire Combination, edging Nelson to the title. They repeated the feat in 1952/53, finishing twelve points ahead of Prescot Cables and also won the Lancashire Junior Cup, beating Lancaster City.

They retained the Lancashire Combination title in 1953/54, this time by fifteen points ahead of Netherfield and again won the Lancashire Junior Cup, beating Horwich RMI. They won the Liverpool Senior non-league cup 1954/55.

Wigan won the Lancashire Junior Cup once more in 1955/56, defeating Nelson 3-1. They were joint winners of the Liverpool Senior Non-League Cup with New Brighton in 1957/58.

In 1959/60, they won the Lancashire Junior Cup by beating Chorley 2–1 and were runners-up in both the Lancashire Combination and the Northern Floodlit League.

They rejoined the Cheshire County League in 1961/62, finishing fifth. In 1962/63, they won the Liverpool Senior Non-League Cup by beating South Liverpool.

Wigan won the Cheshire County League in 1964/65 by five points over Macclesfield Town and claimed the Liverpool Senior Non-League Cup, again beating New Brighton, but lost the Lancashire Junior Cup Final to Chorley.

In 1965/66, they won the Lancashire Junior Cup by beating Netherfield 2–0 and finished as Cheshire County League runners-up, one point behind Altrincham. They also won the Liverpool Senior Non-League Cup, again defeating South Liverpool.

They were runners-up to Altrincham again in 1966/67 and won both the Liverpool Senior Non-League Cup (beating Skelmersdale United) and the Northern Floodlit League.

In 1967/68, Wigan won the Lancashire Junior Cup by beating Marine.

They became founding members of the Northern Premier League in 1968/69–a move they had long campaigned for–and finished runners-up to Macclesfield Town by twelve points.

They were again runners-up to Macclesfield in 1969/70, this time on goal average.

In 1970/71, Wigan finally won the Northern Premier League title, finishing six points ahead of Stafford Rangers.

WHERE THEY PLAYED

Soon after the Second World War, with crowds returning to football grounds in record numbers, the cost of admission became a pressing issue. The Entertainment Tax, introduced in 1917 as a temporary measure, was still in force thirty years later. Some clubs, including Everton, needed to rebuild stadiums that had been bombed during the war.

The new admission price was eventually set at 1s 3d, although some clubs charged 1s 6d. The resumption of football also brought tragedy. A sixth-round FA Cup match at Burnden Park between Bolton Wanderers and Stoke City on 9 March 1946 resulted in a deadly crush, with over 85,000 spectators in attendance. Thirty-three people died and more than 400 were injured.

The official report into the disaster, published in July of that year, mandated ground inspections for stadiums with capacities over 10,000 and safety limits for those over 25,000. Grounds were now required to install turnstiles capable of recording admissions, an internal telephone system and a match control room.

To facilitate the promotion of non-league clubs to the Football League, the League announced in 1969 that it would inspect the grounds of any non-league club applying for election.

In 1971, the Ibrox Stadium disaster–where 66 people died and more than 200 were injured at the end of a Rangers v Celtic match–led to the introduction of the 'Guide to Safety at Sports Grounds' in 1972/73.

ALT PARK, HUYTON

Opened in 1968 by Huyton Rugby League Club, the ground's debut was marred by vandalism from a local gang. A new grandstand was constructed, though it proved smaller than expected and was again vandalised. The site included a social club. Due to ongoing issues with vandalism and maintenance costs, Huyton RLFC relinquished the lease and relocated to the Canal Street ground alongside Runcorn FC.

ANFIELD, LIVERPOOL

In 1957, Anfield installed floodlights, with the first illuminated match played against Everton. In 1962, Liverpool FC announced plans to rebuild the Kemlyn Road Stand at a cost of £150,000, funded in part by a development fund.

By 1963, the original stand had been demolished and construction was underway on a new cantilevered version. As this project neared completion, proposals emerged for redeveloping the Anfield Road Stand into a two-tier structure. This new stand would double the height of the unsanitary and structurally suspect old version.

Despite objections from Anfield residents, the redeveloped Anfield Road Stand opened in 1965. In 1970, plans were drawn up to rebuild the Main Stand and add seating to the Paddock.

BOOTLE STADIUM & SEAFORTH STADIUM

Bootle Stadium, first used by Bootle FC in 1948, could hold up to 30,000 spectators. Located between Southport Road and Stuart Road, it had previously been used by the Army during the war.

In 1951, a declining Bootle FC moved to Seaforth Stadium, which was a covered ground with a capacity of 10,000. Bootle played there until the club folded in 1953.

BROWS LANE, FORMBY

By the end of the 1970s, the ground had a capacity of 4,000, featuring a covered stand and terracing.

BUCKLEY HILL, NETHERTON

In 1966, Bootle Council acquired 46 acres of land formerly owned by Lord Sefton. Thirty acres were set aside for fifteen football pitches, a hockey pitch, hard play areas, a car park and a pavilion. This development compensated for the loss of the Orrell Pleasure Ground, which was being used for construction of the new Giro Bank headquarters.

CANAL STREET, RUNCORN
In 1958, Canal Street underwent renovations: fencing was restored, terracing was added on the reserved side of the ground and the main stand was repainted. Floodlights were installed in 1966.

DOCKERS WEMBLEY, EDINBURGH PARK
Opened in 1953, the complex was funded entirely by a 2s-a-week contribution from over 10,000 dockers, along with loans from the National Dock Labour Board.

It featured two full-size football pitches, a cricket pitch at the centre, two bowling greens, tennis courts and a children's playground. The ornate main gate included motifs of dockers' hooks, ships and anchors. Behind it stood the clubhouses, dressing rooms and a raised embankment capable of hosting national events.

GIGFY PARK, MIDDLEWOOD ROAD, AUGHTON GREEN
Opened in 1964 by Guinness Exports FC, the ground featured covered accommodation behind the goal at the Railway End. There was also spectator seating above the clubhouse, which included a dressing room with a sunken bath.

GOODISON PARK, WALTON
In 1940, bombs struck several areas of Goodison Park. The Gwladys Street Stand sustained significant damage, with all windows blown out and the roof perforated. The Bullens Road school and the surrounding Goodison Avenue/Walton Lane areas were also hit, though damage to the stands was minor. Fortunately, there were no fatalities and few injuries.

Everton installed floodlights in 1957 and in 1958 became the first club in the country to install undersoil heating. The system required 20 miles of electric wire to be laid beneath the pitch, at a cost of around £16,000.

In 1960, the pitch had to be dug up again to add drainage to cope with meltwater from snow and ice.

Around the same time, additional improvements were made: the Gwladys Street End was enclosed to restrict movement without opening gates, extra turnstiles were added for terrace season-ticket holders at the Goodison Road End and the boys' pen was enlarged.

In 1963, the Bullens Road roof was extended to cover the Paddock and new seating and improved dressing rooms were installed. Between 1969 and 1970, Everton built their triple-decker Main Stand on the Goodison Road side. Construction started with the section nearest St Luke's Church. By summer 1970, escalators were being installed for the top balcony.

At the same time, new floodlights were added.

International Matches Held at Goodison Park:

England v Ireland (Home Internationals) – 1947, 1953

Five matches at the 1966 World Cup:

Brazil v Bulgaria (Group 3)

Brazil v Hungary (Group 3)

Brazil v Portugal (Group 3)

Portugal v North Korea (Quarter-final)

West Germany v Soviet Union (Semi-final)

GROVE MOUNT, PENNY LANE

In 1963, the *Liverpool Echo* described the Grove Mount facilities prior to refurbishment:

'Today, the words Penny Lane are synonymous with Liverpool Schoolboys. Here for 17 seasons, city teams have been built and paraded before the public. It is hard to believe that up to two seasons ago, a wooden hut, a tap and a few pails constituted the sum of the amenities for the premier schools' football association team in the country.'

By then, the ground had a pavilion with spacious dressing rooms and showers, flower beds surrounding the site, a full-sized senior pitch with railings and a floodlit all-weather training pitch built on the former Cadby Hall first-team surface.

Here is the second half of the 'Where They Play' section, copy-edited for grammar, clarity and consistency while retaining all original facts:

HAIG AVENUE, SOUTHPORT

Sean McPartlin, in his book *Golden Days – Falling for Southport FC in the Sixties*, described his first visit to Haig Avenue as a youngster in 1963/64:

> '...the continuous roofs and walls of the terracing along the popular side and sweeping round at the Scarisbrick End were of uniform black corrugated iron and the concreted terracing seemed to stretch back forever. From the front of the terracing down to the pitch fencing was sloping compacted earth which fans stood on unless it was raining. Between the popular side and the Blowick End was a small uncovered terrace at an angle to the pitch known as the 'Kop'. The Blowick End was uncovered and consisted of more sloping earth. The Main Stand looked like a long, low, dark and cramped structure which seemed to have more pillars than seats.'

In 1966, the Main Stand was completely destroyed by fire. The 150-yard-long structure housed the club's bars, dressing rooms, showers, offices, gym and boardroom. The blaze also destroyed all playing kits, boots (with Chester City offering use of their spare kit), some floodlights and all club records.

A temporary scaffolding and canvas stand was erected in time for a match in January 1967 and players trained at Meols Cop Secondary School. A new 2,000-seater Main Stand was opened in 1967/68 at a cost of £60,000.

HOGHTON ROAD, ST HELENS

Opened in 1949 by St Helens Town FC and located near Bold Power Station, the Hoghton Road ground had previously been used by St Helens Cricket Club. A group of local businessmen raised £1,000 by public subscription to acquire and develop the ground, which initially had a small stand near the halfway line but few other facilities.

In 1962, a small clubhouse was built on the adjacent training pitch and extended in 1966 to include dressing rooms and a lounge area.

HOLLY PARK, GARSTON
In August 1949, the *Liverpool Echo* described Holly Park as:

'A splendid ground–capable of almost unlimited expansion if South get the right type of football and better served by transport than many senior clubs.'

The site was near two mainline stations and an airport.

In February 1955, a fire destroyed most of the grandstand and the director's office. The blaze was believed to have started in the dressing rooms or canteen area. A temporary 100-seat stand was constructed in 1963.

HOPE STREET, PRESCOT
In 1960, a fire destroyed the 1,800-seat wooden stand. A new stand opened in 1962, accommodating 1,000 spectators and incorporating modern dressing rooms and offices. A new social club was also established at the ground.

NEW BRIGHTON TOWER ATHLETIC GROUND
New Brighton received a Ministry of Works permit in April 1946 and, aided by a £700 supporters' donation, began transforming the former US Forces ground. A new stand was built and terracing added on the south side. An additional £200 was spent on resurfacing the pitch. Two Nissen huts were used as offices and changing rooms.

The following season, covered accommodation for 5,000 fans was built and the pitch issues were resolved. In 1960, plans were introduced to build a 'Kop'-style terrace for 5,000 fans at the Molyneux Drive end. The club also added floodlights, a social club and a restaurant.

ORRELL PLEASURE GROUNDS, BOOTLE JOC LEAGUE
In 1966, Bootle Council purchased 46 acres of land near the former Orrell Pleasure Grounds, part of which had been sold to accommodate the new Giro Bank headquarters. The new site was designated for 15 football and hockey pitches, a pavilion and a car park.

PERCIVAL LANE, RUNCORN

Located near the Manchester Ship Canal, the ground resembled a battlefield when first acquired in 1947. Formerly a World War II balloon site, it had knee-high grass, thirteen craters and a concrete block with surrounding shale at the future centre circle.

Supporters, led by chairman Myer Braverman, launched 'Operation Highbury.' Within eleven weeks, they transformed the site into a functional ground with changing facilities, allowing Runcorn to join the Liverpool County Combination by September 1947.

PRENTON PARK, TRANMERE

After the war, tank traps placed in Borough Road were repurposed to build banking at the Kop end. Floodlights were installed in 1958. A new Main Stand was constructed in 1968 with 4,000 seats at a cost of £80,000. A gale later blew off the roof.

ROSSETT PARK, COLLEGE ROAD, CROSBY

The ground saw improvements including a new tearoom, which | was part of an expanded clubhouse. The players' dressing room featured a large plunge bath and floodlights for training were installed in 1960.

SEALAND ROAD, CHESTER

In 1968, the Popular Side of the ground was extended and covered.
Welsh Cup Finals held at Sealand Road:
Chester v Wrexham (1957/58)
Chester v Swansea Town (Replay and Playoff, 1965/66)
Chester v Cardiff City (1969/70)

SIMMS LANE END, GARSWOOD

Opened in 1967 by Garswood United. The club's first preparations involved a local Ashton councillor learning to operate a ride-on mower to save the council the £20 cost of mowing the pitch.

SIMONSWOOD, KIRKBY
Opened in 1962 by Knowsley Council on behalf of Kirkby FC. Built at a cost of £20,000–£24,000, it had a planned capacity of 12,000. The club paid up to £2,000 annually in rent.

In 1975, the ground's insurance policy was not renewed due to structural defects in the main stand, changing rooms and entrance gates. By the end of the 1970s, Simonswood had a capacity of 10,000 with seating for 500 and covered space for 1,000.

SPRINGFIELD PARK, WIGAN
In April 1953, a fire destroyed the 2,000-seat Main Stand, including dressing rooms, showers, canteen, offices and the boardroom. A fractured gas main caused flames visible across Wigan.

Permission to rebuild was granted by July. Construction of the new double-decker stand began in May 1954, supported by a public subscription fund. The first phase was completed by the start of the 1954/55 season. Floodlights were installed in 1966. By 1970, further improvements were made to the stands and dressing rooms.

SUDLEY RECREATION GROUND (SUDLEY FIELDS), MOSSLEY HILL
In 1945, a further 29 acres were donated to Liverpool City Council upon the death of Miss Emma Holt, supplementing the 26 acres already in use by Mossley Hill Athletic Club.

'VILLA PARK', CROSS LANE, WALLASEY
Opened in 1962, Villa Park became the home of Ashville FC, who had previously played at Wallacre Park. The club moved into the new ground shortly after winning the Wirral Senior Cup.

WEMBLEY STADIUM, LONDON
In 1963, Wembley Stadium underwent a major revamp. A new roof was installed, covering the entire stadium, along with a new

scoreboard, television gantry and tip-up seating. A modern press gallery, upgraded Royal Box, top-class restaurant and lounges were also added.

Local teams who played at Wembley during this time:

Everton – FA Cup Finals (1966, 1968)

Liverpool – FA Cup Finals (1950, 1965, 1971)

Skelmersdale United – FA Amateur Cup Finals (1967, 1971)

WHITE MOSS PARK, SKELMERSDALE

Opened in 1957 by Skelmersdale United, the ground was located near the Mission Hall on Liverpool Road. Previously used by the Skelmersdale Shoe Company team, the 3-acre site replaced Sandy Lane, which was only one acre and council-owned.

White Moss Park cost £1,300 and was purchased outright by the club. The acquisition included a house, later converted into the club's headquarters. Capacity was 10,000, with seating for 200 and covered standing for 1,000.

CHAPTER 5

1972 - 1992

BY THE LATE SIXTIES, WOMEN'S FOOTBALL HAD STARTED TO GROW again. In Manchester, a team called Foden's Ladies had taken over the mantle of the main women's football team from Dick, Kerr's Ladies, and there had been an unofficial Women's World Cup. The Women's FA Cup was first played for in 1970, but it took ten years for the region to get its first winner. On Merseyside, the first women's league appeared with the formation of the Merseyside and Wirral Women's Football League in 1971. Its founder members were Cadbury, Chester, Girobank, Paarden, Plessey (Stoneycroft), Raffles, Squibb (Moreton) and Southport. At the same time, the North West also got a women's league, the North West Women's Regional Football League, of which Foden's Ladies were founder members. This league would soon expand to four divisions. The Merseyside and Wirral Ladies Football League also began its own knockout competition, the exact origin of the name 'Con Rogan Cup' proving elusive, as have some of the tournament's winners.

In men's football in Europe, the UEFA Cup was set up to replace the Inter-Cities Fairs Cup in 1971/72 (see Europe chapter). The following season, 1972/73, saw Liverpool win league title number eight. Liverpool went top in September after beating Sheffield United 5–0 at Anfield and stayed top until February, when they dropped to second place. The league became a three-horse race with Leeds United and Arsenal one point behind. Liverpool needed to beat Arsenal at Anfield to give them breathing space of three points, but a 2–0 defeat left them in second place. Liverpool regained top spot with a 2–1 win against Ipswich and would not relinquish first place again, going on to win the league by three points from Arsenal. The Lancashire Senior Challenge Cup also found a home at Anfield that season. With the league won, the Reds turned to a UEFA Cup final (see Europe chapter).

That same season, the English Schools Shield/Trophy was won again by the Liverpool Schools team when they beat Chelmsford & Mid Essex Schools 8–3 over two legs. That season also saw Wigan Athletic reach the FA Trophy final at Wembley, losing 2–1 to Scarborough after extra time. Southport also won the Fourth Division

The 1972/73 season, saw the two main Liverpool Schools leagues, The Open league that had been running since 1920 and the Catholic Schools league that had run from 1901 amalgamate to become the Liverpool Schools FA leagues.

In 1973/74, Liverpool won the FA Cup, brushing Newcastle United aside in the second half at Wembley to win 3–0. Wigan Athletic won that season's Lancashire Junior Cup/Lancashire Challenge Trophy. In wider football, the last final of the FA Amateur Cup was played, with the FA Challenge Vase (FA Vase) introduced to replace it.

On 1 April 1974, Merseyside County Council came into being, taking in a population of 1,640,500 and 159,750 acres of land. At the time, the district populations were Liverpool 574,000, Knowsley 193,000, St Helens 192,000, Sefton 308,000 and Wirral 352,000. Liverpool had 27,800 acres, Knowsley 24,000, St Helens 33,000, Sefton 36,310 and Wirral 38,630. Knowsley was formed by merging Huyton-with-Roby, Kirkby, Prescot and Whiston with their rural and urban districts. Sefton was formed by the amalgamation of Bootle, Crosby, Formby, Litherland and Southport with their rural and urban districts. St Helens was formed by merging with Ashton-in-Makerfield, Billinge-and-Winstanley, Haydock, Newton-le-Willows, Rainford and Whiston with their rural and urban districts.

The Wirral Sunday Premier Cup began in 1974/75, and that same season the Lal Evans Memorial Trophy was first played for in the Crosby and District Sunday League. Catherine FC donated the trophy in memory of their late club secretary Lal Evans and won it in its first season, beating Allendale United 4–3 in the final after being 3–0 down.

In 1975, the Liverpool Schools left the Lancashire County Schools FA due to the formation of the Merseyside County Schools FA.

In 1975/76, Liverpool won league title number nine. That season they had to juggle a league campaign with a successful run in the UEFA Cup. Liverpool were the league leaders after beating Leeds 2–0 on 7 February and, although they lost top spot again, they stayed in touch with the leaders. From the start of March, they went on a run of nine unbeaten matches, winning eight and drawing one. The league was won on the last game of the season with a 3–1 win at Wolverhampton Wanderers.

A new Merseyside Football League was formed in the 1975/76 season with the following teams: Aytoo, Bootle Reserves, Kirkby Town Reserves, Kirkdale, Lucas Sports, Mount, North Liverpool, Otis (Elevators), Plessey, St Philomena's Reserves, Uniasco Reserves and Woolton Ward, who were the first champions. The same season also saw the Liverpool Schools team win the English Schools Shield/Trophy for the twelfth time, beating Slough Schools 4–3 over two legs. The Football League introduced the Red and Yellow Cards in 1976.

Another season, 1976/77, brought another league title, Liverpool's tenth, while they were also FA Cup runners-up. That season saw the introduction of yellow and red cards for bookings and sendings-off, and goal difference replaced goal average to decide placings. Despite the distractions of the FA Cup and European Cup (see Europe chapter), Liverpool remained unbeaten at home all season. A 2–0 win against Arsenal at Anfield, coupled with Ipswich Town losing 2–1 at Leeds United, sent Liverpool top with a game in hand over Ipswich and with Manchester City three points behind. Although the last four games brought three draws and a defeat, Manchester City could not close the gap and finished one point behind Liverpool. The Reds had another title secured with the European Cup still to play for.

In the FA Cup semi-final at Maine Road, Liverpool faced an Everton side who, just ten days earlier, had lost to Aston Villa in a second replay of the Football League Cup final, 3–2 after extra time at Old Trafford, following a 0–0 draw at Wembley and a 1–1 draw in the first replay. Everton were desperate to return to Wembley, and the semi-final turned out to be controversial, finishing 2–2, with referee Clive Thomas disallowing an Everton goal that would have given them victory. In the replay, again at Maine Road, Liverpool won 3–0, but in the final at Wembley, they lost 2–1 to Manchester United.

That season, the Debenhams Cup was established for the two teams from the Third and Fourth Divisions that progressed furthest in the FA Cup, with Debenhams becoming one of the first sponsors of an FA competition. Chester reached the fifth round of the FA Cup and qualified to play Port Vale over two legs. In the first leg at Vale Park, Chester lost 2–0, but back at Sealand Road, they won 4–1 to take the first Debenhams Cup 4–3 on aggregate.

In the Lancashire Junior Cup/Lancashire Challenge Trophy, Wigan Athletic were winners that season and retained the trophy the following year. That season also saw the women's game gain a knockout competition in the shape of the North West League Cup, with the first games played in 1976/77. The men's game lost a league that season with the end of the Northern Floodlit League.

In the mid-seventies, the Liverpool FA had a trophy returned by persons unknown. Lost since 1910, it was thought to have been a Hospital Cup of some kind. The FA decided to use the renovated trophy for a match for the Lord Mayor of Liverpool's Silver Jubilee Fund on 31 December 1977, inviting Fantail, holders of the Liverpool Sunday Premier Cup, and Waterloo Dock, holders of the Liverpool Challenge Cup, to play for it. Fantail beat Waterloo Dock 2–0 to claim the trophy.

Liverpool retained the European Cup and were runners-up in the first League Cup final in 1977/78, losing to Nottingham Forest. While Liverpool were winning the European Cup, domestic football in 1977/78 saw players finally gain freedom of contract. The campaign for player freedom began in 1960 when PFA chair Jimmy Hill argued for players to have the right to move freely without club control and for a new maximum wage. In 1968, Parliament agreed that the PFA had a case worth hearing, but it was not until April 1978 that players' freedom of contract was finalised.

Before the start of the 1978/79 season, the Cheshire County League added a Second Division, with Bootle, Ford Motors, Kirkby Town, Maghull, Prescot Town, Prescot B.I., Skelmersdale United and Warrington Town among the local clubs helping to form the eighteen-club division.

That season also saw Liverpool win league title number eleven. The title race quickly became a Merseyside affair, with Everton following hot on the heels of their neighbours. At the end of August, Everton and Liverpool were joint top with West Bromwich Albion, with Liverpool ahead due to fewer draws than Everton. By the end of October, Nottingham Forest joined the group of unbeaten teams. By the end of the year, Liverpool led the league on goal difference from Everton.

By the end of January 1979, West Bromwich Albion had returned to the top of the table, with Everton and Liverpool just behind. Everton briefly topped the league in mid-February, but by the end of the month Liverpool were back on top, ahead of Everton and now Arsenal. By April, Everton had dropped out of the title race, leaving Liverpool top with only Nottingham Forest and West Bromwich Albion as real challengers. Liverpool secured the league at the start of May with a 3–0 win at Anfield against Aston Villa, claiming the title unbeaten at home and finishing eight points clear of Nottingham Forest.

In the 1980s, Liverpool dominated domestic and European football and were joined by Everton from 1984 onwards, with both sides winning domestic leagues and European trophies. This success came against the backdrop of the city's economic decline. Between 1972 and 1982, Liverpool lost 80,000 jobs. In 1981, Toxteth suffered a riot, and by 1985 the city had over double the national average unemployment rate. Unemployment benefit was around £18 a week, rising to about £20 a week, and by the mid-1980s it had increased to around £28 for a single person and £45 for a couple.

The cost of a Goodison season ticket for 1980/81 ranged from £32 to £60, with OAPs paying £45. A terrace ticket cost £1.50, and a seat £3. At

Anfield, a season ticket in 1981 cost £63, rising to between £82 and £95 for the 1986/87 season. At Sealand Road, a season ticket was around £48, while Tranmere Rovers set their 1981/82 season tickets at between £29.50 and £38.50, with OAPs paying £22.50. A match ticket for the terraces at Sealand Road cost £1.50 and £1.25 at Prenton Park, with seats at £2.20 and £1.80 respectively. A ticket to watch the 1984 League Cup final at Wembley between Everton and Liverpool cost £4.50 for the terraces, with seats ranging from £11 to £18. For the replay at Maine Road, tickets were £3 on the terraces and £6 to £8 for seats. The average working wage in the 1980s was £124 for men and £78 for women.

Liverpool started the decade by winning their twelfth league title in 1979/80. In 1980/81, Liverpool won the European Cup (see Europe chapter) and secured their first League Cup, beating West Ham 2–1 in a replay at Villa Park after a 1–1 draw at Wembley.

In 1981/82, Queens Park Rangers introduced the first artificial pitch, 'Astroturf', in the Football League. Although the surface had first been used in Islington in 1971, it was the first time it was used for professional football. In March 1981, QPR announced plans to use the pitch at Loftus Road and assured the Football League that they would remove it after three years if it failed commercially. Everton asked the Football League Committee what would happen if a team refused to play on the artificial surface, and were told the tie would be awarded to QPR. In 1985, Everton seconded a motion from Leicester City to ban First and Second Division games on artificial pitches after July 1988, but the motion was defeated.

Liverpool began the 1981/82 season by pursuing league title number thirteen. In their second consecutive League Cup final, they beat Tottenham Hotspur 3–1 in front of 100,000 fans. That season the Football League had introduced three points for a win.

In the amateur game, the North West Counties League was formed in 1982 through the merger of the Cheshire County League, originally founded in 1919, and the Lancashire Combination, founded in 1891. Bootle, Burscough, Formby, Prescot Cables and St Helens Town were the Merseyside teams among the twenty founding members of the league's

First Division. Ellesmere Port & Neston, Kirkby Town, Prescot B.I. and Skelmersdale United were among the twenty founding members of the Second Division. Maghull, Warrington Town, Vulcan Newton and Newton represented the county in Division Three. The league became a feeder to the Northern Premier League, although promotion was not automatic.

The 1982/83 season saw Liverpool win league title number fourteen and their third consecutive League Cup (Milk Cup). At the start of the new year, they were ten points ahead of Watford and Manchester United, increasing their lead to twelve points over United a month later. By March, Liverpool were thirteen points ahead of Watford, who had moved into second place, and by April they were sixteen points clear of Watford, who could no longer catch them. Although Manchester United could still mathematically catch them, Liverpool won the league after Everton beat United 2–0 at Goodison, ending United's hopes. Despite a poor finish to the season, with only one draw from their last six matches, Liverpool secured their fourteenth league title, finishing eleven points ahead of Watford.

In the League Cup final, Liverpool faced Manchester United, with the match going to extra time after a 1–1 draw in 90 minutes. Ronnie Whelan scored the winner, giving Liverpool a third consecutive League Cup triumph. During the close season, Bob Paisley retired after nine successful years, with Joe Fagan, another of Liverpool's Boot Room men, taking over as first-team manager in July 1983.

The 1983/84 season saw Everton join Liverpool in Merseyside's dominance, with Liverpool winning their fifteenth league title as well as the European Cup and Everton lifting the FA Cup. That season also featured the first League Cup final between Everton and Liverpool – the first ever all-Merseyside Wembley affair.

At Goodison, the season had started so poorly that by New Year, 'Kendall Out' had been daubed on manager Howard Kendall's garage doors. Despite this, chairman Sir Philip Carter and the board fully supported him. Attendances had dropped to just over 13,000 for a 0–0 draw against Coventry City on New Year's Eve. However, in the FA Cup and League Cup, Everton's form improved. In the League Cup quarter-final, Adrian

Heath scored from a back pass to earn a draw at Oxford United, a goal credited with changing Everton's fortunes. Everton won the replay 4–1, and in the two-legged semi-final, they defeated Aston Villa 2–1 on aggregate. Liverpool reached their fourth consecutive League Cup final by beating Walsall 4–2 on aggregate.

On Sunday 25 March 1984, Everton and Liverpool met for the first time in a major cup final at Wembley, the Football League Cup, then known as the Milk Cup. Around 100,000 fans, possibly more, travelled to London. The match was largely uneventful, with Everton's Adrian Heath having a goal-bound effort cleared off the line by Liverpool's Alan Hansen, with protests for handball waved away. The match ended 0–0, with the replay at Maine Road three days later drawing over 50,000 fans. Liverpool's Graeme Souness scored the only goal after 21 minutes, securing Liverpool's fourth consecutive League Cup win.

In the league, Liverpool soon regained the lead and by mid-April 1984 were two points clear of Manchester United. They went on to win their fifteenth league title, finishing three points ahead of Southampton. In the FA Cup final at Wembley, Everton beat Watford 2–0 with goals from Graeme Sharp and Andy Gray.

The Lancashire Amateur Cup for 1983/84 was won by Merseyside Police. In the North West Counties League, Ellesmere Port & Neston won the League Cup that season, becoming the second winners of the trophy, which had been inaugurated the previous year. In 1984, the Liverpool Daily Post sponsored a new league in Wales, the Welsh Alliance League.

The 1984/85 season saw Everton win the league title and the European Cup Winners' Cup, while finishing as FA Cup runners-up. The season started inauspiciously for both Everton and Liverpool. By the start of October, Everton had risen to eighth place with Liverpool in eleventh. Things turned around for Everton with a 3–0 win against Leicester at Goodison at the start of November, moving them to the top of the table, one point ahead of Arsenal after four consecutive wins. Liverpool, however, remained in mid-table.

At the start of the new year, Everton were in second place with Liverpool in ninth. Everton moved to the top of the league in mid-January with a 4–0 win against Newcastle United at Goodison and never lost their grip on first place. They won the league with five matches to spare after beating West Ham United 3–0 at Goodison. Liverpool finished second, thirteen points behind, after a late run at the title.

Everton still had to play in their first European final and the FA Cup final. They had reached Wembley by beating Luton Town 2–1 in extra time at Villa Park but were defeated in the final by a Norman Whiteside goal in extra time, losing to a ten-man Manchester United side. This final was played only days after Everton lifted their first European trophy in Rotterdam (see Europe chapter). Liverpool also had a European Cup final to play (see Europe chapter).

On 29 May 1985, Liverpool went to Brussels to play in their fifth European Cup final this time against Italian giant Juventus. Before the game kicked off at the city's Heysel stadium, Liverpool and Juventus fans clashed on the terraces at the designated Liverpool end of the stadium. During the clashes Liverpool fans drove back the Juventus fans causing a crush against the wall at the end of the terracing. The wall soon gave way causing the deaths of thirty-nine Juventus supporters. The aftermath saw the then Prime Minister, Margaret Thatcher, ask the English FA to withdraw English teams from European football. UEFA then imposed an indefinite ban on English teams playing in Europe. This ended up being a five-year ban for all English clubs, with Liverpool being given a ten-year ban which was reduced to six upon appeal.

Joe Fagan left his role as Liverpool manager in May 1985 and was succeeded by club legend Kenny Dalglish. In his first season as player-manager, 1985/86, Everton and Liverpool battled for both the league and FA Cup, with Liverpool winning both to secure their Sixteenth League title and their first league and FA Cup double. This season also saw the sale of alcohol banned at football grounds.

In January 1986, Manchester United led the league by eight points from Liverpool, with Everton five points further back in second. Everton reached the top in early February and looked set to stay there until a 0–0 draw at Old Trafford and a 2–0 Liverpool win at Manchester City on 31 March saw the clubs swap places, with Liverpool moving to the top. Liverpool held onto the lead, briefly losing it when Everton beat Watford 2–0 in mid-April. The title race remained close until 30 April when Liverpool beat Leicester City 2–0 at Anfield while Everton suffered a shock 1–0 defeat away at Oxford United. Liverpool had won all of their last seven league matches, taking the title from Everton by two points.

In the FA Cup, Liverpool beat Southampton 2–1 at White Hart Lane while Everton defeated Sheffield Wednesday 2–1 after extra time at Villa Park, setting up the first all-Merseyside FA Cup final at Wembley.

On 10 May 1986, Everton and Liverpool met at Wembley for the second time in their history, but for the first time in an FA Cup final, with an official attendance of 98,000. Everton opened the scoring through Gary Lineker after twenty-seven minutes. Ian Rush equalised for Liverpool on fifty-six minutes, with Craig Johnston putting Liverpool ahead on sixty-two minutes. Rush added a third for Liverpool on eighty-three minutes, securing the club's first league and FA Cup double.

In the same season, Runcorn finished as runners-up in the FA Trophy final, losing 1–0 to Altrincham at Wembley. In the Lancashire Cup competitions during the eighties, local teams had particular success in the Lancashire Amateur Cup. Between 1981/82 and 1988/89, four teams won the trophy seven times: St Dominics in 1981/82 and 1982/83, Merseyside Police in 1983/84 and 1988/89, Florence Albion in 1985/86, and Earle in 1987/88. Wigan Athletic won the Lancashire Senior Challenge Cup in 1983/84.

After the ban on European competition for English clubs, Everton and Liverpool faced each other in the newly inaugurated Screen Sport Super Cup Final in 1985/86. Liverpool won the short-lived competition 7–2 on aggregate. The Football League had also formed a new competition, the Full Members Cup (meaning a club with full voting rights). Liverpool opted out of the competition but Everton played from 1986/87 onwards and lost in the final in both 1988/89 (to

Nottingham Forest) and 1990/91 (to Crystal Palace). Tranmere Rovers played in the last season of 1991/92.

In 1986/87, Everton won the league again. They reached the top of the table in early February after beating Coventry City 3–1 at Goodison, overtaking leaders Arsenal. Although Everton briefly lost top spot to Liverpool after a 2–1 defeat at Watford in early March, Liverpool then slipped up at the end of March, losing 2–1 at Anfield to Wimbledon, while Everton beat Arsenal 1–0 at Highbury to retake the lead. Everton held onto first place for the remainder of the season, securing the title with a 1–0 win away at Norwich City with two games left, finishing nine points ahead of Liverpool.

In the FA Vase, St Helens Town beat Warrington Town 3–2 at Wembley in 1986/87, becoming the first Merseyside club to win the trophy. Both clubs remain the only Merseyside teams to have played in the final. St Helens Town's campaign included a 5–4 win at home against Colne Dynamoes in the extra preliminary round and a 2–1 home win against General Chemicals in the preliminary round. They then defeated Wren Rovers 2–0 in the first round, Guisborough Town 1–0 in the second round, and Wythenshawe Amateurs 4–1 in the third round, all at home. In the fourth round, they won 2–0 away at Wisbech Town, then beat Rainworth Miners Welfare 4–1 at home in the fifth round. In the quarter-finals, they beat Falmouth Town 1–0 away in a replay after a 1–1 draw. In the semi-final over two legs, St Helens lost 1–0 at home to Emley but won the away leg 2–0 to reach the final.

That summer, Howard Kendall left Everton to join Athletic Bilbao and was replaced by his assistant and former teammate, Colin Harvey, for the 1987/88 season. However, it was Liverpool who won the league, claiming their Seventeenth League title. Liverpool reached the top of the table for the second time at the end of November 1987 after a 4–0 win against Watford at Anfield and never lost the lead for the remainder of the season. This run was supported by a record of twenty-nine league games unbeaten, including twenty-two wins and seven draws, before losing 1–0 to Everton at Goodison Park.

Liverpool secured the title in April with a 1–0 win against Tottenham Hotspur with four games to spare, finishing nine points ahead of

Manchester United. In the FA Cup final, Liverpool were beaten 1–0 by Wimbledon. In wider football, the 1987/88 season saw the introduction of a second division in the Northern Premier League, known as the Multipart League from July 1985.

In April 1988, as part of the Football League's centenary celebrations, a knockout tournament was held at Wembley with matches played over forty minutes. Everton, Liverpool, Tranmere Rovers and Wigan Athletic joined twelve other league clubs in the competition. In the first round, Everton beat Wolverhampton Wanderers on penalties, Liverpool lost to Newcastle United on penalties, Tranmere Rovers beat Wimbledon 1–0, and Wigan Athletic beat Sunderland on penalties. In the quarter-finals, Everton lost 1–0 to Manchester United, Tranmere Rovers beat Newcastle United 2–0, and Wigan Athletic were beaten on penalties by Sheffield Wednesday. In the semi-finals, Nottingham Forest beat Tranmere Rovers on penalties.

In 1988/89, Liverpool lost the league title in the final game of the season at Anfield against Arsenal. However, this season was overshadowed by the tragedy at Hillsborough on 15 April 1989. During the FA Cup semi-final against Nottingham Forest at Hillsborough, congestion outside the ground led police to open the gates to the Leppings Lane terraces, resulting in a crush in the fenced sections. Supporters tried desperately to attract the attention of officials and escape the overcrowding, with the match stopped at 3.06 pm. The disaster led to ninety-seven deaths and almost eight hundred injuries, resulting in the move to all-seater stadiums and a long fight for justice by the families of those affected.

Liverpool and Everton met in the FA Cup final at Wembley, with Liverpool winning 3–2 after extra time. Merseyside Police won the Lancashire Amateur Cup in the 1988/89 season.

In 1989/90, the Liverpool League amalgamated with the SSU League to form the Liverpool SSU League, with two divisions, A and B. Division A included Princess 84, Breck Road and Red Rum from the Liverpool League, joining Tippers, Wellington Road SS A, Greenacres, Oriel Colts, Cabin, Richmond YC A and St Domingo from the SSU League. Division

B featured Speke Legion, Gonzaga and Sixies from the Liverpool League, alongside Wellington Road SS B, Valonia, Peter Marsh, Gray Street Queens, Richmond YC B and Court Hey from the SSU League.

In the 1989/90 season, Everton and Liverpool initially led the league, but Everton dropped away, leaving Liverpool in a title race with Aston Villa and Chelsea. Arsenal entered the race in December and January, but Liverpool led the league by a point from Aston Villa at the start of the new year. By the end of February, Aston Villa had moved into first place, with Liverpool and Villa exchanging the lead weekly until Liverpool went top at the end of March with a 3–2 win against Southampton at Anfield. Liverpool held the lead, winning their eighteenth league title in late April 1990 with a 2–1 win against Queens Park Rangers at Anfield, while Aston Villa could only manage a 3–3 draw against Norwich City. Kenny Dalglish had won three titles in five seasons as player-manager and retired as a player after a career of 835 games for Celtic and Liverpool.

In amateur football, Knowsley United won the North West Counties League Challenge Cup that season. The 1989/90 season also saw the formation of the North West Women's Regional Football League, comprising thirty-five teams across four divisions. Leasowe Pacific won the First Division by five points from Preston Rangers, with Newton finishing fourth and St Helens fifth in the nine-team division. Wigan won the eight-team Second Division.

In 1990, the Football League's 'big five' of the First Division, comprising Everton, Liverpool, Manchester United, Arsenal and Tottenham Hotspur, met with Greg Dyke, Managing Director of London Weekend Television, to discuss television rights for the bigger clubs in England. Dyke favoured more airtime for those clubs, and the meeting sowed the seeds for what would soon become the Premier League.

At the end of the 1990/91 season, the Liverpool Shipping League folded and amalgamated with the Liverpool SSU League, which had only been formed two seasons earlier. The new league featured three divisions. The Premier Division included St Philomena's (first champions), Academicals, Gonzaga, Jabisco, Non Pariel, Devonshire, All Saints, Sportsman OB (formerly Cabin), Turpins, Salisbury Villa and Wellington Road SS A. The First Division comprised Halfie (first winners), Brunswick BC, Winrow Central, Coral Social, Kikrlion, Merebank, Devers, Speke Legion, Greenacres, Blitz, Tippers and Valona. The Second Division featured Foran (first winners), Regals, Stand Farm, Stret Lucas, Peel, Ford Motors, Home Office Reserves, LP Telecom, Winrow Res, Walvale Academicals, Wellington Road SS B and Amberline.

The 1990/91 Lancashire Senior Challenge Cup was won by Wigan Athletic. In 1991, discussions over a new league continued, with the Football League seeking the views of the Football Association before deciding to back the proposal. The FA published a report, 'Blueprint for the Future of Football', supporting a new breakaway league, and by July the First Division clubs had signed an agreement to form it. The league was given the go-ahead in February 1992.

In 1991/92, Sefton Schools lost for the second time in the English Schools Shield/Trophy final, defeated 3–1 over two legs by Barnsley Schools. Merseyside Police won the Lancashire Amateur Cup for the 1991/92 season.

As the men's game prepared for the Premier League, the women's game followed suit. The Women's FA, with a grant from the Sports Council, launched the National League Premier Division. Knowsley United Women's team represented the region in the newly formed eight-team league, finishing fourth in the inaugural 1991/92 season. Other teams included Doncaster Belles, Ipswich Town, Maidstone Tigresses, Millwall Lionesses, Notts Rangers, Red Star Southampton and Wimbledon. Two other eight-team divisions, Division One North and Division One South, were also formed, though no teams from the region participated in these divisions in the first season. In 1991/92, Tranmere Rovers Ladies won the Women's North West Regional League Third Division by one point from Pilkingtons LFC, losing only one game.

The final season of the old Football League First Division ended in 1991/92 with Leeds United as champions. Liverpool finished sixth, with Everton in twelfth. Liverpool also won the FA Cup that season.

TEAMS FORMED OR ACTIVE BETWEEN 1972 AND 1992

AIGBURTH PEOPLES HALL

In 1972/73, former Liverpool League and Central Amateur League side Cumberland joined Aigburth Peoples Hall. The newly amalgamated club gained promotion back to the I Zingari First Division in 1973/74, finishing runners-up to Woolton by three points. In 1974/75, they finished as runners-up to Aintree Villa by two points, and again finished second to Aintree Villa in 1978/79 by five points. They were relegated to the Second Division in 1979/80 but won the newly named First Division title in 1983/84, finishing a point ahead of Florence Albion, and returned to the Premier Division. In 1986/87, they finished runners-up to Unity BCOB in the Premier Division. The I Zingari title returned to Aigburth Peoples Hall in 1989/90, when they won it by three points ahead of Quarry Bank Old Boys, and they won it again in 1991/92 on goal difference from REMYCA United.

AINTREE S.S. (SORTING SIDINGS)

In 1972/73, Aintree finished twelfth in the Liverpool County Combination. In 1975/76, they finished as runners-up by one point to Waterloo Dock in the First Division. In 1976/77, they won the Liverpool Amateur Cup, beating Sefton & District 2–1, and finished top of the First Division by five points from Waterloo Dock, also winning the George Mahon Cup. However, the club faced potential closure, which was avoided after a public meeting. In 1977/78, they finished bottom of the First Division and were relegated to the Second Division, regaining First Division status by 1983/84, finishing eighth. The club resigned from the Liverpool County Combination in January 1985.

AINTREE VILLA

In 1971/72, Aintree Villa won the league by three points from St Andrews United and also won the Liverpool Amateur Cup, beating Marine Reserves. In 1972/73, they retained the league title by eight points from Quarry Bank Old Boys. In 1973/74, they were runners-up to Merseyside Police, before winning the league again in 1974/75 by two points from Aigburth Peoples

Hall, and again in 1978/79 by five points from Aigburth PH, also winning the Liverpool Amateur Cup against Ayone.

They won four out of five I Zingari Challenge Cups between 1979 and 1984: 1979/80 (beating East Villa and League Runners-up), 1980/81 (beating East Villa), 1981/82 (beating Quarry Old Boys and winning the Liverpool Amateur Cup 3–2 against Yorkshire Imperial Metals), and 1983/84 (beating Liverpool Nalgo 4–3), also winning the Premier Division by one point ahead of Walton Village. They were relegated from the Premier Division in 1988/89 but regained status by finishing runners-up to Warbreck in the First Division in 1989/90. In 1990/91, they finished twelfth in the Premier Division.

ALMITHAK

Formed around 1987 when two local sides in the Dingle and Granby areas merged, Almithak joined the Liverpool Sunday League, winning the title and Liverpool Sunday Premier Cup in their first season, 1987/88. They retained the league title in 1988/89 and won the FA National Sunday Cup, beating East Levenshulme 3–1. They won the league for a third time in 1989/90 and won the Liverpool Sunday Premier Cup again in 1990/91.

ASHVILLE

Between 1971/72 and 1991/92, Ashville remained in the West Cheshire League First Division, generally finishing mid-table. In 1973/74, they won the Wirral Amateur Cup, beating Birkenhead Technical College, and in 1989/90 were runners-up in the Wirral Senior Cup, losing to Cammell Laird.

BOOTLE (1973) / LANGTON

By 1971/72, Langton moved to Orrell Mount Park and won the Liverpool County Combination by two points from Dunlop. In 1972/73, they retained the title by three points from Waterloo Dock and won the George Mahon Cup, though they lost the Liverpool Challenge Cup final to Dunlop.

In 1973, Langton changed its name to Bootle FC with Sefton Council's support, retaining the same players. In 1973/74, Bootle won the Liverpool County Combination by seven points from Lucas Sports, also winning the Liverpool Amateur Cup (beating Quarry Bank Old Boys 4–0) and the George Mahon Cup. They joined the Lancashire Combination in 1974/75, finishing third, and won the Lancashire Combination in 1975/76, beating Waterloo Dock in the Liverpool Challenge Cup final and Colne in the Lancashire Combination League Cup final.

Bootle retained the Lancashire Combination in 1976/77 and joined the newly formed Cheshire County League Second Division in 1978/79, winning the division by two points from Curzon Ashton and earning promotion to the First Division, also winning the Liverpool Challenge Cup (beating Waterloo Dock 2–1). In 1981/82, Bootle Reserves left the Merseyside League to join the Liverpool County Combination Second Division.

In 1982/83, Bootle were founder members of the North West Counties League, finishing fourteenth. The reserve team won the Lord Wavertree Cup in 1987. In May 1990, South Liverpool moved to share Bucks Park with Bootle. Plans to move to Buckley Hill, Netherton, to meet ground requirements did not materialise. In 1991/92, Bootle were relegated from the First Division of the North West Counties League after finishing bottom.

BRNESC (BRITISH RAIL NORTH END SOCIAL CLUB)
BRNESC joined the Liverpool County Combination Second Division in 1982/83, winning the division and the Lord Wavertree Cup. In 1983/84, they won the First Division by four points from St Dominics and won the George Mahon Cup. In 1984/85, they retained the league title, edging Waterloo Dock, and were runners-up to Florence Albion in the Liverpool Amateur Cup. They also wn the Lord Wavertree Cup in 183 and 1991.

BROMBOROUGH POOL
Pool were promoted to the First Division after finishing third in the Second Division in 1972/73, and were runners-up to Harrowby in the Wirral

Amateur Cup that season. In 1980/81, they were runners-up to West Kirby in the Wirral Senior Cup, losing 4–1. In 1991/92, they were runners-up to Heswall in the Wirral Senior Cup, losing 2–1, but won the Wirral Amateur Cup by beating Poulton Victoria.

BRUNSWICK BOYS CLUB

Brunswick won the JOC Championship for three consecutive seasons: 1979/80, 1980/81 and 1981/82, the latter on goal difference from 174 Union Club, and won the Everton Cup in 1981/82. The team is believed to have finished in the Bootle JOC after 1987/88, possibly returning as Chaucer Brunswick, though confirmation is outstanding.

BURSCOUGH

In 1971/72, Burscough won the Liverpool Senior Non-League Cup, beating Formby 4–1. In 1973/74, they were runners-up in the same cup, losing to Skelmersdale United, and lost the Cheshire League Cup final to Rossendale United over two legs. In 1974/75, they beat Marine over two legs to win the Cheshire League Cup and were runners-up in the Lancashire Floodlight Trophy to Great Harwood. They remained in the Cheshire County League First Division until the league dissolved in 1981/82, then became founder members of the North West Counties League, winning its first league title in 1982/83 by two points from Rhyl and winning the league's first community shield.

In 1989/90, Burscough were relegated from the First Division after finishing second bottom, but finished fourth in the 1991/92 season, earning promotion back to the First Division, and were runners-up to Ashton United in the North West Counties League Cup, losing 1–0 in the final.

CAMMELL LAIRD (1907)

In 1971/72, they won the Wirral Senior Cup, beating Hoylake Athletic, but lost the Pyke Cup final 3–2 to Poulton Victoria. In 1972/73, they won the Cheshire Amateur Cup by beating Poulton Victoria, and also won the Cheshire Bowl.

They then secured five consecutive championships, starting in 1974/75 by one point from Port Sunlight, and were Wirral Senior Cup runners-up to Poulton Victoria. In 1975/76, they won the title by six points from Poulton Victoria and won the Pyke Cup, beating West Kirby. In 1976/77, they won the league by sixteen points from Heswall and beat Poulton Victoria to win the Wirral Senior Cup, also winning the Pyke Cup against Port Sunlight. In 1977/78, they won the league by nine points from Poulton Victoria and won the Wirral Senior Cup and Pyke Cup, beating Poulton Victoria and Shell respectively. In 1978/79, they won the league by nine points from Poulton Victoria, won the Wirral Senior Cup against Poulton Victoria for the third consecutive season, and won their fourth successive Pyke Cup by beating Heswall 3–2.

In 1979/80, they won the Wirral Senior Cup 2–0 against Poulton Victoria, and lost the Pyke Cup final to Poulton Victoria. They then won four consecutive league titles starting in 1980/81 by eight points from West Kirby, were runners-up to Mersey Royal in the Wirral Amateur Cup, and beat Van Leer to win the Cheshire Amateur Cup. In 1981/82, they won the league by four points from Port Sunlight and won the Cheshire Amateur Cup against Hoylake. In 1982/83, they won the league by a point from West Kirby and were Cheshire Amateur Cup runners-up to West Kirby. In 1983/84, they won the league by four points from Vauxhall Motors and were runners-up in the Wirral Amateur Cup to Poulton Victoria.

In 1984/85, they won the Wirral Amateur Cup against Bronze Social, their reserve side won the Second Division, and they were runners-up to Heswall in the Wirral Senior Cup. They were runners-up again in the Wirral Senior Cup in 1985/86 to Mersey Royal, and their reserves won the Second Division in 1986/87. In 1987/88, they won the Wirral Senior Cup by beating Higher Bebington.

In 1988/89, they began another run of four consecutive league titles, winning the first by four points from Merseyside Police. In 1989/90, they won on goal difference from Mersey Royal and beat Ashville 2–1 to win the Wirral Senior Cup. In 1990/91, they won the league by ten points from Mersey Royal, won the Wirral Senior Cup and Wirral Amateur Cup by beating Heswall, and won the Cheshire Bowl. In 1991/92, they won the league by four points from Shell and won the Pyke Cup by beating Heswall and were Cheshire Amateur Cup runners-up.

CAPENHURST VILLA

Formed in 1985 from a merger between Capenhurst , which had played in the Chester and District League since 1952/53, and Capenhurst Villa, formed in 1980 and playing in the British Nuclear Fuels Inter-Departmental competition. The newly merged club initially played in the South Wirral League Second Division in 1981/82. They were runners-up in the Wirral Amateur Cup to Vauxhall in 1985/86 and moved to the West Cheshire League Second Division for 1988/89, finishing tenth. In 1989/90, they were promoted to the First Division after finishing runners-up on goal difference to Heswall Reserves. In 1990/91, their first season in the First Division, they finished last.

CHESHIRE LINES

Promoted to the Liverpool County Combination First Division in 1977/78, they finished ninth and won the Liverpool Junior Cup by beating Knowsley Social. Relegated in 1978/79 after finishing second from bottom, they were beaten by Plessey in the Liverpool Amateur Cup in 1983/84. In 1984/85, they returned to the First Division, finishing eleventh, and remained there until merging with South Liverpool in July 1992.

CHESTER / CHESTER CITY

In 1972/73, Chester were runners-up in the Cheshire Premier Cup, losing 2–1 to Crewe Alexandra. In 1974/75, they gained their first Football League promotion and reached the League Cup semi-final. After a strong season, they secured promotion to the Third Division on goal average, with their margin over Lincoln City just 0.039.

In 1975/76, they finished seventeenth in the Third Division. In 1976/77, they won the Debenhams Cup, beating Port Vale 4–1, and were runners-up in the Cheshire Premier Cup to Crewe Alexandra. They won the Cheshire Premier Cup in 1977/78, 1978/79 and 1980/81, and were runners-up in 1979/80. In 1981/82, after a seventeen-game winless run, they were relegated to the Fourth Division and were runners-up in the final Cheshire Premier Cup, losing to Tranmere Rovers on penalties.

In 1982/83, they finished thirteenth in the Fourth Division and had added City to their name. In 1983/84, they finished bottom, requiring re-election. In 1985/86, they were promoted to the Third Division, finishing as runners-up to Swindon Town, eighteen points behind. In 1986/87, they finished fifteenth in the Third Division and reached the Freight Rover Trophy Northern final, losing to Mansfield Town.

In November 1989, financial director David Cross announced Sealand Road was for sale. Their final match there was a 2–0 win against Rotherham United at the end of 1989/90. A ground-share with Macclesfield Town followed while plans for a new stadium progressed. In January 1991, planning permission was granted for a new site on Bumper's Lane, with construction starting in January 1992.

CHESTER LADIES
Formed around 1969, they played in the Merseyside and Wirral Ladies Football League.

COLLEGIATE OLD BOYS
Relegated in 1972/73 after finishing second from bottom, they regained I Zingari League First Division status by winning the Second Division in 1974/75, five points ahead of Unity BCOB. Relegated again in 1978/79, they returned by finishing runners-up in 1979/80, but were relegated bottom in 1981/82. They were promoted again in 1982/83, finishing runners-up to Walton Village, and finished as First Division runners-up in 1985/86, four points behind Speke Town.

CROSBY DYNAMO
Won the Crosby Sunday League in 1971/72. In 1972/73, they won the Canon Francis Cup, beating Catherine 2–0, and finished runners-up in the league to Alpha by one point. In 1974/75, they changed their name to Howard Sports.

DINGLE RAIL

Formed in 1967 as Empress, they joined the Liverpool Sunday League and progressed from the Eleventh Division to the First Division by 1975/76. In 1977/78, they won the Premier Division, Premier Cup, and were runners-up in the League Challenge Cup. In 1978/79, they were Premier Cup runners-up and in 1979/80, they won the league, Premier Cup and League Challenge Cup. They also won the South Merseyside Invitation Cup in 1977/78 and 1978/79, and were runners-up in 1979/80.

DUNLOP / SPEKE HALL / SPEKE

In 1972/73, they won the Liverpool Challenge Cup by beating Langton and the Liverpool Amateur Cup by beating Marine. In 1973/74, they retained the Challenge Cup, beating Bootle. Relegated from the First Division in 1980/81, they regained First Division status in 1985/86. In 1986/87, they finished seventh, and in 1987/88, changed their name to Speke Hall, finishing eighth. In 1990/91, they became Speke, finishing eighth in 1991/92.

EARLE

In 1974/75, they won the Liverpool Challenge Cup, beating Kirkby Town. They struggled in the First Division before relegation in 1975/76, finishing bottom with only four wins. In 1977/78, they won the County Combination Second Division and Lord Wavertree Cup, regaining First Division status for 1979/80, finishing eleventh. They were runners-up in 1981/82 and 1982/83, both times behind St Dominics, and in 1987/88, won the Lancashire Amateur Cup, beating BRNESC at Haig Avenue.

EAST VILLA

Won the I Zingari Alliance First Division in 1971/72, earning promotion to the I Zingari League Third Division in 1972/73, finishing fourth. In 1973/74, they were runners-up to Everton Red Triangle in the Third Division, and in 1974/75, finished fifth in the Second Division. In 1975/76, they won the Second Division by five points from Essemay Old Boys. In 1976/77, they were First Division runners-up to Quarry Bank Old Boys by two points.

They won the I Zingari Combination Challenge Cup in 1979/80 and were runners-up in 1980/81. Relegated in 1981/82, they returned to the Premier Division in 1983/84, finishing mid-table. In 1985/86, they were runners-up in the I Zingari Combination Cup. In 1987/88, they finished as Premier Division runners-up, four points behind REMYCA United. In 1989/90, they won the Liverpool Challenge Cup and were runners-up in the Liverpool Amateur Cup. In 1990/91, they were runners-up in the I Zingari Combination Cup and became the first I Zingari club to win the Northern Counties Senior Cup.

EDEN VALE

Originally known as Progress Rovers in the Ormskirk League, Eden Vale joined the Crosby and District Sunday League Third Division (then the Formby, Crosby and District Sunday League) for the 1972/73 season, winning the division at the first attempt. They won the Second Division in 1973/74 and completed a hat-trick by winning the First Division in 1974/75. They won the First Division again in 1976/77, alongside the Lal Evans Memorial Cup, but lost the Canon Francis Cup final to Fairfax.

In 1977/78, they won both the Canon Francis Cup and Lal Evans Memorial Cup again. They dominated league and cup competitions for several seasons: in 1978/79 and 1979/80, they won the First Division, Canon Francis Cup and Lal Evans Memorial Cup; in 1980/81, they won the First Division and Lal Evans Memorial Cup; in 1981/82, they won the First Division; in 1982/83, they won the Canon Francis Cup and Lal Evans Memorial Cup; and in 1983/84, they won the First Division, Canon Francis Cup and Lal Evans Memorial Cup. 1985/86 they won the First Division. They next won the First Division in 1987/88, and the Lal Evans Memorial Cup in 1989/90 and 1990/91, beating Bass Railway 4–0, and added the Canon Francis Cup that season.

ELLESMERE PORT TOWN

In 1971/72, Ellesmere Port finished sixteenth in the Northern Premier League and lost 3–1 to Northwich Victoria in the Cheshire Senior Cup final. In 1973/74, they joined the Lancashire Combination for financial reasons, finishing sixteenth in 1974/75 and eighteenth in 1975/76. They joined the Mid-Cheshire League for 1976/77, finishing tenth, and finished ninth in 1977/78, which proved to be their last season before folding in 1978.

EVERTON

The 1971/72 season was Harry Catterick's last full season in charge, with Everton finishing fifteenth and exiting the FA Cup in the third round. In 1972/73, Catterick retired in April, with Tommy Eglington taking charge for the remainder of the season, which saw Everton finish seventeenth. Billy Bingham was appointed for the 1973/74 season, leading the club to seventh and UEFA Cup qualification for 1974/75 (see Europe chapter). Everton finished fourth in 1974/75 and again qualified for the UEFA Cup for 1975/76.

In 1976/77, Bingham was sacked in January and replaced by Gordon Lee, who took Everton to the League Cup final and led them to third in 1977/78, with Bob Latchford scoring thirty league goals. Everton competed in the UEFA Cup in 1978/79 (see Europe chapter) and, after finishing fourth, secured further UEFA Cup football for 1979/80. However, they fell to nineteenth in the league and were beaten by West Ham United in a twice-replayed FA Cup semi-final. After another bottom-half finish in 1980/81, Gordon Lee was replaced by Howard Kendall.

In 1981/82, Kendall's first season, Everton finished eighth. In 1983/84, Everton won the FA Cup, despite a poor start that saw 'Kendall Out' painted on the manager's garage door in Formby and a lowest attendance of just over 13,000 for a 0–0 draw with Coventry on New Year's Eve. An equaliser from Adrian Heath in a League Cup quarter-final at Oxford, following a back pass from Kevin Brock, is credited with turning the season around, sparking a fifteen-game unbeaten run. Everton reached the League Cup final but lost to Liverpool in a replay. However, they lifted the FA Cup by beating Watford 2–0 at Wembley.

The 1984/85 season saw Everton win the league and European Cup Winners' Cup while finishing as FA Cup runners-up. Despite a poor start, Everton climbed to the top by November and stayed there, clinching the title in May with a 3–0 win over West Ham, finishing thirteen points ahead of Liverpool. They lost the FA Cup final in extra time to Manchester United, shortly after winning their first European trophy.

Everton finished runners-up to Liverpool in both the league and FA Cup in 1985/86 but won the league again in 1986/87. They climbed to second by December and first in February, maintaining their lead to win the title with a 1–0 win at Norwich, finishing nine points ahead of Liverpool.

After two league titles, an FA Cup and a European Cup Winners' Cup, Kendall left for Athletic Bilbao in 1987, with Colin Harvey taking over. Harvey guided Everton to fourth in 1987/88, eighth in 1988/89, and sixth in 1989/90. In October 1990, with Everton in eighteenth, Harvey was replaced first by Jimmy Gabriel, then by Kendall, who returned to lead Everton to ninth and a Zenith Data Systems Cup final, where they lost 4–1 to Crystal Palace.

FANTAIL

Formed in 1974, Fantail joined the Kirkby Newtown Combination for the 1974/75 season, winning the First Division at the first attempt and finishing runners-up in the FA Sunday Junior Cup, losing 1–0 to Stanley Vics. They won the Premier Division on promotion in 1975/76 and joined the Liverpool Sunday League in 1976/77, winning the Fourth Division and the Liverpool Sunday Premier Cup, beating Croxteth Royal British Legion 1–0.

They won the Third Division in 1978/79, the Second Division in 1979/80, and the National Sunday Cup by beating Twin Foxes 1–0. They retained the National Sunday Cup in 1980/81 by beating Mackintosh 1–0 and won the Liverpool Sunday League First Division. In 1982/83, Fantail were runners-up to Eagle FC in the Premier Division.

In 1988, they resigned from the Liverpool Sunday League, returning to the Kirkby Newtown Combination after a disciplinary dispute. In 1989, they joined the Liverpool Business Houses League as Toshiba Sharples and merged with Windmill FC in 1991.

FLORENCE ALBION

Florence Albion won the I Zingari Challenge Cup in 1971/72 but were relegated in 1975/76 after finishing bottom of the I Zingari League First Division. They regained First Division status in 1979/80 by winning the Second Division on goal difference ahead of Collegiate Old Boys. They were runners-up in the 1980/81 Liverpool Amateur Cup, losing 4–0 to St Dominics.

Relegated again in 1982/83, they returned to the First Division in 1983/84 after finishing second to Aigburth Peoples Hall in the Second Division. They won the I Zingari League in 1984/85, finishing two points ahead of Merseyside Police, and won the Liverpool Amateur Cup, beating BRNESC. They finished third from bottom in 1986/87, and the club folded soon after.

FORMBY

Formby joined the Cheshire County League in 1971/72, finishing twentieth of twenty-two clubs. In 1977/78, they won the Liverpool Senior Cup, beating Tranmere Rovers 1–0 at Brows Lane. They remained in the Cheshire League until it dissolved in 1981/82, then became founder members of the North West Counties League in 1982/83, finishing sixteenth in the First Division.

They were runners-up in the 1984/85 Liverpool Senior Cup, losing to Marine, and were relegated to the Second Division of the North West Counties League at the end of 1985/86. After finishing eleventh in their first Second Division season, they were promoted back to the First Division in 1987/88 but were relegated again in 1988/89.

GARSWOOD UNITED

Garswood joined the Warrington Football League in 1972/73 and won the Second Division in 1973/74, also reaching the Guardian Cup final, where they lost to Vulcan. They secured a ten-year lease on their ground that year. In 1974/75, they were runners-up in the First Division to Golborne Sports, and in 1975/76, they finished as runners-up again on goal difference.

In 1976/77, they won the Premier Division and Guardian Cup, beating Greenall Whitley 1–0. They joined the Liverpool County Combination Second Division in 1978/79, beating Rainford North End 2–0 in their first game and finishing as champions, earning promotion to the First Division and winning the Lord Wavertree Cup against Aintree SS.

In 1979/80, they finished as First Division runners-up to St Dominics by one point and won the Liverpool Junior Cup, beating United Welding. Relegated later in the 1980s, they left the league at the end of 1987/88 to join the Mid-Cheshire League Second Division in 1988/89, winning promotion to the First Division in 1989/90 after finishing ten points clear of Linotype Reserves.

HALTON LADIES
Formed in 1972, they played in the Merseyside and Wirral Ladies Football League, losing all but one game during their first season, 1972/73.

HARROWBY
In 1972/73, Harrowby won the Wirral Amateur Cup, beating Bromborough Pool. However, difficulties in securing a suitable ground forced them to withdraw from the West Cheshire League, and the club became defunct.

HESWALL
In 1971/72, Heswall added a reserve side to the West Cheshire League Second Division. In 1976/77, the first team finished as runners-up in the First Division, sixteen points behind Cammell Laird, and won the Wirral Amateur Cup, beating Poulton Victoria. In 1978/79, they lost 3–2 to Cammell Laird in the Pyke Cup final.

In 1984/85, Heswall won the West Cheshire League on goal difference from Mersey Royal and won the Wirral Senior Cup, beating Cammell Laird 1–0 at Prenton Park. They also won the Pyke Cup, beating Poulton Victoria. In 1986/87, they won the Wirral Amateur Cup against Vauxhall Motors and were runners-up in the West Cheshire League, two points behind Cammell Laird.

They regained the league title in 1987/88 by one point from General Chemicals and won the West Cheshire Bowl in 1988/89. In 1989/90, the reserves won the Second Division on goal difference from Capenhurst, and the club were runners-up in the Wirral Amateur Cup, losing to Stork, and won the West Cheshire Bowl again. In 1990/91, the reserves retained the Second Division title, this time by four points from Cammell Laird reserves, while the first team were runners-up in the Wirral Amateur Cup and Wirral Senior Cup. In 1991/92, Heswall won the Wirral Senior Cup, beating Bromborough Pool, but lost the Pyke Cup final to Cammell Laird.

JABISCO
The team disbanded at the end of the 1973/74 season, leaving just one team playing in the Liverpool Shipping League. They won the Liverpool Shipping League in 1990/91.

KIRKBY TOWN AND KNOWSLEY UNITED
In 1971/72, Kirkby Town were relegated to the Lancashire Combination after finishing bottom of the league. They were Lancashire Combination runners-up in 1976/77, finishing fourth in 1977/78, their last season in the competition. They joined the Cheshire County League Second Division for 1978/79, finishing fourth, and were promoted in 1979/80 after finishing third. However, they were relegated from the First Division in 1980/81 after finishing second from bottom, likely due to financial issues, with fans working to keep the club alive.

They finished seventh in their last Cheshire League Second Division season before joining the North West Counties League Second Division in 1982/83. The club resigned at the end of that season, missed 1983/84, but rejoined in 1984/85, winning the Third Division by three points from Colwyn Bay. They won the Second Division in 1985/86 by seven points from Rossendale United and were promoted to the First Division, finishing fourth in 1986/87 and winning the Liverpool Senior Cup.

In 1988, they changed their name to Knowsley United and took over Alt Park from Huyton Rugby League Club. They finished as runners-up in the North

West Counties League in 1988/89, six points behind Rossendale United, and won the North West Counties League Challenge Cup. In 1989/90, they were runners-up, three points behind Warrington Town, and in 1990/91, they won the North West Counties League title by seven points from Colwyn Bay.

In 1991, Knowsley United Ladies formed from Newton Ladies and joined the Women's National League Premier Division, finishing fourth in the league's first season, 1991/92. The men's team started the 1991/92 season in the Northern Premier League, finishing eighth in the First Division.

LEASOWE PACIFIC (LADIES)

Leasowe formed in 1985 when Dolphin five-a-side team merged with Hoylake Ladies (both formed in 1983) to become Leasowe Ladies FC. Under this name, they won the Women's FA Cup at Old Trafford. Later, sponsored by the Pacific Pub in Birkenhead, they became Leasowe Pacific. They joined and won the Merseyside and Wirral Women's League and Cup double twice before moving on to the North West Women's Regional Football League First Division in 1989/90, winning it at the first attempt by five points from Preston Rangers. They retained the title in 1990/91 by one point and won it again in 1991/92 by two points, both times ahead of Preston Rangers and St Helens Ladies respectively.

LEYFIELD

Leyfield were runners-up in the Liverpool League Second Division in 1971/72, earning promotion to the First Division, but were relegated back at the end of 1973/74. In 1976/77, they gained promotion as runners-up and finished as First Division runners-up in 1981/82. They joined the I Zingari Alliance Second Division, winning it at the first attempt and gaining promotion. They finished as runners-up in the First Division and joined the I Zingari League in 1987/88, finishing third in their first season.

LITHERLAND REMYCA

Litherland progressed through the Alliance leagues, winning promotion to the I Zingari League Third Division in 1973/74. They won the Third

Division in 1974/75 by ten points from Warbreck, going unbeaten with twenty-two wins and four draws, and also won the I Zingari Challenge Cup in 1975/76. They were promoted to the First Division in 1976/77 after finishing as Second Division runners-up to Sefton & District.

In 1982/83, they were runners-up to Merseyside Police by one point and won the I Zingari Roy Wade Memorial Trophy in 1984/85. They became Premier Division champions in 1987/88 by four points from East Villa and were runners-up to Netherley Royal British Legion in 1988/89, also winning the I Zingari Challenge Cup against Aigburth Peoples Hall.

In 1990/91, they won the Lancashire Amateur Cup, beating Wythenshawe Amateurs 1–0 after extra time at Burscough, and finished as runners-up to Aigburth Peoples Hall in 1991/92.

LIVERPOOL

In 1972/73, Liverpool won the league and the UEFA Cup (see Europe chapter). They went top in September with a 5–0 win over Sheffield United and stayed top after a strong run of six wins and three draws, despite a defeat at Old Trafford. Their next defeat came on 27 January 1973 against Wolves. The title race was close, with Leeds United and Arsenal one point behind. A 2–0 defeat to Arsenal at Anfield left Liverpool second, but they regained top spot with a 2–1 win against Ipswich and did not relinquish it again, winning the title by three points ahead of Arsenal.

In 1973/74, Liverpool won the FA Cup. Their run began with a 2–2 draw at home against Doncaster on 5 January, followed by a 3–2 replay win on 8 January, with goals from Keegan and Cormack. Another replay was required against Carlisle, with a 0–0 draw at Anfield followed by a 2–0 away win. They beat Ipswich in the fifth round, Bristol City in the quarter-finals, and Leicester in the semi-final replay at Villa Park. Liverpool won the final at Wembley, beating Newcastle United 3–0.

In 1975/76, Liverpool won the league and the UEFA Cup (see Europe chapter), having finished as runners-up the previous season. They reached the top on 20 December with a 2–0 win over QPR, briefly lost it, but regained the lead in February after beating Leeds. From early March, they remained unbeaten, with eight wins and a draw, securing the title with a 3–1 win at Molineux on the final day, finishing one point ahead of QPR.

In 1976/77, Liverpool won the league and the European Cup (see Europe chapter). They hit form at the end of October and remained no lower than second place, staying unbeaten at home all season. In April, a 2–0 win over Arsenal and an Ipswich defeat to Leeds put Liverpool top with a game in hand, with Manchester City three points behind. After beating Ipswich and Manchester United, they secured the title, finishing one point ahead of Manchester City.

In 1977/78, Liverpool won the European Cup (see Europe chapter). In 1978/79, they won the league, having finished runners-up the previous season. A strong start saw them beat Tottenham Hotspur 7–0 at Anfield in September. Liverpool had dominated the league and finished eight points ahead of Nottingham Forest to win another title.

In 1979/80, Liverpool began their title defence with a stuttering start but were top by January, two points ahead of Manchester United with a game in hand. They went on to be just ahead of Manchester United at top spot for the rest of the season and finished the season as Champions, two points ahead of United.

In 1980/81, Liverpool won the European Cup (see Europe chapter) and the League Cup. Their League Cup campaign started slowly as they sat eighth in the league after losing 2–0 to Leicester City before the second-round tie against Bradford City. They lost the away leg 1–0 but won the return at Anfield 4–0 to progress 4–1 on aggregate. Liverpool's form improved as they beat Swindon 5–0 at Anfield in the third round and Portsmouth 4–1 in the fourth round. By the fifth–round tie against Birmingham at Anfield, Liverpool were second in the league and won 3–1 to set up a semi-final against Manchester City. They won the first leg 1–0 at Maine Road through Ray Kennedy and drew 1–1 in the return to win 2–1 on aggregate. In the final at Wembley against West Ham United, Alan Kennedy equalised with two minutes of extra time remaining to force a replay. At Villa Park, Kenny Dalglish and Alan Hansen scored in the first half to secure a 2–1 win and Liverpool's first League Cup. Liverpool finished fifth in the league that season.

In 1981/82, Liverpool returned to title-winning form, claiming the league and League Cup double. Their League Cup defence began with two emphatic wins over Exeter City, 5–0 at Anfield and 6–0 away. In the third round, Liverpool beat Middlesbrough 4–1 at Anfield, with Kevin Sheedy scoring the opener. After a 0–0 draw at Highbury in the fourth round, Liverpool beat Arsenal 3–0 after extra time in the replay at Anfield. A 0–0 draw at Anfield against Barnsley in the fifth round was followed by a 3–1 win in the replay. In the semi-final, Liverpool defeated Ipswich Town 4–2 on aggregate. In the final at Wembley against Tottenham Hotspur, Ronnie Whelan equalised late on before Liverpool scored twice in extra time to secure a second consecutive League Cup. Liverpool won the league title by four points from Ipswich Town.

In 1982/83, Liverpool secured another league and League Cup double. By the end of September, they were top after a 5–0 win over Southampton. In the League Cup, they beat Ipswich Town 4–1 on aggregate in the second round, Tottenham Hotspur 1–0 in the third round, Norwich City in the fourth, and West Ham United 2–1 in the fifth. They defeated Burnley 3–1 on aggregate in the semi-final to set up a final against Manchester United. By then, Liverpool were more than ten points clear at the top of the league. They won the league with five games remaining, finishing eleven points ahead of Watford.

In 1983/84, Liverpool won a treble of the league, European Cup (see Europe chapter) and League Cup. They reached the top of the league in November and never relinquished it. In the League Cup, they beat Brentford 8–1 on aggregate in the second round, Fulham after a replay, Birmingham City after a replay, and Sheffield Wednesday in the fifth round, also after a replay. They beat Walsall 4–2 on aggregate in the semi-final to reach the final against Everton, winning the Milk Cup. Liverpool secured the league title with a 0–0 draw at Notts County, finishing three points ahead of Southampton.

In 1985/86 in the league they were neck and neck with Everton throughout the season. Going into the last game of the season, they needed a win or a draw to win the title. They beat Chelsea at Stamford Bridge, thanks to a Kenny Dalglish goal, to lift the title and in the FA Cup Final a week later at Wembley they beat Everton 3–1 (Rush 2, Johnston 1) to claim the club's first League and FA Cup double.

In 1987/88, Liverpool won their seventeenth league title. They reached the top in October, with QPR and Arsenal close behind. By December, they were seven points clear of Arsenal and unbeaten. At the end of January, they were seventeen points clear of Nottingham Forest. Everton ended their 29-game unbeaten run in March with a 1–0 win at Goodison Park, but Liverpool secured the title with a 1–0 win over Tottenham at Anfield, finishing nine points ahead of Manchester United. Liverpool narrowly missed a double, losing the FA Cup final to Wimbledon.

In 1988/89, Liverpool's season was overshadowed by the Hillsborough tragedy (see separate section). They lost the title in their final match against Arsenal but won the all-Merseyside FA Cup final against Everton 3–2 after extra time.

Liverpool won their eighteenth league title in 1989/90. They reached the top after a 2–1 win over Sheffield Wednesday and remained there for most of the season, despite Aston Villa briefly overtaking them in March. Liverpool secured the title with two games to spare by beating QPR 2–1 at Anfield as Villa could only draw with Norwich. Liverpool finished nine points clear at the top.

Liverpool reserves won the Central League with Five straight wins between 1972/73 and 1976/77 and four straight wins between 1978/79 and 1981/82. They also won two consecutive titles in 1983/84 and 1984/85 and won again in 1989/90.

LIVERPOOL FEDS
Formed in 1991, Liverpool Feds originated as a federation between St Katherine's and Notre Dame Colleges of Hope University.

LIVERPOOL NALGO
The National Association of Local Government Officers (NALGO) were relegated from the I Zingari League First Division in 1973/74. They won

the Liverpool Amateur Cup in 1982/83, beating Aintree Villa, and returned to the Premier Division in 1983/84, finishing fourth, although they lost the I Zingari Challenge Cup to Aintree Villa. They won the Liverpool Amateur Cup again in 1987/88, beating Yorkshire Copper Tubing.

LOBSTER

Lobster won the Premier Division title in 1972/73 but lost the League Cup final 2–0 to Coach. They won the title and Liverpool Sunday Premier Cup in 1973/74. In 1974/75, they became the first winners of the Cup Winners Shield, beating Easby 2–1, and won the league title again. They secured a third consecutive title in 1975/76.

In 1978/79, Lobster became the area's first team to win the FA National Sunday Cup, beating Carlton United 3–2 at Haig Avenue, and also won the Liverpool Sunday League title. In 1980, they were ruled out of the FA National Sunday Cup for not having an enclosed ground. Lobster won the First Division title in 1988/89.

LUCAS SPORTS

In 1972/73, Lucas Sports reserves beat Tinlings 4–0 to win the Liverpool Junior Cup. Following the closure of the Lucas factory in Fazakerley, the team changed its name to Orrell between 1974/75 and 1975/76 while continuing in the Liverpool County Combination. They dropped out shortly after but returned as Lucas Sports in 1980/81, earning promotion to the First Division in 1982/83, where they finished bottom and were relegated.

MAGHULL

In 1971/72, Maghull finished tenth in the Liverpool County Combination before joining the Lancashire Combination in 1972/73, finishing fifteenth. They won the Lancashire Combination Challenge Cup in 1977/78 and joined the Cheshire County League Second Division in 1978/79.

Maghull won the Liverpool Challenge Cup in consecutive years, 1979/80 and 1980/81, beating Bootle and Vulcan respectively. They became founder members of the North West Counties League in 1982/83, placed in the

Third Division, finishing twelfth. They were runners-up in the Liverpool Challenge Cup in 1983/84, losing to St Dominics, and also finished as runners-up in the North West Counties Reserve Division Two. They won the Liverpool Challenge Cup in 1985/86.

Following the removal of the Third Division in 1986/87, Maghull moved into the enlarged Second Division, finishing sixth in 1987/88. Their reserves were runners-up in the North West Counties Reserve Division Challenge Cup in 1986/87, won the Reserve Division in 1987/88, and won the Reserve Division West in 1988/89. In 1991, a fire damaged their clubhouse.

MARINE

In 1971/72, Marine were Cheshire League Cup runners-up, losing 2–1 on aggregate to Oswestry. Their reserves won the Liverpool Challenge Cup, beating Earle, but lost the Liverpool Amateur Cup final the following evening to Aintree Villa. In 1972/73, Roly Howard took over as manager, and Marine finished as Cheshire League runners-up behind Buxton.

The trophies soon followed. In 1973/74, Marine won the Cheshire County League on goal difference from Rossendale United. In 1974/75, they were Cheshire League Cup runners-up, losing 2–1 on aggregate to Burscough, but won the Cheshire Shield, beating Rossendale 3–0. In 1975/76, Marine won the Cheshire County League by one point over Chorley, the Liverpool Senior Non-League Cup against Skelmersdale United 3–0, and retained the Cheshire Shield.

In 1976/77, they won the Liverpool Senior Non-League Cup again, beating St Helens Town 3–2 in the last final before its amalgamation with the Liverpool Senior Cup. In 1977/78, Marine won the Cheshire County League for a third time, finishing four points ahead of Stalybridge Celtic, but were refused entry to the Northern Premier League due to a technicality regarding resignation from the Cheshire League. Their first floodlit game was against Darwen in September 1977.

In 1978/79, Marine finished third in the Cheshire County League, won the Lancashire Junior Cup against Chorley after a replay, and won the

Liverpool Senior Cup against South Liverpool after a replay. They reapplied for the Northern Premier League and, after Atherstone Town resigned, Marine successfully took their place, starting in 1979/80 with a 1–0 loss to Runcorn and finishing their first season in tenth.

In 1980/81, Marine were Northern Premier League Cup runners-up, losing 4–3 to Runcorn. In 1983/84, they were Northern Premier League President's Cup finalists, losing on away goals to Workington. In 1984/85, they won the Northern Premier League Cup against Goole Town and were runners-up in the Peter Swales Shield, while also winning the Liverpool Senior Cup against Formby.

In 1985/86, Marine finished as Northern Premier League runners-up, two points behind Gateshead, and were Northern Premier League Cup runners-up, losing to Hyde United. In 1986/87, they were President's Cup finalists, losing to Macclesfield Town.

Following the expansion of the Northern Premier League in 1987/88, Marine were placed in the Premier Division, winning the Lancashire Trophy against Morecambe and the Liverpool Senior Cup against Southport. In 1988/89, they were Liverpool Senior Cup runners-up, losing to South Liverpool. In 1989/90, they regained the Liverpool Senior Cup, beating South Liverpool.

In 1990/91, Marine won the Lancashire Trophy against Great Harwood but were Liverpool Senior Cup runners-up to Southport. In 1991/92, they finished as Northern Premier League runners-up, fourteen points behind Stalybridge Celtic, won the Northern Premier League Cup against Frickley Athletic, and were Liverpool Senior Cup runners-up, losing to Tranmere Rovers.

MERSEYSIDE POLICE

Known as Liverpool & Bootle Police, they won the league in 1973/74 by three points from Aintree Villa. From 1974/75, they became Merseyside Police. They finished as runners-up to Inter in 1981/82 and won the league in 1982/83 by one point from REMYCA United, also winning the I Zingari Challenge Cup.

In 1983/84, they won the Lancashire Amateur Cup against Broughton Amateurs. In 1984/85, their final season in the league, they finished runners-up to Florence Albion. They joined the West Cheshire League in 1985/86, winning the Second Division at the first attempt and also claiming the West Cheshire Bowl.

In 1988/89, they had a remarkable season, finishing as First Division runners-up to Cammell Laird while winning the Lancashire Amateur Cup against Aigburth Peoples Hall, the Liverpool Amateur Cup against East Villa, and the Pyke Cup against General Chemicals. They won the Lancashire Amateur Cup again in 1991/92, beating Rochdale St Clements.

MERSEY ROYAL

In 1971/72, Mersey Royal were runners-up in the Wirral Combination to Blue Union and won the Wirral Junior Cup. They won the Wirral Combination in 1974/75 and retained it in 1975/76 before joining the West Cheshire League Second Division in 1976/77, finishing fifth.

In 1977/78, they were Wirral Junior Cup runners-up to Shell. In 1980/81, they won the Wirral Amateur Cup against Cammell Laird reserves. They finished as Second Division runners-up in 1981/82 before winning the division in 1982/83 and reaching the Wirral Junior Cup final, where they lost to Mallaby. They won the division again in 1983/84 and earned promotion.

In 1984/85, Mersey Royal won the Cheshire Amateur Cup against West Kirby. In their first First Division season 1984/85 they were League runners-up and 1985/86, they finished runners-up again this time to Heswall on goal difference and won the Wirral Senior Cup against Cammell Laird. They finished runners-up again in 1986/87 to Vauxhall Motors.

In 1987/88, they won the Pyke Cup against Merseyside Police, but in 1988/89, they lost the Wirral Senior Cup final to Higher Bebington. They were runners-up in 1989/90 to Cammell Laird on goal difference, winning the Pyke Cup against Newton, and were runners-up again in 1990/91, ten points behind Cammell Laird.

MOND RANGERS (RUNCORN TOWN FORMED 1968)

Originally CKD, the works team for Castner Kellner's D section, they joined the Runcorn Sunday League in 1968. In 1970, they became Mond , and in 1974, Mond Rangers, joining the Warrington and District League.

They joined the West Cheshire League Second Division in 1984/85, finishing seventh, and by the end of 1991/92 had recorded two sixth-placed finishes.

N.E.L.T.C. (NORTH EAST LIVERPOOL TECHNICAL COLLEGE)

NELTC joined the I Zingari League in 1971/72, finishing sixth in the Third Division, where they remained throughout the 1980s and into the 1990s. In 1989/90, they updated their name from NETC to NELTC.

NEW BRIGHTON

In March 1972, New Brighton's shareholders voted to sell the Tower Grounds for housing, despite attempts by local businessmen and a stock car promoter to save the site for sport. In 1977, the club was wound up and moved to Carr Lane, Hoylake, before re-forming in 1978 as New Brighton, retaining the same team.

They finished second-bottom and were relegated from the Cheshire County League. They moved to Vista Park, Greasby, sharing with Newtown of the West Cheshire League. An administrative error in 1981/82 cost them Cheshire League status, and they joined the South Wirral League Premier Division. Without a permanent home, they played across Wirral until folding in the summer of 1983.

NEWTON

Newton won the Wirral Senior Cup in 1973/74. They spent most of the 1970s and 1980s in the lower half of the West Cheshire League, finishing bottom in 1976/77 and 1978/79, with fourth in 1981/82 being a highlight. They finished bottom again in 1985/86.

NICOSIA

Formed by Liverpool's Cypriot community in the early 1980s, Nicosia joined the Huyton Sunday League and were runners-up in 1982/83. They joined the Business Houses League Second Division in 1983/84, winning it unbeaten and also claiming the Liverpool Sunday Junior Cup and Business Houses Junior Cup.

In 1984/85, they won the First Division unbeaten and were promoted to the Premier Division, which they won for seven consecutive seasons from 1985/86 to 1991/92. During this period, they also won the FA National Sunday Cup in 1990/91, beating London club Ouzavich 3–2 in the final at Wigan.

NORTHERN NOMADS

Northern Nomads spent most of their time in mid-table in the Manchester League before being relegated in 1976/77. They won the First Division in 1978/79 and finished as runners-up to Main Road before folding in 1985.

OLD XAVERIAN

Back in the I Zingari League First Division in 1971/72, Old Xaverian finished ninth and were I Zingari Challenge Cup runners-up. In 1972/73, they moved to Eastway in Maghull. They were relegated to the Second Division in 1973/74. Their reserves were promoted to the I Zingari Combination First Division in 1977/78. In 1981/82, they returned to the First Division as Second Division runners-up, behind Girobank. They were relegated from the Premier Division in 1985/86 but were promoted back for the 1988/89 season.

ORMSKIRK / GUINNESS EXPORTS

In 1972/73, Ormskirk finished 14th in the Cheshire County League. In 1973/74, their final season, they finished 21st out of 22 clubs.

OYSTER MARTYRS

Formed in 1974 by Pat and Shaun McNulty, using the Oyster Pub in Croxteth as their base, Oyster Martyrs joined the Liverpool Sunday League and moved up and down its divisions, reaching the Premier Division by the 1990s.

POULTON VICTORIA

In 1971/72, Poulton won the Cheshire Amateur Cup, Pyke Cup, and West Cheshire League, three points ahead of West Kirby. They won the Wirral Senior Cup in 1972/73, beating Port Sunlight, and were league runners-up by one point. In 1973, they purchased Limekiln Lane in Wallasey, naming it Victoria Park. In 1973/74, they were runners-up in both the Wirral Senior Cup and West Cheshire League and won the West Cheshire Bowl.

Poulton won the Wirral Senior Cup in 1974/75 and the Wirral Amateur Cup, achieving the same double in 1975/76. They finished as league runners-up to Cammell Laird and their reserves won the Second Division. The reserves retained the Second Division title in 1976/77 and 1977/78. Poulton were frequent runners-up in the Wirral Senior Cup and West Cheshire Bowl and won the Wirral Amateur Cup in 1977/78. They won the Cheshire Amateur Cup in 1978/79 and the Pyke Cup and West Cheshire League in 1979/80.

They continued to win cups, including the Wirral Senior Cup in 1982/83, the Pyke Cup and Wirral Amateur Cup in 1983/84, and the Pyke Cup again in 1990/91. In 1991/92, they were Wirral Amateur Cup runners-up and their reserves won the Second Division.

Poulton Victoria first team also League runners-up in 1975/76, 1977/78 and 1978/79

Between 1976/77 to 1979/80 they were Wirral senior cup runners-up to Cammell Lairds.

Wirral senior cup runners-up 1986/87

Wirral Amateur Cup runners-up 1976/77, 1978/79 and 1988/89

PRESCOT B.I.

Prescot B.I. were Liverpool County Combination runners-up in 1977/78 before joining the Cheshire County League Second Division, finishing eighth in 1978/79. They moved into the North West Counties League

Second Division in 1982/83, finishing 18th, and resigned in 1984 due to their artificial pitch being rejected by the league. Many members went on to form Huyton Town in 1985. Prescot B.I. later joined the St Helens Combination in 1985/86, winning the title at the first attempt.

PRESCOT TOWN/PRESCOT CABLES
Prescot Cables were voted out of the Lancashire Combination in 1974/75 after finishing second-bottom. A new owner saved the club, allowing them to join the Mid-Cheshire League in 1975/76, finishing seventh. In 1976/77, they won the league by eight points and in 1977/78 came third, winning the Liverpool Challenge Cup against Waterloo Dock.

They joined the Cheshire County League Second Division in 1978/79, finishing third, and won the division in 1979/80 while also finishing as Liverpool Senior Cup runners-up. In 1980, they reverted to the 'Cables' name. They finished eighth in 1980/81 and Ninth in 1981/82 before joining the North West Counties League in 1982/83, finishing 15th.

Cables were relegated in 1985/86 but returned to the First Division in 1987/88. In 1990, the club's name was changed to Prescot FC.

ROCKVILLE (WALLASEY)
From 1972/73 to 1991/92, Rockville remained in the lower half of the Third Division.

ROMA (ROYAL OAK MUIRHEAD AVENUE)
Originally Mentmore FC, the club became Royal Oak Muirhead Avenue in 1972, using the acronym ROMA. They joined the I Zingari Alliance Second Division in 1971/72 and steadily climbed the league, winning promotion to the I Zingari League in 1977/78. They won the Third Division in 1978/79 and finished third in the Second Division in 1979/80.

Roma won the Liverpool Junior Cup in 1986/87 and secured the Second Division title in 1988/89, finishing eighth in their first Premier Division season in 1989/90.

RUNCORN

Runcorn reserves rejoined the West Cheshire League in 1972. The first team won the Cheshire Senior Cup in 1973/74, beating Macclesfield. In 1974/75, they were Northern Premier League runners-up and won the NPL Challenge Cup and Cheshire Senior Cup. In 1975/76, they won the Northern Premier League and were Cheshire Senior Cup runners-up.

They continued to collect honours, including the NPL Challenge Cup in 1979/80, the NPL and Peter Swales Shield in 1980/81, and promotion to the Alliance Premier League in 1981/82, where they became champions at the first attempt. However, they were denied Football League entry due to Canal Street's facilities.

Runcorn won the Alliance Premier League Bob Lord Trophy in 1982/83 and the Cheshire Senior Cup in 1984/85, 1985/86, 1986/87, 1987/88 and 1988/89, reaching six consecutive finals. Runners up in that cup in 1978/78, 1981/82 and 1983/84. They were FA Trophy runners-up in 1985/86 and Bob Lord Trophy runners-up in 1991/92.

ST. ALOYSIUS

Formed before WW2. They moved on after the war to the Prescot and District League and joined the CMS League in 1957. They joined the Liverpool League in 1962 and won the Liverpool League title in 1984/85. In the Houston cup they won it in 1964/65, 1976/77 and 1983/84 and they also appeared in the Sawyer and Lord Colwyn Cup Finals.

ST DOMINICS

St Dominics won the Fred Micklesfield Cup and George Mahon Cup in 1971/72. They were Liverpool Amateur Cup and George Mahon Cup runners-up in 1974/75, repeating this in 1976/77. After finishing as league runners-up in 1978/79, they won the Liverpool County Combination in 1979/80 and the George Mahon Cup.

They won the Liverpool Amateur Cup in 1980/81 and claimed their first Lancashire Amateur Cup in 1981/82, beating Wythenshawe

Amateurs, while also winning the Liverpool Challenge Cup and the League title. St Dominics won the league and Liverpool Challenge Cup again in 1982/83, plus a second Lancashire Amateur Cup against Wythenshawe.

They were runners-up in 1983/84 but won the Liverpool Challenge Cup again and repeated the win in 1984/85. They took the league title in 1985/86, won a third Lancashire Amateur Cup in 1986/87, and finished runners-up in league and cup competitions across the late 1980s and early 1990s, narrowly missing out on titles in 1990/91 and 1991/92.

ST HELENS LADIES

Formed in 1976, St Helens Ladies joined the Merseyside and Wirral Women's Football League, winning the league and League Cup three seasons in a row from 1977/78 to 1979/80. They won the Women's FA Cup 1–0 against Preston North End at Enfield, but lost the following season's final 4–2 to Southampton Women at Knowsley Road. Moving to the North West Women's Football League, they won the league in 1981/82 and 1982/83, also claiming the League Cup in 1982/83. They won the Divisional Cup in 1983/84 and the league title again in 1986/87. In 1989/90, St Helens competed in the newly renamed North West Women's Regional Football League, finishing fifth. They were runners-up in 1991/92, finishing two points behind Leasowe Pacific.

ST HELENS TOWN

St Helens Town won the Lancashire Combination in 1971/72, finishing six points clear of Accrington Stanley, and were Lancashire Combination League Cup runners-up in 1973/74. They joined the Cheshire League in 1975/76, finishing 14th in their first season. In 1976/77, Town were runners-up in the last Liverpool Senior Non-League Cup Final, losing 3–2 to Marine. A founder member of the North West Counties League in 1982/83, Town finished second from bottom in the First Division, winning only five games. From 1983/84, they remained a mid-table side.

Their reserves finished as runners-up in the North West Counties Reserve Division Two in 1984/85 and in the Reserve Division in 1985/86.

Town remained with the league after the 1986/87 restructure and won the FA Vase in 1986/87, beating Warrington Town 3–2 at Wembley. They finished fifth in the newly formed Division One in 1987/88.

SEAFORTH FELLOWSHIP
Seaforth won the Crosby and District Sunday League Division Four in 1983/84, Division Three in 1984/85, and Division Two in 1985/86.

SKELMERSDALE UNITED
Skelmersdale United spent five seasons in the Northern Premier League, mostly in mid to lower table, but won the Liverpool Senior Non-League Cup in 1973/74 and 1974/75. They left the NPL in 1975/76, replacing their reserve side in the Lancashire Combination, where they finished tenth. After finishing eighth in 1977/78, they joined the Cheshire County League Second Division in 1978/79, finishing 16th. After several lower-half finishes, they joined the North West Counties League in 1982/83, finishing 11th in Division Two, and were League Cup runners-up to Darwen after a replay.

Their reserves won the NWC Reserve Division Cup in 1983/84 and were runners-up in the Reserve Division West in 1988/89 and 1989/90.

SOUTHPORT
Southport won the Fourth Division in 1972/73, clinching promotion with a 2–0 win at Crewe and the title with a final-day 1–1 draw against Hartlepool. They were relegated back to the Fourth Division in 1973/74. They won the Liverpool Senior Cup in 1974/75, beating Liverpool, but lost 7–0 to them in the 1975/76 final.

In 1977/78, Southport dropped out of the Football League after failing re-election, replaced by Wigan Athletic. They joined the Northern Premier League, winning their first match at South Liverpool 1–0 and finishing fifth in their debut season.

In 1980, Southport announced they would enter liquidation unless £25,000 was raised, but were saved by the Hall brothers from Chorley. In

1983/84, they won the Lancashire Floodlit Trophy, and in 1985/86, they were Liverpool Senior Cup runners-up to South Liverpool.

Ground safety measures restricted capacity in 1987, and they were runners-up in the NPL President's Cup in 1987/88, losing to South Liverpool, and in the Liverpool Senior Cup to Marine. In 1990/91, they won the NPL Challenge Cup, beating Buxton 4–1, and the Liverpool Senior Cup, beating Marine 4–0, but were runners-up in the President's Inter-League Cup. In 1991/92, they lost the Lancashire Junior Cup final to Great Harwood.

SOUTH LIVERPOOL

South Liverpool spent much of the 1970s in the lower half of the Northern Premier League. In 1983/84, they won the Liverpool Senior Cup and the Lancashire Junior Cup, and claimed the NPL Challenge Cup on penalties against Hyde United.

They retained the Liverpool Senior Cup in 1985/86, beating Southport. In 1987/88, they won the NPL President's Cup, beating Southport, and won the Liverpool Senior Cup again in 1988/89, beating Marine, but were NPL President's Cup runners-up to Bangor City.

Holly Park was closed in 1990 due to safety issues, and the club moved to share Bucks Park with Bootle. In 1991, the club folded due to debts and resigned from the NPL. A new committee, under the name South Liverpool 1991, preserved the club's name, merging with Cheshire Lines in July 1992 to form Cheshire Lines South Liverpool.

STANTONDALE

Originally the British-American Tobacco team, Stantondale reformed in 1986, joining the Liverpool County Combination Second Division and won it in 1987/88 and in 1988/89, finishing ninth in the First Division. They were Liverpool Junior Cup runners-up that season, losing to Evans. In 1990/91, Stantondale won the league, one point ahead of St Dominics, and the Liverpool Junior Cup, beating Crosfields 3–2. They finished third in their final season in the Combination in 1991/92.

STORK

Stork won the Pyke Cup in 1980/81, beating Runcorn 3–0. They won the Cheshire Amateur Cup in 1986/87, beating Vauxhall Motors 4–3, and the Wirral Amateur Cup in 1989/90, beating Heswall, but lost the Pyke Cup final to Poulton Victoria.

In the West Cheshire League they were mostly mid-table and lost the Pyke cup in 1990/91.

TRANMERE ROVERS

Tranmere were relegated to the Fourth Division in 1974/75 after a draw against Huddersfield. Johnny King took over as manager in April 1975, guiding them to promotion in 1975/76, finishing fourth. They finished 14th in the Third Division in 1976/77 but were relegated in 1978/79 after a draw against Walsall.

In 1979/80, Tranmere won the Cheshire Premier Cup, beating Chester, and retained it in 1981/82. They spent the 1980s mostly in the lower half of the Fourth Division, but finished runners-up in 1988/89, earning promotion to the Third Division.

In 1989 Tranmere moved from their old training ground of the Oval in Bebington that they had used of three decades into a purpose-built training ground at Bidston in Birkenhead. Two outdoor pitches were provided one with floodlights the other with Astroturf. The indoor area had dressing rooms, sauna, treatment clinic. Boot and kit rooms, offices, gymnasium, canteen and leisure/lecture room.

They finished fourth in 1989/90 but lost the play-off final to Notts County. In 1990/91, they finished fifth and won promotion to the Second Division, beating Bolton Wanderers 1–0 in the play-off final after extra time. They finished 14th in the Second Division in 1991/92. They were Associate Members Cup winners in 1990 after beating Bristol Rovers at Wembley, and runners up the following year.

Tranmere Rovers Ladies were promoted twice in two years, winning the Women's North West Regional League Division Four in 1990/91 and Division Three in 1991/92, losing just one game in each season.

UNIASCO

Uniasco won the Liverpool League in 1973/74 but lost to Bronte Old Boys in the Houston Cup Final. However, they won the Liverpool Junior Cup, beating Yorkshire Imperial Metals 2–1. Joining the Liverpool County Combination in 1982/83, they finished third that season, and then won the Liverpool Amateur Cup in 1985/86. In 1986/87, they won the Liverpool Challenge Cup, beating Waterloo Dock 5–4 on penalties. The following season, 1987/88, they won the Liverpool County Combination by nine points from Waterloo Dock, alongside the George Mahon Cup and the Liverpool Challenge Cup, beating St Dominics in the final. They narrowly missed out on a quadruple after losing to Earle in the Lancashire Amateur Cup semi-final. In 1988/89, Uniasco were expelled from the Liverpool County Combination due to unfulfilled fixtures caused by financial difficulties, leading to the club folding.

VAUXHALL MOTORS

In 1972/73, Vauxhall Motors were runners-up in the Pyke Cup Final, losing to Willaston, and added a reserve team in the Second Division. They remained a mid-table West Cheshire League First Division side for much of the 1970s. In 1981/82, they won the Wirral Junior Cup, beating Hoylake Athletic. The following season, they were Wirral Senior Cup runners-up to Poulton Victoria. In 1983/84, they finished as league runners-up, four points behind Cammell Laird, and lost the Wirral Senior Cup to West Kirby. In 1985/86, they won the league by two points ahead of Mersey Royal and also won the Wirral Amateur Cup, beating Capenhurst Villa. The following season, they won the Wirral Senior Cup against Poulton Victoria but lost the Wirral Amateur Cup final to Heswall. In 1987, Vauxhall Motors moved to Rivacre Park and were Cheshire Amateur Cup runners-up to Stork. From 1987/88, they played in both the West Cheshire League and the North West Counties League. They won the NWC Second Division in 1988/89 and finished fourth in 1989/90. In 1990/91, they won the NWC Challenge Cup and finished fifth, but dropped to 13th in 1991/92. In the West Cheshire League, their highest finish from 1987/88 to 1991/92 was fifth.

WALTON VILLAGE

Formed in 1976, Walton Village joined the Liverpool Central Amateur League for the 1976/77 season, reaching the Shallcross Cup Final. They moved to the Prescot and Knowsley League in 1977/78, finishing as First Division runners-up and cup finalists. The following season, they were Premier Division runners-up, won the Premier Cup, and reached the Bardsley Cup Final. In 1979/80, they joined the I Zingari Alliance Second Division, won the Charity Cup, and finished as runners-up in the league. In 1980/81, they won the Liverpool County Intermediate Cup and the I Zingari Alliance First Division, earning promotion to the I Zingari League Third Division. They won the Third Division at the first attempt, four points ahead of Dove, and won the Second Division in 1982/83 by twelve points. In their first Premier Division season in 1983/84, they finished as runners-up to Aintree Villa by one point. They remained in the Premier Division until finishing bottom in 1991/92.

WARRINGTON TOWN

Warrington Town were founder members of the Cheshire County League Second Division in 1978/79, finishing 14th. With the formation of the North West Counties League in 1982/83, they became founder members of the Third Division, finishing as runners-up to Colne Dynamoes and earning promotion to the Second Division, where they finished fourth in 1983/84. In 1986/87, they finished as runners-up to Droylsden in the Second Division, gaining promotion to the First Division, and reached the FA Vase Final at Wembley, losing 3–2 to St Helens Town. In 1989/90, Warrington Town won the NWC League title by three points ahead of Knowsley United, earning promotion to the Northern Premier League. They finished seventh in their first season in the NPL First Division in 1990/91.

WATERLOO DOCK

Waterloo Dock finished third in the Liverpool County Combination First Division in 1971/72 and were runners-up in 1972/73. In 1973/74, they finished fifth and were runners-up in the George Mahon Cup, losing to Bootle. They won the league in 1974/75, five points clear of Ainsdale, and also won the George Mahon Cup, while finishing runners-up in the Lancashire Amateur Cup. In 1975/76, they completed a treble, winning the league, George Mahon Cup, and Liverpool Amateur Cup, and were runners-up in the Liverpool Challenge Cup and Lancashire Amateur Cup. In 1976/77, they won the Liverpool Challenge Cup, beating Prescot, and finished as league runners-up. They won the league again in 1977/78 and George Mahon Cup, and the league again in 1978/79, ahead of Marine Reserves.

In 1980/81, they won the league by five points from St Dominics, and won the George Mahon Cup in 1982/83. They finished as league runners-up in 1984/85 and 1985/86, and won the league again in 1986/87, five points ahead of BRNESC. In 1987/88, they were runners-up to Uniasco, before winning back-to-back titles in 1988/89 and 1989/90. Also winning the Liverpool Challenge Cup in 1988/89. They also won the George Mahon Cup again in 1987 and 991.

WEST KIRBY
They were league runners up in 1980/81 and won the Pyke Cup in 1982/83 and 1985/86 and the Wirral Senior Cup in 1980/81 and 1983/84. They were relegated to Division Two in 1989/90.

WIGAN ATHLETIC
Wigan Athletic won the Northern Premier League Challenge Cup in 1971/72, beating Gainsborough Trinity and won the Lancashire Junior Cup. In 1972/73, they were FA Trophy runners-up to Scarborough and NPL Shield runners-up. In 1973/74, they won the Lancashire Junior Cup and the NPL Shield and finished as league runners-up by one point. They won the NPL in 1974/75, four points ahead of Runcorn, and the Shield again in 1975/76. Further Lancashire Junior Cup wins came in 1976/77 and 1977/78, with Wigan finishing runners-up in the NPL in 1977/78.

In 1978, Wigan were elected to the Football League, joining the Fourth Division and finishing sixth in their first season. In 1981/82, they finished third and were promoted to the Third Division, where they finished 18th in 1982/83. Wigan won the Football League Trophy in 1984/85 and reached the

Third Division play-offs in 1986/87, losing to Swindon Town in the semi-finals. The 1991/92 Lancashire Senior Challenge Cup was won by Wigan Athletic.

WHERE THEY PLAYED

The 1975 Safety of Sports Grounds Act allowed the Secretary of State for Sport to designate any sports ground with accommodation for more than 10,000 spectators, or 5,000 for Football League clubs, as requiring a safety certificate to admit spectators, with the safety certificates administered by local authorities. Clubs were given two years to bring their grounds up to the safety standards set out in the Act. They were also permitted to set up club lotteries to raise money for ground improvements. Additionally, the pools companies donated 10% of their incomes to a new Football Grounds Improvement Trust that was established that same year.

Ground grading was introduced in the 1980s, initially by the Vauxhall Conference, before expanding to cover all s. There are at least eight levels of grading for non-league teams. Grades A and B applied to the Conference National Division and the Conference North and South divisions. A Grade A ground must be capable of being upgraded to meet the criteria of the Football League and must allow fans to view the match, either standing or seated, along the full length of at least three sides of the pitch.

Grades C and D applied to the Northern Premier League, Premier Division, and First Division, requiring the same potential for upgrade to National League System standards. All grounds were required to have a clubhouse facility either on or adjacent to the ground, providing refreshments to spectators on matchdays. The ground must be located near the conurbation that bears the club's name, or to the place they are traditionally associated with, subject to the approval of the FA and the Board of Directors of the Football Conference. All clubs were required to disclose plans and details of any proposed future move to a new stadium or any significant alteration to their existing ground.

All pitches had to be of grass unless otherwise authorised, and any slope was not to exceed a gradient of 1:41 in any direction. The pitch dimensions were required to be a minimum of 100 metres by 64 metres, with goalposts and goal net supports of professional manufacture. Each technical area had to accommodate either eleven people with a minimum width of 5.5 metres or eight people with a minimum width of 4 metres. Clubs had to provide a safe, unimpeded passage for players and officials between the dressing rooms and the pitch, such as a permanent or retractable tunnel.

Dressing rooms had to be located within the enclosed area of the ground, be of sound construction, and be a minimum of 18 square metres, excluding shower and toilet areas. The referees' dressing room had to be a minimum of six square metres, containing at least one showerhead, one hand basin, and one toilet. New builds were required to provide separate rooms for male and female referees.

The Popplewell Report of July 1985 was commissioned by the government following the Bradford City stadium fire and the violence at the Birmingham City v Leeds United match at St Andrew's, where a wall collapse killed a 14-year-old fan. The inquiry also considered the Heysel Stadium disaster. Justice Popplewell's report, delivered on 24 July 1985, made recommendations on fire safety and crowd safety at football grounds. Among these were the immediate demolition of wooden football stands, the introduction of ID cards for football fans, the banning of away fans from matches, and the erection of perimeter fencing at grounds.

The Taylor Report of 1990, published in the wake of the Hillsborough disaster, made further significant recommendations. These included scrapping the supporters' ID card scheme, requiring all-seater stadiums for First and Second Division clubs by the end of 1994, the removal of spikes from perimeter fences, banning ticket touting, encouraging early kick-offs for high-risk games, increasing Sunday kick-offs, and providing better training for police and stewards.

Following the Taylor Report, the Football Licensing Authority (FLA) was established, with its primary role being the awarding of licences to football grounds in England and Wales. The FLA also advised the government on the introduction of all-seater stadiums and maintained the standards of grounds that retained terraces, while overseeing the implementation of the 1975 Safety of Sports Grounds Act.

ALT PARK, HUYTON

Huyton Town briefly moved into Alt Park, as did Eagle FC, a Sunday League team from the Eagle and Child Pub in Huyton. This club also suffered from vandalism at Alt Park, including a fire that destroyed the changing block in June 1986. Despite the Eagle Club's efforts, the ground had become somewhat dilapidated by the time Knowsley United took over in 1988. The Orr family, owners of Knowsley United, purchased Alt Park while searching for a home for Kirkby Town and set about renovating the stadium, adding new dressing rooms, improving the pitch, and installing various facilities to secure a licence to play matches there after starting the season with seven consecutive away games. A new pitch was necessary, as during its use by Huyton Rugby League Club, the ground was either muddy in winter or a dust bowl in summer due to poor drainage and its proximity to the River Alt. In 1991, Knowsley United's owners revamped Alt Park, using its reopening in July 1991 to confirm Knowsley United and its Ladies team as the rightful successors to Kirkby Town. The £850,000 revamp gave the ground a capacity of 9,000, with seating for 350 and covered standing for 3,500.

ANFIELD, LIVERPOOL

In 1970, plans were drawn up to rebuild the Main Stand, including the seating of the paddock area. By Liverpool's first match of the 1971-1972 season, on 14 August 1971 against Nottingham Forest, the spectator side of the Main Stand, which cost £500,000, was ready for use. The new stand added 4,000 seats, and the players had new dressing rooms, although the boardroom, offices, and treatment rooms were not yet completed; the stand was formally opened in March 1973. In 1977, fences were erected around the pitch perimeter, and in 1978, the Boys' Pen was closed to create more room for supporters. In 1980, the Main Stand became fully seated, including the paddock area. In 1981, most of the terraced housing in Kemlyn Road was demolished, apart from No. 26, where Joan and Nora Mason refused to move until 1990. In 1982, the Anfield Road Stand gained 4,380 seats, leaving a smaller standing area for 2,600 away supporters. In

1990, construction began on the Kemlyn Road Stand, which was opened on 1 September 1992 by UEFA President Lennart Johansson and renamed the "Centenary Stand."

BROWS LANE, FORMBY
By the late 1970s, the ground had a capacity of 4,000 with a covered stand and terracing. In the early hours of 15 September 1990, the social club and offices were destroyed by fire, with damages estimated at £100,000.

CANAL STREET, RUNCORN
In 1974, the FA awarded the ground a "B" rating, although the Football League downgraded it to a "C" in 1979. In 1981, Runcorn undertook £150,000 worth of refurbishment, including spending £10,000 on replacing benches with tip-up seating in the Wivern Place Stand, using new timber and cantilever steel, and adding a VIP and boardroom complex at the back. Other improvements included an updated public address system, a new path around the training pitch, and new turnstiles at the Social Club side. The new social club featured two main rooms, a large concert area for 200 people, and a lounge for 90.

BUCKS PARK, NETHERTON
Opened by Bootle FC in August 1978 at Copy Lane, Netherton, the ground hosted its first home game against Ford Motors. With a capacity of around 6,000, it lacked significant seating or covered standing but featured a clubhouse. An £8,000 Sports Council grant was used to build dressing rooms, and a new stand was planned for the following year. Bucks Park also became home to South Liverpool after their sale of Holly Park, bringing with them floodlights. The ground, with a 5,000 capacity, offered 400 seats and covered standing for 1,400. In 1984, a new stand accommodating 200 seats and a directors' box was constructed, along with new turnstiles.

GIGFY PARK, MIDDLEWOOD ROAD, AUGHTON GREEN
By 1978, the Guinness-owned factory site had enclosed the ground in glass, and according to some reports, the ground even featured a heated stand.

GOODISON PARK, WALTON

In 1972, Everton improved the Bullens Road roof and installed the ground's first computer ticketing system. The Boys' Pen was closed in 1977 to increase capacity, and at the end of the 1977-1978 season, ten-foot-high perimeter fences were installed around the terraces, removing the semi-circles at either end to create more space. In 1981, ten executive boxes were added in front of the Main Stand, available at £5,000 per season or £15,000 for three seasons, while the Upper Bullens received new seating. In 1986, the Bullens Road and Gwladys Street roofs were joined. The Main Stand's Enclosure was converted to all-seating in 1987-1988, becoming the Family Enclosure. Following the Taylor Report, Everton began converting Goodison into an all-seater stadium, having already removed the fences after the Hillsborough disaster. The last match with the lower Gwladys Street as a standing terrace was in May 1991, a 1–0 win against Luton Town. The Bullens Road Paddock also became all-seated, leaving only the lower Park End Stand with standing areas.

GROVE MOUNT, PENNY LANE

A 1990 Liverpool Echo report described Grove Mount, Penny Lane succinctly: "There are no stands at Penny Lane, not even a public toilet, just a plain brick clubhouse."

HAIG AVENUE, SOUTHPORT

By the time Southport left the Football League in 1978, the covered terraced area behind one of the goals had been condemned as unsafe and closed. At that time, the ground had a capacity of 21,000, with seating for 1,800 and covered standing for 11,000 spectators. Following the 1986 Popplewell Report into the Bradford Fire, Southport had to demolish the covered terracing on the Popular Side and behind the Scarisbrick New Road Stand, leaving only the main grandstand intact. Sean McPartlin, in his book Golden Days: Falling for Southport FC in the Sixties, described the remaining grandstand as having "looked tatty and faintly ridiculous in its new reduced surroundings."

HOGHTON ROAD, ST HELENS

In 1977, the dressing rooms were improved, and the clubhouse received a new lounge, sauna, and snooker/games area. During the 1977-1978 season, a walled running track was laid around the ground, which now had a capacity of 7,600 with seating for 200 fans. During the 1980s, the club revamped the clubhouse and sold off the sauna, added a directors' box on the Hoghton Road side, and constructed a new players' entrance. Floodlights were also added and upgraded again in the mid-1990s.

HOLLY PARK, GARSTON

In May 1984, a fire damaged Holly Park's Main Stand, and the Northern Premier League ordered the ground closed until repairs were completed. The ground reopened for matches on 2 October 1984. By May 1985, ahead of the League's next inspection, the club had installed new floodlights.

HOPE STREET, PRESCOT

Between 1977 and 1979, Hope Street underwent significant improvements, including a better playing surface, improved fencing, and new dressing rooms. The 1,500-seater stand was reopened, and floodlights were installed.

NEW BRIGHTON TOWER ATHLETIC GROUND

Programme notes from a 1972 home match noted that a crowd of 240 spectators was asked to keep noise levels down when goals were scored due to complaints from nearby residents. New Brighton left the Tower Ground at the end of the 1975-1976 season, moving to a new ground in Hoylake.

ORRELL MOUNT PARK, ORRELL

Sefton Council opened Orrell Mount Park in 1973, converting eight acres of the former Silcock's animal foodstuff factory sports ground into a public park. The pitch was first used by Langton FC, then by Bootle FC. In May 1976, the Liverpool Echo described the ground, then used by Bootle FC, as "the club's biggest handicap," citing its sloping pitch, lack of covered accommodation, and the ease with which spectators could avoid paying the 15p admission due to gaps in the fencing. Bootle had already secured a 30-year lease on another site, Bucks Park.

PRENTON PARK, TRANMERE

In 1972, a gale blew the roof off the Cowshed End, which was replaced with a new roof featuring three spans instead of five. A squash court and indoor bowls club were constructed behind the Kop in 1976 but sold off in 1981 to raise funds. In 1985, the capacity of the Main Stand was reduced to 1,000. New exit gates were added in the early 1980s, and a snack bar was installed in the late 1980s.

ROSSETT PARK, COLLEGE ROAD, CROSBY

In 1976, planning permission was granted to install floodlights at Rossett Park, and by September 1977, at a cost of £14,000, the lights were operational, debuting in a match against Darwen. In 1978, as part of an effort to join the Northern Premier League, the pitch was moved towards the Rossett Road side of the ground, necessitating the removal of spectator accommodation on that side.

SEALAND ROAD, CHESTER

In 1979, a new Main Stand was constructed at Sealand Road at a cost of £500,000, providing seating for 2,500 spectators. The stand was built directly behind the old stand, which, once demolished, left a gap between the new stand and the pitch. Fences were installed in 1985. By the 1988-1989 season, the ground's capacity stood at 8,474. As the club's debts mounted, Sealand Road was put up for sale, and Chester played their final match there in April 1990, a 2–0 win over Rotherham in the Third Division.

SIMMS LANE END, GARSWOOD

By 1977, Garswood's clubhouse had been renewed, with plans for further extensions and the addition of squash courts under consideration.

SIMONSWOOD, KIRKBY
By the late 1970s, Simonswood had a capacity of 10,000, with seating for 500 and covered accommodation for 1,000 spectators. In 1982, Kirkby Town left Simonswood to ground-share with Prescot Cables. The Liverpool Echo reported on 2 May 1986 about the scandal surrounding the Simonswood Ground.

SPRINGFIELD PARK, WIGAN
In 1985, the Safety of Sports Grounds Act reduced Springfield Park's capacity from 20,000 to 10,800.

MIDDLEWOOD ROAD, TOWN GREEN, AUGHTON
Following the disbandment of Ormskirk in 1974, when a proposed move to Clubmoor failed, the Town Green ground at Middlewood Road became a community sports facility.

VICTORIA PARK, BURSCOUGH
Burscough installed floodlights at Victoria Park in 1972. During the 1986-1987 season, the ground underwent a revamp: the old stand, originally constructed in 1926 using materials from Everton's Bullens Road Stand, was dismantled, a new grandstand with seating for 250 was built, and the old canteen was demolished. The floodlights, which had been damaged in a gale, were replaced.

WEMBLEY STADIUM, LONDON
Between 1987 and 1989, Wembley Stadium added 29 executive boxes and a new seating level known as the Olympic Gallery, located just below the roof and accommodating 4,000 spectators. Twenty-eight new hospitality lounges were created, and new electronic screens were installed. In 1989, the stadium's perimeter fences were removed in line with changes at many grounds across the country.

Local Teams Who Played at Wembley During This Period:

Everton: FA Cup Finals (1984, 1985, 1986, 1989), League Cup Final (1977).

Liverpool: FA Cup Finals (1974, 1977, 1986, 1988, 1989, 1992), League Cup Finals (1978, 1981, 1982, 1983, 1984, 1987).

Runcorn: FA Trophy Final (1986).

St Helens Town: FA Vase Final (1987).

Tranmere Rovers: Football League Trophy Finals (1990, 1991), Third Division Play-Off Finals (1990, 1991).

Warrington Town: FA Vase Final (1987).

Wigan Athletic: Football League Trophy Final (1985).

WHITE MOSS PARK, SKELMERSDALE

In the summer of 1977, White Moss Park hosted baseball games when the Liverpool Tigers (formerly Liverpool NALGO Tigers) relocated from Bootle to Skelmersdale.

CHAPTER 6

MEN'S PREMIER LEAGUE, WOMEN'S SUPER LEAGUE AND INTO THE FUTURE

1992–PRESENT

The clubs forming the then Football League First Division resigned en masse on 20 February 1992 in order to force the issue of a new league. Everton and Liverpool were joined in the inaugural season of the Premier League by Arsenal, Aston Villa, Blackburn Rovers, Chelsea, Coventry City, Crystal Palace, Ipswich Town, Leeds United, Manchester City, Manchester United, Middlesbrough, Norwich City, Nottingham Forest, Oldham Athletic, Queens Park Rangers, Sheffield United, Sheffield Wednesday, Tottenham Hotspur, Southampton and Wimbledon.

The Football League redesignated its divisions for the start of the 1992/93 season, with the former Second Division becoming the First Division, the Third Division becoming the Second Division, and the Fourth Division becoming the Third Division. Meanwhile, the back-pass rule was changed in 1992, preventing goalkeepers from picking up the ball from a teammate's deliberate back-pass, except when received from a throw-in, header, chest pass, or deflection. In 1994, substitutions allowed for two outfield players plus a goalkeeper, with this expanding to three substitutes in 1995.

The women's league added two teams to each division for the 1992/93 season. Leasowe Pacific and St Helens joined the ten-team Northern Division, with Leasowe winning the division at the first attempt and St Helens finishing in fifth place. Knowsley United Ladies reached the Women's League Cup final in 1992/93, having defeated local rivals Leasowe Pacific 5–4 in the semi-final. The final, played before the Men's Third Division Play-Off Final at Wembley on 29 May 1993, saw Knowsley beaten 3–0 by Arsenal Ladies.

That season, the Liverpool Schools team won the English Schools Shield/ Trophy, defeating Sheffield Schools 3–2 over a two-leg final. Seymour added their name to the growing list of Liverpool teams to win the FA National Sunday Cup by beating Bedfont Sunday 1–0. In 1993/94, the Women's FA Cup came under the organisation of the Football Association, with Knowsley United Ladies finishing as runners-up. In mid-1994, Liverpool FC took over the running of Knowsley United Ladies, renaming the team Liverpool Ladies, while Everton did the same with Leasowe Pacific, renaming them Everton Ladies by the end of the year. The Women's National League Premier Division also became the Women's Premier League, while in the men's game, the Northern Premier League became known as the Unibond League.

In 1994/95, Everton won the FA Cup, and Liverpool secured the League Cup (Coca-Cola Cup) for the fifth time, defeating Bolton Wanderers 2–1 at Wembley with both goals scored by Steve McManaman. Paul Rideout scored the only goal in Everton's 1–0 FA Cup final victory over Manchester United. Gary Ablett became the first Merseyside player to win the FA Cup with both Everton and Liverpool, having previouslywon it with the Reds in 1989.

That same season, Liverpool Women reached the Women's FA Cup final, losing 3–2 to Arsenal at Prenton Park. In 1995/96, they were again runners-up, losing 3–2 on penalties to Croydon at The New Den after a 1–1 draw following extra time. This season also saw the inaugural Lancashire Women's Challenge Cup, with St Helens Garswood becoming its first winners.

The Men's Premier League reduced to twenty clubs for the 1995/96 season by relegating four clubs and promoting only two. Everton started the season as FA Community Shield holders, while both Liverpool Men's and Women's teams ended the season as FA Cup runners-up, with Manchester

United defeating the men's side 1–0 at Wembley and the women's team losing on penalties to Croydon at The New Den. That season, Croxteth & Gilmoss Royal British Legion lost 2–1 to St Joseph's (Luton) in the FA National Sunday Cup final.

In 1996, UEFA awarded England the hosting of the tenth European Football Championship (Euro 96). Anfield was one of the host venues, alongside Old Trafford, for Group C matches featuring the Czech Republic, Germany, Italy, and Russia. Anfield's fixtures included Italy's 2–1 win over Russia on 11 June, a 2–1 defeat for Italy against the Czech Republic on 14 June, and a 3–3 draw between the Czech Republic and Russia on 19 June. Anfield also hosted a quarter-final between France and the Netherlands on 22 June, with France advancing on penalties after a goalless draw.

In 1996, the Central League introduced a cup competition, with Tranmere Rovers Reserves participating from its first season (1996/97). In May 1997, the Liverpool Schools team defeated Islington and Camden Schools 5–3 on aggregate in the English Schools Shield/Trophy final. Ahead of the 1997/98 season, football laws were revised, focusing on goalkeepers: they could now move along the goal line during penalties, could no longer handle a teammate's throw-in, could score directly from a goal kick, and were limited to holding the ball for six seconds before an indirect free kick was awarded.

That season, Southport finished as FA Trophy runners-up, losing 2–0 to Cheltenham Town at Wembley. Everton Ladies won the Women's National League Premier Division, finishing three points ahead of Arsenal, while the Northern Combination Women's Football League was established as a feeder league for the National League Northern Division, with no regional teams included in its inaugural twelve-team season. Tranmere Rovers won the 1998/99 Central League Cup, defeating Stockport County 2–1 at Prenton Park. That year Wigan Athletic won the Lancashire Senior Cup.

The UEFA Regions Cup began in 1999, replacing the UEFA Amateur Cup, with Mid-Cheshire representing England but failing to progress beyond the group stage. To date, no team from the region has participated in the tournament.

In 1999/2000, the North West Women's Regional Football League (NWWRFL) restructured its divisions, renaming the First Division as the Premier Division, the Second Division as Division One, and the Third and Fourth Divisions as Division Two North and Division Two South. Chester City Ladies finished as Premier Division runners-up, with Liverpool Feds in third, Wigan ninth, and Liverpool District tenth. Newsham won Division One, while Brazil finished sixth. Wigan Latics placed third in Division Two North, and Liverpool Feds Reserves finished tenth in Division Two South.

That season, Tranmere Rovers Men were League Cup runners-up, losing 2–1 to Leicester City at Wembley, while Vauxhall Motors won the North West Counties League, then sponsored by First North Western.

At the turn of the millennium, Merseyside's population was over 1.3 million. In 2000/01, Liverpool won the FA Cup for the sixth time and the League Cup (Worthington Cup) for the sixth time, defeating Birmingham City 5–4 on penalties after a 1–1 draw at Cardiff's Millennium Stadium. In the FA Cup final, Liverpool defeated Arsenal 2–1, also at the Millennium Stadium. They completed a treble by beating Alvaves to win the UEFA Cup (see European chapter). That season, Tranmere Rovers Ladies reached the Women's League Cup final, losing 3–0 to Arsenal Ladies at the Deva Stadium in Chester.

From 2001 to 2006, the FA Community Shield was played at the Millennium Stadium while Wembley was redeveloped, returning to the new Wembley upon its reopening. The Shield was renamed from the Charity Shield to the Community Shield in 2002 following a complaint from the Charity Commission. Liverpool won the 2001 FA Community Shield.

In 2001/02, Chester City Ladies became the first regional team to join the Northern Combination Women's Football League, joining Blackburn Rovers, Blackpool Wren Rovers, Bradford City, Chester-le-Street, Huddersfield, Leeds City Vixens, Manchester United, Middlesbrough, Newcastle, Scunthorpe United, and Stockport County in a twelve-team league, finishing seventh in their debut season. That season, Britannia won the FA National Sunday Cup, beating Little Paxton 2–0.

In 2002/03, Liverpool won the League Cup (Worthington Cup) for the seventh time, defeating Manchester United 2–0 in the final at Cardiff, with goals from Gerrard and Owen. Prescot Cables won the North West Counties League, finishing four points ahead of Clitheroe. That year, Allerton lost 3–1 to Northampton's Duke of York in the FA National Sunday Cup final.

Following the 2003/04 season, the Football Conference added Northern and Southern Divisions, with the top division renamed the National Division. Runcorn Halton and Vauxhall Motors joined the newly formed Northern Division. Chester won the 2004 Football Conference. For 2004/05, the Football League rebranded its divisions: the First Division became the Championship, the Second Division became League One, and the Third Division became League Two. Wigan Athletic finished as Championship runners-up, seven points behind Sunderland, earning promotion to the Premier League.

That season, Everton Ladies were FA Cup runners-up, losing 1–0 to Charlton Athletic at Upton Park. The men's Conference League expanded to three divisions: Conference National, Conference North, and Conference South, with Southport joining the Conference North and winning the division in its first season. Nicosia won the FA National Sunday Cup, defeating UK Flooring 3–1.

The FA Inter-League Cup, created in 2003/04 to select England's representative for the UEFA Regions Cup, was won by Mid-Cheshire, who defeated Cambridgeshire County League 2–0, representing England in the 2005 tournament but again failing to reach the final stages.

In 2005, Liverpool came back rom 3–0 down to win the European Champions League Final against Milan, in what came to be known as 'the Miracle of Istanbul' (see European chapter).

At the start of 2005/06, the NWWRFL restructured its divisions into the Premier Division, Division One North, and Division One South. Liverpool Feds finished third, Wigan Ladies fourth, and Wirral fifth in the Premier Division. St Domingo won Division One North, with Wigan Athletic in fourth, Knotty Ash sixth, Burscough Dynamo eleventh, and Liverpool Feds Reserves last. That season, Liverpool won the FA Cup for the seventh time, defeating West Ham United 3–1 on penalties after a 3–3 draw at Cardiff, while Wigan Athletic were League Cup runners-up, losing

4–0 to Manchester United. Everton Women finished as Women's Premier League runners-up, six points behind Arsenal.

The Liverpool Schools team won the English Schools Shield/Trophy (U15 Trophy) that season, defeating Swansea Schools 3–0 on aggregate. Cammell Laird won the North West Counties League.

As FA Cup holders, Liverpool won the FA Community Shield at the start of the 2006/07 season. That season also saw the merger of the Liverpool County Combination and the I Zingari League, forming the Liverpool County Premier League with two divisions. A merger proposal had been rejected by the I Zingari League four years earlier despite the Liverpool County Combination's agreement, but in 2005, both leagues voted to dissolve and merge in time for the 2006/07 season.

The founder members of the Premier Division of the Liverpool County Premier League were: Waterloo Dock (who won the league by thirteen points from East Villa), East Villa, St Aloysius, Croxteth Red Rum, N.E.L.T.C., South Sefton Borough, Lucas Sports, Old Xaverians, Speke, Penlake, Ford Motors, Roma, Birchfield, Collegiate Old Boys, and Mackets.

The founder members of Division One were: Aigburth Peoples Hall, Alsop Old Boys, BRNESC, Cheshire Lines, Copperas Hill, Hill Athletic, Kingsley United, Liverpool NALGO, Mossley Hill Athletic, Page Celtic, Quarry Bank Old Boys, St Ambrose, South Liverpool, Stoneycroft, Vision, and Warbreck. South Liverpool won the First Division by five points ahead of BRNESC, with both clubs promoted to the Premier Division. The season ended with fifteen clubs after St Ambrose dropped out and had their record expunged.

The newly formed Second Division consisted of seventeen clubs as founder members: Albany Athletic, Blueline, Edge Hill BCOB, Eli Lilly, Essemmay Old Boys, Finn Harps, Jubilee Triangle, Leisure Sports Orchard, Leyfield, Lionians, Lydiate Weld, Old Holts, REMYCA United, Redgate Rovers, Rockville, Rolls Royce, and Sacre Coeur Former Pupils. REMYCA United won the division by three points ahead of Albany Athletic, with both clubs promoted to the First Division.

Everton Ladies continued their series of second-place finishes in 2006/07, finishing fourteen points behind an unbeaten Arsenal. In 2007/08, the Northern Premier League expanded its First Division into Division One North and Division One South. Skelmersdale United joined the eighteen-team Division One North, while Cammell Laird were placed in Division One South. In the same season, Everton Ladies again finished second to Arsenal, this time by five points, but won the League Cup, defeating Arsenal 1-0 in the final at the Matchroom Stadium in London in front of over 5,000 spectators. That season also saw the Liverpool Schools team defeat Brighton & Hove Schools 4-2 in the English Schools Shield/Trophy (U15 Trophy) final.

In 2008/09, Everton were FA Cup Final runners-up, losing 2-1 to Chelsea at Wembley, with Louis Saha scoring one of the fastest goals in FA Cup Final history. Everton Ladies again finished second to Arsenal that season, this time on goal difference. In 2009, the North West Counties League renamed its divisions to the Premier Division and Division One.

The 2009/10 season saw Everton Ladies win the Women's FA Cup. They began with a 6-2 home win against QPR, followed by a 7-0 home victory over Portsmouth in the fifth round, and a 2-1 win against Blackburn Rovers in the quarter-final. In the semi-final at Haig Avenue, Everton defeated Barnet 2-0, and in the final at the City Ground, Nottingham, in May 2010, they beat Arsenal Ladies 3-2 with a last-minute extra-time goal by Natasha Dowie. They also finished as league runners-up to Arsenal by eleven points that season. The Liverpool Schools team defeated Cambridge and District Schools 8-0 in the final of the English Schools Shield/Trophy (U15 Trophy). That season, the Liverpool County Premier League reached the final of the FA Inter-League Cup but were defeated 5-2 by the Priaulx League (Channel Islands).

In 2010, the Women's Super League (WSL) was formed, with its first season played in 2011. The new eight-team summer league, played from April to August, featured Everton and Liverpool, alongside Arsenal, Birmingham City, Bristol Academy, Chelsea, Doncaster Rovers Belles, and Lincoln Ladies. Everton Ladies finished third, while Liverpool Ladies finished eighth in the inaugural season. The WSL also introduced its own League Cup, the WSL Continental Cup, sponsored by Continental Tyres.

2010 saw the Fenway Sports Group, headed by John W Henry, buy Liverpool from fellow Americans, Tom Hicks and George Gillet jr, whose running of the club brought it to the brink of financial collapse.

In 2010/11, Oyster Martyrs became the latest Liverpool side to win the FA National Sunday Cup, beating fellow Liverpool side Paddock 1–0 in the final, marking the beginning of five successive finals featuring Liverpool clubs. In 2011/12, Liverpool won the League Cup (Carling Cup) for the eighth time and were FA Cup runners-up. In the League Cup, Liverpool began in the second round with a 3–1 away win at Exeter City, followed by a 2–1 victory at Brighton & Hove Albion in the third round. They defeated Stoke City 2–1 away in the fourth round, beat Chelsea 2–0 away in the quarter-final, and progressed to the final after a 1–0 away win against Manchester City in the semi-final first leg and a 2–2 draw at Anfield in the second leg. Liverpool won the final at Wembley, defeating Cardiff City 3–2 on penalties after a 2–2 draw following extra time.

In the FA Cup that season, Liverpool beat Oldham Athletic 5–1 in the third round at Anfield, defeated Manchester United 2–1 in the fourth round at Anfield, overcame Brighton & Hove Albion 6–1 in the fifth round, and beat Stoke City 2–1 in the quarter-final at Anfield. They defeated Everton 2–1 in the semi-final at Wembley before losing 2–1 to Chelsea in the final at Wembley.

In 2011/12, UEFA introduced its Financial Fair Play (FFP) regulations, limiting clubs to a maximum loss of €5 million over three years unless covered by the owner or third parties. The Premier League and Football League adopted similar regulations with modifications to align with UEFA's rules.

In 2012/13, Wigan Athletic won the FA Cup, defeating Manchester City 1–0 in the final. That same season, Canada lost 5–1 to Hetton Lyons Cricket Club in the FA National Sunday Cup Final. The introduction of goal-line technology, using Hawk-Eye, began in 2012 and was implemented in the Premier League from the 2013/14 season.

In 2013/14, the Premier League introduced its own FFP rules, allowing clubs to sustain a maximum loss of £105 million over three seasons

(2013/14, 2014/15, and 2015/16), while the Football League introduced its own FFP regulations with the same financial threshold. In the 2012/13 season, Oyster Martyrs won the FA National Sunday Cup for the second time, defeating Barnes Albion 4–3 in the final, before losing 5–2 to Humbledon Plains Farm in the 2013/14 final.

The Liverpool Schools team defeated Cambridge and District Schools in the 2013/14 English Schools Shield/Trophy (U15 Trophy) final. The Liverpool Women's Challenge Cup also began that season. Everton Ladies were FA Cup runners-up in 2013/14, losing 2–0 to Arsenal in the final at Milton Keynes Stadium.

At the end of the 2013/14 season, the Crosby and District Sunday League dissolved after forty-six years, citing rising costs, reduced player interest, and the closure of supporting pubs and clubs. Teams increasingly preferred five-a-side formats, and referee availability became a challenge. Saltbox had remained with the league throughout its existence, while The YBM became the only team to win the league's four major trophies in its final season.

In 2014, the Liverpool City Region was established, comprising the City of Liverpool, Halton, Knowsley, St Helens, Sefton, and Wirral, with a combined population of 1.5 million. These six authorities pooled responsibilities for economic development, transport, employment, skills, culture, housing, and physical infrastructure. Unlike Merseyside, which excluded Halton and consisted of twenty-two former local government districts, the Liverpool City Region created a more streamlined structure for regional cooperation.

The Women's Super League added a second division in 2014 and that same season Liverpool Women won the title for the second season in a row, qualifying for the Women's Champions League. Everton Ladies, however, finished eighth and were relegated to the new Women's Super League Two. The Northern Combination Women's Football League folded after the 2013/14 season with Mossley Hill Ladies finishing the final season in third place, Tranmere Rovers Ladies in fourth and Liverpool Feds in eighth. This was part of the restructuring of the women's football pyramid. Liverpool Feds, Mossley Hill and Tranmere Rovers were placed into the newly formed Women's Premier League Northern Division One for the start of the 2014/15 season. In that first season, Liverpool Feds finished as runners-up by two points from Guiseley Vixens Women, Mossley Hill Athletic finished seventh and Tranmere Rovers Ladies finished ninth.

The National League Plate was added to the Women's Premier League in 2014/15 due to the increase in teams, running alongside the Women's Premier League Cup. Liverpool Feds took part but lost in the first round to Huddersfield Town. In Sunday football, Campfield lifted the FA National Sunday Cup for the first time by beating OJM 2–0. The Wirral Schools team reached the final of the English Schools Shield/Trophy (U15 Trophy) in 2014/15, losing on penalties to Aldershot and Farnborough Schools after a 4–2 defeat.

In men's football, the North West Counties League began a sponsorship deal with Hallmark Securities in 2015 for three years. At the same time the Conference League was rebranded as the National League. In the 2015/16 English Schools Shield/Trophy (U15 Trophy) final, Liverpool Schools beat Bristol and South Gloucestershire Schools 1–0. The following season, 2016/17, Wirral Schools won the same competition by beating Swansea Schools 2–1. City of Liverpool won their first trophy in 2016/17 when they won the North West Counties First Division Challenge Cup by beating Sandbach United 1–0 and also lifted the North West Counties Challenge Cup by beating Barnoldswick Town on penalties.

In 2016, long term Everton chairman/ owner, Bill Kenwright, invited Farhad Moshiri, an Anglo- Iranian businessman to invest in and then takeover the club. Moshiri had close financial ties with the Russian oligarch, Alisher Usmanov. Upon the outbreak of war in Ukraine in 2022, UK government sanctions were placed on Usmanov, and Everton were put up for sale. After three turbulent years, the club was sold to the American-owned Friedkin Group in late-2024.m

In 2018 the Premier League voted to introduce Video Assistant Referee (VAR) technology to aid refereeing decisions. It was trialled in fifteen matches during the 2018/19 season and fully introduced for the 2019/20 season to review clear and obvious errors for goals, penalties, straight red cards and mistaken identity. VAR had first been trialled in 2016 in a friendly between PSV Eindhoven and FC Eindhoven after being developed in the Netherlands in the early 2010s.

Liverpool won the European Champions League again in 2019 (see European chapter).

In 2018/19 the Women's Super League Two changed its name to the Championship, with Liverpool joining the league for the 2020/21 season after being relegated from the Super League at the end of the Covid-hit 2019/20 season. Liverpool finished third, having started with a 1–1 home draw against Durham. The men's North West Counties League returned to three divisions with 60 clubs including AFC Liverpool, Bootle, Burscough, Cammell Laird 1907, City of Liverpool, Ellesmere Rangers, Litherland REMYCA, Lower Breck, St Helens Town, Runcorn Town and Vauxhall Motors. In 2018/19 Liverpool Feds became the first local team to play in the Women's National League Plate, losing 5–1 to West Bromwich Albion at Butlin Road, Rugby.

The Covid pandemic heavily affected the 2019/20 and 2020/21 seasons. On 13 March 2020 the Premier League was suspended, initially until 3 April, following Everton, Arsenal and Leicester City players self-isolating. The Football League and women's leagues were also suspended. Everton's last match before suspension was a 4–0 defeat away to Chelsea on 8 March while Liverpool's was a 2–1 home win over Bournemouth on 7 March, putting them 25 points clear of Manchester City with nine matches remaining.

Unlike the men's Premier League which resumed under Project Restart, the women's leagues ended early, with Everton moved up to sixth on sporting merit and Liverpool relegated without another match played. Project Restart was first discussed on 17 April 2020, with non-contact training beginning on 20 May and contact training from 27 May. Players and staff were tested twice weekly and teams needed sterile routes into stadiums. The league resumed on 17 June 2020 with Everton and Liverpool drawing 0–0 behind closed doors at Goodison Park on 21 June 2020 under strict protocols including separated entry routes. Liverpool eventually won a twentieth league title, finishing eighteen points ahead of Manchester City.

The women's FA Cup was also delayed, with Everton beating London
Bees 1–0 in the fourth round and Bristol City 5–0 in the fifth round before
suspension. The postponed quarter-final against Chelsea was played in
September 2020 with Everton winning 2–1, followed by a 3–0 semi-final
win against Birmingham City. Everton lost the final 3–1 after extra time to
Manchester City at Wembley in November 2020.

The Northern Premier League restructured several times, moving to
Division One East and West in 2019/20, then to Division One North West
and South East, and finally to Division One West, East and Midlands for
2021/22. Campfield won the FA National Sunday Cup for the second time
in 2019/20 by beating St Joseph's of Luton 1–0.

In 2020 the Liverpool Business Houses League (founded 1926) merged
with the Liverpool Sunday League (founded 1964) creating a six-division
structure with twelve to fourteen clubs per division and eleven new clubs
added.

The Northern Premier League was abandoned in March 2020 with
Marine third in Division One West, Runcorn Linnets tenth, Prescot
Cables fourteenth and City of Liverpool seventeenth. The following season
was also abandoned with Marine sixth, Runcorn Linnets seventh, City
of Liverpool tenth and Prescot Cables in Division One North West. The
North West Counties League was abandoned at the end of March 2020
with Bootle third, Runcorn Town seventh, Skelmersdale United sixteenth,
Burscough eighteenth and Litherland REMYCA nineteenth in the Premier
Division. Lower Breck topped Division One North, AFC Liverpool were
second and St Helens Town bottom. Vauxhall Motors led Division One
South with Cammell Laird thirteenth. The 2020/21 season was suspended
in December 2020 and abandoned in February 2021.

The 2020/21 season began on 12 September 2020 without fans and
under strict Covid protocols. Liverpool beat Leeds United 4–3 at Anfield
while Everton lost 1–0 at Tottenham Hotspur. Fans returned in December
2020 with Liverpool supporters watching a 1–0 win over Wolves on
6 December and 2,000 Everton fans seeing their team beat Chelsea 1–0 on
12 December.

In 2021 Marine were drawn at home in the FA Cup third round to Tottenham Hostpur, the lowest ranked club to reach that stage as the competition. Due to Covid-19 restrictions, fans were prohibited from watching live. Instead, the football world came together to buy over 30,000 virtual tickets for the game – transforming the Crosby club's financial fortunes.

In 2021 concussion substitutes were introduced and teams were allowed five substitutes with an additional one in extra time, using only three opportunities during play to make changes.

In 2021/22 Liverpool won the League Cup (Carabao Cup) for the ninth time and the FA Cup for the eighth time. Liverpool started in the third round of the League Cup with a 3–0 win at Norwich City, followed by a 2–0 win at Preston North End and a penalty shootout victory against Leicester City after a 3–3 draw. They reached the final after a 2–0 win away to Arsenal and beat Chelsea 11–10 on penalties at Wembley after a 0–0 draw. Liverpool also won the FA Community Shield that season.

The Wirral Schools team won the EFSA Champions Cup (formerly the English Schools Shield/Trophy U15 Trophy) in both 2021/22 and 2022/23, beating Mid Sussex Schools 1–0 in 2021/22 and Chester-le-Street, Washington and Derwentside Schools 2–1 in 2022/23.

In 2022/23 the National League expanded the North and South Divisions as planned pre-Covid, with Chester and Southport in the 24-team North Division. In 2023/24 Everton were deducted ten points for breaching Financial Fair Play rules, reduced to six on appeal, and were later docked a further two points in January 2024. Liverpool won the League Cup for the tenth time, which was Jürgen Klopp's last trophy before stepping down. In the 2022/23 FA National Sunday Cup final Aigburth Arms of the Business Houses League lost 3–2 to St Joseph's of Luton at Pride Park, Derby.

On 14 August 2023 Michael Jones an Everton fan died due to an accident while working on the building of Everton's new stadium at Bramley Moore Dock.

In the 2023/24 EFSA Champions Cup final the Liverpool Schools team faced Aldershot and Farnborough. In June 2024 the Wirral District FA announced its disbandment after 139 years.

In 2023/24 Liverpool won the League Cup. In that season's FA National Sunday Cup final Home Bargain FC were beaten 2–1 by Trooper FC.

In 2024 the I Zingari Combination became known as the I Zingari Veterans league. The Liverpool Old Boys League changed its name to the Liverpool Football League for the 2024/25 season.

In January 2025, Liverpool played their six thousandth competitive match since their formation in 1892 against Brentford. Liverpool won their record-equalling twentieth League title with four games remaining, beating Tottenham Hotspur 5–1, and manager Arne Slot became the first manager to win a title in his first season with a club. They secured the title ten points ahead of second-placed Arsenal.

Celebrations for their last Premier League title win in 2019/20 had to be postponed due to Covid-19, but this time the club and fans were determined to celebrate properly. The team enjoyed an open-topped bus tour of Liverpool on 26 May 2025. The tour had only just finished when a car drove down Water Street in Liverpool city centre at the same time as fans were leaving the tour route. This resulted in over one hundred people being injured, with a man being charged with dangerous driving, grievous bodily harm and malicious wounding. At the time of writing, a trial had been set for November 2025.

In 2025 Runcorn Linnets won the Cheshire Senior Cup for the first time.

Since 2010 Merseyside teams played in the Lancashire Senior Cup Final on six occasions, winning it four times: Liverpool 2009/10, Everton 2015/16, Liverpool 2016/17 and Liverpool 2021/22. Wigan Athletic were runners-up in 2013/14 and 2020/21.

In early July 2025, Liverpool player Diogo Jota and his brother Andre Silva were killed as they drove from their home in Portugal back to pre-season training at their respective football clubs. The car suffered a blow-out as it overtook another vehicle in the province of Zamora in Spain. Diogo was just twenty-eight years of age, recently married, and had three children. He had played over one hundred and twenty matches for Liverpool, scoring forty-seven goals, and had won the Premier League in 2024/25, the FA Cup in 2021/22, and the League Cup in 2021/22 with Liverpool. He had also won the Championship with Wolverhampton Wanderers in 2017/18 and claimed the UEFA Nations League with Portugal in 2018/19 and 2024/25. Liverpool announced that his number 20 would be retired by the club.

In February 2025 Marine announced plans to move to a new 5,000 capacity stadium on an eight-acre site at Edge Lane, Crosby. In May that year, Everton's men's team ended a 133 year stay at Goodison Park with a 2–0 home win against Southampton. It was announced that Goodison would become the new home of Everton's Women's team from the start of the 2025/26 season onwards. Liverpool's men's team won a record equalling twentieth title, finishing ten points ahead of second-placed Arsenal.

As well as a new era at Everton a new era had started at Southport with new owners announced at the end of the 2024/25 season.

In July 2025 Liverpool Women's forward Olivia Smith became the first £1m female footballer when she transferred from Liverpool to Arsenal. Swedish striker Alexander Isak became Liverpool's most expensive signing and the areas most expensive, when on deadline day September 2025 he signed from Newcastle United in a deal worth a reported £120m.

Liverpool and Everton's women's side played their first game of the 2025/26 season at Anfield with Everton winning 4–1 after a hattrick by Ornella Vignola. It was the first hattrick by an Everton player against Liverpool since Dixie Dean in September 1931 at Anfield.

The start of the 2025/26 season saw Liverpool continue their pursuit of another League title winning their first two league matches, Tranmere Rovers climbing the League Two table, and a new era beginning at Everton at their newly named Hill Dickinson Stadium on Regent Road. They kicked off at their new home with a near full house, fan plaza, personalised paving slabs and fireworks, with sticky blue iced doughnuts for a treat and a 2–0 win against Brighton & Hove Albion. Iliman Ndiaye had the distinction of being the last scorer at Goodison Park (against Southampton in May 2025) and the first at the Hill Dickinson Stadium.

THE TEAMS THAT PLAYED AND WERE FORMED 1992-

AFC LIVERPOOL

In February 2008 ten fans of Liverpool met to form a new club intended as a more affordable alternative to Liverpool FC. Its first match was a friendly at Ashton Town's ground on 16 July 2008 against St Helens Town, ending 1-1 in front of 600 fans. They shared Prescot Cables' ground and joined the North West Counties League First Division for the 2008/09 season, winning their first match 5-0 against Darwen. They finished the season in fourth place. They gained promotion to the Premier Division at the end of 2010/11 by finishing fourth and played in their third First Division Cup Final, losing to Atherton Collieries, having previously beaten Padiham 1-0 in 2008/09 and Cheadle Town in 2009/10.

Their first season in the Premier Division, 2011/12, saw them finish ninteenth. In 2012/13 AFC Liverpool reached the Liverpool Senior Cup Final against Bootle, drawing 2-2 before losing 4-3 on penalties. In 2014/15 they lost 5-4 to Skelmersdale United in the Liverpool Senior Cup Final. The same season they moved to share College Road with Marine.

They spent seven seasons in the Premier Division before being relegated in twentieth place at the end of 2017/18. The following season, 2018/19, they finished third in Division One North and were promoted back to the Premier Division in 2021/22 after the two Covid-hit seasons, finishing fourteenth, then sixth in 2022/23 and fourteenth in 2023/24. The AFC Liverpool Ladies team joined the North West Women's Regional League in 2010/11, finishing fifth in Division One South in their first season, and left the league after the 2014/15 season, finishing eighth. 2019/2020 lost to Sandbach United in the same cup. Not promoted due to COVID

The men's side finished the 2024-25 season in ninth in the North West Counties Premier Division table.

AIGBURTH PEOPLES HALL

The I Zingari Premier Division title returned to Peoples Hall in 1991/92 ahead of REMYCA United, and in 1992/93 four points ahead of Selwyn. In 1996/97 they won six I Zingari trophies, including the league, four points ahead of Stoneycroft, the I Zingari Combination and Cup, the I Zingari Alliance and Cup and the I Zingari Senior Cup. They won the league three more times, in 1998/99 by six points from REMYCA United, in 1999/2000 by three points from East Villa and in 2001/02 by two points from Old Xaverians. They won the I Zingari Challenge Cup in 1997/98, beating St Philomenas, before leaving the I Zingari League at the end of 2002/03.

They joined the Liverpool County Combination for 2003/04, playing at Cheshire Lines' ground in Allerton, and finished twelfth. In 2004/05 they finished bottom, and in the final season of the Combination, 2005/06, they finished thirteenth. Following the amalgamation of the Liverpool County Combination and I Zingari League in 2006/07, they were placed in Division One of the Liverpool County Premier League, finishing thirteenth. In 2007/08 they won the First Division by two points from Page Celtic and were promoted. In 2008/09 they finished as runners-up in the Premier Division to Waterloo Dock but beat Waterloo Dock 2–1 to win the Liverpool Challenge Cup. In 2009/10 they won the Liverpool Challenge Cup, beating St Aloysius 3–1, and the I Zingari Challenge Cup. In 2011/12 they won their first Liverpool County Premier League title with three games to spare and a thirteen-point margin over East Villa. Two seasons later, in 2013/14, they won the first of four consecutive league titles, finishing seven points ahead of Waterloo Dock, and also won the I Zingari Combination Cup on penalties against Waterloo Dock. In 2014/15 they won the league by three points from East Villa, followed by a title in 2015/16 by two points from Waterloo Dock and another I Zingari Combination Cup, beating Page Celtic 6–1. Their fourth title came in 2016/17 by three points from Lower Breck. They left the league at the end of 2017/18.

Their reserves were also successful, winning the I Zingari Combination in 1947/48, 1949/50, 1950/51, 1952/53, 1954/55, 1955/56, 1956/57, 1960/61, 1963/64, 1989/90, 1992/93, 1994/95, 1995/96, 1996/97, 1997/98, 1998/99, 2001/02 and 2002/03, totalling eighteen championships.

They also won the George Mahon Cup in 2008, 2012 and 2013.

AINTREE VILLA

They were relegated from the Premier Division at the end of 1992/93 but were promoted back as runners-up to Jabisco in 1993/94, finishing tenth in 1994/95. They were relegated again at the end of 1995/96 and left the league after 1996/97. In 1998/99 they joined the West Cheshire League Third Division, finishing as runners-up to BICC Elsby, and repeated this in 1999/2000 in the Second Division, seven points behind BICC Elsby. In 2000/01 they won the Second Division by four points from Manweb. They were runners-up in the First Division in 2005/06, three points behind Poulton Victoria. In 2008/09 they resigned mid-season from the West Cheshire League but continued in the I Zingari Combination. In 2012/13 they joined the Liverpool County Premier League, finishing second from bottom in Division Two, and despite never being promoted from that division, they returned to the West Cheshire League after 2017/18. In 2018/19 they won the Third Division by six points from South Sefton Borough and also won the West Cheshire Shield. They were promoted from the Second Division in 2019/20 and finished thirteenth and ninth in 2021/22 and 2022/23. Their reserves rejoined the West Cheshire League Third Division in 2019/20, winning it in 2022/23 to gain promotion.

They finished in sixth place in the West Cheshire League First Division at the end of the 2024-2025 season.

ASHVILLE

Ashville won the Wirral Amateur Cup in 1993/94, beating Cammell Laird. In 2002/03 their reserves won the West Cheshire League Third Division, four points ahead of FC Pensby, and also the Pyke Cup. They were runners-up in the Wirral Amateur Cup in 2005/06, losing to West Kirby. The first team were relegated in 2008/09. In 2009/10 their reserves won the West Cheshire Shield, beating Vauxhall Motors Sports and Social Club, while the first team were runners-up in the Wirral Senior Cup in 2010/11, losing to Vauxhall Motors, but won the Second Division and West Cheshire Bowl, beating Capenhurst Villa 6–1. Promoted to the First Division, Ashville won it in 2011/12 by thirteen points from Marine Reserves and won the Wirral Senior Cup, beating Heswall, and the Wirral Amateur Cup, beating New Brighton. In 2013/14 they lost the Pyke Cup, to Newton 3–2, and the Wirral Amateur Cup, beating Woodlands Santos. They were relegated in 2014/15.

In 2015/16 they won the West Cheshire Bowl, beating Maghull Reserves, and in 2016/17 they won the Second Division and the Wirral Amateur Cup, beating Ellesmere Port Town, but were runners-up in the Wirral Senior Cup, losing to Newton. In 2017/18 they were again runners-up in the Wirral Senior Cup, losing to Newton, while the reserves won the West Cheshire Bowl, beating Vauxhall Motors Sports and Social Club. In 2018/19 Ashville won the Wirral Senior Cup, beating Neston Nomads. In 2021/22 they were promoted to the North West Counties League First Division South for 2022/23 after finishing as runners-up to Mersey Royal, but lost the Pyke Cup Final 2–0 to Mossley Hill Athletic. They finished their first season in the North West Counties League in twelfth place.

They finished seventh at the end of the 2024-2025 North West Counties League Division One South season.

BIRKENHEAD LADIES
Birkenhead Ladies joined the North West Women's Regional League at the start of 2009/10, finishing fifth in their first season. They were promoted to the Premier Division after winning the 2013/14 season by sixteen points from Ellesmere Port Town. In 2014/15 they finished eighth in their first season in the top division. At the end of 2016/17 they finished bottom of the Premier Division and left the league.

BOOTLE

In 1992/93 Bootle finished as runners-up in the North West Counties League Division Two, gaining promotion after beating Maghull 3–1 at Bucks Park. In July 1993 Bootle's social club went bankrupt, putting the club's future in doubt. For 1993/94 Bootle returned to the First Division of the North West Counties League and won the Floodlit Trophy. By 1996/97 the lack of facilities and the size of Bucks Park caught up with the club. Despite a mid-table finish in the First Division, they were relegated to the Second Division due to ground grading issues, including unsuitable floodlights donated by South Liverpool and the ground's limited size.

They spent one season, 1997/98, in the Second Division before promotion back to the First Division, spending two seasons there before being relegated at the end of 1999/2000. In 2002 Bootle left Bucks Park and shared Edinburgh Park with Waterloo Dock. In 2002/03 they returned to the Liverpool County Combination, finishing fifth, and were second from bottom in 2003/04. In the final season before the league merged with the I Zingari League, 2005/06, Bootle finished third.

In 2006 Bootle moved to New Bucks Park and returned to the North West Counties League Second Division for 2006/07. They were Vodkat League Challenge Cup runners-up in the newly named First Division in 2007/08 and gained promotion to the Premier Division, also finishing as runners-up in the NWC Challenge Cup and First Division Cup, while the reserves won the Vodkat League Reserve Division. The reserves finished as runners-up in 2008/09 but the First team won the First Division and came third in their first Premier Division season in 2009/10 and the reserves again won their division.

In 2012/13 Bootle faced AFC Liverpool in the Liverpool Senior Cup Final, drawing 2–2 before winning 4–3 on penalties. They finished as Premier Division runners-up in 2016/17, eight points behind Atherton Collieries, and again in 2018/19, two points behind City of Liverpool. After the Covid-hit seasons of 2019/20 and 2020/21, Bootle were promoted to the Northern Premier League Division One West. In their first season, 2021/22, they finished seventh, followed by a fourth-place finish in 2023/24, losing in the play-off semi-finals. At the end of the 2024-2025 season Bootle finished fourteenth in the Norther Premier League Division One West table.

BRAZIL LADIES (WALTON)

Formed in Walton, Brazil Ladies joined the North West Women's League in 1997/98 and remained for three seasons. They won the Second Division in 1998/99 and achieved their highest finish of sixth in the First Division in their final season, 1999/2000.

BROMBOROUGH POOL

Bromborough Pool finished as runners-up in the West Cheshire League First Division in 1993/94, one point behind Cammell Laird. In 1994/95 they were Pyke Cup runners-up, losing 3–2 to Christleton. They left the West Cheshire League at the end of 1998/99 and became defunct after 115 years in local football.

BRNESC

In 1995/96 BRNESC were relegated from the Liverpool County Combination First Division after finishing bottom and receiving a three-point deduction. In 1996/97 they narrowly missed promotion back to the First Division on goal difference, but in 1997/98 they regained their place as runners-up in the Second Division. Two seasons later, 1999/2000, they left the Combination after finishing bottom and joined the I Zingari League, finishing third in the Premier Division in 2003/04. They finished bottom in the I Zingari League's final season, 2005/06, and were placed in the Liverpool County Premier League First Division for 2006/07, finishing runners-up to South Liverpool.

In 2007/08 they finished second from bottom in the Premier Division and were relegated. In 2017/18, despite finishing tenth in Division One, they were promoted back to the Premier Division for 2018/19, finishing fourth, and won the George Mahon Cup by beating FC Pilchy 3–1. They lost the I Zingari Cup Final 3–2 against Waterloo Dock. BRNESC remained in the Premier Division until merging with East Villa in 2023 to form East Villa Rail.

In 2021/22 BRNESC Women won the Women's Liverpool Challenge Cup.

BURSCOUGH

In the North West Counties League, Burscough finished mid-table in the First Division in 1992/93 and lost 2–1 to Southport in the Liverpool Senior Cup Final at Goodison Park. They won the North West Counties Challenge Cup Final 2–1 against Nantwich Town. They finished third in 1993/94. In 1995/96 they finished mid-table but won the North West Counties Challenge Cup Final 1–0 against Fixton at Gigg Lane and also won the North West Counties Community Shield, beating Fixton 1–0.

In 1997/98 Burscough finished as runners-up in the First Division, five points behind Kidsgrove Athletic, and were promoted to the Northern Premier League for 1998/99, also winning the Floodlit Trophy and finishing as runners-up to Liverpool in the Liverpool Senior Cup. They finished mid-table in the Second Division of the Northern Premier League in 1998/99 and were promoted to the Premier Division in 1999/2000 after finishing as runners-up on goal difference. They remained mid-table in 2000/01 and won the Liverpool Senior Cup, beating Southport 1–0.

In 2002/03 Burscough won the FA Trophy, beating Tamworth 2–1 at Villa Park. In 2003/04, the final season before the Conference North and South were formed, they reached the play-offs but lost 2–0 to Bradford Park Avenue in 2004/05. In 2006/07 Burscough won the Northern Premier League Premier Division on goal difference and were promoted to the Conference North, also winning the Lancashire Challenge Trophy against Marine.

In their first Conference North season, 2007/08, they finished eighth but were relegated back to the Northern Premier League Premier Division in 2008/09 after finishing second from bottom. In 2009/10 they finished mid-table before being relegated to the Northern Premier League Division

One North in 2011/12 after finishing bottom. In 2016/17 they finished bottom again and returned to the North West Counties League Premier Division, finishing eighteenth in 2017/18 and as League Cup runners-up to Widnes. In 2023, Victoria Park was shared with Skelmersdale United. Burscough finished in eleventh in the North West Counties Premier Division at the end of 2024/25.

CAMMELL LAIRD (1907)

In 1992/93 Cammell Laird won the Cheshire Amateur Cup, beating Capenhurst, and the Pyke Cup. The reserves won the West Cheshire Second Division, retaining the title in 1993/94 by one point from Bromborough Pool, while the first team were runners-up in the Wirral Amateur Cup to Ashville and again won the Pyke Cup. In 1994/95 they beat Vauxhall Motors 2–1 in the Wirral Senior Cup Final. 1995/96 saw them as runners-up in the Wirral Senior Cup.

In 1998/99 the first team won the West Cheshire First Division, three points ahead of Heswall, also winning the Pyke Cup and West Cheshire Bowl. The following season they beat Vauxhall Motors to win the Wirral Senior Cup and were League runners-up. In 2000/01 they won the First Division by twenty-one points from Christleton and the West Cheshire Bowl. In 2001/02 they finished as runners-up, two points behind Christleton, won the Wirral Senior Cup against Poulton Victoria and the Pyke Cup, and retained the West Cheshire Bowl in 2002/03.

In 2003/04 they were League runners-up and beat Heswall to win the Wirral Senior Cup and retained it in 2004/05 by beating Castrol Social before leaving to join the North West Counties League Second Division in 2004/05, winning the division by ten points from Silsden and also winning the League Cup. In 2005/06 they won the First Division of the North West Counties by eleven points from Skelmersdale United, gaining promotion to the Northern Premier League.

In 2006/07 they reached the play-off final but lost 2–1 to Eastwood Town, winning the Cheshire Senior Cup 3–1 against Northwich Victoria. With league restructuring, they were placed in the First Division South in 2007/08, finishing as runners-up behind West Kirby and losing the Cheshire Amateur Cup Final to Poulton Victoria.

In 2008/09 they finished eighteenth in the Premier Division and were relegated, winning the Wirral Senior Cup against Newton. In 2009/10 they switched to the First Division North, winning the West Cheshire League from West Kirby. They finished as runners-up to Skelmersdale United in 2012/13, sixteen points behind, and lost the play-off final to Trafford on penalties.

At the end of 2013/14 they rebranded as Cammell Laird 1907. In 2014/15 they finished as runners-up in the First Division, gained promotion to the Premier Division and won the Pyke Cup. In 2016/17 they were relegated back to the First Division South. In 2021/22 they won the Wirral Senior Cup 3–0 against Heswall, repeating the win in 2023/24 against Capenhurst Villa.

The ladies team joined the North West Women's Football League in 2017/18, finishing as runners-up in Division One North, four points behind Penrith AFC, before leaving the league in 2018/19 after finishing fifth. In 2021/22 they lost to FC Isle of Man in the First Division Cup and to Charnock Richard in the 2022/23 League Challenge Cup before winning the 2023/24 Wirral Senior Cup 3–0 against Capenhurst Villa. 2015/16 saw them as runners-up in the Wirral Senior Cup. The finished 2024/25 in tenth place in the North West Counties Division One South.

CAPENHURST VILLA

In 1992/93 Capenhurst Villa won the Wirral Senior Cup, beating Mersey Royal 2–1, and were runners-up the following season, losing 1–0 to Poulton Victoria. The reserves finished as runners-up in the West Cheshire Second Division in 1995/96, one point behind Poulton Victoria reserves. They added Villa to their name in 2000. In 2000/01 they were relegated to the Second Division after finishing second from bottom in the First Division.

In 2003/04 they won the West Cheshire Bowl, finishing as runners-up in the same competition in 2010/11. In 2013/14 they won the West Cheshire

Second Division, twelve points clear of Helsby. In 2014/15 the reserves lost the Wirral Amateur Cup Final to Willaston, also finishing as runners-up in the Third Division in 2016/17.

In 2018/19 the first team finished as runners-up in the Second Division, four points behind Page Celtic, and lost the West Cheshire Bowl Final. In 2022/23 they won the Wirral Senior Cup, beating Mersey Royal 1–0, but lost the 2023/24 final 3–0 to Cammell Laird 1907. Villa finished the 2024/25 West Cheshire League First Division season in eleventh.

CHESHIRE LINES

After demerging from South Liverpool, Cheshire Lines remained in the First Division in 1994/95, finishing bottom and being relegated. They played in the single division in 1999/2000, finishing fifteenth, and were relegated again when the Second Division reformed in 2000/01. They were in the single division again in 2002/03, finishing thirteenth.

On the formation of the Liverpool County Premier League in 2006/07 they were placed in the First Division, finishing seventh, and were promoted after finishing third in 2007/08. They won the Lord Wavertree Cup in 1997 and 2014.

Following difficulties, they left the Premier Division during 2012/13 and had their record expunged. They returned in 2013/14, finishing as runners-up in the Second Division behind Litherland REMYCA reserves, but disbanded soon after. The facilities were taken by Woodstreet, who later merged back with former members to reform Cheshire Lines.

The revived club joined the West Cheshire League Third Division in 2015/16, finishing eleventh, and gained promotion after finishing third in 2016/17. In 2017/18 they finished fourth in the Second Division. They remained in the Second Division for five seasons before leaving the league at the end of 2022/23.

CHESHIRE LINES SOUTH LIVERPOOL

The combined Cheshire Lines and South Liverpool side played in the Liverpool County Combination in 1992/93 and 1993/94. They were runners-up in the Second Division in 1992/93 behind Beesix FC, earning promotion to the First Division, where they finished sixth. The partnership ended after 1993/94 with Cheshire Lines and South Liverpool demerging and going their separate ways.

CHESTER/CHESTER CITY

At the end of the 1992/93 season Chester were relegated from the Second Division of the Football League. In 1993/94 they were runners-up in the Third Division, five points behind Shrewsbury Town, and promoted back to the Second Division. Back in the Second Division for 1994/95 they finished second from bottom and were relegated again. In 1995/96 they finished eighth in the Third Division and in 1996/97 reached the play-offs, finishing sixth but losing the semi-final against Swansea City.

In 1999 the club was saved from going bust with help from the fans and American Terry Smith, a former New England Patriots player and car dealer in North Carolina, who took over in July. On the last day of the 1999/2000 season Chester were relegated from the Football League after a 1–0 home defeat to Peterborough United. They needed to better the results of Carlisle United and Shrewsbury Town to stay up, but despite Carlisle losing 1–0, Shrewsbury won 2–1 and Chester's defeat sent them down after sixty-nine years in the league.

The 2000/01 season saw their first game outside the Football League, a 2–0 away defeat to Rushden and Diamonds, and they finished eighth in the Conference Premier Division. Off-field issues dominated, and in 2001 the American owners sold up. In 2002/03 Chester finished fourth and qualified for the play-offs against Doncaster Rovers, drawing 2–2 over two legs but losing 4–3 on penalties.

In 2003/04 Chester were promoted, with a 0–0 draw at Shrewsbury followed by a 1–0 home win against Scarborough courtesy of a Darryn Stamp goal, securing the title by a point from Hereford. Back in the Football League in 2004/05, they opened with a 1–1 draw at Notts County with Ray Mathias as caretaker manager after Mark Wright's resignation, with Ian Rush later appointed.

In 2008/09 Chester were relegated from the Football League after a 2–2 draw at Aldershot Town, finishing second from bottom, four points off Grimsby Town. The club entered administration, leading to a ten-point deduction for the following season. Though taken out of administration, a further fifteen-point deduction was imposed when a CVA was rejected by HMRC, and the FA refused to accept the new ownership structure.

By November 2009 fans formed the City Fans United group and began protesting as debts mounted, including unpaid bills to Wrexham and Vauxhall Motors. During a home match against Eastbourne Borough, fans invaded the pitch in the 72nd minute with Chester leading 3–2, leading to the match being abandoned. In February 2010 the home match against Ebbsfleet United proved to be Chester's last. The club failed to fulfil their next two fixtures as players refused to play against Forest Green and the match against Wrexham was cancelled due to unpaid police bills. The Conference expelled Chester and expunged their record. In March 2010, with unpaid taxes exceeding £26,000, the High Court ordered Chester to be wound up, ending 126 years of history.

In 2010 the club was reformed by fans as Chester FC and joined the Northern Premier League Division One North for 2010/11, starting with a 1–1 away draw at Warrington on 24 August 2010. They finished the season as champions and were promoted to the Premier Division. In 2011/12 Chester won the Premier Division, sealing promotion to the Conference North after a 1–1 draw against Northwich Victoria, finishing seventeen points clear.

In 2012/13 Chester won their opening Conference North match and secured the title with a 1–0 win over Boston United on 6 April, sixteen points clear of Guiseley, and also won the Cheshire Senior Cup against Stalybridge Celtic. In 2013/14 they finished fourth from bottom, but were reprieved after Hereford United and Salisbury City were expelled from the Conference.

In the National League Premier Division in 2015/16 Chester finished seventeenth. In 2017/18 they were relegated to the National League North after finishing second from bottom. Following the Covid-hit 2019/20 and 2020/21 seasons, Chester finished third in 2022/23 and tenth in 2023/24 in the National League North. Finished the National League North 2024/25 season in fourth, however they lost in the Play-off Semi-Final 2–1 to Scunthorpe United.

Chester FC Women were formed in 2015. The earlier Chester Ladies joined the North West Women's Football League Fourth Division in 1994/95, finishing as runners-up and earning promotion. They finished third in the Third Division in 1995/96, gaining promotion to the Second Division for 1996/97, and were promoted to the Premier Division after finishing third in 1997/98. They were runners-up in 1999/2000 and won the league unbeaten in 2000/01. They returned to the Premier Division in 2008/09, finishing fifth, but were relegated to Division One South in 2011/12, before returning to the Premier Division in 2012/13 after winning Division One South by nineteen points. They left the league after the 2013/14 season but returned in Division One South in 2018/19.

CITY OF LIVERPOOL

City of Liverpool FC was formed in 2015, with roots going back to 2008 discussions between Paul Manning, Peter Furmedge and others about the lack of non-league representation in Liverpool and the effects of football's globalisation. A 2014 meeting targeted August 2016 for the club's first season, and by early 2015 a website and social media presence were established. A public meeting on 21 September 2015 at the Quakers Meeting Rooms in Liverpool saw around fifty attendees agree to form the club as a Community Benefit Society owned by its members.

Working with Supporters Direct, the club formalised its structure and sought entry to the North West Counties Football League. In November 2015 an agreement was reached with Bootle FC to groundshare at the Delta Taxi Stadium, enabling the club to apply before the 31 December deadline. After an initial rejection by the FA, which placed them in the Liverpool County Premier League, Northwich Manchester Villa's resignation opened a spot. Following an appeal meeting at Wembley on 8 June 2016, the FA admitted the club to the NWCFL for the 2016/17 season.

City of Liverpool finished fourth in their first season in Division One and won promotion to the Premier Division after a 3–0 play-off final win over Litherland REMYCA. They also won the North West Counties Football Challenge Cup against Barnoldswick Town on penalties and the First Division Cup with a 1–0 win over Sandbach United, completing a treble.

In their first Premier Division season in 2017/18 they finished fourth. In 2018/19 City of Liverpool won the league by two points from Bootle, earning promotion to the Northern Premier League Division One North West. They finished seventeenth in the Covid-hit 2019/20 season and were tenth in 2020/21 when the season was halted again due to Covid. They finished ninth in 2021/22 and twelfth in 2022/23.

In 2023/24 City of Liverpool finished fifth, losing 2–0 to Prescot Cables in the Division One West play-off final, and were beaten 2–0 by Marine in the Liverpool Senior Cup Final, their first appearance in the final.

The women's team joined the North West Women's Football League Division One South in 2017/18, finishing bottom, and repeated this the following season before leaving the league. In 2023/24 City of Liverpool reached their first Liverpool Senior Cup Final, losing to Marine. The 2024-2025 season saw them end the season bottom of the Northern Premier League Division One West and relegated back to the North West Counties League.

COLLEGIATE OLD BOYS

In the now named Premier Division they were relegated bottom in 1996/97 season. They regained Premier Division status in 2002-2003.

In the newly created Liverpool County Premier League, Collegiate began the 2006/07 season in the Premier Division and finished in fifteenth place out of sixteen teams. The following season, 2007/08 they finished bottom of the Premier Division and were relegated to the First Division. Their reserve side finished as runners-up in the Lord Wavertree Cup losing 4–0 to Alder in 2010/11.

In 2013-2014 they finished as runners-up in the First Division and were promoted to the Premier Division for the 2014/15 season finishing in twelfth place. They left the league at the end of that season.

EAST VILLA (RAIL)

In the I Zingari League Villa finished sixth in the 1992/93 season and they won the I Zingari Challenge Cup in 1995/96. They won the I Zingari League in 1997/98 and again in 2004/05.

In 2006/07 they were one of the founder members of the newly formed Liverpool County Premier League starting in the Premier Division and finishing as runners-up to Waterloo Dock by thirteen points. The following season, 2007/08 they finished as runners-up again to Waterloo Dock this time by two points and they won the Liverpool Challenge Cup beating Speke 3–2. They won the George Mahon Cup in 2007 and the Lord Wavertree Cup in 2009.

In 2014/15 they finished as runners-up by three points to Aigburth Peoples Hall and they finished as runners-up again in 2017/18 fifteen points off Lower Breck and were runners-up to Lower Breck in the I Zingari Challenge Cup losing 4–3, and in 2018/19 they were runners-up to Waterloo Dock by six points.

In 2023 East Villa merged with BRNESC Football Club to become East Villa Rail Football Club. They beat the Naylo 2–0 at Bootle's New Bucks Park to win the 2023/24 George Mahon Cup.

EDEN VALE

In the rest of the 1990s the trophies kept coming, they won the title six times in a row between 1993/94 and 1998/99, together with five Canon Francis Cups in 1992/93 and 1994/95 through to 1997/98. Vale also claimed the FA Sunday Premier Cup in 1997/98. By the 2000s Vale had moved back to the Ormskirk Sunday League.

ELLESMERE PORT TOWN

Another new Ellesmere Port Town was formed in 1992 and played two seasons in the second division of the North West Counties League, playing at a ground in Thornton Road, but folded in 1994.

In 2011 the newest incarnation of Ellesmere Port Town started life in the Chester and District League and gained promotion in the league each season between 2011/12 and 2013/14.

The women's side joined the North West Women's Regional League in 2012/13 and finished as runners-up in the South Division in 2013/14 and 2014/15, and won the Cheshire County FA Ladies Cup that same season.

The men's side joined the West Cheshire League in division three for the start of the 2015/16 season. The following season, 2016/17, they were promoted to the West Cheshire League second division and were runners-up to Ashville in the Wirral Amateur Cup.

They finished in third place the following season, 2017/18, to be promoted to the West Cheshire League First Division, finishing seventh at the end of the season. In 2020/21 Town beat Heswall to win the Wirral Senior Cup Final.

EVERTON

Everton's first game in the Premier League was a 1-1 home draw against Sheffield Wednesday and they finished the 1992/93 season in thirteenth spot. The following season, 1993/94, they stayed in the Premier League on the last day of the season at home to Wimbledon. Needing to win to stand a chance of staying up, they fell two goals behind in the first half but fought back with a penalty from Graham Stuart to make it 2-1 before a volley by Barry Horne levelled the match. With time running out, another goal by Graham Stuart made it 3-2, ensuring Everton remained in the Premier League.

A poor start to the 1994/95 season saw former Goodison forward Joe Royle replace Mike Walker as manager, finishing in seventeenth place. They would go on to win the FA Cup that season, the winning goal scored by Paul Rideout. They also won the Liverpool Senior Cup in 1996, 2003, 2005 and 2007.

That same season the women's side, formerly Leasowe Pacific, were part of the Women's Premier League, finishing fourth. In 1995/96 Everton finished sixth. Joe Royle was replaced by captain Dave Watson in March 1997 and the club finished fifteenth at the end of the 1996/97 season. The women's side were runners-up in the League Cup, losing 2-1 to Millwall Lionesses.

Former manager Howard Kendall returned for a third stint for the 1997/98 season but had to rely on a final day 1–1 draw at Coventry to avoid relegation on goal difference from Bolton Wanderers. The women's side won the Women's Premier League National Division, finishing three points clear of Arsenal. Walter Smith replaced Kendall for the 1998/99 season, leading the team to fourteenth spot while the women's team finished as runners-up in the League Cup, losing 3–1 to Arsenal at Prenton Park.

Smith kept Everton mid-table for three seasons but was replaced by Preston North End manager David Moyes at the end of 2001/02, who steered the club to fifteenth. In 2002/03 Everton finished seventh but in 2003/04 flirted with relegation, finishing seventeenth. In contrast, Everton finished fourth in 2004/05, qualifying for the Champions League for the first time in the club's history. The women's team finished runners-up to Arsenal by six points in 2005/06 and again finished second in 2006/07 to an unbeaten Arsenal, this time by fourteen points.

Everton announced they were leaving Bellefield in 2006 and moved onto their new purpose-built training facility at Finch Farm in Halewood in October 2007 together with their youth teams and Women's side.

In 2007/08 Everton were again second to Arsenal, this time by five points, but beat them 1–0 to win the League Cup. In 2008/09, Everton finished second to Arsenal on goal difference and in 2009/10 finished as runners-up to Arsenal again, this time by eleven points, while also winning the Women's FA Cup and finishing runners-up in the League Cup, losing 3–1 to Leeds United.

By the time Moyes left for Manchester United in 2012/13, Everton had spent most seasons in the top half of the table. Wigan Athletic manager Roberto Martinez replaced him for 2013/14, leading Everton to fifth place and European qualification. In 2014/15 Everton fell to eleventh and in 2015/16 Martinez was replaced by David Unsworth and Joe Royle, with Everton finishing eleventh.

In 2016/17 Dutch legend Ronald Koeman took Everton to seventh but a poor start to 2017/18 saw him replaced by David Unsworth, then Sam

Allardyce, with the club finishing eighth. Allardyce was replaced by Marco Silva for 2018/19, guiding Everton to eighth.

In 2019/20 Silva was replaced by Duncan Ferguson, then by Carlo Ancelotti, who led Everton to twelfth. In 2020/21 Everton finished tenth. Ancelotti resigned and rejoined Real Madrid, with Rafael Benitez appointed for 2021/22. Benitez was replaced in January 2022 by Duncan Ferguson, then Frank Lampard, who guided Everton to sixteenth. Lampard was replaced in January 2023 by Sean Dyche during a turbulent 2022/23 season.

During 2023/24, Everton were docked ten points in October for breaching the Premier League's Profit and Sustainability Rules, reduced to six on appeal, before a further two-point deduction in April 2024 following a second tribunal. This was also appealed but dropped once Premier League survival was secured for the 2024/25 season.

In 2017 Everton's women's team won the WSL2 Spring series and were promoted back to WSL1 for the newly reorganised 2017/18 season.

At the end of the 2024/25 season Everton's women's side finished in eighth in WSL1.

The women's side also won the Women's Liverpool Senior Cup in 2004/05, 2005/06, 2006/07, 2007/08, 2008/09, 2010/11, 2011/12 and 2012/13.

EVERTON ST DOMINGO'S/ST DOMINGO'S LADIES

St Domingo's Ladies joined the North West Women's Football League's Third Division in 2003/04, finishing runners-up in their first season. In 2004/05 they were runners-up to Burnley FC Girls and Ladies by six points in Division Two. In 2005/06 they won Division One North by three points from Burnley. They finished as runners-up twice in 2007/08 and 2008/09 in Division One North before leaving the league at the end of 2008/09.

FC ST HELENS

Formed in 2014 when the St Helens Town reserve side split to form a new team, FC St Helens joined the West Cheshire League Third

Division in 2014/15, finishing sixth, before moving to the Cheshire League for 2015/16, finishing fourth in Division Two and earning promotion to Division One for 2016/17, finishing fifth. They were promoted to the Premier Division at the end of 2017/18, finishing fourteenth in 2018/19.

After the Covid-hit seasons of 2019/20 and 2020/21, St Helens were promoted to the North West Counties League after winning the 2021/22 Cheshire League title. They finished third in their first season in the North West Counties League Division One North in 2022/23 and won the Division One North title in 2023/24, nine points ahead of Atherton LR. In their first season in the North West Counties League Premier Division 2024/25 they finished in eighth place.

FORMBY

Formby won the Lamot Pils Trophy in 1994/95. In 1999/2000 they won both North West Counties League Cups, including a penalty shootout win over Curzon Ashton at Gigg Lane, and were Worthington Trophy winners in 2001.

In 2002 they moved to Altcar Road but were told the ground did not meet North West Counties League standards, so they rejoined the Liverpool County Combination for 2002/03, finishing ninth. They returned to the North West Counties League in 2003/04, finishing third in Division Two, earning promotion to the First Division for 2004/05, finishing twentieth. They remained in the renamed Premier Division until relegation in 2010/11.

In 2012/13 Formby won Division One of the North West Counties League by five points from Abbey Hey but were denied promotion due to ground compliance issues. They ground-shared with Burscough but folded on 2 June 2014 due to financial difficulties despite finishing runners-up in 2013/14.

Formby FC was revived in March 2022, joining the Liverpool County Premier League Championship Division for 2022/23, finishing sixth, and finished third in 2023/24.

GARSWOOD UNITED

In 1994/95 Garswood were beaten by Waterloo Dock in the Liverpool Challenge Cup final. In 1995/96 they won the Mid-Cheshire League, finishing nine points ahead of Barnton, and beat Merseyside Police 3–1 to win the Liverpool Challenge Cup. They joined the North West Counties League Second Division for 1996/97, finishing third, but returned to the Mid-Cheshire League at the end of 1997/98 after finishing eighth.

In 2005/06 they won the Mid-Cheshire First Division League Cup and the Wigan Cup. When the Mid-Cheshire League became the Cheshire League in 2007/08, United remained with the league and won the Wigan Cup again, repeating the feat in 2009/10. They won the Cheshire League title in 2013/14, finishing four points ahead of Eagle Sports, and won the Liverpool Challenge Cup and the Wigan Cup the same season. They were relegated in 2016/17.

HALEWOOD APOLLO

Formed around 2014 by a group of friends, Halewood Apollo joined the Warrington and District League Fifth Division for 2014/15, winning the division at the first attempt. In 2016/17 they won the Second Division. Apollo joined the Liverpool County Premier League First Division in the Covid-hit 2020/21 season and were promoted to the Premier Division for 2021/22, finishing eighth.

In 2022/23 they finished runners-up to MSB Woolton by five points in the Premier Division and won the I Zingari Challenge Cup, beating Warbreck 5–2. They won the Premier Division title in 2023/24, finishing one point ahead of East Villa Rail.

JABISCO

Jabisco joined the I Zingari League in 1992/93, winning the Second Division title by one point from Blacklow Brow. They made it two promotions in a row by winning the First Division title in 1993/94, one point ahead of Aintree Villa. In their first season in the Premier Division in 1994/95, Jabisco finished fifth.

The club was renamed Jabisco Boulevard before the 1996/97 season, finishing sixth, and was renamed again as Kirkby Boulevard before 1997/98, finishing eleventh. They left the league at the end of 1998/99 after finishing bottom of the I Zingari Premier Division.

KNOTTY ASH LADIES

Knotty Ash Ladies joined the North West Women's Football League in 1989/90 in the Third Division, finishing third and earning promotion to the Second Division. They remained there until relegation back to the Third Division at the end of 1993/94.

They won the Third Division in 1997/98, earning promotion to the renamed First Division, where they finished runners-up in 1998/99 and were promoted to the Premier Division. They remained in the Premier Division until relegation to the First Division at the end of 2002/03, leaving the league at the end of 2007/08.

KNOWSLEY UNITED LADIES

Knowsley United Ladies finished third in the Premier Division in 1992/93 and were runners-up in the League Cup, losing 3–0 to Arsenal at Wembley. They reached the Women's FA Cup final in 1993/94, losing 1–0 to Doncaster Belles at Glanford Park, Scunthorpe, having beaten Leyton Orient, Huddersfield Town, Arsenal and Stanton Rangers along the way.

In their final season as Knowsley United Ladies, 1994/95, they finished third in the Premier Division. Before the 1995/96 season they became Liverpool Women's, becoming the women's team of Liverpool FC.

LEYFIELD

They joined the Liverpool League Third Division and won promotion to the Second Division at the end of the 1967/68 season. They were runners-up in the Second Division in 1971/72, gaining promotion to the Liverpool League First Division, but were relegated back to the Second Division at the end of the 1973/74 season. In 1976/77 they gained promotion to the First Division as runners-up and came runners-up of the First Division in

1981/82. They joined the I Zingari Alliance Second Division, winning it at the first time of asking and gaining promotion. They finished as runners-up of the First Division and eventually joined the I Zingari League proper in 1988/89, reaching the First Division after winning the Second Division two seasons later, and gained Premier Division status as winners of the First Division in 1992/93. They won the Liverpool Junior Cup in 1993/94 and in 1996/97 Leyfield were relegated to the First Division of the I Zingari League. In 2012/13 Leyfield resigned from the league mid-season and left the league with their record expunged. They reappeared in 2014/15 in the Second Division, winning the division, but after one season in the First Division in 2015/16, finishing seventh, they again resigned from the league during 2016/17. Despite reappearing in the Second Division in 2017/18, they again resigned and this time did not reappear.

LITHERLAND REMYCA/REMYCA UNITED/LITHERLAND UNITED

They finished runners-up to Aigburth Peoples Hall in 1991/92 and were Premier Division champions in 1993/94, four points clear of Liver Vaults, also winning the I Zingari Challenge Cup by beating Maghull, though they lost 2–1 to Maghull in the Liverpool Challenge Cup final. They retained the Premier Division in 1994/95 by six points from Aigburth Peoples Hall and won the I Zingari Challenge Cup, beating Blacklow Brow 7–4. In 1995/96 they were champions again, one point clear of Aigburth Peoples Hall, and won the I Zingari Challenge Cup in 1998/99, beating East Villa 4–1.

In 2000/01 they joined the newly reformed Second Division of the Liverpool County Combination but left in 2002/03 before returning to the I Zingari League Second Division in 2005/06, winning the division in its final season before the merger. On the formation of the Liverpool County Premier League, they were placed in the Third Division, becoming its first champions in 2006/07, three points ahead of Albany Athletic. In 2009/10 they were promoted from the Second Division to the Premier Division.

The club changed its name to Litherland REMYCA in 2013. In 2013/14 they finished fifth in the Liverpool County Premier League and were promoted to the North West Counties League, while the reserves won the Third Division. A fifty-seater stand was added at Litherland Sports Park to meet ground requirements for the NWCFL, joining the First Division in 2014/15 and finishing ninth. In 2016/17 they finished third and lost 3–0 to City of Liverpool in the play-off final.

In 2017/18 they finished runners-up to Silsden by four points and were promoted to the Premier Division, finishing fifteenth in 2018/19. They were sixteenth when the 2019/20 season was abandoned due to Covid and were bottom after four games when 2020/21 was also abandoned. In 2021/22 they finished second from bottom but were reprieved from relegation due to points-per-game calculations after the abandoned seasons. REMYCA finished nineteenth in the North West Counties League Premier Division for 2024/25.

LIVERPOOL

Liverpool's first Premier League match in 1992/93 was a 1–0 away defeat at Nottingham Forest, finishing sixth that season. In 1993/94 they finished eighth, with Graeme Souness replaced by Roy Evans in January 1994. Evans guided Liverpool to the League Cup in 1994/95, third in 1995/96, fourth in 1996/97 and third in 1997/98. Liverpool's women's side were runners-up in three FA Cup finals in 1994 (as Knowsley United, 1995 and 1996. Liverpool had adopted the women's side Knowsley United as their new women's side in 1994.

At the start of 1998/99, Evans was joined by Gérard Houllier in joint management, but Evans resigned in November, leaving Houllier in sole charge as Liverpool finished seventh. They finished fourth in 1999/2000 and third in 2000/01, also winning multiple trophies. Houllier fell ill in October 2001, with Phil Thompson taking over until March 2002, guiding Liverpool to second, seven points behind Arsenal. Liverpool won the League Cup in 2002/03 and fourth in 2003/04 before being replaced by Rafael Benítez.

In 2004/05 Benítez led Liverpool to a Champions League title, followed by third in 2005/06 and 2006/07 and fourth in 2007/08. In 2008/09 Liverpool finished runners-up to Manchester United by four points. They finished seventh in 2009/10, after which Benítez was replaced by Roy Hodgson, who was replaced mid-season by Kenny Dalglish in

2010/11, guiding them to sixth. Dalglish led Liverpool to eighth in 2011/12 before Brendan Rodgers took over for 2012/13, finishing seventh. Their women's team won their first title in 2013, having previously won the National League North on three occasions (2004, 2007 and 2010).

In 2013/14 Liverpool finished runners-up to Manchester City by two points, their women's team went one better and won their second back-to-back title in 2014. They finished sixth in 2014/15, and Rodgers was replaced in October 2015 by Jürgen Klopp, who guided Liverpool to eighth in 2015/16 and fourth in both 2016/17 and 2017/18. In 2018/19 they finished second to Manchester City by one point and won the Champions League. In 2019/20 Liverpool amassed ninety-nine points to win the league by eighteen points in a season affected by Covid. In 2020/21 they finished third and were runners-up to Manchester City in 2021/22.

Liverpool finished fifth in 2022/23. In 2023/24 they won their tenth League Cup, defeating Leicester City, Bournemouth, West Ham and Fulham to reach the final against Chelsea at Wembley. After a 0–0 draw, Virgil van Dijk scored the winner in extra time, marking Klopp's final trophy before stepping down at the end of a season where Liverpool finished third, having challenged Manchester City for the title.

Liverpool's women's side were relegated from the WSL1 at the end of the Covid-19 hit season of 2019/20. The They returned to WSL1 by winning the WSL2 title at the end of the 2021/22 season and after finishing fourth in 2023/24 they finished the 2024/25 season in seventh place. The women's U21 team also won the Liverpool Women's Senior Cup in 2023/24 and 2024/25.

At the end of the 2024/25 season Liverpool won a twentieth League title. They began the season with a new manager Arne Slot, a Dutchman who had come from managing Feyenoord. They hit the top after ten games and never looked back with the only real threat coming from Arsenal. Liverpool won their record equalling twentieth League title with four games left beating Tottenham Hotspur 5–1 and manager Arne Slot became the seventh manager to win a title in the first season with a club. They won the title ten points ahead of second placed Arsenal.

Liverpool announced that they were leaving Melwood in 2017 and had moved into a new training facility in Kirkby on the same site as their Academy side. The Academy had moved to Kirkby back in 1998 and the first team joined them from November 2020 due to COVID-19 regulations delaying the move over to the site by a month.

LIVERPOOL CITY LADIES' COMMUNITY
Liverpool City Ladies joined the North West Women's Football League in 1993/94 in Division Four and reached the Premier Division by 1998/99, remaining until leaving the league at the end of 1999/2000 after seven seasons.

LIVERPOOL FEDS WOMEN'S
Liverpool Feds joined the North West Women's Regional League in 1993, winning the Fourth Division at the first attempt, six points ahead of Newsham Park. They won the Third Division in 1993/94 by one point from Lancaster/Morecambe and the Second Division in 1995, two points ahead of Blackburn Rovers. On reaching the First Division in 1996, they finished second from bottom. In 2001 they were runners-up to Chester City in the Premier Division and won the Premier Division in 2002, four points ahead of Bolton Wanderers.

They returned to the Premier Division in 2003/04, finishing third, and were runners-up in 2004/05 and again in 2007/08. In 2009/10 they won the Premier Division and were promoted to the Women's Northern Combination League, finishing sixth in 2010/11 and eighth in 2013/14, the final season of the Northern Combination.

In 2014/15 Liverpool Feds were runners-up in the newly formed Women's National League Northern Division One, linking with men's team Marshall FC (formed 1998) until 2018. They were runners-up again in 2016 to Middlesbrough and in 2017 to Guiseley Vixens. Initially playing at Hope University's Marsh Campus in Aigburth, they moved to Jericho Lane in 2018.

In 2018/19 they were runners-up in the Women's National League Plate, losing 5–1 to West Bromwich Albion in the final. In 2021/22 they won the division by three points over Newcastle United and were promoted to the National League Premier Division, finishing ninth in 2022/23.

LOWER BRECK

Formed in summer 2010 in Tuebrook, they won the South Liverpool Youth Division in 2010/11 and the West Cheshire Youth Division and Plate in 2011/12. In 2012/13, they joined with Grapes FC, joining the Liverpool County Premier League Second Division, winning it at the first attempt by four points from Old Xaverians Reserves.

In 2013/14 they were promoted to the Premier Division, finishing eleventh in 2014/15. In 2016/17 they finished runners-up to Aigburth Peoples Hall by three points, winning the George Mahon Cup and the I Zingari Challenge Cup. In 2017/18 they won the Premier Division by fifteen points from East Villa, also winning the Liverpool Challenge Cup, the George Mahon Cup (beating Custy's 7–0) and the I Zingari Challenge Cup (beating East Villa 4–3).

They joined the North West Counties League in 2018/19, finishing fourth in Division One North. In the Covid-hit 2019/20 season, Lower Breck were top when the league was abandoned, with the 2020/21 season also abandoned. They were promoted to the Premier Division for 2021/22, finishing nineteenth.

They finished the 2024/25 season as runners-up in the North West Counties League Premier Division three points behind Bury and won the subsequent play-off final 2–0 against Padiham and were promoted to the Northern Premier League for the 2025/26 season, they were runners-up to Everton in the Liverpool Senior Cup losing 4–1.

LUCAS SPORTS

Upon regaining First Division status for the 1992/93 season, they finished runners-up, five points behind St Dominics, and won the George Mahon Cup beating Yorkshire Copper Tubing. They finished runners-up to St Dominics in the league again in 1993/94 and were runners-up in the George

Mahon Cup (Peter Coyne Cup) losing to Crawfords. In 1998/99 they lost to Stockbridge in the George Mahon Cup but won the cup the following season, 1999/2000. They won the George Mahon cup in 2002/03. They remained in the Liverpool County Combination until the league finished at the end of the 2005/06 season and were placed in the Premier Division of the newly formed Liverpool County Premier League, finishing seventh in its inaugural season, 2006/07. In 2010/11 they were relegated to the First Division after finishing bottom of the Premier Division and remained there until the club folded at the end of the 2014/15 season.

MAGHULL

In 1992/93 they won the North West Counties Second Division but were unable to be promoted due to ground limitations and were Lamont Pils Trophy runners-up. In 1993/94 they were North West Counties Reserve Division Challenge Cup runners-up and Lamont Pils Trophy runners-up, won the Liverpool Challenge Cup beating Litherland REMYCA United 2–1, but were I Zingari Challenge Cup runners-up to Litherland REMYCA United. In 1999/2000 Maghull joined the West Cheshire League, finishing eleventh in their first season. In 2001/02 the reserves won the Third Division. In 2003/04 they were Liverpool Junior Cup runners-up and in 2005/06 West Cheshire Bowl runners-up. They were West Cheshire League runners-up in 2006/07, sixteen points behind West Kirby, they also won the Cheshire Bowl. They were again runners-up in 2010/11, four points behind West Kirby, while beating Newton 3–0 to win the Pyke Cup. In 2011/12 they beat Ellesmere Port 3–0 to win the Pyke Cup. In 2013/14 they won the West Cheshire League by fifteen points ahead of Hale, were West Cheshire League Bowl winners and Wirral Senior Cup runners-up. Between then and 2023/24 they regularly finished in the top half of the First Division. They were Runners up in 2023/24 and promoted to North West Counties League Div 1 North finishing tenth. And finished as West Cheshire League First Division runners-up in 2023/24 and were promoted to the North West Counties League Division One North finishing in tenth in 2024/25.

MARINE

In 1992/93 they were Northern Premier League Shield runners-up, losing on penalties to Stalybridge Celtic after a 1–1 draw, and were runners-up to Everton in the Liverpool Senior Cup final. In 1993/94 Marine won the Northern Premier League by one point from Leek Town and won the Peter Swales Shield, beating Guiseley, and the Liverpool Senior Cup, beating Southport 2–1 at Goodison Park. They won the Northern Premier League again in 1994/95, four points clear of Morecambe, won the league shield against Spennymoor, the Peter Swales Shield against Lancaster City, but lost the Liverpool Senior Cup to Tranmere Rovers.

In 1999/2000 they won the Liverpool Senior Cup, beating Tranmere 1–0, and the Lancashire Challenge Trophy, beating Bamber Bridge 5–0. In 2002/03 they won the Northern Premier League Cup against Gateshead but lost the Peter Swales Shield to Accrington Stanley. In 2004/05 they were Liverpool Senior Cup runners-up, beaten by Everton. In 2007 the reserves left the Lancashire League to join the West Cheshire League. In 2007/08 Marine won the Liverpool Senior Cup, beating Liverpool 1–0. In 2012 new floodlights were erected at Rossett Park.

In 2015/16 Marine won the Northern Premier League Cup, beating Scarborough Athletic 2–1. In 2017/18 they were Liverpool Senior Cup runners-up, losing to Prescot Cables. In 2018/19 they were relegated to the Northern Premier League First Division North West. The following two seasons were abandoned due to Covid, with Marine in third in 2019/20 and sixth in 2020/21.

In 2021/22 Marine were promoted back to the Premier Division after beating Runcorn Linnets in the play-off final and won the Liverpool Senior Cup, beating Runcorn Linnets on penalties. In 2022/23 Marine finished ninth in the Premier Division and won the Liverpool Senior Cup again. In 2023/24 Marine won the Premier Division play-off final against Macclesfield to gain promotion to the National League North and won the Liverpool Senior Cup for the second year running, beating City of Liverpool 2–0. In the National League North, they finished fifteenth at the end of the 2024/25 season.

MERSEYSIDE POLICE

They finished as runners-up in the West Cheshire League in 1992/93, four points behind Christleton, and won the Lancashire Amateur Cup, beating Wythenshawe Amateurs. They won the Lancashire Amateur Cup again in 1997/98, beating Crawfords 2–1. They were relegated from the First Division in 1999/2000 but won the Second Division in 2003/04, six points ahead of Cammell Laird reserves, regaining top-flight status. In 2004/05 they won the Lancashire Amateur Cup, beating St Dominics. In 2010/11 they rejoined the West Cheshire League, finishing eighth in the Third Division, but left the league during the 2013/14 season with their record expunged. In 2021/22 they became founder members of the Emergency Services League North West of England League.

MERSEY GIRLS LADIES

Joined the North West Women's Football League in 2014/15, finishing third.

MERSEYRAIL BOOTLE LADIES

Joined the North West Women's Football League in 2015/16 in Division One South, finishing fourth. In 2016/17 they won the division by five points from FC United of Manchester and finished fifth in their first Premier Division season in 2017/18. In 2021/22 they won the Premier Division by ten points from Tranmere Rovers Ladies, earning promotion to the Women's National League Division One North for 2022/23, where they finished bottom.

MERSEY ROYAL

In 1992/93 they lost the Wirral Senior Cup to Capenhurst. In 1995/96 they won the Pyke Cup and were runners-up in the Wirral Senior Cup in 1996/97, losing to Heswall. They were relegated from the First Division in 2001/02 and from the Second Division in 2002/03. In 2003/04 they finished fifth in the Third Division. In 2007/08 they were Wirral Amateur Cup runners-up to FC Pensby. In 2011/12 they were promoted to the Second Division but were relegated in 2012/13 and 2013/14.

They were promoted back to the Second Division in 2018/19 and quickly promoted to the First Division in 2019/20. In 2021/22 they won the West Cheshire League First Division by four points from Ashville and won the Cheshire Amateur Cup. In 2022/23 they won the league again, two points ahead of Mossley Hill Athletic, but lost the Pyke Cup final to them. They also won the Northern Counties Association Cup, beating Sefton, and retained the Cheshire Amateur Cup, beating Broadheath Central. In 2023/24 they finished sixth.

MSB WOOLTON LADIES

Joined the North West Women's Football League Division One North in 2013/14, finishing bottom. They switched to Division One South in 2014/15, finishing sixth, and won the division in 2015/16, six points ahead of FC United of Manchester. In 2016/17 they finished sixth in the Premier Division and eighth in 2017/18 before leaving the league.

(LIVERPOOL) NALGO (NATIONAL ASSOCIATION OF LOCAL GOVERNMENT OFFICERS)/ ALDER

Became a founder member of the Liverpool Premier League in 2006/07, finishing tenth, before changing their name to Alder FC. They finished second in the First Division in 2014/15, six points behind Waterloo GSOB, earning promotion to the Premier Division. The NALGO name returned for the 2016/17 season. In 2019/20 they won the George Mahon Cup, beating MSB Woolton 2–0. They won the league in 2020/21 and were runners-up the following season. They won the league in 2024/25.

NEW BRIGHTON

Reformed in August 1993, joining the Birkenhead and Wirral League before moving to the South Wirral Premier Division. In 1995/96 they were Wirral Amateur Cup runners-up and won the Wirral Junior Cup. They joined the West Cheshire League in 1996/97, finishing third in the Second Division. They finished seventh in 1997/98 and won the Wirral Amateur cup and finished fourth in 1998/99, with their reserves finishing fifth in the Third

Division. They won the West Cheshire Shield in 2001/02 and 2002/03. In 2004/05 they won the Second Division and the West Cheshire Bowl, winning the bowl again in 2007/08. In 2009/10 they were Wirral Amateur Cup runners-up to West Kirby. The club became defunct in 2012 after being Wirral Amateur Cup runners-up.

NEWTON

After spending most of the 1990s in the lower half of the table, they won the West Cheshire league in 2003/04, seven points ahead of Cammell Laird. They won the Pyke Cup in 2008/09 and were Wirral Senior Cup runners up and won the Pyke Cup again in 2013/14. They won back-to-back Wirral Senior Cups in 2016/17 and 2017/18, beating Ashville both times, and won the league in 2016/17, nine points clear of Mossley Hill Athletic, and the Pyke Cup in 2017/18. They won the league again in 2018/19, twelve points clear of Rainhill Town. At the end of the 2024/25 season, they finished third in the West Cheshire League First Division.

OLD XAVERIANS

Having been relegated in 1993/94, in 1997/98 Old Xaverians were promoted to the Premier Division after finishing as First Division runners-up to Edge Hill on goal difference. They finished eighth in 1998/99 and were Premier Division runners-up in 2001/02, two points behind Aigburth Peoples Hall, and won the I Zingari Challenge Cup. In 2002/03 the reserves won the I Zingari Combination Third Division. In 2003/04 they won the I Zingari Premier Division by eighteen points ahead of East Villa and were Challenge Cup runners-up, while the reserves won the I Zingari Combination Second Division.

In 2004/05 they were Premier Division runners-up, one point behind East Villa, and the reserves won the I Zingari Combination Challenge Cup. In 2005/06 they won the last I Zingari Premier Division title by one point from East Villa and the reserves won the Challenge Cup again. On the formation of the Liverpool County Premier League they were placed in the Premier Division in 2006/07, finishing ninth.

In 2007/08 they won the first North West Counties FA Challenge Cup, beating St Aloysius 1–0.

In 2010/11 they were League runners-up. In 2015/16 the reserves won the Liverpool County Premier League and retained it in 2016/17. In 2022/23 they won the George Mahon Cup, beating MSB Woolton on penalties.

POULTON VICTORIA

Vics won the Wirral Amateur Cup in 1992/93, beating West Kirby, and the Wirral Senior Cup in 1993/94, beating Capenhurst. They won the Cheshire Amateur Cup in 1994/95 and were West Cheshire League Runners-up behind Vauxhall Motors and the West Cheshire League Second Division with the reserves in 1995/96, six points ahead of Heswall, and won the West Cheshire Bowl. In 1996/97 they won the Cheshire Amateur Cup and the West Cheshire League, four points ahead of Heswall. In 1997/98 they won the West Cheshire League by eleven points from Ashville, won the Pyke Cup and were runners-up in the Wirral Senior Cup, losing to Heswall.

In 1999/2000 they won the West Cheshire League by twelve points from Cammell Laird and won a fourth title in 2000/01, beating Mersey Royal and winning the Pyke Cup and Wirral Senior Cup winners. They were Wirral Senior Cup runners-up in 2001/02, losing to Cammell Laird. In 2002/03 2002/03 runners-up in league and the reserves won the Second Division. In 2003/04 Vics won the Pyke Cup. They won the Wirral Senior Cup again in 2005/06, beating Ellesmere Port, won the West Cheshire League by three points from Aintree Villa and won the West Cheshire Bowl. They won the Pyke Cup and Wirral Amateur Cup, beating Manor Athletic in 2006/07. The reserves won the Second Division again in 2007/08. The club folded in 2009 but was revived in 2018. They were 2019/20 Runners-up in third division and again in 2022/23. They left the league in 2024.

In the Cheshire Amateur Cup they were winners in 1998/99 and 2007/08. They were runners-up in 1997/98, 2003/04 and 2008/09.

Earlier honours include West Cheshire Division Two titles in 1976, 1977, 1978, 1982, 1992 and 1996, and West Cheshire Bowl wins in 1974, 1977, 1978, 1979, 1982, 1995 and 1996.

PRESCOT B.I.

Also known as Prescot BICC, they were relegated from the Premier Division of the St Helens Combination by 1994/95 and remained there until returning to the Liverpool County Combination Second Division in 1997/98 as Prescot BICC, finishing fifth. They left the County Combination Second Division at the end of 1998/99.

PRESCOT CABLES

1992/93 North West Counties League. In 1995 the club reverted to the Prescot Cables name. In 1998/99 they were North West Counties Challenge Cup runners-up, losing to Vauxhall Motors. In 2001/02 they won the North West Counties Challenge Cup, beating Atherton Collieries, and were North West Counties League Division One runners-up, five points behind Kidsgrove Athletic. In 2002/03 they won the Division One title by four points from Clitheroe.

In 2003/04 they finished twelfth in their first Northern Premier League Division One season and were promoted to the Northern Premier League Premier Division following the creation of the National League and the league restructure. In 2004/05 they finished fifth in the Northern Premier League Premier Division and lost in the play-off semi-final to Workington. In 2008/09 Prescot were relegated to Northern Premier League Division One North after finishing bottom, with only five wins and thirteen points off second bottom Leigh Genesis. In 2010/11 the reserves joined the West Cheshire League. In 2015/16 they were runners-up in the Liverpool Senior Cup, losing to Everton U23s. In May 2016 Hope Street was renamed Volair Park. In 2016/17 they won the Liverpool Senior Cup, beating Southport 2-0.

In 2017/18 they retained the cup, beating Marine 4-0, and reached the Northern Premier League North Division play-off final, losing 1-0 to Bamber Bridge. In 2018 Knowsley Council purchased the 99-year lease on Volair Park after the club fell behind on payments. In 2018/19 they lost the Liverpool Senior Cup final on penalties to Southport. In November 2019 the stadium was renamed the IP Truck Parts Stadium. In 2023/24

Prescot finished third in Northern Premier League Division One West and won promotion to the Premier Division by beating City of Liverpool 2–0 in the play-off final. Cables finished in tenth place at the end of the 2024/25 Northern Premier League Premier Division season.

R.O.M.A. (ROYAL OAK MUIRHEAD AVENUE)

Roma remained mid-table in the I Zingari Premier Division until the league merged with the Liverpool County Premier League in 2006/07. They won the I Zingari Challenge Cup in 2004/05. In 2006/07 Roma were placed in the Premier Division, finishing thirteenth. In 2008/09 they were relegated from the Premier Division but were promoted back after finishing third in the First Division in 2010/11. They were relegated from the Premier Division again in 2015/16, and further relegated to the Second Division after finishing second bottom in 2019/20. They regained First Division status for 2021/22 but were relegated again at the end of 2022/23. In 2023/24 they resigned record expunged mid-season.

RUNCORN

In 1991/92 they were runners-up to Wycombe Wanderers in the Bob Lord Trophy. In 1992/93 they were in the Conference league and they were FA Trophy runners-up, losing 4–1 to Wycombe Wanderers at Wembley, and again runners-up in 1993/94, losing 2–1 to Woking. They were runners-up in the Cheshire Senior Cup, losing to Northwich Victoria. In 1995/96 they were relegated to the Northern Premier League after finishing second bottom, and in 1996/97 were runners-up in the Northern Premier League President's Cup, losing to Blyth Spartans, but won the trophy in 1997/98, beating Guiseley. They were runners-up to Macclesfield in the Cheshire Senior Cup, losing 1–0. In 2000 Canal Street was sold and in 2001 the club was renamed Runcorn Halton, ground-sharing at Lowerhouse Lane with Widnes RLFC. In 2004/05 they joined the new Conference North. In 2005/06 they rejoined the Northern Premier League Premier Division before becoming defunct in 2006.

RUNCORN LINNETS

Formed in 2006 by fans of the former Runcorn FC, who met at the Quayside Bar on the site of the old Canal Street ground. They remodelled an existing supporters' trust, joined the North West Counties League Division Two in 2006/07, playing at Witton Albion's ground, and finished as runners-up, earning promotion to Division One, where they finished twelfth in 2007/08. In 2010/11 the reserves joined the West Cheshire League, winning it in their first season.

In 2011/12 they won the West Cheshire Bowl. In 2012/13 they beat Formby to win the North West Counties League Challenge Cup. They were league runners-up in 2013/14, 2014/15 and 2015/16 before winning the North West Counties Premier League in 2017/18, earning promotion to the Northern Premier League. In 2018/19 they finished sixth in their first Northern Premier League Division One West season. After the Covid-hit seasons of 2019/20 and 2020/21, they lost the 2021/22 Division One West play-off final to Marine and the 2022/23 play-off final to Workington, also losing the Liverpool Senior Cup final on penalties to Marine. The ladies team joined the North West Women's Football League Division One South in 2020/21, finishing eighth. In 2022/23 the Linnets lost the Liverpool Senior Cup final on penalties. They were 2023/24 League runners-up and in 2024/25 finished in eleventh and won the Cheshire Senior Cup.

RUNCORN TOWN

Promoted to the West Cheshire League First Division after finishing runners-up to Vauxhall Motors Reserves in 1994/95, they finished second bottom in 1995/96. In 1998/99 the club added a reserve team to the new Third Division. The first team were relegated to the Second Division after finishing bottom in 2001/02. In 2004/05 they finished runners-up to New Brighton in the Second Division, their last season as Mond Rangers before returning to the Runcorn Town name for 2005/06. They finished second bottom and were relegated, but were promoted back to the First Division as champions in 2006/07. In 2007/08 they won the West Cheshire Shield. They remained in the First Division until 2009/10 when they joined the

North West Counties League. In 2010/11 they were promoted from Division One after finishing runners-up, while the reserves won the West Cheshire League Third Division. In 2011/12 they finished runners-up in the Premier Division, four points behind Ramsbottom United. In 2021/22 they were relegated from the North West Counties Premier Division to Division One North after finishing bottom. They finished thirteenth in 2023/24 and moved to Division One South for 2024/25.

St. ALOYSIUS

They joined the Second Division of the Liverpool County Combination in 1998/99 winning the division at the first attempt in what was a great season for them as they also won the Liverpool Junior Cup and the Lord Wavertree Cup. They won the Liverpool Challenge Cup the following season and the Liverpool County Combination in 2001/02. They came tenth at the end of the last Liverpool County Combination season 2005/06 and started in the Premier Division of the new Liverpool County Premier League, finishing third in 2006/07. They finished runners-up in 2010/11 but the following season they resigned mid-season with their record expunged.

ST DOMINICS

They won the Liverpool County Combination title in 1992/93 by five points from Lucas Sports and again in 1993/94, beating Lucas Sports on goal difference, and added the Lancashire Amateur Cup, beating Wythenshawe Amateurs on penalties after a 3–3 draw. They won a third title in 1994/95, seven points ahead of Waterloo Dock. In 1996/97 they won the Liverpool Challenge Cup, beating Crawfords 2–1, and the Lancashire Amateur Cup. In 1997/98 they won the league by five points from Crawfords and retained it the following season, twelve points clear of Manweb. They won the Lord Wavertree Cup in 2000, 2001 and 2006.

In 1998/99 they won the league but lost the Lancashire Amateur Cup to Merseyside Police. In 2001/02 and 2002/03 they won the Lancashire Amateur Cup. In 2004/05 they were runners-up to Waterloo Dock on goal difference. They joined the Liverpool County Premier League on its formation, finishing third in 2006/07 and eighth in 2007/08 before being demoted to Division Two for 2008/09, where they resigned mid-season with their record expunged.

ST HELENS LADIES / GARSWOOD SAINTS

In 1992/93 they joined the National Women's League Northern Division, finishing fifth. At the end of 1993/94 St Helens changed their name to Garswood Saints. In 1997/98 they finished as runners-up to Ilkeston Town by twelve points in the now named Women's Premier League Northern Division. In 2002/03 they were relegated after finishing bottom of the Northern Division and in 2003/04 joined the Women's National Combination League, finishing second from bottom. They returned to the North West Women's Regional League Premier Division and won the 2004/05 title by seven points from Liverpool Feds. The club disbanded shortly after a fire at their clubhouse in 2006.

ST HELENS TOWN

They finished runners-up in 1993/94 and were North West Counties League Challenge Cup runners-up to Rossendale United, losing 1–0. They won the reserve league in 1994/95 and were runners-up again in 1995/96. In 1997/98 they were runners-up to Burscough in the North West Counties Floodlit Trophy, losing 2–1. In 1999/2000 St Helens Town left Hoghton Road to ground-share with St Helens RLFC at Knowsley Road, with their last Hoghton Road game a 1–0 win over Vauxhall Motors.

In 2009/10 they left Knowsley Road when St Helens RLFC moved to Langtree Park, leading to a nomadic period ground-sharing with Atherton Collieries, Ashton Town and Ashton Athletic. In 2014/15 they were relegated to the North West Counties League Division One after finishing second from bottom of the Premier Division. In April 2016 it was announced they would move to the council-owned Ruskin Drive. They shared Prescot Cables' ground in 2016/17, with hopes of moving to Ruskin Drive delayed until July 2017 due to upgrade works, after playing fixtures at Prescot Cables' Volair Park and Ashton Town.

In 2018/19 the First Division of the North West Counties League split into North and South, with Town placed in Division One North, finishing seventeenth of twenty. They left the league after finishing bottom in 2021/22, moving to the Liverpool County Premier League Premier Division for 2022/23, finishing bottom. For 2023/24 they moved to the Cheshire Football League. They won the League 2 title in 2024/25.

SKELMERSDALE UNITED
In 1995/96 United finished bottom and were relegated to the North West Counties Second Division. In 1997/98 they were Second Division runners-up and promoted back to the First Division. In 1999/2000 they won the North West Counties League Cup, beating Newcastle Town. The reserves were runners-up in the North West Counties Reserve Division in 2001/02, and the club left White Moss Park at the end of that season. In 2002/03 the reserves were again runners-up and won the NWC Reserve Division Cup, and in 2004 the reserves returned to the NWC Reserve League from the Liverpool County Combination. In 2004 they moved to the West Lancashire College Stadium at Selby Place (Stormy Corner).

In 2004/05 they were North West Counties League Cup runners-up, losing to Cammell Laird, while the reserves won the Reserve Division and League Trophy. In 2005/06 they were promoted to the Northern Premier League as runners-up to Cammell Laird, joining Division One for 2006/07, finishing fifteenth. In 2007/08 they were placed in Division One North, finishing third. In 2008/09 they finished runners-up by one point to Durham City and won the Lancashire Challenge Cup, beating Radcliffe Borough 2–1. They finished runners-up again in 2010/11 on goal difference to Chester. In 2012/13 they won the Northern Premier League Division One North by sixteen points from Cammell Laird and were promoted to the Premier Division, finishing sixth in 2013/14. In 2014/15 they won the Liverpool Senior Cup, beating AFC Liverpool 5–4.

In 2016/17 Skelmersdale were relegated after a 6–0 defeat to Buxton, with their ground access denied by the owners. By October 2017, Chequer Properties blocked use of Stormy Corner, but a last-day deal to ground-share with Prescot Cables saved their league status. They finished second bottom in 2017/18 and bottom in 2018/19 in Division One West, leading to relegation to the North West Counties League. In 2019/20 they moved to JMO Sports Park, and when the league was abandoned due to Covid-19 they were sixteenth. In 2021/22 they finished runners-up in the Premier Division and won an inter-step play-off at Cinderford Town 5–1 to earn promotion to the Northern Premier League Division One West for 2022/23, where they finished eleventh but were relegated due to ground grading issues, moving to share with Burscough at Victoria Park. In 2023/24 they finished bottom of the North West Counties Premier Division and were relegated to Division One North. Sadly, at the end of the 2024/25 season of the North West Counties Division One North they finished bottom and were relegated to the Liverpool County Premier League Premier Division.

SOUTH LIVERPOOL

The newly demerged South Liverpool joined the Liverpool County Combination Division Two in 1994/95, finishing runners-up, three points behind Plessey. In 1995/96 they finished sixth in Division One. In 2001/02 they won the George Mahon Cup, beating Royal Seaforth 4–2 on penalties after a 3–3 draw.

In 2006/07 they joined the new Liverpool County Premier League, winning the First Division by five points from BRNESC and earning promotion to the Premier Division, where they finished sixth in 2007/08. In 2008/09 they won the George Mahon Cup, beating Lucas Sports 1–0, and in 2010/11 won the I Zingari Cup, beating Waterloo Dock 1–0.

In 2011/12 they joined the West Cheshire League Third Division, winning it by nine points from Helsby, helped by winning every away game. In 2012/13 they won the Second Division by four points from Mallaby, and in 2013/14 finished fourth, losing the Liverpool Challenge Cup final 2–1 to Garswood United. In 2014/15 they won the West Cheshire League by twelve points from Cammell Laird 1907 Reserves and were Pyke Cup runners-up, losing to the same team. The reserves were promoted from Division Three.

In 2015/16 they retained the West Cheshire League by seven points from Chester Nomads, won the Pyke Cup, beating Mossley Hill Athletic 2-1, and won the Liverpool Challenge Cup, beating Richmond Raith Rovers 4-2. They retained the Liverpool Challenge Cup in 2016/17, beating Byrom 5-0. In 2017/18 they won the West Cheshire League by thirteen points from Vauxhall Motors. When the league was stopped due to Covid-19 in 2019/20, South Liverpool were top after sixteen games, eight points clear of Mossley Hill Athletic and won the Pyke Cup. In 2020/21, the first full season post-Covid, they won the West Cheshire League and were promoted to the North West Counties League Division One North for 2021/22, finishing thirteenth.

At Jericho Lane, their new home, they finished fifth in 2023/24 but won the play-off final 3-1 against Ashton Town to secure promotion to the Premier Division. They finished the 2024/25 season in twentieth in the North West Counties League Premier Division.

SOUTHPORT

In 1992/93 Southport won the Northern Premier League and were promoted to the Conference League, also winning the Peter Swales Shield, the Lancashire Junior Cup, beating Chorley 5-2 at Burnden Park, and the Liverpool Senior Cup, beating Burscough 2-1 at Goodison. In 1993/94 they won the Northern Premier League Shield and the Lancashire Challenge Trophy, again beating Chorley 5-2. 1993/94 runners-up in Lancs Challenge Trophy to Morecambe and Lancs senior cup runners-up.

In 1996/97 they joined the Football Conference and won the Lancashire Challenge Trophy, beating Accrington Stanley 3-0. In 1997/98 they were FA Trophy runners-up, losing 1-0 to Cheltenham Town at Wembley, and won the Lancashire Challenge Trophy, beating Morecambe 2-0. In 1998/99 they won the Liverpool Senior Cup, beating Burscough 6-3. In 2000/01 they won the Lancashire Challenge Trophy, beating Lancaster City 1-0, and were Liverpool Senior Cup runners-up, losing to Burscough. In 2002/03 they were relegated from the Conference League to the Northern Premier League, finishing sixth in 2003/04.

In 2004/05 they won the Conference League North, and in 2005/06 won the Lancashire Challenge Trophy, beating Lancaster City 1–0, before being relegated from the Conference National in 2006/07. They won the Lancashire Challenge Trophy again in 2007/08, beating Chorley 4–1. In 2009/10 they won the Conference League North, pipping Fleetwood Town after a tense title race, sealing the title with a 3–0 win at Eastwood Town. They also won the Lancashire Challenge Trophy, beating Clitheroe 4–0 at the Reebok Stadium.

In 2010/11 they survived in the Conference National despite finishing in the relegation places due to Rushden & Diamonds' expulsion, and won the Liverpool Senior Cup, beating Everton 2–0. In 2012 Haig Avenue was renamed the Merseyrail Community Stadium under a sponsorship deal. In 2016/17 they were relegated from the National League Premier, confirmed after a 3–0 defeat at Dover Athletic, having earned only five points from fourteen games. They were Liverpool Senior Cup runners-up, losing to Prescot Cables.

Back in the National League North in 2017/18, they finished fifteenth, and in 2018/19 won the Liverpool Senior Cup, beating Prescot Cables on penalties after a 0–0 draw, and the Lancashire Challenge Trophy, beating Colne 3–1. They retained the Lancashire Challenge Trophy in 2021/22, beating West Didsbury & Chorlton 2–1, and again in 2022/23, beating Atherton Collieries on penalties. 2024/25 Lancashire Challenge Trophy winners and finished in eighteenth place in the National League North.

SOUTHPORT LADIES

In 2000/01 they moved to the North West Women's Regional Football League, finishing ninth in their first season. In 2001/02 they played in the Third Division North, finishing fourth, and were promoted to the Second Division for 2002/03, finishing fifth. They finished third in 2003/04.

SPEKE (FORMERLY DUNLOP)

In 1992/93 Speke finished twelfth in the First Division, but the following season finished bottom and were relegated to the Second Division. They regained First Division status by winning the Second Division in 1997/98.

They were runners-up in the First Division in 2000/01 to St Aloysius by six points, and won the title in 2002/03, five points ahead of Waterloo Dock. The following season, 2003/04, the positions were reversed, with Speke finishing second to Waterloo Dock by fourteen points. Speke won the last Liverpool County Combination First Division title, finishing eight points ahead of Waterloo Dock in 2005/06. They were founder members of the Liverpool County Premier League Premier Division in 2006/07, finishing tenth. They left the league during 2008/09, with their record expunged.

STANTONDALE

In 1992/93 they joined the North West Counties League Second Division, finishing fifth and winning the Second Division Cup, beating Maghull. They finished fourth in 1993/94. Their last season in the league was 1997/98, finishing twentieth. They left and folded, citing the lack of floodlights as preventing promotion to the First Division. Their final seasons were played at Formby's Brows Lane ground.

STORK

In 1994/95 Stork won the Wirral Amateur Cup, beating Heswall. In 1998/99 they lost to Heswall in the Wirral Senior Cup and lost to Heswall in the Wirral Amateur Cup. Stork resigned mid-season in 2002/03.

TRANMERE ROVERS

In 1992/93 the men's team played in the Football League First Division, finishing fourth and losing in the play-off semi-final. The women's team finished third in Division Two of the Women's North West Regional League. In 1993/94 the men finished fifth and again lost in the play-off semi-finals, while the women finished fifth in the WNWRL First Division. In 1994/95 the men again finished fifth and lost in the play-off semi-finals, while Tranmere Rovers Ladies won the Women's North West Regional League Division One by one point from Wigan Ladies. They won the Central League Cup in 1999.

In 1995/96 Tranmere Rovers Ladies won the Women's FA Premier League Northern Division by five points from Huddersfield Town, earning promotion to the National Division, and won their first Cheshire Shield. In 1996/97 they finished eighth in the National Division. In 1999/2000 Tranmere Rovers lost at Wembley 2–1 to Leicester City in the League Cup Final.

In 2000/01 Tranmere Rovers Ladies reached the League Cup final, finishing as runners-up to Arsenal, while the men's team finished bottom of the First Division and were relegated. At the end of 2003/04, Tranmere Ladies were relegated to the Premier League Northern Division. In 2004/05 the men finished third in League One but lost in the play-off final on penalties to Hartlepool United. At the end of 2008/09 Tranmere Ladies were relegated from the Northern Division after finishing eleventh, joining the Women's Northern Combination and being relegated again in 2010/11.

In 2012/13 Tranmere Ladies won the North West Regional League Premier Division by two points from Blackpool. In 2013/14 the men finished bottom of League One and were relegated, while the women returned to the Premier League for 2014/15.

In 2014/15 the men finished bottom of League Two and were relegated out of the Football League. In 2015/16, their first season outside the Football League, the men finished sixth in the National League and were runners-up in the Cheshire Senior Cup, losing to Stockport County. In 2016/17 they finished runners-up in the National League, four points behind Lincoln City, but lost the play-off final to Forest Green. The women were relegated after finishing bottom of Division One North.

In 2017/18 the men finished second in the National League, ten points behind Macclesfield, and won the play-off final against Boreham Wood to return to the Football League. In 2018/19 they finished sixth in League Two and won the play-off final, beating Newport County at Wembley. In 2019/20 They were relegated from League One to League Two.

In 2020/21 the men were EFL Trophy runners-up, losing 1–0 to Sunderland at an empty Wembley due to Covid restrictions. In 2021/22 Tranmere Ladies finished as runners-up to Merseyrail in the North West Women's Regional League Premier Division, ten points behind. The men finished 2024/25 in Twentieth spot.

TUEBROOK LADIES

Joined the North West Women's Football League Fourth Division in 1992/93, finishing runners-up in their first season. In 1993/94 they finished fourth in the Third Division but were relegated back to the Fourth Division in 1995/96 after finishing bottom. They left the league at the end of 1996/97.

VAUXHALL MOTORS

In 1992/93 Vauxhall finished third in the West Cheshire League. In 1993/94 they were Cheshire Amateur Cup runners-up, losing to Cammell Laird. In 1994/95 they won the West Cheshire League, four points ahead of Poulton Victoria, the reserves won the Second Division, and they lost the Wirral Senior Cup to Cammell Laird.

In 1995/96 they joined the North West Counties League Division Two, winning it by eight points from Atherton Collieries, and were promoted to Division One, while retaining a team in the West Cheshire League. In 1997/98 they were North West Counties League Challenge Cup runners-up, and in 1998/99 they won the competition. In 1999/2000 they won the league by nine points from Newcastle Town, earning promotion to the Northern Premier League, while also winning the Floodlit Cup and Pyke Cup but losing the Wirral Senior Cup final to Cammell Laird.

In 2000/01 they joined the Northern Premier League Division One, finishing runners-up to Bradford Park Avenue. In 2001/02 they were runners-up again, this time to Burton Albion.

In 2002/03 the reserves won the West Cheshire League. In 2003/04 they lost the Wirral Amateur Cup to Heswall.

They joined the new Conference North for 2004/05, finishing fifteenth, won the Pyke Cup, but lost the Wirral Amateur Cup final to Willaston. In 2007/08 they avoided relegation due to Boston United's financial issues, and in 2009/10 were saved from relegation by Farsley Celtic's expulsion. In 2010/11 they won the Wirral Senior Cup, beating Ashville, and won it again in 2012/13, beating West Kirby.

At the end of 2013/14, they resigned from the Conference North due to financial difficulties and rejoined the West Cheshire League for 2014/15, finishing fourth and winning the Wirral Senior Cup against Mallaby. 2015/16 lost Wirral amateur cup to West Kirby and Wasps. In 2017/18 they were Pyke Cup runners-up to Newton and lost the Cheshire Amateur Cup final to Knutsford. They left the West Cheshire League to join the restructured North West Counties League Division One South in 2018/19, finishing as runners-up to Rylands.

They were top of the table when the 2019/20 season was abandoned due to Covid, and the following season was also abandoned. In 2021/22 they were promoted to the Premier Division, finishing eighth. In 2022/23 they won the title, eight points ahead of Avro, and started the 2023/24 season in the Northern Premier League Division One West. Vauxhall finished fourth in the Northern Premier League Division One West at the end of the 2024/25 season but lost in the play-off semi-final to Hednesford Town.

WALTON VILLAGE
In 1992/93 they finished second from bottom of the First Division, repeating the position in 1993/94, before finishing mid-table in 1994/95. After two further seasons of bottom-half finishes, they left the I Zingari League at the end of 1996/97.

WARRINGTON TOWN
In 1991/92 the reserves won the Northern Combination Supplementary Cup on penalties against Harwood reserves. At the end of 1996/97 they finished second from bottom and were relegated to the North West Counties First Division, and the following season were relegated again to the Second Division.

In 1999/2000 they won the Second Division Trophy, beating Tetley Walker, and were promoted as champions, two points ahead of Tetley Walker. As part of Conference North and South restructuring, they were promoted back to the Northern Premier League First Division after finishing fifth. In 2007/08 they were placed in the First Division South but switched to the First Division North in 2008/09.

In 2013/14 they finished third and reached the play-offs, losing in the semi-finals. In 2014/15 they reached the FA Cup Second Round and won the Northern Premier League Challenge Cup, beating Farsley Celtic on penalties. In 2015/16 they won the First Division North title by fifteen points from Spennymoor Town, earning promotion to the Premier Division.

Before the Covid-hit seasons of 2019/20 and 2020/21, Warrington finished third in both 2017/18 and 2018/19, winning the play-off final against South Shields but losing the super play-off against King's Lynn Town, missing out on promotion. In 2022/23 they finished runners-up to South Shields by eight points and won promotion to the National League North after beating Bamber Bridge 1–0 in the play-off final. They finished thirteenth in their first season, 2023/24. They finished twenty third in 2024/25.

WATERLOO DOCK

In the Liverpool County Combination, Dock finished fifth three seasons in a row between 1991/92 and 1993/94, then finished as runners-up in 1994/95, seven points behind St Dominics, and again in 1995/96, one point behind Stockbridge. They won the title in 1996/97, eight points ahead of Stockbridge. Dock won the final title of the century in 1999/2000, ten points ahead of Yorkshire Copper Tube. In 2000/01 Yorkshire Copper Tube finished ten points ahead of Dock, while in 2002/03 Speke finished five points ahead, but Dock reclaimed the title in 2003/04, fourteen points clear of Speke, and again in 2004/05, on goal difference from St Dominics. They also won the Liverpool Challenge Cup four times in a row from 2003 to 2007, and again in 2012. In the final Liverpool County Combination season, 2005/06, they were runners-up to Speke by eight points. There were six further George Mahon Cups (1992, 1996, 1997, 2001, 2005 and 2010).

Following the transition to the Liverpool County Premier League in 2006/07, Waterloo Dock continued their success, winning the inaugural title by thirteen points from East Villa. They retained the title in 2007/08, finishing two points ahead of East Villa, and made it three in a row in

2008/09, eighteen points ahead of Aigburth Peoples Hall. That season, they were runners-up to Liverpool Reserves in the Liverpool Senior Cup, losing 1–0 at Marine's College Road. They won a fourth successive title in 2009/10, ten points clear of St Aloysius, and a fifth in 2010/11, twenty-one points ahead of Old Xaverians. Dock finished as runners-up in 2012/13, 2014/15 and 2015/16 before winning the title again in 2018/19, six points clear of East Villa. After the Covid-19 affected seasons of 2019/20, which was voided, and 2020/21, in which they were nominal runners-up, Dock finished third in 2021/22 and seventh in 2022/23. Dock in 2023/24 and 2024/25 finished in tenth.

WEST KIRBY

Promoted in second place in the Second Division in 2002/03, they went onto win the League in three times between 2006 and 2009 and again in 2010/11. The Pyke Cup was claimed 2005/06 and 2012/13. Six Wirral Senior Cups were won between in 2002 and 2014 and when they changed their name briefly to West Kirby and Wasps in 2015/16. Changing back to West Kirby in 2017 they remain in the West Cheshire League.

WEST KIRBY LADIES

Joined the North West Women's Regional League after winning the Cheshire Women's League Premier Division in 2018/19. Their first two seasons, 2019/20 and 2020/21, were affected by Covid-19, and they finished bottom of the league in their third season, 2021/22.

WIGAN ATHLETIC

In 1992/93 they were relegated from the Second Division. In 1996/97 they won the Third Division title on goal difference from Fulham. Wigan also won the Lancashire Senior Cup in 1998/99 but lost in the 2013/14 and 2020/21 finals.

In 2002/03 they won the Second Division, fifteen points ahead of Crewe Alexandra. In 2004/05 they were runners-up in the Championship to Sunderland.

After promotion from the Championship as runners-up, they began their first Premier League season in 2005/06 with a 1–0 home defeat to Chelsea, finishing the season in tenth place under Roberto Martinez. In 2006/07 they flirted with relegation before finishing seventeenth. They spent a further six seasons in the Premier League under Martinez, finishing fourteenth in 2007/08, eleventh in 2008/09, sixteenth in both 2009/10 and 2010/11, and fifteenth in 2011/12. Their Premier League tenure ended in 2012/13 when they were relegated with two games to go, despite winning the FA Cup Final that season. Martinez left for Everton at the end of the season. They were relegated in 2014/15 second from bottom, but came back up after winning League 1 by two points from Burton Albion in 2015/16. In 2016/17 they were relegated again from the Championship. And in 2017/18 they won League 1 by two points from Blackburn Rovers. Again in 2019/20 they were relegated to League 1 and in 2021/22 they won League 1. 2022/23 saw them Relegated from the Championship. 2024/25 they finished fifteenth in League 1.

Wigan Athletic unofficially adopted a women's team of the same name in 1999. This women's team joined the North West Women's Regional League Division Two North in 1999/2000, finishing third, and remained in Division Two until leaving at the end of 2003/04. They rejoined the league in the Premier Division for the 2018/19 season. They left the NWWRL at the end of the 2021/22 season. In the summer of 2024 Wigan athletic announced that they would form their own official women's team played in the Lancashire Women's County League for the 2024/25 season and won the title at the first attempt.

WIRRAL LADIES

Joined the North West Women's Regional League Fourth Division at the start of 1994/95 and were promoted from the now named Second Division South at the end of 2000/01, finishing runners-up to Broughton Aerospace on goal difference. They changed their name back to Wirral and finished runners-up to Hopwood by nine points, earning promotion to Division One. They finished as runners-up to Rochdale by twelve points in 2003/04, securing promotion to the Premier Division for 2004/05. They left the league at the end of the 2009/10 season.

WHERE THEY PLAY

ARCOFRAME STADIUM, RUSKIN DRIVE, ST HELENS

Opened by Pilkington in 2018, the Arcoframe Stadium features a 200-seat covered stand, a refreshments kiosk, and a fully licensed bar and clubhouse known as 'The Sticky Wicket'. The ground, shared with St Helens Town, includes hard-standing areas for spectators.

ALTCAR ROAD, FORMBY

Opened by Formby for the 2003/04 season, the ground included a glass-fronted cabin for media, a wooden covered standing area behind one goal, and a covered seated area near the sole turnstile. A portable classroom from Brows Lane was relocated for use on site. It had a capacity of two thousand.

ALT PARK, HUYTON

In 1994, Knowsley United chair Paul Orr appealed to the Huyton public to help stop ongoing vandalism at Alt Park, which had included the destruction of a Portakabin by fire, damage to stand seating, the demolition of walls in front of dugouts, and theft of PA equipment and kits, costing the club around £45,000. By 1997 Orr criticised Knowsley Council's lack of support, which he said had forced the club's resignation from the Unibond League, and he personally paid £4,000 to refit floodlights and £4,000 for 500 new stand seats.

ANFIELD, LIVERPOOL

In 1992, the Kemlyn Road Stand was rebuilt with a second tier and cantilever roof, renamed the Centenary Stand to mark the club's centenary, and opened in September, holding 11,000 fans with executive boxes and function rooms. The Kop hosted standing fans for the final time on 30 April 1994, a 1–0 defeat to Norwich, before becoming an all-seater stand for over 12,800 supporters.

In 2016 the Main Stand was expanded to add 8,500 seats, becoming a three-tier structure with a capacity of over 20,600. In 2017 the Centenary

Stand was renamed the Sir Kenny Dalglish Stand. Work on expanding the Anfield Road Stand began in 2021, traditionally housing away supporters, but delays meant it remained incomplete until early 2024.

BRAMLEY-MOORE DOCK STADIUM, LIVERPOOL (HILL DICKINSON STADIUM)

At Everton's AGM in January 2017, chair Bill Kenwright confirmed Bramley-Moore Dock as the preferred site for a new stadium, alongside proposals for a new railway station and road funded by Liverpool City Council. In November that year Everton agreed a 200-year lease with Peel Holdings, and in 2018 plans for a 52,000-seat stadium, potentially expandable to 62,000, were submitted. Construction of the 52,888-capacity stadium began in July 2021, following preparatory work from June, with ground broken on 10 August 2021. The dock infill began on 1 October using 450,000 cubic metres of sand and was completed by December, allowing the first stadium structures to rise.

On 17 February 2025, the first compulsory test event was held, with 10,000 fans selected by ballot from shareholders, season ticket holders, and members attending a friendly between Everton U18s and Wigan Athletic U18s. Only the South Stand, the new home end, was open. Wigan took a 2–0 lead before sixteen-year-old Ray Robert scored Everton's first goal at the new ground, converting a penalty at the South Stand end. A second test event, admitting 25,000 fans, Everton U21s against a Bolton Wanderers U21 lasted only sixty-five minutes with the score at 1–1 due to a mandatory evacuation practice.

A third test game was held on 9 August 2025 against AS Roma the other team owned by Everton owners Friedkin group. The game ended 0–1 to Roma with a full capacity crowd watching on of over fifty thousand. The day included a fifty-minute Everton veterans v AS Roma veterans' game. A behind closed doors game had already been played against Port Vale earlier in July.

On 16 May 2025 Everton announced that local solicitors Hill Dickinson would sponsor Bramley Moore Dock.

After a final test event against AS Roma in early-August, the new stadium opened for Premier League Football on 24 August 2025 in a 2–0 victory over Brighton & Hove Albion.

BROWS LANE, FORMBY

By its closure in summer 2002, Brows Lane had a 2,000 capacity, with a small wooden stand for 200 seated supporters and covered areas for a further 500. Formby moved to Altcar Road for the 2002/03 season. The site became Formby Pool in January 2007.

BUCKLEY HILL, NETHERTON

In November 1992, the pavilion that had stood since the 1960s was destroyed by fire. A new pavilion was built with ten self-contained dressing rooms with showers for home and away teams and a referee's room.

CANAL STREET, RUNCORN

The 1993/94 season saw multiple incidents at Canal Street. During an FA Cup first-round match against Hull City, the away fans' celebrations after a goal led to a wall collapse, injuring 16 people, including a police officer with a broken leg. The club faced expulsion from the league unless improvements were made, spending £14,000 to retain its status. In March 1994, the 255-seat main stand was destroyed by fire, forcing home games to Witton Albion's ground, and the West Terrace roof was later blown off. Pressured by Halton Borough Council, Runcorn moved to the Halton Stadium with Widnes Rugby League Club in the 1990s. The last competitive match at Canal Street was a 2–1 defeat to Gateshead on 5 May 2001.

1885 ARENA (DEVA STADIUM), CHESTER

Chester City moved into the Deva Stadium in 1992, situated near Bumpers Lane, crossing the Welsh border. Planning permission was granted in late 1991, with the first sod cut on 28 January 1992. The main stand seated 2,134 beneath a blue-clad cantilever roof, with the west stand seating 1,274. The two end stands each accommodated 1,296 standing. By the early 2000s, the ground had a capacity of 6,000, with over 3,000 seated and covered terracing for 2,600.

Between 2004 and 2007 it was known as the Saunders Honda Stadium. In 2006 the North Terrace was renamed the Harry McNally

Terrace. In May 2010, the lease was awarded to the reformed Chester FC. On the stadium's anniversary in 2017, the club shared construction statistics: 6,500 tons of concrete, 52,000 blocks, 48,000 bricks, 2,000 litres of paint, 40 miles of cable, 100 sockets, 550 light fittings, 171 doors, 1.5 miles of drainage pipes, 16 standards of timber, and 4.5 tons of nails and screws. Before the 2019/20 season, it was renamed the 1885 Arena.

DOCKERS WEMBLEY, EDINBURGH PARK, LIVERPOOL
In September 2020, plans were approved for housing development on what remained of the Edinburgh Park site.

GOODISON PARK, WALTON
The Park End Stand saw standing one last time in January 1994, against Bolton Wanderers, in an FA Cup replay. From February onwards the stand was rebuilt and the new 6,000-seater Park End Stand opened later that year and Goodison was now all-seated. Improvements for accessibility and fan experience continued to be made until May 2025, when the men's team played their last game ending 133 years at the stadium.

The 'Old Lady', however, had a stay of execution, becoming the home of Everton's Women's team from 2025/26 onwards. Goodison and the Everton Women were now owned by The Friedkin Group's parent company.

HARRISON PARK, NEW BRIGHTON
First used in around 1993 by the reformed New Brighton club, the ground featured fenced-off pitches and changing facilities, upgraded in 1996 before joining the West Cheshire League.

HAIG AVENUE, SOUTHPORT
In 1993, new terracing was added, funded partly by a £75,000 Football Trust grant towards the £200,000 cost, which also helped reseat the 1,900-capacity Main Stand. By the early 2000s, the ground held 6,000,

with seating for 1,660 and covered standing for 1,100. In 2018, the Main Stand was reroofed, with new gangways and railings added.

JERICHO LANE FOOTBALL HUB, OTTERSPOOL
Opened in October 2018 as part of the FA Parklife initiative, the site has three floodlit artificial pitches, changing facilities, parking, and health and fitness amenities.

JMO SPORTS PARK, BLAGUEGATE PLAYING FIELDS, SKELMERSDALE
First used by Skelmersdale United in the 2019/20 season, the venue was disused by the club in 2023 due to the artificial surface not meeting FA standards.

KIRKLANDS STADIUM, ROCK FERRY
By 2012, Kirklands featured a seated stand with a roof and executive area, open hard standing on either side, the covered First Bus Wash Family Stand, and a covered standing area known as the Volleyball Net End.

LINNETS STADIUM, RUNCORN
Opened in 2010 by Runcorn Linnets in partnership with Millbank Management, initially named the Millbank Linnets Stadium, with a 1,600 capacity. In 2017, a new clubhouse was built, and the surrounding pitches were fenced off for junior teams.

MOOR LANE, CROSBY
In 2023/24, housing was developed at the front of Moor Lane Playing Field, the base of Liverpool Ramblers, while the pitch remained in place.

NEW BUCKS PARK, VESTY ROAD, BOOTLE
Bootle moved to New Bucks Park in 2006 after leaving Bucks Park for redevelopment. Initially using Portacabins, they soon constructed a clubhouse with changing rooms and offices. The northern side featured

three stands (one seated, two covered terraces), with a small covered stand, 'The Dodge Kop', behind the western goal, and open standing at the opposite end. Turnstiles were located in the north-west corner, alongside a refreshment bar. City of Liverpool FC shared the ground from 2016 until moving on in 2021.

PRENTON PARK, TRANMERE

In 1993, three sides were redeveloped simultaneously to meet the 1994 all-seater deadline. Since 2018, Liverpool FC Women have used Prenton Park, having previously played at Kirkby Sports Stadium and Skelmersdale United. The ground has hosted women's internationals, including England v Spain (1996), England v Scotland (2005), and England v Russia (2017).

ROSSETT PARK, COLLEGE ROAD, CROSBY

In 1994, turnstiles and toilet blocks were upgraded, followed by a new 400-seat cantilever stand at the College Road end in 1999/2000, funded partly by the Football Trust. This replaced an eighty-year-old stand and left uncovered terracing divided into three blocks. In 2006, it was renamed the Arriva Stadium. The BBC described the ground in 2009 as "hemmed in by gardens" on one side, with dugouts, floodlights, and netting, while the opposite side featured shallow covered terracing and good elevated views behind the goals. In 2012, new floodlights were installed. The ground was renamed the Marine Travel Arena in 2015. In 2019, the club's tea room, 'The Gallery', was replaced by a modern café, and in 2022, a 3G pitch was installed. In 2024, Marine announced plans to move to a new 5,000-capacity stadium to meet growing demand.

STORMY CORNER, SKELMERSDALE

Used by Skelmersdale United from 2004, the ground had a capacity of 2,300 (240 seated, 500 covered). In November 2017, the owner locked the club out over lease disputes. In 2018, Southport FC used it for training, and it suffered an arson attack later that year. There were plans for the new Skelmersdale AFC to take over the ground.

VALERIE PARK, HOPE STREET, PRESCOT

By 2002, Valerie Park had a 4,400 capacity, with 550 covered spaces and seating for 200. By 2016, it featured a large main stand, covered terracing behind the Hope Street goal, and open standing on the opposite side and goal end.

VICTORIA PARK, BURSCOUGH

In 1996, admission prices were £2.50 adults, £1.25 concessions, allowing a family of four to attend, buy a programme, and have refreshments for under £10. Facilities included a grandstand for 200+, covered terracing for 1,000, floodlights, a snack bar, and a club shop.

By 2007, the ground was no longer meeting modern requirements, and proposals were made to replace it, but by 2010, redevelopment costs were prohibitive, leading to its sale to Chequer Properties Ltd, with the club renting it back at a peppercorn rate. Burscough briefly shared White Moss Park with Skelmersdale United in 2010/11 before returning. The ground was demolished in 2020. In 2023, it was shared with Skelmersdale United, and a new ground opened in 2024.

WALTON HALL PARK, WALTON

In 1999, Liverpool Schoolboys moved from Penny Lane to Walton Hall Park, where a new £2.7 million complex had been built, including a £1.8 million National Lottery grant. Sir Trevor Brooking, as Chair of Sport England, officially opened the facility, which had taken ten years to come to fruition. The complex featured two floodlit show pitches, a fully enclosed synthetic pitch, three training pitches, extensive changing facilities, a performance unit, lecture rooms for referee courses, and administrative offices for the Liverpool County FA.

In 2019, Everton constructed a 500-capacity stadium at the park for Everton Women's home matches, which was expanded to a 2,200-capacity venue by 2021. However, shortly after these improvements, the stadium suffered an arson attack.

From 2025/26 Everton's women's team moved to Goodison Park.

WEMBLEY STADIUM, LONDON

The final match at the old Wembley Stadium was a 1–0 defeat for England against Germany on 7 October 2000. Demolition of the old stadium began in September 2002, with the iconic Twin Towers coming down by December. The new Wembley was handed over to the FA in March 2007 and officially opened in May with the FA Cup Final between Chelsea and Manchester United. The new stadium has a capacity of nearly 90,000.

Local teams who played at Wembley during this period:

Everton: FA Cup Finals (1995, 2009); FA Cup Semi-Finals (2009, 2012, 2016).

Everton Women: Women's FA Cup Final (2020)

Liverpool: FA Cup Finals (1992, 1996, 2012, 2022); League Cup Finals (1995, 2012, 2016, 2022, 2024); FA Cup Semi-Finals (2012, 2015, 2022).

Runcorn: FA Trophy Finals (1993, 1994).

Southport: FA Trophy Final (1998).

Tranmere Rovers: League Cup Final (2000); Football League Two Play-Off Final (2019); National League Play-Off Finals (2017, 2018).

Wigan Athletic: FA Cup Final (2012); FA Cup Semi-Final (2013).

WINDLESHAW SPORTS GROUND, DENTONS GREEN, ST HELENS

Windleshaw has hosted sport since the 1890s, including the first rugby league match between St Helens RFC and Wigan RLFC, and served as the home of St Helens RFC until 1890/91. It was also the base of St Helens Cricket Club. FC St Helens took over in 2014, adding two seated stands, two covered stands, floodlighting, and a PA system by summer 2024. The ground also features a clubhouse and a food kiosk.

Stadiums that didn't happen

EVERTON: King's Dock, Kirkby, Walton Hall Park

In 1996, Everton Chairman Peter Johnson announced plans to leave Goodison Park, identifying Liverpool's King's Dock in 2001 as the site for a proposed 55,000-seater stadium, but funding issues prevented its progression. In June 2006, Everton entered talks with Knowsley Council and Tesco regarding a 55,000-capacity stadium in Kirkby, alongside a Tesco supermarket. However, the plans were vetoed by central government. In 2014, Everton explored a new stadium at Walton Hall Park in partnership with Liverpool City Council and Liverpool Mutual Homes, but this proposal also failed to progress.

LIVERPOOL: Stanley Park

In 2003, Liverpool were granted planning permission for a new 55,000-seater stadium on Stanley Park, with completion targeted for 2006. In 2007, under new American owners Tom Hicks and George Gillett Jr., final planning permission was granted in June 2008, but funding could not be secured. When Fenway Sports Group took over in 2010, the plans were reviewed but did not proceed. By 2012, the Stanley Park stadium plans were abandoned, with only minor groundwork completed.

Teams with Limited Available Information

The following teams yielded minimal information upon research, allowing only for brief mentions:

Chester College - In 1881, when the *Field* newspaper reported on an association football match between Birkenhead and Liverpool, it included Chester College amongst the teams that surrounded the local Liverpool area and were within easy travelling distance for spectators. The team appears to date back to the late 1860s, as a match reported in the *Cheshire Observer* was held on college grounds in 1869, which saw an eleven from the College beat Officers from the Garrison 3–2 after an hour and a half's play. This was surely an Association game from the brief description given. The team joined the Cheshire FA in 1914 and played at various times throughout most of the period this book covers. It could be said that Chester College is the area's earliest known team.

Albion FC - Played in the Bootle League and Bootle JOC in the 1920s, winning the Senior JOC Division in 1926/27, 1927/28 and 1928/29.

Blundellsands FC - Formed circa 1882 and played in both the I Zingari League and Liverpool League. They won the Liverpool Amateur Cup in 1921/22, the Liverpool League title in 1925/26 and the Houston Cup in 1928/29.

Bronte Old Boys FC - Formed in the 1960s and joined the Liverpool League, winning the Third Division and Second Division before claiming the First Division title in 1972/73 and 1974/75. They also won Houston Cups on many occasions and secured two Liverpool Junior Cups in 1974/75 and 1976/77.

Crossens FC - Won the Southport League on six occasions during the 1920s and 1930s: 1925/26, 1931/32, 1932/33, 1933/34, 1936/37 and 1938/39.

Pentagon Association FC - Won the Senior Division of the Bootle JOC League in 1969/70, 1970/71, and 1972/73, as well as winning the First Division and Everton and Liverpool cups on five occasions.

Planter's FC - Won the Birkenhead League in 1928/29 and 1929/30 and the Wirral Senior Cup in the same seasons.

Sefton & District FC - Formed in 1919 and played in the I Zingari League from the 1920s onwards, winning the title in 1980/81 as well as claiming the Liverpool Amateur Cup in both 1980/81 and 1986/87.

St. Sylvester's FC - A team that won five Liverpool League titles: 1965/66, 1966/67, 1968/69, 1969/70 and 1970/71.

CHAPTER 7

MERSEYSIDE TEAMS IN EUROPE AND BEYOND

Pre-European/UEFA Competitions

Before European/UEFA competitions, Merseyside teams would arrange to play teams during tours of Europe. These usually took place over Easter and in early summer, with the first such tour coming in 1902, made by the Old Xaverians.

Old Xaverian Tour of Holland 1902

Their first match was in April 1902 against Amsterdam AFC, with Old Xaverians winning 7–2 and reporting that they had a 'right royal reception' before and after the game. In The Hague the following Saturday, they played the 'International' champions, Handt Braef Stant AFC and in 'hurricane' winds Old Xaverians lost the game 3–1. On the Sunday they played and lost to an All Holland eleven. On Easter Monday they played in Nijmegen against an Eastern Holland XI who fought back to level things at 3–3 by full time. As the Old Xaverians left the ground in their carriages, a group of locals threw stones at them and at one point the police had to stop a lump of timber being hurled at them. However, this incident didn't stop the Old Xaverians being full of praise for how they had been treated by the Dutch teams, officials and fans alike.

Everton Tour of Austria, Czechoslovakia and Hungary 1905

After being offered £600 for a tour, Everton set off for a seven-match tour of the old Austro-Hungary from Exchange Station on 27 April, playing their first match three days later against 'Athletikai' Club and beating them 11–2. They won 4–0 at Vienna FC, played and beat an Austrian XI on 5 May, beat Tottenham Hotspur 2–0 on 7 May, beat Athletiklub Sparta 6–3 and Sportklub Slavia 5–0 before a final 1–0 win against fellow tourists Tottenham Hotspur.

Liverpool Balmoral Football Club

Toured Belgium during Easter 1907 and took part in the Beerschot Toernooi, losing to the Old Mancunians 3–1 in the final. The following Easter, 1908, they took part in the same tournament but lost in the earlier rounds and entered the same tournament again in 1909.

Old Xaverian Tour of Belgium 1908

Invited to Belgium over the Easter holiday for the inaugural competition of the Dupuich Cup. This was a cup donated by Adolphe Dupuich in memory of his son Jean, who had died at the age of 20 and had played for Leopold CB Football Club, who were hosting the tournament. The tournament was the successor to the Coupe Van der Straeten Ponthoz, which had been formed in 1900 in Belgium for European clubs to play in.

Old Xaverians joined Belgian clubs Leopold CB, Union Saint Gilloise and Racing Club of Brussels, French club US Tourquennoise, German clubs Preussen FC of Berlin and Preussen FC Duisburg and Dutch club Dijxhoorn XI in the tournament. Playing first against the host club Leopold of Belgium, they beat them 2–1. In the second round they lost 3–2 against Club Union of St Gilloise in a match that police had to stop due to crowd trouble. The Old Xaverians were leading with twenty minutes to go when the Belgian side started to play roughly – so much so that three of the Old Xaverians were kicked so hard that they could no longer play, whilst another was taken off injured. The English in the crowd invaded the pitch and the match was abandoned by English referee Kyle from Sussex. They played a third match, a friendly this time against Belgique Club in Brussels, achieving a 2–0 win.

Northern Nomads Tour of Scandinavia 1908

They played five games during the tour: drew 2–2 to Boldklubben 1893, won 3–2 against BK Frem København, drew 1–1 against a København Select team, won 2–0 against AIK Stockholm and beat Örgryte IS 4–1 in Göteborg. The Nomads made further tours to the Low Countries in 1910, 1911, 1912, 1913 and to Hungary in 1914.

Liverpool Tour of Scandinavia 1910

Liverpool left for Copenhagen on 11 May 1910 for a fortnight's tour of Denmark. On 18 May, they played a local team in Copenhagen and beat them 3–1; however, the next game was postponed due to the death of King Edward VII. When Liverpool next played, they were beaten 3–0 by a combined Danish Football Union Eleven. In the postponed game, Liverpool beat another combined Danish Football Union Eleven 1–0. On the way back home they were joined by Manchester United.

Old Xaverian Tour of Spain 1913

Old Xaverians beat Deportivo in Bilbao 3–2 and a Basque XI 1–0 in San Sebastián.

Liverpool Tour of Scandinavia 1914

Liverpool took three days to get to their first game in Gothenburg on 10 May 1914. The game was played on a skating pond which had its water run off in the summer and the surface covered with gravel and rolled. Liverpool won 4–1, but they had Terris injured when he got his foot caught in a hole and twisted his ankle. Their second match was played in Stockholm, this time in front of 16,000, with Liverpool scoring three goals and having one disallowed.

At the end of this tour, Liverpool found that they had fallen foul of new laws on touring drawn up by the Football Association which required their consent for teams to take part in foreign tours. Liverpool had failed to do so and were fined five guineas. They further fell foul of the FA's laws on expenses, having paid the players more than the £5 per man limit. Liverpool in future would be limited to 5s per day in expenses.

Orrell Football Club

Toured Belgium at Easter 1914 and won the Pasternooi Tournament, beating FC Brugeois.

After World War One, further tours of Europe were made by Merseyside clubs. Orrell went back to Belgium in 1920 and 1921 for the Pasternooi Tournament. The Northern Nomads toured Germany in 1921, with Everton in Denmark and Liverpool facing Milan, Modena, Pisa, Vercelli, Genova and Pisa in May and June 1922. The following season, Liverpool made a champions' tour of Paris in May 1923. Northern Nomads went back to Belgium in 1925 and toured Germany in 1926 and 1927. Everton toured Switzerland in May 1928.

In the 1930s the European tours continued. Liverpool toured Denmark in May 1932 and Everton toured Germany. Everton toured Scandinavia in May 1933, Spain in May 1934 and Switzerland in May 1935. Liverpool toured Praha, Zagreb, Beograd twice, Bucharest and Timişoara in May 1936, with Everton touring Germany the same year. Everton were next touring in Denmark in May 1937. In the year that World War Two started, Liverpool toured in Stockholm and Borås, with Everton in Switzerland and the Netherlands.

After World War Two, both Everton and Liverpool toured in Sweden in 1950 and 1951 respectively. Liverpool toured in Austria and Spain in 1952. Everton toured in Denmark in 1954 and in 1955, adding the Netherlands and Germany to the tour that year. Liverpool toured in France in 1956 and in Spain in 1958.

UEFA Formation and Early Competitions

UEFA, the Union of European Football Associations, was founded in Basel, Switzerland in June 1954. Their first competitions were the European Cup (now called UEFA Champions League), first held in 1955/56 and the Inter-Cities Fairs Cup in 1955, set up to promote trade fairs in Europe. The UEFA Cup replaced the Inter-Cities Fairs Cup for the 1971/72 season.

The European Cup Winners' Cup's first season was in 1960/61 for the winners of national cups to take part in. Another European competition was formed in 1968: the Coppa Ottorino Barassi, named after Italian sports official Ottorino Barassi (1898-1971). He helped organise the 1934 World Cup that was played in Italy and also helped Italy win the following World Cup in 1938. During the war he kept the original World Cup safe in a bank in Rome during World War Two. After the war he helped organise the 1950 World Cup and helped form UEFA in the 1950s. The cup competition itself was between the winners of England's Amateur Cup Final and the Italian equivalent Coppa Italia Dilettanti.

UEFA brought in a ruling that away goals counted double for the start of the 1965/66 season of the European Cup Winners' Cup before bringing it into the other European competitions. In the Fairs' Cup the rule started in 1966/67 and in the European Cup the rule came in at the start of the 1967/68 competition.

In 1969 the Anglo-Italian Cup began as compensation to those third division teams such as Swindon Town who had won the English League Cup but were not allowed to play in European competitions, due to only first and second tier sides being eligible. Swindon won the 1969 Anglo-Italian League Cup over two legs against AS Roma. The following season, due to violence marring the competition, Swindon were declared winners.

A British competition inaugurated in 1970 was sponsored by petrol giants Texaco and known as the Texaco Cup. It was made up of clubs who had finished outside of the European places in England, Scotland and both Northern Ireland and the Republic of Ireland. UEFA inaugurated the European Super Cup in 1972 between the winners of the European Cup and the winners of the UEFA Cup.

European Qualification Issues

European qualification rules proved problematic to both Everton and Liverpool. Everton had finished in fourth place in the League at the end of the 1974/75 season, which left them in the UEFA Cup places for the 1975/76 season. However, with Liverpool finishing second in the League, this meant that Everton fell foul of the Football League's one club per city rule and Stoke City, who finished fifth, were put forward by the league instead. Everton argued that this was unfair and refused to give up their place. When nominations for the UEFA Cup were put forward, Stoke City were refused the right to play in the Cup by UEFA and Everton were reluctantly put forward by the league instead.

EVERTON IN EUROPE

Inter-Cities Fairs Cup 1962/63

Merseyside's first representatives in the Inter-Cities Fairs Cup were Everton in the 1962/63 season. They were drawn in the first round against Scottish club Dunfermline Athletic, winning the first leg at Goodison Park 1-0 through a Dennis Stevens goal. The second leg at East End Park saw Dunfermline secure a 2-0 win on the night and a 2-1 victory on aggregate.

European Cup 1963/64

Having finished as champions in 1962/63, Everton were the first Merseyside representatives in the European Cup for the 1963/64 season. They entered the preliminary round playing Inter Milan over two legs. The first leg at Goodison Park on 18 September 1963 saw them play out a 0-0 draw in front of a crowd of just over 62,000. The following week, on 25 September 1963, Everton travelled to the San Siro in Milan to play the second leg in front of just over 59,000. Everton went out of the competition 1-0, with the goal being scored by Jair early into the second half.

Inter-Cities Fairs Cup 1964/65

The following season, Everton were in the Inter-Cities Fairs Cup. In the first round, Norwegian side Vålerenga were beaten 9–4 on aggregate and they then beat Scottish side Kilmarnock 6–1 over the two legs in the second round. In the third round they were drawn against Manchester United, losing 3–2 on aggregate.

Inter-Cities Fairs Cup 1965/66

Again in the Inter-Cities Fairs Cup, Everton played Nürnberg in the first round, winning 2–1 on aggregate, but came unstuck in the second round against Újpest Dózsa of Hungary, losing 3–0 away and only winning the second leg at Goodison 2–1 to go out 4–2 on aggregate.

European Cup Winners' Cup 1966/67

Aalborg BK of Denmark were beaten 2–1 on aggregate in the first round and in the second round it was Spanish team Real Zaragoza who provided the opposition. The Blues lost the first leg in Spain 2–0 but could only win 1–0 in the second leg and went out of the competition.

European Cup 1970/71

Everton entered the 1970/71 European Cup, beating Icelandic side Keflavík 9–2 on aggregate (6–2 and 3–0 respectively). In the second round the Blues faced German side Borussia Mönchengladbach. Both legs finished 1–1 and they won what proved to be the first European penalty shoot-out 4–3 at Goodison Park. The Blues were knocked out by Panathinaikos of Greece in the quarter-finals.

Texaco Cup 1973/74

Everton were Merseyside's only representatives in the Texaco Cup. They entered the competition in 1973/74 as part of then-manager Billy Bingham's plans to give the team more competitive games. They were drawn in the first round against Scotland's Heart of Midlothian, lost 1–0 at home and drew the second leg 0–0 to go out of the competition.

UEFA Cup 1975/76

Everton were drawn against AC Milan, with Everton at home achieving a
0–0 draw, but went out of the competition after a 1–0 loss in Milan in the
second leg.

UEFA Cup 1978/79

In the UEFA Cup, Everton started their campaign with a 5–0 first-round
first-leg victory against Irish minnows Finn Harps. In the second leg at
Goodison Park, Everton again recorded a 5–0 win and moved on to the
second round against Czech side Dukla Praha, losing on away goals after
winning 2–1 and losing 1–0.

UEFA Cup 1979/80

Everton returned to European action in the UEFA Cup and were drawn
against Dutch side Feyenoord, losing both legs 1–0.

European Cup Winners' Cup 1984/85

Having won the FA Cup in May 1984, Everton entered the European
Cup Winners' Cup for the 1984/85 season. Their first game was against
University College Dublin and they could only manage a 0–0 draw in the
first leg. In the second leg a fortnight later, Everton managed a 1–0 win with
a goal by Graeme Sharp. The second round took Everton to Czechoslovakia
(now Slovakia) against Inter Bratislava in the first leg, with Paul Bracewell
giving them a 1–0 win. The second leg saw a more comfortable 3–0 win at
Goodison. The quarter-final saw Everton up against Dutch side Fortuna
Sittard and the first leg at Goodison gave Everton a three-goal lead going
into the second leg courtesy of an Andy Gray hat-trick. The two-leg tie was
completed a fortnight later in the Netherlands with a 2–0 win through
goals by Peter Reid and Graeme Sharp. The semi-final was against German
maestros Bayern Munich. The first leg saw Everton play out a 0–0 draw,
with the second leg producing one of Goodison's all-time atmospheres
under the floodlights. Everton came back from 1–0 down to win through to
their first European final with a 3–1 win. The final, held in the Netherlands

at the Feyenoord Stadion in Rotterdam against Austrian side Rapid Vienna, saw Everton win 3–1 with goals by Andy Gray, Trevor Steven and Kevin Sheedy.

European Cup Winners' Cup 1995/96

Everton returned to the Cup Winners' Cup and were drawn against Icelandic team KR Reykjavík in the first round. The Blues travelled to the Icelandic capital in the first leg and returned with a 3–2 win thanks to goals by John Ebbrell, David Unsworth and Daniel Amokachi. In the second round, Everton played Feyenoord, a team that included future Everton manager Ronald Koeman, losing 1–0 on aggregate.

UEFA Champions League/UEFA Cup 2005/06

The 2005/06 season was Everton's first time in the UEFA Champions League for the men's team and they entered the competition at the third qualifying round stage, drawn against Spanish side Villarreal. Everton lost both legs 2–1, but the second leg proved controversial when a late equaliser by Duncan Ferguson was ruled offside, meaning Everton dropped into the first round of the UEFA Cup against Dinamo Bucharest. They lost the first leg away heavily 5–1 but only won the second leg 1–0, meaning their European adventures were over.

Women's UEFA Cup 2007/08

Everton Ladies represented English teams in the 2007/08 tournament. They were drawn in qualifying group A with Swiss club Zuchwil, Northern Irish team Glentoran Ladies and Lithuanians Gintra-Universitetas. The early years of women's European competition saw the early group games being played in one location and Everton Ladies travelled to Šiauliai and Pakruojis in Lithuania. Everton's first group game saw them beat Gintra Universitetas 4–0, their second game was even more one-sided with Everton beating Glentoran 11–0 and finally a 5–0 win against Zuchwil saw Everton Ladies top the group with twenty goals for and none against. In the second round, Everton were in Group B3 with Frankfurt of Germany, Rapide Wezemaal of

Belgium and Icelandic club Valur. They lost their first two matches against Rapide 2–1 and Frankfurt 2–1 but beat Valur 3–1 to finish third in the group.

UEFA Cup 2007/08 (Men)
The same season, Everton's men successfully negotiated the first round against Metalist Kharkiv and group A of the UEFA Cup against FC Nürnberg, Zenit Saint Petersburg, AZ and Larissa. They beat Norwegian side Brann in the round of thirty-two and reached the round of 16 against Fiorentina, being beaten on penalties after the tie finished 2–2. The following season the men's team went out of the UEFA Cup in the first round.

UEFA Cup 2008/09
Everton went out in the first round of the UEFA Cup to Standard Liège.

Women's Champions League 2009/10
Everton Ladies were back in Europe once again, this time in group G being played in Croatia between 30 July and 4 August. Everton were drawn against Norwegian team Strømmen, Estonians Levadia Tallinn and Croatians Osijek. Against the home side, Croatian team Osijek, Everton won 3–1. Against Estonia's Levadia Tallinn, Everton gained a comfortable 7–0 win and in the final game they beat Norway's Strømmen 1–0 to finish top of the group. In the round of 32, there was more Norwegian opposition, this time Røa from Oslo. Everton lost the game 3–2 on aggregate to go out of the competition.

UEFA Europa League 2009/10 (Men)
Everton's men played in that season's UEFA Europa League, beating Sigma Olomouc in a play-off and then negotiating Group I against Benfica, BATE Borisov and AEK Athens before being beaten by Sporting CP of Portugal in the round of thirty-two.

Women's Champions League 2010/11
In the 2010/11 season, Everton Ladies found they were drawn in the first-round group being held in Lithuania. The opposition was provided

by Klaksvík of the Faroe Islands, Macedonian side ZFK Borec and Lithuanians Gintra Universitetas. Everton Ladies finished top of the group after winning all three games: 6–0 against KÍ Klaksvík, 10–0 against Borec Veles and 7–0 against Gintra Universitetas. In the round of 32 they were up against Hungarian side MTK Hungária, beating them easily over two legs 7–1. Brøndby IF provided the next opposition. In the quarter-final they met German side Duisburg, losing 5–2 on aggregate.

UEFA Europa League 2014/15

Everton entered the group stage of the competition in Group H against Wolfsburg, Krasnodar and Lille. They won three and drew two of their games, only losing to Krasnodar away, meaning they finished in top spot in the group to move into the knockout stages. They were drawn against Swiss side Young Boys, beating them 4–1 and 3–1 over the two legs. For their round of sixteen game, they were drawn against Dynamo Kiev. Winning the first leg at Goodison 2–1, they lost heavily in Ukraine 5–2 to go out of the competition.

UEFA Europa League 2017/18

Everton started the competition at the third qualifying round stage against Slovak side Ružomberok, beating them 1–0 in both legs of the tie. They moved forward to the play-off round, beating Hajduk Split 3–1 on aggregate (2–1 and 1–1) and were drawn in Group E against Atalanta, Lyon and Apollon Limassol for the next stage. However, Everton lost four, drew one and won only one game and dropped out of the competition in third place in the group.

LIVERPOOL IN EUROPE

European Cup 1964/65

Liverpool's first taste of European competition came in the 1964/65 season in the European Cup. Their first competitive game came in the preliminary round against Reykjavík, first away with an easy 5–0 win, then with a 6–1 win at Anfield. In the first round proper anderlecht were beaten 3–1 and 1–0 respectively and in the second round they faced Cologne. The first leg ended in a 0–0 draw and the second leg finished 2–2 after extra time. The game ended in stalemate and a coin toss decided the winner, with even that needing a second coin toss before Liverpool went through to the semi-final, where they faced Inter Milan. Winning the first leg 3–1, they lost the second leg 3–0 to miss out on a first European final.

European Cup Winners' Cup 1965/66

Liverpool were the first Merseyside team to enter the European Cup Winners' Cup competition in 1965/66 and the first to reach a final. They were drawn in the first round against Juventus, losing the first leg in September by a Leoncini goal in the last ten minutes at the Stadio Olimpico in Turin. A fortnight later, Liverpool wasted no time in getting the aggregate score level, with Lawler scoring after twenty minutes. Five minutes later, Strong scored what proved to be the winner. The second round saw Liverpool drawn against Belgian side Standard Liège. They won 3–1 at Anfield and in the second leg won 2–1 to face Honvéd of Budapest in the quarter-final. They drew 0–0 in Budapest and a week later beat the Hungarians 2–0 at Anfield in front of over 54,000, with goals from Chris Lawler and Ian St. John to move into a semi-final against Celtic. After losing 1–0 in Glasgow, they beat Celtic 2–0 at Anfield to move into their first European final. The final was at Hampden Park in Scotland against Borussia Dortmund. The Reds went behind to a Held goal after 61 minutes but equalised six minutes later. The game, played in front of over 41,000, went into extra time where Liverpool succumbed to a Libuda goal after 107 minutes and Dortmund took the cup.

European Cup 1966/67

For the European Cup in the 1966/67 season, this time starting in the first round, Liverpool played Romanian side Petrolul Ploiești, beating them 2–0 at Anfield and getting a vital away goal in a 3–1 defeat at the Stadionul Petrolul in Ploiești to make the tie 3–3 on aggregate. A play-off game at the Heysel Stadium in Brussels saw Liverpool win 2–0 to progress into the second round, where they met Ajax. On 7 December 1966, Liverpool lost the first leg in Amsterdam 5–1 and they drew the second leg 2–2 at Anfield, losing on aggregate 7–3.

Inter-Cities Fairs Cup 1967/68

Liverpool started their Inter-Cities Fairs Cup games in 1967/68, drawn against Malmö FF of Sweden in the first round. They secured a 2–0 first-leg lead in Sweden courtesy of two Tony Hateley goals. At Anfield they scored two more with Malmö scoring a late consolation goal. In the second round, eight goals at Anfield effectively saw off TSV 1860 München of Germany before Liverpool added an away goal in a 2–1 defeat in the second leg in Germany. In the third round, Ferencváros of Hungary got the better of them, winning both legs 1–0.

UEFA Cup 1972/73 - First European Trophy

Liverpool played in the Inter-Cities Fairs Cup four times between 1967/68 and 1970/71. An appearance in the Cup Winners' Cup followed in the 1971/72 season before Liverpool finally won a European trophy the following season, 1972/73. In September 1972, Kevin Keegan and Emlyn Hughes got Liverpool off to a winning start to their first season in the UEFA Cup, both scoring in a 2–0 defeat of Eintracht Frankfurt in the first round first-leg game at Anfield. In the second leg, Liverpool played out a 0–0 draw. The second round saw a 6–1 aggregate win against Greek side AEK Athens. Rounds three and four saw Liverpool travel behind 'the Iron Curtain' for games against East German sides Dynamo Berlin and Dynamo Dresden respectively. In the semi-final, Tottenham Hotspur provided the opposition. Alec Lindsay got Liverpool off to the perfect start, scoring after seventeen minutes. In the second leg, Tottenham won 2–1, but Heighway had got the all-important away goal. Liverpool moved on to the final against German side Borussia Mönchengladbach. The first leg was at home with Liverpool winning 3–0 in front of a crowd of more than 41,000. In the second leg, Liverpool lost 2–0, but they had done enough over two legs and Emlyn Hughes lifted Liverpool's first European trophy.

UEFA Cup 1975/76 - Second European Trophy

Liverpool went out in the second round of the European Cup in 1973/74 and in the Cup Winners' Cup in 1974/75 before reaching another final in 1975/76. They would have to juggle a league campaign with what became a successful run in the UEFA Cup. Their first tie came against Scottish side Hibernian, with the Reds losing 1–0 away and 3–1 at home to face Real Sociedad in the second round, winning the tie 3–1 and 6–0 respectively. In the third round they faced Śląsk Wrocław and beat them 2–1 away and 3–0 at home. In the quarter-final they faced Dynamo Dresden, drawing the first leg away 0–0 and winning the second leg 2–1 to reach the semi-final against Barcelona. At the Nou Camp in the first leg, Liverpool won 1–0 in front of 70,000 with a John Toshack goal. In the second leg, the Reds drew 1–1 and made it through to the final. In the final they faced FC Bruges, winning at Anfield in the first leg 3–2 and drawing the second leg 1–1, securing the club's second European trophy.

European Cup 1976/77 - First European Cup

In the 1976/77 European Cup-winning season, in the first round they faced Crusaders from Northern Ireland, beating them 2–0 at Anfield and 5–0 away to face Trabzonspor in the second round. They lost 1–0 away in Turkey before beating them 3–0 at Anfield. In the quarter-final they faced French side Saint-Étienne and lost 1–0 in the first leg in France. In the second leg they won a tense game at Anfield thanks to a goal by 'Super Sub' David Fairclough, who came off the bench to score with six minutes to go. In the semi-final they beat Swiss side FC Zürich 3–1 away and then 3–0 at Anfield to progress to the final in the Stadio Olimpico in Rome against German side Borussia Mönchengladbach. The Reds won their first European Cup 3–1 thanks to goals by McDermott, Smith and Neal.

European Cup 1977/78 - Second European Cup

The following season, 1977/78, they received a bye in the European Cup's first round of matches and so they started their defence of the trophy in the second round with a 5–1 home win against Dynamo

Dresden and a 2–1 defeat in the away leg. In the quarter-final they beat Benfica away 2–1 and 4–1 at Anfield. In the semi-final against Borussia Mönchengladbach, they lost the first leg 2–1 but won at Anfield 3–0 to face FC Bruges at Wembley in the final. In the final they beat Bruges 1–0 with a Kenny Dalglish goal.

European Cup 1980/81 - Third European Cup

Liverpool had two unsuccessful appearances in the European Cup in 1978/79 and 1979/80 but were successful again in 1980/81. For the start of their European campaign, they travelled to Finland to face Oulu Palloseura on 17 September, coming away with a 1–1 draw. In the second leg of the tie at Anfield, with Graeme Souness getting Liverpool off the mark in the fifth minute, he would score a hat-trick, as would Terry McDermott, as the Reds won the game 10–1. In the second round they faced Aberdeen, beating them 1–0 at Pittodrie in the first leg and 4–0 in the return leg at Anfield. In March came the quarter-final two legs against CSKA Sofia. Liverpool won the first leg of the tie 5–1 at Anfield, with Souness getting a hat-trick. Liverpool finished off the quarter-final winning 1–0 in Sofia, making it 6–1 on aggregate to face a semi-final tie against Bayern Munich.

At Anfield for the semi-final first leg, they drew 0–0 in front of nearly 45,000 fans. Away in the second leg in Munich in front of 75,000, Ray Kennedy scored the equaliser for the Reds to give them a 1–1 draw and they were in the European Cup final against Real Madrid on away goals. In the final at Parc des Princes in Paris, Liverpool lifted the cup thanks to a goal by Alan Kennedy.

European Cup 1983/84 - Fourth European Cup

The Reds went out of the European Cup in the quarter-final stage in 1981/82 and 1982/83 before another final beckoned in 1983/84. The Reds started their campaign with a two-leg aggregate 6–0 win over Odense BK. In the second round they recorded a 0–0 draw in the first leg away against Athletic Bilbao and in the return leg at Anfield they won the tie 1–0 thanks to an Ian Rush goal. The third round saw them play Portuguese side Benfica, beating them 1–0 at Anfield in the first leg and in the second leg recording an emphatic 4–1 win away. In the semi-final they won the first leg at Anfield 1–0 against Dinamo Bucharest and in the second leg they reached the final thanks to a 2–1 win. In the final at the Stadio Olimpico in Rome they faced AS Roma and finished the ninety minutes 1–1, winning the resulting penalties 4–2.

1984/85 HEYSEL STADIUM DISASTER

After crowd trouble before the 1985 European Cup Final between Liverpool and Juventus resulted in the deaths of 39 supporters, all English clubs were banned from Europe indefinitely.

Liverpool only returned to Europe in the UEFA Cup of 1991/92, followed by the Cup Winners' Cup in 1992/93 and went on to play in the UEFA Cup again in 1995/96, 1997/98 and 1998/99 and the Cup Winners' Cup again in 1996/97.

UEFA Cup 2000/01 - Fifth European Trophy

After a season outside of European competition, Liverpool started away at Rapid Bucharest, coming away with a 1–0 win in the UEFA Cup 2000/01 season. In the second leg they finished all square at Anfield 0–0, winning the tie 1–0 on aggregate. The second round saw them face Slovan Liberec, winning the first leg at Anfield 1–0 with the second leg finishing 3–2 to the Reds. In the third round, Liverpool won the tie 4–2 against Olympiacos, the first leg finishing 2–2 away and the second leg at Anfield 2–0. In the fourth round, Liverpool beat AS Roma 2–0 away but lost the second leg at Anfield 1–0. In the quarter-final, Porto held the Reds 0–0 at their ground with the Reds winning the second leg at Anfield 2–0. In the semi-final they faced Barcelona in the first leg at the Nou Camp, coming away with a 0–0 draw. At Anfield the Reds won 1–0 to a Gary McAllister penalty. The final at the Westfalenstadion saw a high-scoring game against Alavés of Spain. The ninety minutes finished at 4–4 with the Reds winning 5–4 late into extra time thanks to an own goal.

Champions League 2004/05 - Miracle of Istanbul

Two more seasons in the Champions League followed in 2001/02 and 2002/03 and UEFA Cup in 2002/03 and 2003/04. For the 2004/05 'Miracle of Istanbul' season, Liverpool started in the third qualifying round, winning the two legs 2–1 against Graz AK. In the group stage they were in the same group as AS Monaco, Olympiacos and Deportivo. The Reds won their first group game at Anfield 2–0 against AS Monaco. In their second game they lost away at Olympiacos 1–0. Their third group game saw a 0–0 draw against Deportivo at Anfield. Away against Deportivo in the fourth group game they won 1–0. In the fifth match at AS Monaco, they lost 1–0 and they beat Olympiacos 3–1 at home. In the knockout stage they faced Bayer Leverkusen, winning 3–1 at Anfield and 3–1 away. In the quarter-final they faced Juventus at home, beating them 2–1 and away they finished 0–0 to move to a semi-final against Chelsea. The first leg at Stamford Bridge saw a 0–0 draw with the Reds winning the second leg 1–0 at Anfield.

In the final in Istanbul the Reds faced AC Milan and were 3–0 down at half-time, but with goals from Gerrard, Šmicer and Alonso in the second half, the Reds took the game to extra time and won the cup 3–2 on penalties.

Champions League 2006/07

After an unsuccessful Champions League journey in 2005/06, they started their 2006/07 Champions League campaign in the third qualifying round. The Reds beat Maccabi Haifa 2–1 over two legs. They faced PSV Eindhoven (0–0 and 3–0), Galatasaray (3–2 and 2–3) and Bordeaux (1–0 and 3–0) in the group matches. In the first group game they were held away 0–0 at PSV Eindhoven. The second group game saw them win 3–2 at Anfield against Galatasaray. In the third game they beat Bordeaux 1–0. In the quarter-final they again faced PSV Eindhoven, beating them 3–0 away and 1–0 at home. In the semi-final they again faced Chelsea, with the Reds losing the first game at Stamford Bridge 1–0 but winning the second leg 1–0 after ninety minutes and after extra time, with the Reds winning 4–1 on penalties. In the final at the Olympic Stadium in Athens, the Reds lost 2–1 to AC Milan.

Women's Champions League 2014/15

Liverpool's women's team started their first season in Europe with a game in August 2014 in the Champions League round of 32 against Linköping of Sweden. Liverpool suffered a heavy 3-0 defeat in Sweden in the first leg and despite going another goal down on aggregate after 24 minutes of the second leg at the Select Security Stadium in Widnes, they managed to win the game, scoring twice during the second half. However, it wasn't enough to progress further.

Women's Champions League 2015/16

The following season, 2015/16, Liverpool's women were drawn against Brescia again in the round of 32, this time in Italy. A mistake by goalkeeper Danielle Gibbons, punching Sara Gama's shot into her own net, was the difference between the clubs in the first leg in Italy. The second leg at Halton Stadium in Widnes was manager Matt Beard's last game in charge of the team before moving to the US. The game saw Liverpool lose to a goal midway through the first half and despite having most of the play and having a goal disallowed, Liverpool couldn't claw the lead back and went out of their second season in Europe 2-0 on aggregate in front of a crowd of 387.

Europa League 2015/16

The men's team had spent four seasons in the Champions League in 2007/08, 2008/09, 2009/10 and 2014/15 (in seasons 2009/10 and 2014/15 dropping into the Europa League) and two in the Europa League in 2010/11 and 2012/13 before reaching four finals in the next four years.

Liverpool started the 2015/16 Europa League competition in Group B together with Sion of Switzerland, Russian side Rubin Kazan and French side Bordeaux. Drawing their first three matches 1-1 with Bordeaux, 1-1 with Sion and 1-1 with Rubin Kazan, they won the next two games 1-0 at Rubin Kazan and 2-1 at home to Bordeaux and drew the last 0-0 away at Sion to top the group. They beat German club FC Augsburg 1-0 on aggregate in the round of 32 to face Manchester United in the last 16. They beat United 3–1 on aggregate (2–0 and 1–1) to face Borussia Dortmund in the quarter-finals. Drawing 1–1 in Germany, Liverpool scored an injury-time winner to beat the German side 4–3 at Anfield after going 2–0 down after nine minutes. In the semi-final they faced Spanish side Villarreal, who beat them at El Madrigal 1–0 before Liverpool won the tie with three goals at Anfield. In the final they faced Sevilla and were beaten 3–1.

Champions League 2017/18

After missing out on Europe altogether in the 2016/17 season, the Reds entered the 2017/18 Champions League competition at the play-off stage using the League Route. They were drawn against German club 1899 Hoffenheim, beating them 2–1 in Germany and 4–2 at Anfield. In the group stage they were in Group E with Spaniards Sevilla, Russian side Spartak Moscow and Slovenian side Maribor. They drew 2–2 at Anfield against Sevilla, 1–1 in Russia against Spartak Moscow and hammered Maribor in Slovenia 7–0 in the first three games. In the return games they beat Maribor 3–0 at Anfield, drew away 3–3 against Sevilla and hammered Spartak Moscow at Anfield 7–0 to top the group. In the round of 16 they faced FC Porto and beat them 5–0 in the away leg and drew 0–0 at Anfield before facing Manchester City in the quarter-final. At Anfield the Reds won 3–0 and then beat City 2–1 at the City of Manchester Stadium to win through to the semi-final 5–1 on aggregate. In that semi-final they faced Italian side AS Roma and beat them 5–2 in the first leg at Anfield and although they lost the away leg 4–2, they had made it through to the final. In the final they faced and lost to Real Madrid 3–1.

Champions League 2018/19 - Sixth European Cup

They won the European Cup/Champions League for a sixth time in 2018/19. The Reds started in Group C against Paris Saint-Germain, Napoli and Red Star Belgrade. The first group game at Anfield saw the Reds beat Paris Saint-Germain 3–2. In the second game they lost 1–0 to Napoli in Naples. In the third group game at Anfield, they beat Red Star Belgrade 4–0. In the fourth game they lost 2–0 to Red Star away and in the fifth match away at Paris

Saint-Germain the Reds lost 2–1. In the final game at Anfield, they beat Napoli 1–0 to progress to the knockout stages in second place in the group.

In the knockout stages Liverpool were held 0–0 at Anfield by Bayern Munich, but the Reds won 3–1 in Germany to play a quarter-final against FC Porto. The Reds won the first leg at Anfield 2–0 and won emphatically 4–1 in Portugal. In the semi-final the Reds lost 3–0 away at the Nou Camp against Barcelona but won heavily at Anfield, winning 4–0. In the final in Madrid against Tottenham Hotspur, the Reds won 2–0.

Champions League 2021/22

After finishing in the Champions League round of sixteen and quarter-final in the previous two seasons, 2021/22 saw them as Champions League runners-up. Starting the tournament in Group B against Spanish side Atlético Madrid, Portuguese side FC Porto and Italian side AC Milan, at Anfield in the first group game they beat AC Milan 3–2 before beating FC Porto 5–1 away in their second group game. In the third match they beat Atlético Madrid 3–2 away and beat them again 2–0, this time at Anfield, in the return games. In the fifth game they beat FC Porto 2–0 again at Anfield and in the last group game they beat AC Milan 2–1 in the San Siro. In the round of 16 they faced Inter Milan and beat them away 2–0 but held on at Anfield, losing only 1–0 to progress to the quarter-final against Benfica in Portugal. The first leg away saw the Reds win 3–1 and then at Anfield they drew a goal-packed game 3–3 to progress to the semi-final. There they faced Villarreal, beating them in the first leg at Anfield 2–0 and winning the second leg away 3–2 to move into another Champions League final. In the final they met Real Madrid but lost 1–0 to a Vinícius goal.

Recent European Campaigns

In 2022/23 they reached the round of sixteen in the Champions League and the following season they reached the quarter-final of the UEFA Europa League. In 2023/24 they reached the quarter-finals of the Europa League and in 2024/25 they reached the Champions League round of sixteen.

They also won the UEFA Super Cup in 1977, 2001, 2005 and 2019.

SKELMERSDALE UNITED

Skelmersdale United won the Copa Ottorino Barassi in 1971. Skelmersdale played Montebelluna, an amateur club founded in 1919 who played near Venice. Both clubs, however, had become professional clubs not long before the game. Montebelluna stayed in Blackpool the night before the game before travelling to Skelmersdale's White Moss Park for the first leg. United won the game on 29 September 1971, 2–0. For the second leg, Skelmersdale United complained about being £1,000 out of pocket for expenses for the tie. Normally, the Football Association had helped teams with the expense of playing in the games. However, this time Skelmersdale had to come up with the money themselves. The second leg in Montebelluna saw the home side pull one back overall with a tenth-minute goal in front of a crowd of 7,000. Skelmersdale, though, held onto the aggregate lead and won the cup, having survived a late penalty claim by the home side. The Montebelluna side had a player brought down inside or near the penalty area, with the referee being jeered when he gave a free kick outside the area.

TRANMERE ROVERS

The first Anglo-Italian Cup games were played between 1970 and 1973 when no Merseyside clubs had taken part. When the competition returned in 1992/93, Tranmere Rovers were Merseyside's representatives. Tranmere played Peterborough United and Wolverhampton Wanderers in a three-team round-robin group, with the top club qualifying to play the Italian clubs in the international round. Tranmere played and drew 0–0 away at Peterborough, beating Wolverhampton Wanderers at Prenton Park 2–1 on their way to topping the group with 3 points to qualify for the international round in the English Group B.

In a complicated group system, they needed to better the results of Derby County, West Ham United and Bristol City – these teams made up the English clubs in the group. Tranmere, however, would play only the Italian teams in the group: Cosenza, Cremonese, Pisa and AC Reggiana.

The first game in Europe that Tranmere played was against AC Reggiana on 11 November 1992, coming away with a 0–0 draw. Tranmere's first

European win came in Pisa on 8 December 1992 in front of a crowd of just 700, with a Kenny Irons goal securing a place in the history books, scoring the only goal against a side that included a young Patrick Vieira. The following season, 1993/94, Tranmere were drawn in the English preliminary group round against Sunderland and Bolton Wanderers. They lost 2–0 to Sunderland away, meaning that they needed to beat Bolton Wanderers by a heavy score in their final game to qualify to play against the Italian teams. However, Rovers lost away 2–1 to crash out of the cup.

The Anglo-Italian Cup was revamped slightly for the 1994/95 season, with six of the Football League First Division teams who finished outside of the promotion places playing in just the international round. Tranmere were drawn in Group A with Ascoli, Atalanta, Lecce and Venezia of Italy and with English clubs Notts County, Swindon Town and Wolverhampton Wanderers. Playing just the Italian sides, Tranmere drew only one match at home in the first game against Venezia and lost to Ascoli, Atalanta and Lecce, finishing bottom of their eight-team group. The Anglo-Italian Cup finished in 1996.

WIGAN ATHLETIC
After winning the FA Cup in 2013, Wigan played in the 2013/14 Europa League, playing in Group D with Rubin Kazan, Maribor and Zulter Waregem. Wigan finished in last place in the group, only winning one game against Maribor at Home and drawing two other games.

INTERCONTINENTAL CUP
Inaugurated in 1960 by UEFA and CONMEBOL, the Cup began as a two-legged tie between the European Cup winners and the South American Copa Libertadores winners.

Liverpool's Intercontinental Cup Appearances
Liverpool first played in the Intercontinental Cup against Brazilian team Flamengo in 1981 after initially declining to play in the 1977 and 1978 editions of the competition. Against Flamengo they lost 3–0 in the National

Stadium in Tokyo. Three years later the Reds lost 1–0 against Argentine team Independiente, again at the National Stadium in Tokyo.

FIFA CLUB WORLD CUP

The FIFA Club World Cup began in 2000 under the name FIFA Club World Championship. Financial difficulties, particularly the bankruptcy of FIFA's marketing partner International Sport and Leisure (ISL), forced the tournament's cancellation between 2001 and 2004. When it resumed in 2005, FIFA established it as a yearly competition that ran through 2023. The format has since been overhauled for 2025 onwards, transforming it into a four-yearly tournament with an expanded structure reminiscent of the FIFA World Cup.

Liverpool's Tournament History

Liverpool played in the revamped World Club Cup in 2005 held in Japan. They first played Costa Rican Club Saprissa, who were the Concacaf Champions, after starting the Cup at the semi final stage, beating them 3–0 in Yokohama. In the final Liverpool met Brazilian side Sao Paolo in Yokohama losing 1–0, Liverpool would finally get their hands on the World Club Cup in Qatar 2019. They played Mexican side Monterrey in the Semi-Final beating them 2–1 in Doha. In the final they faced Flamengo again but this time beat them 1–0 again in Doha to carry off the Cup for the first time

EUROPEAN SUPER LEAGUE

In April 2021, Liverpool announced that they would take part in a newly proposed European League with AC Milan, Arsenal, Atlético Madrid, Barcelona, Chelsea, Inter Milan, Juventus, Manchester City, Manchester United, Real Madrid and Tottenham Hotspur. However, the idea was soon met with fan protests and a meeting with other Premier League clubs unhappy with the announcement. The idea was dropped soon afterwards.

CHAPTER 8

MISCELLANEOUS

Rockford Files

Tranmere's use of the theme tune from American TV series *The Rockford Files* is thought to date back to games Rovers played on Friday nights in 1979 (to avoid clashes with fixtures at Goodison or Anfield). When club Chairman Bill Bothwell was asked why attendances were lower than expected, his reply was: 'I can only conclude that the people of Wirral prefer to watch *The Rockford Files* on TV on a cold Friday night than support their local football team.' The club's PA announcer soon adopted the tune to the amusement of supporters, and it has been used ever since.

You'll Never Walk Alone

Liverpool's 'You'll Never Walk Alone' first appeared in the 1945 Rodgers and Hammerstein musical *Carousel*. The version the club adopted was the 1963 recording by Liverpool band Gerry and the Pacemakers. This came about when manager Bill Shankly chose the song during his 1965 appearance on BBC radio's *Desert Island Discs*. Soon afterwards, the club's supporters began singing the tune and have continued the tradition ever since.

Z Cars

Everton's use of the *Z Cars* theme began as a tribute to TV actor Leonard Williams, a cast member of the police drama, who attended Everton's

5–0 victory over Blackpool at Goodison Park on 10 November 1962. The club played the tune knowing he was in attendance. When Williams passed away just five days later, the club again played the tune in tribute. Everton won that match too, beating Sheffield United. After fans wrote asking the club to keep the tune, Everton agreed and went on to win the league title that same season.

Everton have used the tune for all seasons except 1994/95, when the chairman changed the walk-out music to '2001: A Space Odyssey,' followed by 'Bad Moon Rising' at the next game. Following supporter complaints, Everton reinstated *Z Cars*, which has remained ever since.

APPENDIX

PROFESSIONAL

LEAGUE POSITIONS BY SEASON

Season	Teams in League	Bootle	Everton	Liverpool	New Brighton Tower
1888/89	12	N/A	8	N/A	N/A
1889/90	12	N/A	2	N/A	N/A
1890/91	12	N/A	1	N/A	N/A
1891/92	14	N/A	5	N/A	N/A
1892/93	28	24	3	N/A	N/A
1893/94	31	N/A	6	17	N/A
1894/95	32	N/A	2	16	N/A
1895/96	32	N/A	3	17	N/A
1896/97	32	N/A	7	5	N/A
1897/98	32	N/A	4	9	N/A
1898/99	36	N/A	4	2	23
1899/00	36	N/A	11	10	28
1900/01	36	N/A	7	1	22
1901/02	36	N/A	2	11	N/A
1902/03	36	N/A	12	5	N/A
1903/04	36	N/A	3	17	N/A
1904/05	36	N/A	2	19	N/A
1905/06	40	N/A	11	1	N/A
1906/07	40	N/A	3	15	N/A
1907/08	40	N/A	11	8	N/A
1908/09	40	N/A	2	16	N/A
1909/10	40	N/A	10	2	N/A
1910/11	40	N/A	4	13	N/A
1911/12	40	N/A	2	17	N/A
1912/13	40	N/A	11	12	N/A
1913/14	40	N/A	15	16	N/A
1914/15	40	N/A	1	13	N/A
1919/20	44	N/A	16	4	N/A
1920/21	66	N/A	7	4	N/A

N/A: Team drops out of league football

Season	Teams in League	Everton	Liverpool	Southport	Tranmere Rovers	New Brighton	Chester/ Chester City	Wigan Borough
1920/21	66	7	4	N/A	N/A	N/A	N/A	N/A
1921/22	64N	20	1	53N	62N	N/A	N/A	61N
1922/23	64N	5	1	61N	60N	N/A	N/A	49N
1923/24	66N	7	12	51N	56N	62N	N/A	54N
1924/25	66N	17	4	48N	65N	47N	N/A	55N
1925/26	66N	11	7	64N	51N	56N	N/A	61N
1926/27	66N	20	9	56N	53N	54N	N/A	62N
1927/28	66N	1	16	52N	49N	54N	N/A	64N
1928/29	66N	18	5	56N	51N	58N	N/A	48N
1929/30	66N	22	12	53N	56N	57N	N/A	62N
1930/31	66N	23	9	49N	48N	63N	N/A	54N
1931/32	65N	1	10	51N	48N	64N	47N	N/A
1932/33	66N	11	14	56N	55N	65N	48N	N/A
1933/34	66N	14	18	62N	51N	59N	54N	N/A
1934/35	66N	8	7	65N	50N	60N	47N	N/A
1935/36	66N	16	19	65N	47N	66N	46N	N/A
1936/37	66N	17	18	58N	63N	59N	47N	N/A
1937/38	66N	14	11	60N	45N	57N	53N	N/A
1938/39	66N	1	11	48N	44N	60N	50N	N/A
1946/47	66N	10	1	65N	54N	62N	47N	N/A
1947/48	66N	14	11	59N	62N	66N	64N	N/A
1948/49	66N	18	12	65N	55N	61N	62N	N/A
1949/50	66N	18	8	60N	49N	58N	56N	N/A
1950/51	68N	22	9	65N	48N	68N	57N	N/A
1951/52	68N	29	11	61N	55N	N/A	63N	N/A
1952/53	68N	38	17	50N	57N	N/A	64N	N/A
1953/54	68N	24	22	55N	58N	N/A	68N	N/A
1954/55	68N	11	33	55N	63N	N/A	68N	N/A
1955/56	68N	15	25	49N	60N	N/A	61N	N/A
1956/57	68N	15	25	66N	67N	N/A	65N	N/A
1957/58	68N	16	26	67N	55N	N/A	65N	N/A
1958/59	92	16	26	92	51	N/A	81	N/A

N/A: Team drops out of league football

Season	Teams in League	Everton	Liverpool	Southport	Tranmere Rovers	Chester/ Chester City	Wigan Athletic
1959/60	92	15	25	89	64	88	N/A
1960/61	92	5	25	82	65	92	N/A
1961/62	91	4	23	85	83	91	N/A
1962/63	92	1	8	81	76	89	N/A
1963/64	92	3	1	89	75	80	N/A
1964/65	92	4	7	88	73	76	N/A
1965/66	92	11	1	78	73	75	N/A
1966/67	92	6	5	70	72	77	N/A
1967/68	92	5	3	58	63	90	N/A
1968/69	92	3	2	52	51	82	N/A
1969/70	92	1	5	68	60	79	N/A
1970/71	92	14	5	76	62	73	N/A
1971/72	92	15	3	75	64	88	N/A
1972/73	92	17	1	69	54	83	N/A
1973/74	92	7	2	67	60	75	N/A
1974/75	92	4	2	79	68	72	N/A
1975/76	92	11	1	91	72	61	N/A
1976/77	92	9	1	91	58	57	N/A
1977/78	92	3	2	91	56	59	N/A
1978/79	92	4	1	N/A	67	64	74
1979/80	92	19	1	N/A	83	53	74
1980/81	92	15	5	N/A	89	62	79
1981/82	92	8	1	N/A	79	68	71
1982/83	92	7	1	N/A	87	81	62
1983/84	92	7	1	N/A	78	92	59
1984/85	92	1	2	N/A	74	84	60
1985/86	92	2	1	N/A	87	70	48
1986/87	92	1	2	N/A	88	59	48
1987/88	92	4	1	N/A	82	59	51
1988/89	92	8	2	N/A	70	52	61
1989/90	92	6	1	N/A	48	60	62
1990/91	92	9	2	N/A	49	63	54
1991/92	92	12	6	N/A	36	62	59

N/A: Team drops out of league football

Season	Teams in League	Everton	Liverpool	Tranmere Rovers	Chester/ Chester City	Wigan Athletic
1992/93	92	13	6	26	70	69
1993/94	92	17	8	27	72	89
1994/95	92	15	4	27	69	84
1995/96	92	6	3	33	76	78
1996/97	92	15	4	31	74	69
1997/98	92	17	3	34	82	55
1998/99	92	14	7	35	82	50
1999/00	92	13	4	33	92	48
2000/01	92	16	3	44	N/A	50
2001/02	92	15	2	56	N/A	54
2002/03	92	7	5	51	N/A	45
2003/04	92	17	4	52	N/A	27
2004/05	92	4	5	47	N/A	22
2005/06	92	11	3	62	N/A	10
2006/07	92	6	3	53	N/A	17
2007/08	92	5	4	55	N/A	14
2008/09	92	5	2	51	N/A	11
2009/10	92	8	7	63	N/A	16
2010/11	92	7	6	61	N/A	16
2011/12	92	7	8	56	N/A	15
2012/13	92	6	7	55	N/A	18
2013/14	92	5	2	65	N/A	25
2014/15	92	11	6	92	N/A	43
2015/16	92	11	8	N/A	N/A	45
2016/17	92	7	4	N/A	N/A	43
2017/18	92	8	4	N/A	N/A	45
2018/19	92	8	2	74	N/A	38
2019/20	92	12	1	65	N/A	43
2020/21	92	10	3	75	N/A	64
2021/22	92	16	2	77	N/A	45
2022/23	92	17	5	80	N/A	44
2023/24	92	15	3	84	N/A	56
2024/25	92	13	1	88	N/A	59

N/A: Team drops out of league football

EUROPEAN TROPHY WINNERS

Season	Winner	Competition
1970/71	Skelmersdale United	Otto Barassi Cup
1972/73	Liverpool	UEFA Cup
1975/76	Liverpool	UEFA Cup
1976/77	Liverpool	European Cup
1977/78	Liverpool	European Cup
1980/81	Liverpool	European Cup
1983/84	Liverpool	European Cup
1984/85	Everton	European Cup Winners Cup
2000/01	Liverpool	UEFA Cup
2004/05	Liverpool	European Champions League
2018/19	Liverpool	European Champions League

FA CUP WINNERS

Season	Winners	Season	Winners
	1872-1888		**1888-1915**
1871/72	Wanderers	1888/89	Preston Noth End
1872/73	Wanderers	1889/90	Blackburn Rovers
1873/74	Oxford University	1890/91	Blackburn Rovers
1874/75	Royal Engineers	1891/92	West Bromwich Albion
1875/76	Wanderers	1892/93	Wolverhampton Wanderers
1876/77	Wanderers	1893/94	Notts County
1877/78	Wanderers	1894/95	Aston Villa
1878/79	Old Etonians	1895/96	The Wednesday
1879/80	Clapham Rovers	1896/97	Aston Villa
1880/81	Old Carthusians	1897/98	Nottingham Forest
1881/82	Old Etonians	1898/99	Sheffield United
1882/83	Blackburn Olympic	1899/00	Bury
1883/84	Blackburn Rovers	1900/01	Tottenham Hotspur
1884/85	Blackburn Rovers	1901/02	Sheffield United
1885/86	Blackburn Rovers	1902/03	Bury
1886/87	Aston Villa	1903/04	Manchester City
1887/88	West Bromwich Albion	1904/05	Aston Villa

Season	Winners	Season	Winners
1905/06	**Everton**	1947/48	Manchester United
1906/07	The Wednesday	1948/49	Wolverhampton Wanderers
1907/08	Wolverhampton Wanderers	1949/50	Arsenal
1908/09	Manchester United	1950/51	Newcastle United
1909/10	Newcastle United	1951/52	Newcastle United
1910/11	Bradford City	1952/53	Blackpool
1911/12	Barnsley	1953/54	West Bromwich Albion
1912/13	Aston Villa	1954/55	Newcastle United
1913/14	Burnley	1955/56	Manchester City
1914/15	Sheffield United	1956/57	Aston Villa
		1957/58	Bolton Wanderers
	1920-1939	1958/59	Nottingham Forest
1919/20	Aston Villa	1959/60	Wolverhampton Wanderers
1920/21	Tottenham Hotspur	1960/61	Tottenham Hotspur
1921/22	Huddersfield Town	1961/62	Tottenham Hotspur
1922/23	Bolton Wanderers	1962/63	Manchester United
1923/24	Newcastle United	1963/64	West Ham United
1924/25	Sheffield United	1964/65	**Liverpool**
1925/26	Bolton Wanderers	1965/66	**Everton**
1926/27	Cardiff City	1966/67	Tottenham Hotspur
1927/28	Blackburn Rovers	1967/68	West Bromwich Albion
1928/29	Bolton Wanderers	1968/69	Manchester City
1929/30	Arsenal	1969/70	Chelsea
1930/31	West Bromwich Albion	1970/71	Arsenal
1931/32	Newcastle United	1971/72	Leeds United
1932/33	**Everton**		
1933/34	Manchester City		**1973-1992**
1934/35	Sheffield Wednesday	1972/73	Sunderland
1935/36	Arsenal	1973/74	**Liverpool**
1936/37	Sunderland	1974/75	West Ham United
1937/38	Preston North End	1975/76	Southampton
1938/39	Portsmouth	1976/77	Manchester United
		1977/78	Ipswich Town
	1946-1972	1978/79	Arsenal
1945/46	Derby County	1979/80	West Ham United
1946/47	Charlton Athletic	1980/81	Tottenham Hotspur

Season	Winners	Season	Winners
1981/82	Tottenham Hotspur	2002/03	Arsenal
1982/83	Manchester United	2003/04	Manchester United
1983/84	**Everton**	2004/05	Arsenal
1984/85	Manchester United	2005/06	**Liverpool**
1985/86	**Liverpool**	2006/07	Chelsea
1986/87	Coventry City	2007/08	Portsmouth
1987/88	Wimbledon	2008/09	Chelsea
1988/89	**Liverpool**	2009/10	Chelsea
1989/90	Manchester United	2010/11	Manchester City
1990/91	Tottenham Hotspur	2011/12	Chelsea
1991/92	**Liverpool**	2012/13	**Wigan Athletic**
		2013/14	Arsenal
	1993-Present	2014/15	Arsenal
1992/93	Arsenal	2015/16	Manchester United
1993/94	Manchester United	2016/17	Arsenal
1994/95	**Everton**	2017/18	Chelsea
1995/96	Manchester United	2018/19	Manchester City
1996/97	Chelsea	2019/20	Arsenal
1997/98	Arsenal	2020/21	Leicester City
1998/99	Manchester United	2021/22	**Liverpool**
1999/00	Chelsea	2022/23	Manchester City
2000/01	**Liverpool**	2023/24	Manchester United
2001/02	Arsenal	2024/25	Crystal Palace

Season	Women's Winners	Season	Women's Winners
1970/71	Southampton	1979/80	**St.Helens**
1971/72	Southampton	1980/81	Southampton
1972/73	Southampton	1981/82	Lowestoft
1973/74	Fodens	1982/83	Doncaster Belles
1974/75	Southampton	1983/84	Howbury Grange
1975/76	Southampton	1984/85	Friends of Fulham
1976/77	QPR	1985/86	Norwich
1977/78	Southampton	1986/87	Doncaster Belles
1978/79	Southampton	1987/88	Doncaster Belles

Season	Women's Winners	Season	Women's Winners
1988/89	**Leasowe Pacific**	2006/07	Arsenal
1989/90	Doncaster Belles	2007/08	Arsenal
1990/91	Millwall Lionesses	2008/09	Arsenal
1991/92	Doncaster Belles	2009/10	**Everton**
		2010/11	Arsenal
	1993-Present	2011/12	Birmingham City
1992/93	Arsenal	2012/13	Arsenal
1993/94	Doncaster Belles	2013/14	Arsenal
1994/95	Arsenal	2014/15	Chelsea
1995/96	Croydon	2015/16	Arsenal
1996/97	Millwall Lionesses	2016/17	Manchester City
1997/98	Arsenal	2017/18	Chelsea
1998/99	Arsenal	2018/19	Manchester City
1999/00	Croydon	2019/20	Manchester City
2000/01	Arsenal	2020/21	Chelsea
2001/02	Fulham	2021/22	Chelsea
2002/03	Fulham	2022/23	Chelsea
2003/04	Arsenal	2023/24	Manchester United
2004/05	Charlton Athletic	2024/25	Chelsea
2005/06	Arsenal		

COMBINATION WINNERS

Season	Winners	Season	Winners
1890/91	Gorton Villa	1900/01	Wrexham
1891/92	**Everton Reserves**	1901/02	Wrexham
1892/93	**Everton Reserves**	1902/03	Wrexham
1893/94	**Everton Reserves**	1903/04	**Birkenhead**
1894/95	Ashton North End	1904/05	Wrexham
1895/96	**Everton Reserves**	1905/06	Whitchurch
1896/97	**Everton Reserves**	1906/07	Whitchurch
1897/98	**Everton Reserves**	1907/08	**Tranmere Rovers**
1898/99	**Everton Reserves**	1908/09	**Chester**
1899/00	Chirk AAA	1909/10	Crewe Alexandra Reserves
		1910/11	Whitchurch

LANCASHIRE LEAGUE WINNERS

Season	First Division Winners	Second Division Winners
1949/50	Blackpool	N/A
1950/51	Preston North End	N/A
1951/52	Stockport County	N/A
1952/53	Burnley	N/A
1953/54	Rochdale	N/A
1954/55	Manchester United	N/A
1955/56	Oldham Athletic	Burnley
1956/57	Burnley	Bolton Wanderers
1957/58	Rochdale	**Everton**
1958/59	Preston North End	**Everton**
1959/60	Bolton Wanderers	**Everton**
1960/61	Burnley	Bolton Wanderers
1961/62	Burnley	**Liverpool**
1962/63	**Everton**	**Everton**
1963/64	**Everton**	**Everton**
1964/65	**Everton**	Manchester United
1965/66	**Liverpool**	**Liverpool**
1966/67	**Everton**	Manchester City
1967/68	**Liverpool**	**Liverpool**
1968/69	**Liverpool**	Manchester City
1969/70	**Everton**	Manchester United
1970/71	**Everton**	Blackburn Rovers
1971/72	**Liverpool**	Manchester United
1972/73	Stockport County	**Liverpool**
1973/74	**Wigan Athletic**	**Everton**
1974/75	**Everton**	**Everton**
1975/76	Oldham Athletic	**Liverpool**
1976/77	Oldham Athletic	**Liverpool**
1977/78	**Liverpool**	Burnley
1978/79	Port Vale	Burnley
1979/80	**Tranmere Rovers**	**Everton**
1980/81	Oldham Athletic	Burnley
1981/82	**Wigan Athletic**	Blackburn Rovers
1982/83	**Liverpool**	Oldham Athletic
1983/84	Manchester United	Morecambe

Season	First Division Winners	Second Division Winners
1984/85	Manchester United	Blackburn Rovers
1985/86	Manchester City	Oldham Athletic
1986/87	Manchester United	Preston North End
1987/88	Manchester United	Oldham Athletic
1988/89	**Everton**	Manchester United
1989/90	Manchester United	Blackpool
1990/91	Manchester United	Crewe Alexandra
1991/92	Crewe Alexandra	Crewe Alexandra
1992/93	Manchester United	**Liverpool**
1993/94	Burnley	Preston North End
1994/95	Manchester United	Manchester City
1995/96	Manchester United	Blackburn Rovers
1996/97	Manchester United	Manchester United
1997/98	Manchester United	Blackburn Rovers B
1998/99	**Tranmere Rovers**	
1999/00	**Southport**	

LEAGUE CHAMPIONS

Season	Winners	Season	Winners
	1888-1915	1901/02	Sunderland
1888/89	Preston North End	1902/03	The Wednesday
1889/90	Preston North End	1903/04	The Wednesday
1890/91	**Everton**	1904/05	Newcastle United
1891/92	Sunderland	1905/06	**Liverpool**
1892/93	Sunderland	1906/07	Newcastle United
1893/94	Aston Villa	1907/08	Manchester United
1894/95	Sunderland	1908/09	Newcastle United
1895/96	Aston Villa	1909/10	Aston Villa
1896/97	Aston Villa	1910/11	Manchester United
1897/98	Sheffield United	1911/12	Blackburn Rovers
1898/99	Aston Villa	1912/13	Sunderland
1899/00	Aston Villa	1913/14	Blackburn Rovers
1900/01	**Liverpool**	1914/15	**Everton**

Season	Winners	Season	Winners
	1919-1939	1959/60	Burnley
1919/20	West Bromwich Albion	1960/61	Tottenham Hotspur
1920/21	Burnley	1961/62	Ipswich Town
1921/22	**Liverpool**	1962/63	**Everton**
1922/23	**Liverpool**	1963/64	**Liverpool**
1923/24	Huddersfield Town	1964/65	Manchester United
1924/25	Huddersfield Town	1965/66	**Liverpool**
1925/26	Huddersfield Town	1966/67	Manchester United
1926/27	Newcastle United	1967/68	Manchester City
1927/28	**Everton**	1968/69	Leeds United
1928/29	The Wednesday	1969/70	**Everton**
1929/30	Sheffield Wednesday	1970/71	Arsenal
1930/31	Arsenal	1971/72	Derby County
1931/32	**Everton**		
1932/33	Arsenal		**1973-1992**
1933/34	Arsenal	1972/73	**Liverpool**
1934/35	Arsenal	1973/74	Leeds United
1935/36	Sunderland	1974/75	Derby County
1936/37	Manchester City	1975/76	**Liverpool**
1937/38	Arsenal	1976/77	**Liverpool**
1938/39	**Everton**	1977/78	Nottingham Forest
		1978/79	Liverpool
		1979/80	Liverpool
	1947-1972	1980/81	Aston Villa
1946/47	**Liverpool**	1981/82	**Liverpool**
1947/48	Arsenal	1982/83	**Liverpool**
1948/49	Portsmouth	1983/84	**Liverpool**
1949/50	Portsmouth	1984/85	**Everton**
1950/51	Tottenham Hotspur	1985/86	**Liverpool**
1951/52	Manchester United	1986/87	**Everton**
1952/53	Arsenal	1987/88	**Liverpool**
1953/54	Wolverhampton Wanderers	1988/89	Arsenal
1954/55	Chelsea	1989/90	**Liverpool**
1955/56	Manchester United	1990/91	Arsenal
1956/57	Manchester United	1991/92	Leeds United
1957/58	Wolverhampton Wanderers		
1958/59	Wolverhampton Wanderers		

Season	Winners	Season	Winners
Premier League 1993-2025		2008/09	Manchester United
1992/93	Manchester United	2009/10	Chelsea
1993/94	Manchester United	2010/11	Manchester United
1994/95	Blackburn Rovers	2011/12	Manchester City
1995/96	Manchester United	2012/13	Manchester United
1996/97	Manchester United	2013/14	Manchester City
1997/98	Arsenal	2014/15	Chelsea
1998/99	Manchester United	2015/16	Leicester City
1999/00	Manchester United	2016/17	Chelsea
2000/01	Manchester United	2017/18	Manchester City
2001/02	Arsenal	2018/19	Manchester City
2002/03	Manchester United	2019/20	**Liverpool**
2003/04	Arsenal	2020/21	Manchester City
2004/05	Chelsea	2021/22	Manchester City
2005/06	Chelsea	2022/23	Manchester City
2006/07	Manchester United	2023/24	Manchester City
2007/08	Manchester United	2024/25	**Liverpool**

WOMEN'S PREMIER LEAGUE AND WOMEN'S SUPER LEAGUE

Women's Premier	Champions	Women's Premier	Champions
1992-2010		2008/09	Arsenal
1991/92	Doncaster Belles	2009/10	Arsenal
1992/93	Arsenal	**WSL**	**Champions**
1993/94	Doncaster Belles	2011	Arsenal
1994/95	Arsenal	2012	Arsenal
1995/96	Croydon	2013	**Liverpool**
1996/97	Arsenal	2014	**Liverpool**
1997/98	**Everton**	2015	Chelsea
1998/99	Croydon	2016	Manchester City
1999/00	Croydon	2017	Chelsea
2000/01	Arsenal	2017/18	Chelsea
2001/02	Arsenal	2018/19	Arsenal
2002/03	Fulham	2010/20	Chelsea
2003/04	Arsenal	2020/21	Chelsea
2004/05	Arsenal	2021/22	Chelsea
2005/06	Arsenal	2022/23	Chelsea
2006/07	Arsenal	2023/24	Chelsea
2007/08	Arsenal	2024/25	Chelsea

LEAGUE CUP WINNERS

Season	Winners	Season	Winners
1960/61	Aston Villa	1993/94	Aston Villa
1961/62	Norwich City	1994/95	**Liverpool**
1962/63	Birmingham City	1995/96	Aston Villa
1963/64	Leicester City	1996/97	Leicester City
1964/65	Chelsea	1997/98	Chelsea
1965/66	West Bromwich Albion	1998/99	Tottenham Hotspur
1966/67	Queen's Park Rangers	1999/00	Leicester City
1967/68	Leeds United	2000/01	**Liverpool**
1968/69	Swindon Town	2001/02	Blackburn Rovers
1969/70	Manchester City	2002/03	**Liverpool**
1970/71	Tottenham Hotspur	2003/04	Middlesbrough
1971/72	Stoke City	2004/05	Chelsea
1972/73	Tottenham Hotspur	2005/06	Manchester United
1973/74	Wolverhampton Wanderers	2006/07	Chelsea
1974/75	Aston Villa	2007/08	Tottenham Hotspur
1975/76	Manchester City	2008/09	Manchester United
1976/77	Aston Villa	2009/10	Manchester United
1977/78	Nottingham Forest	2010/11	Birmingham City
1978/79	Nottingham Forest	2011/12	**Liverpool**
1979/80	Wolverhampton Wanderers	2012/13	Swansea City
1980/81	**Liverpool**	2013/14	Manchester City
1981/82	**Liverpool**	2014/15	Chelsea
1982/83	**Liverpool**	2015/16	Manchester City
1983/84	**Liverpool**	2016/17	Manchester United
1984/85	Norwich City	2017/18	Manchester City
1985/86	Oxford United	2018/19	Manchester City
1986/87	Arsenal	2019/20	Manchester City
1987/88	Luton Town	2020/21	Manchester City
1988/89	Nottingham Forest	2021/22	**Liverpool**
1989/90	Nottingham Forest	2022/23	Manchester United
1990/91	SheffieldWednesday	2023/24	**Liverpool**
1991/92	Manchester United	2024/25	Newcastle United
1992/93	Arsenal		

Season	Women's Winners	Season	Women's Winners
1991/92	Arsenal	2008/09	Arsenal
1992/93	Arsenal	2009/10	Leeds Carnegie
1993/94	Arsenal	2011	Arsenal
1994/95	Wimbledon	2012	Arsenal
1995/96	Wembley	2013	Arsenal
1996/97	Millwall Lionesses	2014	Manchester City
1997/98	Arsenal	2015	Arsenal
1998/99	Arsenal	2016	Manchester City
1999/00	Arsenal	2017/18	Arsenal
2000/01	Arsenal	2018/19	Manchester City
2001/02	Fulham	2019/20	Chelsea
2002/03	Fulham	2020/21	Chelsea
2003/04	Charlton Athletic	2021/22	Manchester City
2004/05	Arsenal	2022/23	Arsenal
2005/06	Charlton Athletic	2023/24	Arsenal
2006/07	Arsenal	2024/25	Chelsea
2007/08	**Everton**		

LIVERPOOL SENIOR CUP WINNERS

Season	Winners	Season	Winners
1882/83	Bootle	1896/97	Rock Ferry
1883/84	Everton	1897/98	Everton
1884/85	Earlestown	1898/99	Everton
1885/86	Everton	1899/00	Everton
1886/87	Everton	1900/01	Liverpool
1887/88	Bootle	1901/02	Liverpool
1888/89	Bootle	1902/03	Liverpool
1889/90	Everton	1903/04	Everton
1890/91	Everton	1904/05	Liverpool
1891/92	Everton	1905/06	Liverpool
1892/93	Liverpool	1906/07	Liverpool
1893/94	Everton	1907/08	Everton
1894/95	Everton	1908/09	Liverpool
1895/96	Everton	1909/10	Everton/Liverpool

Season	Winners	Season	Winners
1910/11	Everton	1946/47	Liverpool
1911/12	Everton/Liverpool	1947/48	Liverpool
1912/13	Liverpool	1948/49	Tranmere Rovers
1913/14	Everton	1949/50	Tranmere Rovers
1914/15	Liverpool	1950/51	Liverpool
1915/16	WW1	1951/52	Liverpool
1916/17	WW1	1952/53	Everton
1917/18	WW1	1953/54	Everton
1918/19	Everton	1954/55	Tranmere Rovers
1919/20	Liverpool	1955/56	Everton
1920/21	Everton	1956/57	Everton
1921/22	Everton	1957/58	Everton/Southport
1922/23	Everton	1958/59	Everton
1923/24	Everton	1959/60	Everton
1924/25	Liverpool	1960/61	Everton
1925/26	Everton	1961/62	Liverpool
1926/27	Liverpool	1962/63	Southport
1927/28	Everton	1963/64	Liverpool/Southport
1928/29	Liverpool	1964/65	Not Finished
1929/30	Liverpool	1965/66	Not Finished
1930/31	Southport	1966/67	Not Finished
1931/32	Southport	1967/68	Liverpool
1932/33	New Brighton	1968/69	Not Finished
1933/34	Tranmere Rovers	1969/70	Tranmere Rovers
1934/35	New Brighton	1970/71	Not Finished
1935/36	Everton/Liverpool	1971/72	Not Finished
1936/37	Liverpool	1972/73	Tranmere Rovers
1937/38	Everton	1973/74	Tranmere Rovers
1938/39	Liverpool	1974/75	Southport
1939/40	Everton	1975/76	Liverpool
1940/41	Not Played	1976/77	Liverpool
1941/42	Liverpool	1977/78	Formby
1942/43	Liverpool	1978/79	Marine
1943/44	Southport	1979/80	Liverpool
1944/45	Everton	1980/81	Liverpool
1945/46	Liverpool	1981/82	Everton/Liverpool

Season	Winners	Season	Winners
1982/83	Everton	2004/05	Everton
1983/84	South Liverpool	2005/06	Tranmere Rovers/Marine
1984/85	Marine	2006/07	Everton
1985/86	South Liverpool	2007/08	Marine
1986/87	Kirkby Town	2008/09	Liverpool
1987/88	Marine	2009/10	Liverpool
1988/89	South Liverpool	2010/11	Southport
1989/90	Marine	2011/12	Tranmere Rovers
1990/91	Southport	2012/13	Bootle
1991/92	Tranmere Rovers	2013/14	Tranmere Rovers
1992/93	Southport	2014/15	Skelmersdale United
1993/94	Marine	2015/16	Everton
1994/95	Tranmere Rovers	2016/17	Prescot Cables
1995/96	Everton	2017/18	Prescot Cables
1996/97	Liverpool	2018/19	Southport
1997/98	Liverpool	2019/20	Covid-19
1998/99	Southport	2020/21	Covid-19
1999/00	Marine	2021/22	Covid-19
2000/01	Burscough	2022/23	Marine
2001/02	Liverpool	2023/24	Marine
2002/03	Everton	2024/25	Everton
2003/04	Liverpool		

MOST SUCCESSFUL LEAGUE MANAGERS BY TROPHIES WON

Bob Paisley (Liverpool) 1974-1983
First Division 1975/76, 1976/77, 1978/79, 1979/80, 1981/82 and 1982/83
FA Cup runners-up 1976/77
League Cup 1980/81, 1981/82 and 1982/83 runners-up 1977/78
European Cup winners 1976/77, 1977/78 and 1980/81
UEFA Cup 1975/76
UEFA Super Cup winners 1977
UEFA Super Cup runners-up 1978
Intercontinental Cup runners-up 1981
Six charity shields

Bill Shankly (Liverpool) 1959-1974
First Division 1963/64, 1965/66 and 1972/73 -Second Division 1961/62
FA Cup 1964/65 and 1973/74
UEFA Cup 1972/73
Three Charity Shields

Kenny Dalglish (Liverpool) 1985-1991 & 2011-2012
First Division 1985/86, 1987/88 and 1989/90
FA Cup 1985/86 (completing a league and cup double) and 1988/89
League Cup 2011/12
Football League Super Cup 1986
Four Charity Shields (Two of which were shared)

Gerard Houllier (Liverpool) 1998-2004
FA Cup 2000/01
League Cup 2000/01 & 2002/03
UEFA Cup 2000/01
UEFA Super Cup 2001
One Charity Shield

Jürgen Klopp (Liverpool) 2015-2024
Premier League 2019/20
FA Cup 2021/22
League Cup 2021/22 and 2023/24 runners-up 2015/16
UEFA Champions League 2018/19 and runners-up in 2017/18 and 2021/22
UEFA Super Cup 2019
FIFA Club World Cup 2019
UEFA Europa League runners-up 2015/16
One Community Shield

Howard Kendall (Everton) 1981-1987, 1990-1993 & 1997-1998
First Division 1984/85 and 1986/87
FA Cup won 1983/84 and runners-up 1984/85 and 1985/86
League Cup runners-up 1983/84
European Cup Winners Cup won 1984/85
Three Charity Shield (One of which was shared)

Harry Catterick (Everton) 1961-1973
First Division 1962/63 and 1969/70
FA Cup 1965/66 and runners-up 1967/68
Two Charity Shields

Joe Fagan (Liverpool) 1983-1985
First Division 1983/84
League Cup 1983/84
European Cup 1983/84

Rafael Benitez (Liverpool) 2004-2010
FA Cup 2005/06
UEFA Champions League 2004/05 and runners-up 2006/07
UEFA Super Cup 2005
League Cup runners-up 2004/05
FIFA Club World Championship runners-up 2005
One Community Shield

Arne Slot (Liverpool) 2024-
Premier League 2024/25

Joe Royle (Everton) 1994-1997 – Caretaker 2016
FA Cup 1994/95
One Charity Shield

Graeme Souness (Liverpool) 1991-1994
FA Cup 1991/92

Roberto Martinez (Wigan Athletic) 2009-2013
FA Cup 2012/13

Roy Evans (Liverpool) 1994-1998
League Cup 1994/95

Colin Harvey (Everton) 1987-1990
FA Cup runners-up 1988/89
One Charity Shield

David Moyes (Everton) 2002-2013 & 2025-
FA Cup runners-up 2008/09

Gordon Lee (Everton) 1977-1981
League Cup runners-up 1976/77

John Aldridge (Tranmere Rovers) 1996-2001
League Cup runners-up 1999/00

Jimmy Meadows (Southport) 1971-1973
Fourth Division winners 1972/73

John King (Tranmere Rovers) 1975-1980 & 1987-1996
Fourth Division runners-up 1988/89 and promotion 1975/76
Third Division Play-off winners 1990/91
Associate Members Cup runners-up 1991

Billy Bingham (Southport) 1965-1968
Fourth Division runners-up 1966/67

Harry McNally (Chester City) 1985-1992
Fourth Division runners-up 1985/86

Ken Roberts (Chester) 1968-1976
Fourth Division promotion 1974/75

Manager of the year awards
1973 Bill Shankly (Liverpool)
1976 Bob Paisley (Liverpool)
1977 Bob Paisley (Liverpool)
1979 Bob Paisley (Liverpool)
1980 Bob Paisley (Liverpool)
1982 Bob Paisley (Liverpool)
1983 Bob Paisley (Liverpool)
1984 Joe Fagan (Liverpool)
1985 Howard Kendall (Everton)
1986 Kenny Dalglish (Liverpool)
1987 Howard Kendall (Everton)
1988 Kenny Dalglish (Liverpool)
1990 Kenny Dalglish (Liverpool)
2003 David Moyes (Everton)
2005 David Moyes (Everton)
2009 David Moyes (Everton)
2014 Brendan Rodgers (Liverpool)
2020 Jürgen Klopp (Liverpool)
2022 Jürgen Klopp (Liverpool)
2025 Arne Slot (Liverpool)

WOMEN'S TEAM MANAGERS BY TROPHIES WON

MATT BEARD (LIVERPOOL WOMEN) 2012-2015 and 2021-2025
Women's Super League 1 2013 and 2014
Women's Championship 2021/22
WSL Manager of the Season 2013 and 2023/24

KEITH MARLEY (EVERTON WOMEN) 1998-2002
Women's Premier League 1997/98
Women's Premier League Cup runners-up 1996/97 and 1998/99

MAUREEN 'MO' MARLEY (EVERTON WOMEN) 2002-2012
Women's FA Cup 2009/10 runners-up 2004/05
Women's Premier League Cup 2007/08
Women's Premier League runners-up 2005/06, 2006/07, 2007/08, 2008/09 and 2009/10
2 Women's Community Shields

ANDY SPENCE (EVERTON WOMEN) 2012-2015 and 2016-2018
Women's WSL 2 Spring Series 2017
Women's FA Cup runners-up 2013/14

LIZ DEIGHAN (St. HELENS WOMEN) 1976-1989
Women's FA Cup 1979/80 runners-up 1980/81, 1982/83 and 1986/87

BILLY JACKSON (LEASOWE PACIFIC) 1988-1998
Women's FA Cup 1988/89 runners-up 1987/88

ANGIE GALLIMORE (LIVERPOOL WOMEN) 1993-1995
Women's FA Cup runners-up 1993/94, 1994/95

JOBY HUMPHRIES (LIVERPOOL WOMEN) 1995-1996
Women's FA Cup runners-up 1995/96

WILLIE KIRK (EVERTON WOMEN) 2018-2021
Women's FA Cup runners-up 2019/20

H I G H E S T   A T T E N D A N C E

Everton	78,299 Goodison Park 18 September 1948 First Division v Liverpool
Liverpool	61,905 Anfield 2 February 1952 FA Cup Fourth Round v Wolverhampton Wanderers
Wigan Athletic	27,536 Springfield Park 12 December 1953 FA Cup Second Round v Hereford United
Tranmere Rovers	24,424 Prenton Park 5 February 1972 FA Cup Fourth Round v Stoke City
Southport	20,010 Haig Avenue 26 January 1932 FA Cup Fourth Round Replay v Newcastle United
Bootle	c20,000 Hawthorne Road 26 December 1889 Friendly Match v Everton
New Brighton	c16,000 Tower Ground FA Cup 5 January 1957 Third Round v Torquay United
New Brighton Tower	c10,000 Tower Ground 14 January 1899 Second Division v Manchester City

R E C O R D   G O A L   S C O R E R S

Name	Goals	Club	Seasons
William Ralph Dean	383	Everton	1925-1937
Ian Rush	346	Liverpool	1980-1987 & 1988-1996
Ian Muir	180	Tranmere Rovers	1985-1994
Stuart Rimmer	150	Chester/Chester City	1984-1988 & 1991-1998
Alan Spence	108	Southport	1961-1968
Andy Liddell	70	Wigan Athletic	1998-2004

AMATEUR

BOOTLE JOC EVERTON CUP

Season	Winners	Season	Winners
1936/37	Linacre Gasworks	1965/66	Bootle St.James
1937/38	Miranda	1966/67	Aintree Royal
1938/39	Linacre Gasworks	1967/68	Winifred Sports
1939/40	St.James's	1968/69	Dryden Athletic
1945/46	Victoria	1969/70	Pentagon Association
1946/47	Knowsley Vics.	1970/71	Bootle Y.M.C.A.
1947/48	Victoria	1971/72	Pentagon Association
1948/49	Seaforth Fellowship	1972/73	Pentagon Association
1949/50	Seaforth Fellowship	1973/74	Netherton United
1950/51	Seaforth Fellowship	1974/75	Alexandra (Bootle)
1951/52	Bootle Celtic	1975/76	Kirkdale Centre
1952/53	Benson's	1976/77	The Vale
1953/54	Benson's	1977/78	Cabbage
1954/55	Benson's	1978/79	Atlanta
1955/56	Salisbury Athletic	1979/80	St.Philomena's
1956/57	Queen's Park	1980/81	St.Raymond's
1957/58	Bootle St.James	1981/82	Brunswick Boys Club
1958/59	Winifred Sports	1982/83	Barratt
1959/60	Alexandra Royal	1983/84	B.O.C. Roughwood
1960/61	Benson's	1984/85	Corry Rangers
1961/62	Park Villa	1985/86	Killern Park
1962/63	Aintree Royal	1986/87	St.Philomena's
1963/64	Aintree Royal	1987/88	Mariners
1964/65	Aintree Royal	1988/89	Chaucer Brunswick

B O O T L E   J O C   L E A G U E   W I N N E R S

Season	Winners	Season	Winners
1926/27	Albion	1961/62	Hilton United
1927/28	Albion	1962/63	Hilton United
1928/29	Albion	1963/64	Bootle St. James
1929/30	Walton Conservatives	1964/65	Bootle St. James
1930/31	Bank Albion	1965/66	St.Philomena's
1931/32	Litherland Amateurs	1966/67	Benson's
1932/33	Litherland Amateurs	1967/68	Mount
1933/34	Bootle Labour	1968/69	Benson's
1934/35	Miranda	1969/70	Pentagon Association
1935/36	Miranda	1970/71	Pentagon Association
1936/37	Miranda	1971/72	Pentagon Association
1937/38	Miranda	1972/73	Pentagon Association
1938/39	Derby Wanderers	1973/74	Netherton United
1945/46	Victoria	1974/75	Netherton United
1946/47	Seaforth Fellowship	1975/76	Kirkdale Centre
1947/48	Seaforth Fellowship	1976/77	Lee Jones Old Boys
1948/49	Seaforth Fellowship	1977/78	Carters Arms
1949/50	Seaforth Fellowship	1978/79	Doric United
1950/51	Seaforth Fellowship	1979/80	Brunswick Boys Club
1951/52	Hornby	1980/81	Brunswick Boys Club
1952/53	Alhambra	1981/82	Brunswick Boys Club
1953/54	Bootle Celtic	1982/83	Barratt
1954/55	Queens Park	1983/84	B.O.C. Roughwood
1955/56	Benson's	1984/85	Corry Rangers
1956/57	Salisbury Athletic	1985/86	Corry Rangers
1957/58	Salisbury Athletic	1986/87	Mainbrace
1958/59	Winifred Sports	1987/88	Selwyn
1959/60	Bootle Labour	1988/89	Doric United
1960/61	Alexandra		

BOOTLE JOC LIVERPOOL CUP

Season	Winners	Season	Winners
1938/39	Everton 'B'	1967/68	Walsingham
1939/40	Lydiate	1968/69	Christchurch
1946/47	Alhambra	1969/70	Andrew Sports
1947/48	Walton Lane Social	1970/71	Wimpey S&S
1948/49	Elm Bank	1971/72	St. Robert Bellarmine
1949/50	Bootle Celtic	1972/73	St. Robert Bellarmine
1950/51	Bootle Celtic	1973/74	Atlanta
1951/52	Park Villa	1974/75	Holy Ghost
1952/53	Salisbury Athletic	1975/76	The Vale
1953/54	Queen's Park	1976/77	Sandown United
1954/55	Rea United	1977/78	Hamlet
1955/56	Winifred Sports	1978/79	Non Pariel
1956/57	Rea United	1979/80	C 4th Cabs
1957/58	Rea United	1980/81	Marian Villa
1958/59	Bootle Labour	1981/82	St. Saviours Old Boys
1959/60	Cambridge United	1982/83	Corry
1960/61	Hilton United	1983/84	D.A.M.S.
1961/62	Cambridge United	1984/85	Red Lion
1962/63	Pentagon	1985/86	Litherland Labour
1963/64	Pheonix Albion	1986/87	Selwyn
1964/65	St. Philomena's	1987/88	Doric
1965/66	St. Andrew's	1988/89	Lansett
1966/67	Pentagon Association		

CROSBY AND DISTRICT LEAGUE

Season	Winners	Season	Winners
1967/68	Crosby Dynamo	1976/77	Eden Vale
1968/69	Crosby Dynamo	1977/78	Wheatsheaf
1969/70	Park Villa	1978/79	Eden Vale
1970/71	Park Villa	1979/80	Eden Vale
1971/72	Crosby Dynamo	1980/81	Eden Vale
1972/73	Alpha	1981/82	Eden Vale
1973/74	Catherine	1982/83	Merton Villa
1974/75	Eden Vale	1983/84	Eden Vale
1975/76	Allendale United	1984/85	Merton Villa

Season	Winners	Season	Winners
1985/86	Eden Vale	2000/01	Osset Sound
1986/87	Valend	2001/02	Saltbox
1987/88	Eden Vale	2002/03	Saltbox
1988/89	Merton Villa	2003/04	Dickie Lewis
1989/90	Lion Hotel	2004/05	Seaburn
1990/91	Lion Hotel	2005/06	Seaburn
1991/92	Lion Knowsley	2006/07	Saltbox
1992/93	Lion Hotel	2007/08	North Mersey Lions
1993/94	Eden Vale	2008/09	Seaburn
1994/95	Eden Vale	2009/10	Salisbury Athletic
1995/96	Eden Vale	2010/11	Salisbury Athletic
1996/97	Eden Vale	2011/12	Oak Tree Pub
1997/98	Eden Vale	2012/13	Oak Tree Pub
1998/99	Eden Vale	2013/14	The YBM
1999/00	Woodpecker		

GEORGE MAHON CUP WINNERS

Season	Winners	Season	Winners
1909/10	Garston Gas Works	1931/32	Liverpool Cables
1910/11	Buckley Engineers	1932/33	Everton 'A'
1911/12	Garston North End	1933/34	Everton 'A'
1912/13	Earlestown Rovers	1934/35	Skelmersdale United
1913/14	Southport Park Villa	1935/36	Everton 'A'
1919/20	Saltney United	1936/37	Prescot Cables
1920/21	Burscough Rangers	1937/38	Earlestown Bohemians
1921/22	Whiston Parish	1938/39	Everton 'A'
1922/23	Wigan Borough Reserves	1939/40	Skelmersdale United
1923/24	Prescot	1940/41	Burscough Victoria
1924/25	Skelmersdale United	1941/42	Liverpool
1925/26	Burscough Rangers	1942/43	Marine
1926/27	Prescot	1943/44	Marine
1927/28	Bootle Celtic	1944/45	Marine
1928/29	Whiston Parish	1945/46	Prescot B.I.
1929/30	Blundellsands	1946/47	Ellesmere Port Town
1930/31	Marine	1947/48	Burscough

409

Season	Winners	Season	Winners
1948/49	St. Helens Town	1986/87	Waterloo Dock
1949/50	Haydock C&B	1987/88	Uniasco
1950/51	Hoylake Athletic	1988/89	Avon Athletic
1951/52	Skelmersdale United	1989/90	Ayone
1952/53	Everton 'A'	1990/91	Waterloo Dock
1953/54	Liverpool 'A'	1991/92	Waterloo Dock
1954/55	Liverpool 'A & Skelmersdale United (Shared)	1992/93	Lucas Sports
		1993/94	Crawfords
1955/56	Unit Construction	1994/95	Crawfords
1956/57	Dunlop (Speke)	1995/96	Waterloo Dock
1957/58	Aintree S.S.	1996/97	Waterloo Dock
1958/59	South Liverpool Reserves	1997/98	Stockbridge
1959/60	Guiness Exports	1998/99	Stockbridge
1960/61	Guiness Exports	1999/00	Lucas Sports
1961/62	Guiness Exports	2000/01	Waterloo Dock
1962/63	Guiness Exports	2001/02	South Liverpool
1963/64	Guiness Exports	2002/03	Lucas Sports
1964/65	Formby	2003/04	Halewood Town
1965/66	Aintree S.S. & Prescot B.I. (Shared)	2004/05	Waterloo Dock
1966/67	Langton	2005/06	St Dominics
1967/68	Langton	2006/07	East Villa
1968/69	Langton	2007/08	Aigburth People's Hall
1969/70	Langton	2008/09	South Liverpool
1970/71	Dunlop (Speke)	2009/10	Waterloo Dock
1971/72	St. Dominic's	2010/11	East Villa
1972/73	Langton	2011/12	Aigburth People's Hall
1973/74	Bootle	2012/13	Aigburth People's Hall
1974/75	Waterloo Dock	2013/14	Page Celtic
1975/76	Waterloo Dock	2014/15	Page Celtic
1976/77	Aintree S.S.	2015/16	West Everton Xaviers
1977/78	Waterloo Dock	2016/17	Lower Breck
1978/79	Ayone	2017/18	Lower Breck
1979/80	St. Dominic's	2018/19	BRNESC
1980/81	Gleneagles	2019/20	Liverpool Nalgo
1981/82	Ayone	2020/21	Not Played Covid
1982/83	Waterloo Dock	2021/22	Liver Academy
1983/84	BRNESC	2022/23	Old Xaverians
1984/85	Littlewoods Athletic	2023/24	East Villa Rail
1985/86	Earle	2024/25	The Grenadier

I ZINGARI LEAGUE WINNERS

Season	First/Premier Division Winners	Second/First Division Winners	Third/Second Division Winners
1895/96	Walton		
1896/97	Liverpool Casuals		
1897/98	Liverpool Casuals	Trinity Bible Class	
1898/99	Melrose	Melrose Reserves	
1899/00	Kirkdale	Melrose Reserves	
1900/01	Melrose	Melrose Reserves	Bromborough Pool Reserves
1901/02	Anfield Recreation	Marine	Balmoral
1902/03	Marine	Valkyrie	Cardwell
1903/04	Marine	Balmoral	Waterloo Melville
1904/05	Helsby Athletic	Liverpool Caledonians	St.James (Toxteth)
1905/06	Kirkdale	Widnes Wesley Guild	St.Cleopas
1906/07	Widnes Wesley Guild	Dingle Recreation	Melrose
1907/08	Bromborough Pool	Liscard	Carisbrooke
1908/09	Valkyrie	Liscard Central	St.Lawrence
1909/10	Balmoral	St.Cleopas	Seafield
1910/11	Marine	St.Cleopas	Florence Albion
1911/12	St.Cleopas	Beresford Old Boys	All Saints (Stoneycroft)
1912/13	Orrell	All Saints (Stoneycroft)	Aughton Wanderers
1913/14	Orrell	Liverpool Scottish	St.Chads
1919/20	Marine	Cowley	Earle
1920/21	Marine	Bon Marche	SS Simon & Jude
1921/22	Orrell	Earle	Thorndale
1922/23	Marine	Cadby Hall	Orrell Athletic
1923/24	Marine	Orrell Athletic	Pembroke
1924/25	Orrell	Pembroke	Oakmere
1925/26	Cadby Hall	Harrowby	Southport Trinity
1926/27	Liverpool Police Athletic	Southport Trinity	Olympic
1927/28	Cadby Hall	The Casuals	Salop Athletic
1928/29	Cadby Hall	Maghull	West Derby Union
1929/30	Orrell	West Derby Union	Britannia
1930/31	Earle	Bromborough Pool	Port Sunlight 'A'
1931/32	Thorndale	Port Sunlight	Lander Old Boys

Season	First/Premier Division Winners	Second/First Division Winners	Third/Second Division Winners
1932/33	The Casuals	Formby	North Western
1933/34	Orrell	Maghull	Stoneycroft
1934/35	Earle	Stoneycroft	Lucem
1935/36	Cadby Hall	Oakmere	Blundellsands
1936/37	Earle	Harrowby	Waterloo G.S.O.B.
1937/38	Port Sunlight	Oakmere	Sefton & District
1938/39	Earle	Waterloo G.S.O.B.	Port Sunlight Gym
1946/47	Liverpool Police Athletic	Aigburth Peoples Hall	Melling
1947/48	Aigburth People's Hall	Westminster	Unity Old Boys
1948/49	Collegiate Old Boys	Westminster	St.Margaret Marys
1949/50	Aigburth People's Hall	Old Xaverians	Alsop Old Boys
1950/51	Collegiate Old Boys	Alsop Old Boys	Liverpool Tech. Students
1951/52	Collegiate Old Boys	Liverpool Tech. Students	Fazakerley
1952/53	Aigburth People's Hall	Litherland B.C.O.B.	Liverpool Police
1953/54	Aigburth People's Hall	Liverpool Police	Florence Albion
1954/55	Maghull	Florence Albion	Essemmay Old Boys
1955/56	Maghull	St.Mathews O.S.A.	Gateacre
1956/57	Collegiate Old Boys	Odyssey	West Toxteth
1957/58	Aigburth People's Hall	Essemmay Old Boys	Old Bootlelians
1958/59	Florence Albion	West Toxteth	Aintree Villa
1959/60	Aigburth People's Hall	Aintree Villa	Beaconsfield
1960/61	Aigburth People's Hall	Rockville (Wallasey)	St. Annes (Aigburth)
1961/62	Florence Albion	Old Bootleians	Sefton & District
1962/63	League Abandoned	No Competition	No Competition
1963/64	Aigburth People's Hall	Quarry Bank Old Boys	Hilltop
1964/65	University of Liverpool	Aintree Villa	Celtic
1965/66	Liverpool Police Athletic	Hilltop	Gateacre
1966/67	Aintree Villa	Sefton & District	York House Old Boys
1967/68	Aintree Villa	Liverpool Telecoms	Molyneux
1968/69	Aintree Villa	Gateacre	Bootle Cricket
1969/70	Florence Albion	St. Andrews United	Fazakerley Villa
1970/71	Aintree Villa	Crosby	Unifruit
1971/72	Aintree Villa	Alsop Old Boys	Waterloo G.S.O.B.
1972/73	Aintree Villa	Liverpool Telecoms	Woolton

Season	First/Premier Division Winners	Second/First Division Winners	Third/Second Division Winners
1973/74	Liverpool & Bootle Police	Woolton	Everton Red Triangle
1974/75	Aintree Villa	Collegiate Old Boys	REMYCA United
1975/76	St. Andrew's United	East Villa	St.Francis de Salle
1976/77	Quarry Bank Old Boys	Sefton & District	Old Cathinians
1977/78	Quarry Bank Old Boys	St. Mary's C.O.B.	Woolton
1978/79	Aintree Villa	Woolton	ROMA
1979/80	Mossley Hill	Florence Albion	All Souls
1980/81	Sefton & District	Inter (F.S.)	Girobank
1981/82	Inter	Girobank	Walton Village
1982/83	Merseyside Police	Walton Village	Selbac United
1983/84	Aintree Villa	Aigburth Peoples Hall	Parkside Albion
1984/85	Florence Albion	Parkside Albion	English Rose
1985/86	Speke Town	English Rose	Highfieldonians
1986/87	Unity BCOB	South End Vics.	Zodiac
1987/88	REMYCA United	Zodiac	Breckside Park
1988/89	Netherley Royal British Legion	ROMA	Liver Vaults
1989/90	Aigburth People's Hall	Warbreck	Shrewsbury House Old Boys
1990/91	Netherley Royal British Legion	Liver Vaults	Selwyn
1991/92	Aigburth People's Hall	Selwyn	De la Salle Old Boys
1992/93	Aigburth People's Hall	Leyfield	Jabisco
1993/94	REMYCA United	Jabisco	NELTC
1994/95	REMYCA United	St. Mary's C.O.B.	East Lancs Crown
1995/96	REMYCA United	East Lancs Crown	Sacre Coeur F.P.
1996/97	Aigburth People's Hall	Sacre Coeur F.P.	New Heys Old Boys
1997/98	East Villa	Edge Hill B.C.O.B.	Old Holts
1998/99	Aigburth People's Hall	Mills	Kinsela's
1999/2000	Aigburth People's Hall	Hill Athletic	Child
2000/01	Mills	Warbreck	Alsop Old Boys
2001/02	Aigburth People's Hall	Alsop Old Boys	Turpins
2002/03	NELTC	Turpins	Rolls Royce
2003/04	Old Xaverians	Liverpool NALGO	Allerton
2004/05	East Villa	Red Rum	Copperas Hill
2005/06	Old Xaverians	St. Ambrose	REMYCA United

I ZINGARI COMBINATION WINNERS

Season	Winners	Season	Winners
1904/05	Kirkdale	1951/52	Collegiate Old Boys
1905/06	Valkyrie	1952/53	Aigburth Peoples Hall
1906/07	Hale Bank Athletic	1953/54	Stoneycroft
1907/08	Hale Bank Athletic	1954/55	Aigburth Peoples Hall
1908/09	New Brighton TA	1955/56	Aigburth Peoples Hall
1909/10	Orrell	1956/57	Aigburth Peoples Hall
1910/11	Kirkby United	1957/58	Maghull
1911/12	Southport YMCA	1958/59	Maghull
1912/13	Orrell	1959/60	Crosby
1913/14	Harrowby	1960/61	Aigburth Peoples Hall
1919/20	Marine	1961/62	Florence Albion
1920/21	Marine	1962/63	No Competition
1921/22	Marine	1963/64	Aigburth Peoples Hall
1922/23	Marine	1964/65	Crosby
1923/24	Cadby Hall	1965/66	Liverpool Police
1924/25	Cadby Hall	1966/67	Liverpool Police
1925/26	Orrell	1967/68	Liverpool & Bootle Police
1926/27	Earle	1968/69	Aintree Villa
1927/28	Orrell	1969/70	Aintree Villa
1928/29	Thorndale	1970/71	Aintree Villa
1929/30	The Casuals	1971/72	Aintree Villa
1930/31	Thorndale	1972/73	Aintree Villa
1931/32	Collegiate Old Boys	1973/74	Aintree Villa
1932/33	Port Sunlight	1974/75	Quarry Bank Old Boys
1933/34	Earle	1975/76	Aintree Villa
1934/35	Collegiate Old Boys	1976/77	Quarry Bank Old Boys
1935/36	Earle	1977/78	Quarry Bank Old Boys
1936/37	Orrell	1978/79	Sefton & District
1937/38	Cadby Hall	1979/80	East Villa
1938/39	Collegiate Old Boys	1980/81	Quarry Bank Old Boys
1946/47	Maghull	1981/82	Quarry Bank Old Boys
1947/48	Aigburth Peoples Hall	1982/83	Merseyside Police
1948/49	Thorndale	1983/84	Aintree Villa
1949/50	Aigburth Peoples Hall	1984/85	East Villa
1950/51	Aigburth Peoples Hall	1985/86	Unity BCOB

Season	Winners	Season	Winners
1986/87	Merseyside Police	2004/05	Speke
1987/88	Liverpool Nalgo	2005/06	Old Xaverians
1988/89	East Villa	2006/07	South Liverpool
1989/90	Aigburth Peoples Hall	2007/08	NELTC
1990/91	Quarry Bank Old Boys	2008/09	Old Xaverians 'A'
1991/92	Warbreck	2009/10	Manweb
1992/93	Aigburth Peoples Hall	2010/11	Old Xaverians Reserves
1993/94	Aigburth Peoples Hall	2011/12	Liver Academy
1994/95	Aigburth Peoples Hall	2012/13	Jaymc
1995/96	Aigburth Peoples Hall	2013/14	Essemay Old Boys
1996/97	Aigburth Peoples Hall	2014/15	East Liverpool
1997/98	Aigburth Peoples Hall	2015/16	Mount Athletic
1998/99	Aigburth Peoples Hall	2016/17	The Saddle
1999/00	Old Xaverians	2017/18	Stoneycroft
2000/01	BRNESC	2018/19	Empress
2001/02	Aigburth Peoples Hall	2019/20	Covid-19
2002/03	Aigburth Peoples Hall	2020/21	Frames
2003/04	Speke	2021/22	Springwood

I ZINGARI CHALLENGE CUP WINNERS

Season	Winner	Score	Runner up
1911/12	Bromborough Pool	2-1	Beresford Old Boys
1912/13	St. Cleopas		Marine
1913/14	Marlborough Old Boys		Bromborough Pool
1919/20	Marine		Bootle Albion
1920/21	Marine	5-1	North Western
1921/22	Hightown	2-0	Marine
1922/23	Marine	2-0	Earle
1923/24	Marine	4-1	Orrell
1924/25	Cadby Hall	3-1	Orrell
1925/26	Liverpool Police		Harrowby
1926/27	Earle	1-0	Orrell
1927/28	Hightown	2-0	Orrell
1928/29	Olympic	1-0	Britannia

Season	Winner	Score	Runner up
1929/30	Cadby Hall		Harrowby
1930/31	The Casuals	2-1	Earle
1931/32	The Casuals	5-3	Harrowby
1932/33	Earle/Formby Joint		
1933/34	Bromborough Pool	5-0	The Casuals
1934/35	Maghull	2-1	Earle
1935/36	Earle	2-0	Maghull
1936/37	Earle	6-2	Bromborough Pool
1937/38	Earle	3-0	Port Sunlight
1938/39	Collegiate Old Boys	3-0	Cadby Hall
1947/48	Aigburth Peoples Hall		Maghull
1948/49	Aigburth Peoples Hall	3-1	Collegiate Old Boys
1949/50	Aigburth Peoples Hall	2-0	Collegiate Old Boys
1950/51	Collegiate Old Boys	5-2	Aigburth Peoples Hall
1951/52	Aigburth Peoples Hall	6-2	Collegiate Old Boys
1952/53	Aigburth Peoples Hall		
1953/54	Stoneycroft		Liverpool Police
1954/55	Florence Albion		Collegiate Old Boys
1955/56	Florence Albion	4-2	Collegiate Old Boys
1956/57	Florence Albion		Essemay Old Boys
1957/58	Florence Albion	5-1	Essemay Old Boys
1958/59	Rockville (Wallasey)	3-2	Aigburth Peoples Hall
1959/60	Florence Albion	2-1	Old Xaverians
1960/61	University of Liverpool		Essemay Old Boys
1961/62	Liverpool Police		Florence Albion
1962/63	Aigburth Peoples Hall		Nalgo
1963/64	Crosby		
1964/65	University of Liverpool		
1965/66	Liverpool Police		Crosby
1966/67	Florence Albion		University of Liverpool
1967/68	Florence Albion		Stoneycroft
1968/69	Aintree Villa/ Molyneux Joint		
1969/70	Florence Albion		Sefton & District
1970/71	Aintree Villa		St. Andrews United
1971/72	Florence Albion		Liverpool Police
1972/73	Alsop Old Boys		Old Xaverians

Season	Winner	Score	Runner up
1973/74	Woolton		Merseyside Police
1974/75	Woolton		Aintree Villa
1975/76	REMYCA United		Quarry Bank Old Boys
1976/77	Alsop Old Boys		Merseyside Police
1977/78	Quarry Bank Old Boys		
1978/79	St. Andrews United		Collegiate Old Boys
1979/80	Aintree Villa		East Villa
1980/81	Aintree Villa		East Villa
1981/82	Aintree Villa		Quarry Bank Old Boys
1982/83	Merseyside Police		Alsop Old Boys
1983/84	Aintree Villa		NALGO
1984/85	Parkside Albion		Speke Town
1985/86	Alsop Old Boys		East Villa
1986/87	Speke Town		Aigburth Peoples Hall
1987/88	Quarry Bank Old Boys		Aigburth Peoples Hall
1988/89	REMYCA United		Aigburth Peoples Hall
1989/90	Netherley Royal British Legion	3-0	Aigburth Peoples Hall
1990/91	Netherley Royal British Legion		East Villa
1991/92	Selwyn		Shrewsbury House Old Boys
1992/93	Jabisco		REMYCA United
1993/94	REMYCA United		Essemay Old Boys
1994/95	REMYCA United		Blacklow Brow
1995/96	East Villa		Sacre Coeur FP
1996/97	Mills		St. Philomenas
1997/98	Aigburth Peoples Hall		St. Philomenas
1998/99	REMYCA United		East Villa
1999/00	NELTC		
2000/01	NELTC		
2001/02	Old Xaverians		Quarry Bank Old Boys
2002/03	Warbreck		
2003/04	Allerton		
2004/05	ROMA		
2005/06	St. Ambrose		Red Rum
2006/07	East Villa		Waterloo Dock
2007/08	Waterloo Dock		Red Rum

417

Season	Winner	Score	Runner up
2008/09	Waterloo Dock		South Liverpool
2009/10	Aigburth Peoples Hall		
2010/11	South Liverpool		Waterloo Dock
2011/12	Ford Motors		Croxteth
2012/13	South Sefton Borough		
2013/14	Aigburth Peoples Hall		Waterloo Dock
2014/15	East Villa		Page Celtic
2015/16	Aigburth Peoples Hall		Page Celtic
2016/17	Lower Breck		Page Celtic
2017/18	Lower Breck		East Villa
2018/19	Waterloo Dock		BRNESC
2019/20	Page Celtic		BRNESC
2020/21	COVID		COVID
2021/22	The Empress		Waterloo Dock
2022/23	Halewood Apollo		Warbreck
2023/24	MSB Woolton		Halewood Apollo
2024/25	MSB Woolton		

LANCASHIRE AMATEUR LEAGUE WINNERS

Season	Winners
1899/00	**Old Xaverians**
1900/01	**Melling**
1901/02	**Melling**
1902/03	**Old Xaverians**
1903/04	Blackburn Crosshill
1904/05	**Wigan Grammar School Old Boys**
1905/06	**Old Xaverians**
1906/07	**Southport Holy Trinity Old Boys**
1907/08	**Old Xaverians**
1908/09	Preston Winckley
1909/10	**Southport YMCA**

LIVERPOOL AMATEUR CUP WINNERS

Season	Winners	Season	Winners
1905/06	Liverpool Balmoral	1953/54	Aigburth Peoples Hall
1906/07	Widnes Wesley Guild	1954/55	Collegiate Old Boys
1907/08	Old Xaverians	1955/56	Alsop Old Boys
1908/09	Merton	1956/57	Collegiate Old Boys
1909/10	Marine	1957/58	Aintree S.S.
1910/11	Bromborough Pool	1958/59	Florence Albion
1911/12	Old Xaverians	1959/60	Unit Construction
1912/13	St. Cleopas	1960/61	Waterloo G.S.O.B.
1913/14	Orrell	1961/62	Unit Construction
1919/20	Marine	1962/63	Maghull
1920/21	Orrell	1963/64	Guinness Exports
1921/22	Blundellsands	1964/65	Dunlop (Speke)
1922/23	Marine	1965/66	Langton
1923/24	Marine	1966/67	Langton
1924/25	Harlandic	1967/68	Langton
1925/26	Cadby Hall	1968/69	Langton
1926/27	Marine	1969/70	Florence Albion
1927/28	Marine	1970/71	Marine
1928/29	Marine	1971/72	Aintree Villa
1929/30	Formby	1972/73	Dunlop (Speke)
1930/31	Marine	1973/74	Bootle
1931/32	Garston Gas Works	1974/75	A.C. Delco
1932/33	Aintree S.S.	1975/76	Waterloo Dock
1933/34	Marine	1976/77	Aintree S.S.
1934/35	Maghull/Garston Woodcutters	1977/78	Sefton and District
1935/36	Cadby Hall	1978/79	Aintree Villa
1936/37	Earle	1979/80	Sefton and District
1937/38	Dee-Jay	1980/81	St. Dominics
1938/39	Earlestown Bohemians	1981/82	Aintree Villa
1945/46	Earle/Marine	1982/83	Liverpool NALGO
1946/47	Earle	1983/84	Plessey
1947/48	Formby	1984/85	Florence Albion
1948/49	Formby	1985/86	Uniasco
1949/50	Collegiate Old Boys	1986/87	Sefton and District
1950/51	Collegiate Old Boys	1987/88	Liverpool NALGO
1951/52	Aigburth Peoples Hall	1988/89	Merseyside Police
1952/53	Marine Reserves	1989/90	No Competition

LIVERPOOL CHALLENGE CUP WINNERS

Season	Winners	Season	Winners
1908/09	Tranmere Rovers	1949/50	South Liverpool Reserves
1909/10	Widnes Wesley Guild	1950/51	Burscough
1910/11	South Liverpool	1951/52	Formby
1911/12	Skelmersdale United	1952/53	Everton 'A'
1912/13	South Liverpool	1953/54	Liverpool 'A'
1913/14	Skelmersdale United	1954/55	Burscough
1914/15	Burscough Rangers	1955/56	Everton 'A'
1919/20	Skelmersdale United	1956/57	New Brighton
1920/21	Skelmersdale United	1957/58	South Liverpool
1921/22	Furness Whithy	1958/59	Liverpool 'A'
1922/23	New Brighton Reserves	1959/60	Liverpool 'A'
1923/24	New Brighton Reserves	1960/61	Liverpool 'A'
1924/25	New Brighton Reserves	1961/62	Prescot Cables
1925/26	Harlandic	1962/63	Guinness Exports
1926/27	Burscough Rangers	1963/64	Formby
1927/28	Prescot	1964/65	Langton
1928/29	Prescot Cables	1965/66	Guinness Exports
1929/30	Prescot Cables	1966/67	South Liverpool
1930/31	Peasley Cross 'A'	1967/68	Formby
1931/32	Everton 'A'	1968/69	Kirkby Town
1932/33	New Brighton Reserves	1969/70	Lucas Sports
1933/34	Everton 'A'	1970/71	Prescot B.I.
1934/35	B.I. Social (Prescot)	1971/72	Marine Reserves
1935/36	Miranda	1972/73	Dunlop (Speke)
1936/37	South Liverpool Reserves	1973/74	Dunlop (Speke)
1937/38	Miranda	1974/75	Earle
1938/39	Skelmersdale United	1975/76	Bootle
1939/40	Skelmersdale United	1976/77	Waterloo Dock
1942/43	Marine	1977/78	Prescot Town
1943/44	R.A.F. (Padgate)	1978/79	Bootle
1944/45	Marine	1979/80	Maghull
1945/46	Skelmersdale United	1980/81	Maghull
1946/47	Skelmersdale United	1981/82	St. Dominics
1947/48	Burscough	1982/83	St. Dominics
1948/49	Prescot Cables	1983/84	St. Dominics

Season	Winners	Season	Winners
1984/85	St. Dominics	2005/06	Waterloo Dock
1985/86	Maghull	2006/07	Waterloo Dock
1986/87	Uniasco	2007/08	East Villa
1987/88	Uniasco	2008/09	Aigburth Peoples Hall
1988/89	Waterloo Dock	2009/10	Aigburth Peoples Hall
1989/90	East Villa	2010/11	East Villa
1990/91	Ford Motors	2011/12	Waterloo Dock
1991/92	Stanton Dale	2012/13	South Sefton Borough
1992/93	Lucas Sports	2013/14	Garswood United
1993/94	Maghull	2014/15	Eagle Sports
1994/95	Waterloo Dock	2015/16	South Liverpool
1995/96	Garswood United	2016/17	South Liverpool
1996/97	St. Dominics	2017/18	Lower Breck
1997/98	Manweb	2018/19	Richmond Raith Rovers
1998/99	Waterloo Dock	2019/20	Covid-19
1999/00	Yorkshire Copper Tube	2020/21	Covid-19
2000/01	Waterloo Dock	2021/22	East Villa
2001/02	St. Aloysius	2022/23	BRNESC
2002/03	Royal Seaforth	2023/24	Liverpool Nalgo
2003/04	Waterloo Dock	2024/25	The Grenadier The Gren
2004/05	Waterloo Dock		

LIVERPOOL JUNIOR CUP WINNERS

Season	Winners	Season	Winners
1887/88	Aintree Church	1898/99	Melrose Reserves
1888/89	5th Irish	1899/00	Formby Rangers
1889/90	Prescot First Team	1900/01	Ellesmere Port
1890/91	Kirkdale	1901/02	Garston North End
1891/92	Wavertree	1902/03	Garston Gasworks
1892/93	Saltney Borderers	1903/04	Valkyrie
1893/94	Liverpool Casuals	1904/05	Garston North End
1894/95	L&N.W. Locos	1905/06	Prescot Wire Works
1895/96	Hudson's	1906/07	Liverpool Rovers
1896/97	Kirkdale	1907/08	Warrington Albions
1897/98	Hawthorne	1908/09	Widnes Wesley Guild

Season	Winners	Season	Winners
1909/10	Diamond Match	1951/52	Everton 'B'
1910/11	Banks Road	1952/53	Elm Bank
1911/12	Skelmersdale Mission	1953/54	Unit Construction
1912/13	Westhead Juniors	1954/55	Birkdale Athletic
1913/14	Crystal Athletic	1955/56	Coronation
1914/15	Alexandra Vics	1956/57	Salisbury Athletic
1917/18	Allerton (War Fund)	1957/58	Rylands (Warrington)
1918/19	Haydock Colliery	1958/59	Birkdale Athletic
1919/20	Poulton Rovers	1959/60	St Dominics Cyms
1920/21	Furness Whithy	1960/61	Rockville Wallasey
1921/22	Howsons	1961/62	Guinness Exports
1922/23	Bootle St James	1962/63	Albright & Wilson
1923/24	Mellanear	1963/64	Norwest
1924/25	Aintree S.S.	1964/65	Aintree Villa
1925/26	Linacre Gasworks	1965/66	Newton
1926/27	Parkhill Wesley	1966/67	St.Dominics
1927/28	Garston Protestant Reformers	1967/68	Pegasus Old Boys
1928/29	Derby Crescent	1968/69	Tillotsons
1929/30	LMS Langton Dock	1969/70	A.C. Delco
1930/31	Earlestown White Star	1970/71	Waterloo Dock
1931/32	Haydock Athletic	1971/72	Longview Labour
1932/33	Blue Circle Cement	1972/73	Lucas Sports
1933/34	Miranda	1973/74	Uniasco
1934/35	Beacon	1974/75	Bronte Old Boys
1935/36	Everton Amateurs	1975/76	Fleet
1936/37	Haydock Villa	1976/77	Bronte Old Boys
1937/38	Burscough Vics.	1977/78	Cheshire Lines
1938/39	High Park	1978/79	Longview Labour
1942/43	Fleetwood Hesketh	1979/80	Garswood United
1943/44	Derbyshire Hill Rovers (St. Helens)	1980/81	Whitbread Falcon
1944/45	Derbyshire Hill	1981/82	Inter
1945/46	High Park	1982/83	Plessey
1946/47	Aigburth Peoples Hall	1983/84	Shrewsbury House
1947/48	High Park & Victoria	1984/85	Littlewoods
1948/49	Parr & Hardshaw	1985/86	Speke BCOB
1949/50	Fleetwood Hesketh	1986/87	Roma
1950/51	Everton 'B'	1987/88	Ventmond

Season	Winners	Season	Winners
1988/89	Evans	2007/08	Mossley Hill Athletic
1989/90	Beesix	2008/09	Knowsley South
1990/91	Stantondale	2009/10	Hale
1991/92	Aigburth Peoples Hall	2010/11	Liverpool North
1992/93	Eagle Sports	2011/12	Allerton
1993/94	Leyfield	2012/13	New Street
1994/95	Selwyn	2013/14	New Street
1995/96	Stockbridge	2014/15	Vulcan
1996/97	South Liverpool	2015/16	Quarry Bank Old Boys
1997/98	Child	2016/17	Netherley Wood Lane Legion
1998/99	St. Aloysius	2017/18	Quarry Bank Old Boys
1999/00	Child	2018/19	Marshalls FC
2000/01	Pilkington FC	2019/20	
2001/02	Tuebrook	2020/21	
2002/03	Birchfield	2021/22	FC Salle
2003/04	Halewood Town	2022/23	St.Margaret's Old Boys
2004/05	Pilkington FC	2023/24	South Liverpool Third team
2005/06	South Liverpool Reserves	2024/25	Clay Brow Clay Brow Saturday
2006/07	Rainhill Town		

LIVERPOOL COUNTY COMBINATION WINNERS

Season	Winners	Runners Up
1909/10	Garston Gasworks	Prescot Wire Works
1910/11	Skelmersdale United	Prescot Wire Works
1911/12	Garston North End	Skelmersdale United
1912/13	Garston Gasworks	Prescot Wire Works
1913/14	Skelmersdale United	Wallasey Borough
1919/20	Skelmersdale United	Frodsham Athletic
1920/21	Whitson Parish Church	Burscough Rangers
1921/22	Burscough Rangers	Frodsham
1922/23	New Brighton Reserves	Wigan Borough Reserves
1923/24	New Brighton Reserves	Ormskirk
1924/25	Port Sunlight Athletic	Everton 'A'
1925/26	Burscough Rangers	Whiston Parish Church

Season	Winners	Runners Up
1926/27	Burscough Rangers	New Brighton Reserves
1927/28	Marine	Whiston
1928/29	Whitson	Marine
1929/30	Liverpool 'A'	Bootle Celtic
1930/31	Marine	Everton 'A'
1931/32	Everton 'A'	Whiston
1932/33	Whiston	Everton 'A'
1933/34	Marine	Everton 'A'
1934/35	Marine	Everton 'A'
1935/36	Everton 'A'	Skelmersdale United
1936/37	Everton 'A'	Earlestown Bohemians
1937/38	Everton 'A'	Hoylake Athletic
1938/39	Skelmersdale United	Everton 'A'
1945/46	Skelmersdale United	Marine
1946/47	Liverpool 'A'	Skelmersdale United
1947/48	Earlestown	Formby
1948/49	Formby	Everton 'A'
1949/50	Burscough	Skelmersdale United
1950/51	Skelmersdale United	Everton 'A'
1951/52	Skelmersdale United	Formby
1952/53	Everton 'A'	Formby
1953/54	Skelmersdale United	Everton 'A'
1954/55	Everton 'A'	Liverpool 'A'
1955/56	Liverpool 'A'	Marine Reserves
1956/57	Unit Construction	South Liverpool Reserves
1957/58	Dunlop (Speke)	Marine Reserves
1958/59	Guinness Exports	Burscough Rangers
1959/60	Guinness Exports	Unit Construction
1960/61	Rylands Recreation	Guinness Exports
1961/62	Guinness Exports	Langton
1962/63	Guinness Exports	Langton
1963/64	Guinness Exports	Unit Construction
1964/65	Langton	Formby
1965/66	Lucas Sports	Maghull
1966/67	Maghull	Dunlop (Speke)
1967/68	Langton	Maghull
1968/69	Langton	Guinness Exports Reserves
1969/70	Langton	Lucas Sports

Season	Winners	Runners Up
1970/71	Langton	Lucas Sports
1971/72	Langton	Dunlop (Speke)
1972/73	Langton	Waterloo Dock
1973/74	Bootle	Lucas Sports
1974/75	Waterloo Dock	Ainsdale
1975/76	Waterloo Dock	Aintree S.S.
1976/77	Aintree S.S.	Waterloo Dock
1977/78	Waterloo Dock	Prescot B.I.
1978/79	Waterloo Dock	St. Dominics
1979/80	St. Dominics	Garswood United
1980/81	Waterloo Dock	St. Dominics
1981/82	St. Dominics	Earle
1982/83	St. Dominics	Earle
1983/84	BRNESC	St. Dominics
1984/85	BRNESC	Waterloo Dock
1985/86	St. Dominics	Waterloo Dock
1986/87	Waterloo Dock	BRNESC
1987/88	Uniasco	Waterloo Dock
1988/89	Waterloo Dock	St. Dominics
1989/90	Waterloo Dock	St. Dominics
1990/91	Stantondale	St. Dominics
1991/92	Yorkshire Copper Tube	St. Dominics
1992/93	St. Dominics	Lucas Sports
1993/94	St. Dominics	Lucas Sports
1994/95	St. Dominics	Waterloo Dock
1995/96	Stockbridge	Waterloo Dock
1996/97	Waterloo Dock	Stockbridge
1997/98	St. Dominics	Crawfords United Biscuits
1998/99	St. Dominics	Manweb
1999/00	Waterloo Dock	Yorkshire Copper Tube
2000/01	Yorkshire Copper Tube	Waterloo Dock
2001/02	St.Aloysius	Speke
2002/03	Speke	Waterloo Dock
2003/04	Waterloo Dock	Speke
2004/05	Waterloo Dock	St. Dominics
2005/06	Speke	Waterloo Dock

LIVERPOOL COUNTY PREMIER LEAGUE WINNERS

Season	Premier Division Winners	Premier Division Runners Up
2006/07	Waterloo Dock	East Villa
2007/08	Waterloo Dock	East Villa
2008/09	Waterloo Dock	Aighburth Peoples Hall
2009/10	Waterloo Dock	St. Aloysius
2010/11	Waterloo Dock	Old Xaverians
2011/12	Aighburth Peoples Hall	East Villa
2012/13	West Everton Xaviers	Waterloo Dock
2013/14	Aighburth Peoples Hall	Waterloo Dock
2014/15	Aighburth Peoples Hall	East Villa
2015/16	Aighburth Peoples Hall	Waterloo Dock
2016/17	Aighburth Peoples Hall	Lower Breck
2017/18	Lower Breck	East Villa
2018/19	Waterloo Dock	East Villa
2019/20	Covid-19	Covid-19
2020/21	Liverpoo Nalgo	Waterloo Dock
2021/22	Sefton Athletic	Liverpool Nalgo
2022/23	MSB Woolton	Halewood Apollo
2023/24	Halewood Apollo	East Villa Rail
2024/25	MSB Woolton	Liverpool Nalgo

LIVERPOOL OLD BOYS LEAGUE

Season	Winners	Season	Winners
1923/24	Collegiate Old Boys	1952/53	Old Bootleians
1924/25	Birkenhead Institute Old Boys	1953/54	Old Bootleians
1925/26	Birkenhead Institute Old Boys	1954/55	Old Bootleians
1926/27	Marlborough Old Boys	1955/56	Old Maricollians
1927/28	Marlborough Old Boys	1956/57	Prescot Grammar School Old Boys
1928/29	Liobians	1957/58	Prescot Grammar School Old Boys
1929/30	Old Holts	1958/59	Old Bootleians
1930/31	Ormskirk Grammar School Old Boys	1959/60	Old Wallaseyans
1931/32	Old Holts	1960/61	Old Instonians
1932/33	Ormskirk Grammar School Old Boys	1961/62	Prescot Grammar School Old Boys
1933/34	Waterloo Grammar School Old Boys	1962/63	Void
1934/35	Ormskirk Grammar School Old Boys	1963/64	Old Wallaseyans
1935/36	Ormskirk Grammar School Old Boys	1964/65	Old Swan Technical College
1936/37	Ormskirk Grammar School Old Boys	1965/66	Walton Technical College
1937/38	Ormskirk Grammar School Old Boys	1966/67	De La Salle Old Boys
1938/39	Ormskirk Grammar School Old Boys	1967/68	Old Wallaseyans
1940/46	No Competition	1968/69	Blue Coat Old Boys
1946/47	Essemmay Old Boys	1969/70	Prescot Grammar School Old Boys
1947/48	Essemmay Old Boys	1970/71	Prescot Grammar School Old Boys
1948/49	Prescot Grammar School Old Boys	1971/72	Hillfoot Hey Old Boys
1949/50	Alsop Old Boys	1972/73	Hillfoot Hey Old Boys
1950/51	Old Bootleians	1973/74	Kirkby CFE
1951/52	Old Bootleians	1974/75	Quarry Bank Old Boys

427

Season	Winners	Season	Winners
1975/76	Riversdale COT	2001/02	Old Xaverians
1976/77	Old Wallaseyans	2002/03	Old Xaverians
1977/78	Old Bootleians	2003/04	Hope Park
1978/79	Old Bootleians	2004/05	Collegiate Old Boys
1979/80	Kirkby CFE	2005/06	Bankfield Old Boys
1980/81	Kirkby CFE	2006/07	Bankfield Old Boys
1981/82	Old Wallaseyans	2007/08	Naylorsfield
1982/83	Shorefields FP	2008/09	Old Bootleians
1983/84	Old Bootleians	2009/10	Waterloo Grammar School Old Boys
1984/85	Salesian Old Boys	2010/11	Roby College Old Boys
1985/86	Salesian Old Boys	2011/12	DLS Academy
1986/87	Kirkby CFE	2012/13	Old Holts
1987/88	Kirkby CFE	2013/14	Quarry Bank Old Boys
1988/89	Kirkby CFE	2014/15	Quarry Bank Old Boys
1989/90	Quarry Bank Old Boys	2015/16	Bankfield Old Boys
1990/91	Old Wallaseyans	2016/17	Quarry Bank Old Boys
1991/92	Old Wallaseyans	2017/18	Alumni
1992/93	Old Wallaseyans	2018/19	Quarry Bank Old Boys
1993/94	Royal Insurance	2019/20	Oakes Institute
1994/95	Walker Park	2020/21	South Liverpool
1995/96	FC Salle	2021/22	FC Salle
1996/97	Hillfoot Hey Old Boys	2022/23	Abbey Road
1997/98	Hugh Baird TCSS	2023/24	Mersey Harps First Team
1998/99	Hope Park	2024/25	Mersey Harps First Team
1999/00	Hope Park		
2000/01	Walker Park		

LIVERPOOL SENIOR NON LEAGUE CUP WINNERS

Season	Winners	Season	Winners
1949/50	Bootle	1963/64	New Brighton
1950/51	Bootle	1964/65	Wigan Athletic
1951/52	Prescot Cables	1965/66	Wigan Athletic
1952/53	Prescot Cables	1966/67	Wigan Athletic
1953/54	South Liverpool	1967/68	South Liverpool
1954/55	Wigan Athletic	1968/69	Marine
1955/56	Burscough	1969/70	South Liverpool
1956/57	New Brighton	1970/71	Ornskirk
1957/58	New Brighton/Wigan Athletic	1971/72	Burscough
1958/59	Prescot Cables	1972/73	Ornskirk
1959/60	New Brighton	1973/74	Skelmersdale United
1960/61	Prescot Cables	1974/75	Skelmersdale United
1961/62	New Brighton	1975/76	Marine
1962/63	Wigan Athletic	1976/77	Marine

LORD WAVERTREE CUP WINNERS

Season	Winner	Season	Winner
1910/11	Banks Road Garston	1931/32	Liverpool 'A'
1911/12	L& NWR Par Way	1932/33	Skelmersdale United
1912/13	Wallasey Borough	1933/34	Prescot Cables
1913/14	Burscough Rangers	1934/35	Liverpool 'A'
1915/20	No Competition	1935/36	Earlestown Bohemians
1920/21	Chester Reserves	1936/37	Skelmersdale United
1921/22	Burscough Rangers	1937/38	Skelmersdale United
1922/23	Wigan Borough Reserves	1938/39	Tushinghams Brickworks
1923/24	N/A	1944/45	Marine Reserves
1924/25	Port Sunlight	1945/46	Marine Reserves
1925/26	N/A	1946/47	Castner Kellner
1926/27	N/A	1947/48	Marine Reserves
1927/28	Whiston	1948/49	Runcorn Athletic
1928/29	Whiston	1949/50	Everton 'B'
1929/30	Liverpool 'A'	1950/51	Everton 'B'
1930/31	Liverpool 'A'	1951/52	Everton 'B'

Season	Winner	Season	Winner
1952/53	Everton 'B'	1989/90	Royal Seaforth
1953/54	Liverpool 'B'	1990/91	BRENSC Reserves
1954/55	Aintree S.S.	1991/92	BRENSC Reserves
1955/56	Unit Construction & Liverpool 'A'	1992/93	Halewood Town
1956/57	South Liverpool Reserves	1993/94	Royal Seaforth
1957/58	South Liverpool Reserves	1994/95	Eldonians
1958/59	Dunlop (Speke)	1995/96	Selwyn
1959/60	South Liverpool Reserves	1996/97	Cheshire Lines
1960/61	Langton	1997/98	Prescot BICC
1961/62	Waterloo Ramblers	1998/99	St. Aloysius
1962/63	Waterloo Ramblers	1999/00	St. Dominics
1963/64	Guinness Exports Reserves	2000/01	St. Dominics
1964/65	Lucas Sports	2001/02	Tuebrook
1965/66	Prescot Town Reserves	2002/03	Waterloo Dock
1966/67	Gleneagles	2003/04	Halewood Town
1967/68	Burscough Reserves	2004/05	Speke
1968/69	No Competition	2005/06	St. Dominics
1969/70	No Competition	2006/07	Edge Hill BCOB
1970/71	No Competition	2007/08	Old Holts
1971/72	No Competition	2008/09	East Villa Reserves
1972/73	No Competition	2009/10	N/A
1973/74	No Competition	2010/11	Alder
1974/75	No Competition	2011/12	Kingsley United
1975/76	No Competition	2012/13	Holy Cross
1976/77	UGB (St Helens) Recreation	2013/14	Cheshire Lines
1977/78	Earle	2014/15	Woolton
1978/79	Garswood United	2015/16	Custys
1979/80	Cardinal Allen Old Boys	2016/17	Mount Athletic
1980/81	Harrison Line	2017/18	The Saddle
1981/82	Otis	2018/19	Marshalls Roby
1982/83	BRENSC	2019/20	Covid-19
1983/84	Liverpool Maritime Terminals	2020/21	Covid-19
1984/85	BEESIX	2021/22	Joey Orr's The Edge
1985/86	Avon Athletic	2022/23	N/A
1986/87	Bootle Reserves	2023/24	N/A
1987/88	Lucas Sports	2024/25	Flathouse
1988/89	Ford Motors		

NORTH WEST WOMEN'S REGIONAL FOOTBALL LEAGUE

Season	Winners	Season	Winners
1971	Preston North End	1980/81	Preston North End
1972	Preston North End	1981/82	**St. Helens**
1973	Preston North End	1982/83	**St. Helens**
1973/74		1983/84	Preston Rangers
1974/75	Barrow	1984/85	Preston Rangers
1975/76	Preston North End	1985/86	Broadoak
1976/77	Preston North End	1986/87	**St. Helens**
1977/78	Preston North End	1987/88	**Leasowe Pacific**
1978/79	Bronte	1988/89	**Leasowe Pacific**
1979/80	Preston North End		

NORTH WEST WOMEN'S REGIONAL LEAGUE

Season	Winners	Season	Winners
1989/90	**Leasowe Pacific**	2007/08	Blackpool Wren Rovers
1990/91	**Leasowe Pacific**	2008/09	**Liverpool Feds**
1991/92	**Leasowe Pacific**	2009/10	**Mossley Hill**
1992/93	**Wigan Ladies**	2010/11	Fletcher Moss Rangers
1993/94	Manchester Belle Vue	2011/12	Chorley
1994/95	**Tranmere Rovers**	2012/13	**Tranmere Rovers**
1995/96	Manchester United	2013/14	Morecambe
1996/97	Bangor City	2014/15	Blackpool Wren Rovers
1997/98	Preston North End Women	2015/16	Crewe Alexandra
1998/99	Blackpool Wren Rovers	2016/17	Bolton Wanderers
1999/00	Manchester City	2017/18	Burnley FC Girls & Ladies
2000/01	**Chester City**	2018/19	Stockport County
2001/02	**Liverpool Feds**	2019/20	Covid-19 FC United of Manchester
2002/03	**Newsham Peoples Hall**	2020/21	**Covid-19 Tranmere Rovers**
2003/04	Preston North End Women	2021/22	**Merseyrail**
2004/05	Garswood Saints	2022/23	FC United of Manchester Women
2005/06	Stretford Victoria	2023/24	Cheadle Town Stingers
2006/07	Rochdale AFC	2024/25	Wythenshawe Women

OTTO BARRASI CUP

Season	Winner	Season	Winner
1967/68	Leytonstone	1972/73	Walton & Hersham
1968/69	North Shields/Roma	1973/74	Not Played
1969/70	Enfield	1974/75	Staines Town
1970/71	**Skelmersdale United**	1975/76	Soresinese
1971/72	Hendon		

PYKE CUP WINNERS

Season	Winners	Season	Winners
1900/01	Wheatland	1927/28	Ellesmere Port Cement
1901/02	Liverpoool Caledonians	1928/29	Ellesmere Port Town
1902/03	Rock Ferry St. Pauls	1929/30	Shell Mex
1903/04	Ellesmere Port	1930/31	Rhyl/Colwyn Bay
1904/05	West Kirby	1931/32	No Competition
1905/06	Garston Gasworks	1932/33	Heswall
1906/07	Ergremont Social	1933/34	Hoylake Athletic
1907/08	African Royal/Harrowby	1934/35	Shell Mex
1908/09	Harrowby	1935/36	Shell Mex
1909/10	Harrowby	1936/37	Helsby B.I.
1910/11	Hoylake Athletic	1937/38	Bromborough Pool
1911/12	Harrowby	1938/39	Heswall
1912/13	Egremont	1939/40	Ellesmere Port Town
1913/14	Garston Gasworks	1946/47	Flint Town
1914/15	Wirral Railway	1947/48	Port Sunlight
1919/20	West Kirby	1948/49	Hoylake Athletic
1920/21	Ellesmere Port	1949/50	Stork
1921/22	Garston Gasworks	1950/51	Shell/Stork
1922/23	Poulton Rovers	1951/52	Newton
1923/24	Chester 'A'	1952/53	Bromborough
1924/25	West Kirby	1953/54	Tranmere Rovers 'A'
1925/26	Runcorn	1954/55	Liverpoool 'C'
1926/27	Victoria Lodge	1955/56	Stork

Season	Winners	Season	Winners
1956/57	Stork	1991/92	Cammell Laird
1957/58	New Brighton	1992/93	Cammell Laird
1958/59	Runcorn Reserves	1993/94	Cammell Laird
1959/60	Runcorn Reserves	1994/95	Christleton
1960/61	Runcorn Reserves	1995/96	Mersey Royal
1961/62	Newton	1996/97	Heswall
1962/63	Stork	1997/98	Poulton Victoria
1963/64	West Kirby	1998/99	Cammell Laird
1964/65	West Kirby/Newton	1999/00	Vauxhall Motors
1965/66	Ellesmere Port	2000/01	Poulton Victoria
1966/67	West Kirby	2001/02	Cammell Laird
1967/68	Port Sunlight	2002/03	Ashville
1968/69	Chester College	2003/04	Poulton Victoria
1969/70	Cammell Laird	2004/05	Vauxhall Motors
1970/71	Christleton	2005/06	West Kirby
1971/72	Poulton Victoria	2006/07	Poulton Victoria
1972/73	Willaston	2007/08	Castrol Social
1973/74	Port Sunlight	2008/09	Newton
1974/75	Port Sunlight	2009/10	Castrol Social
1975/76	Cammell Laird	2010/11	Maghull
1976/77	Cammell Laird	2011/12	Maghull
1977/78	Cammell Laird	2012/13	West Kirby
1978/79	Cammell Laird	2013/14	Newton
1979/80	Poulton Victoria	2014/15	Cammell Laird 1907
1980/81	Stork	2015/16	South Liverpool
1981/82	Christleton	2016/17	Redgate Rovers
1982/83	West Kirby	2017/18	Newton
1983/84	Poulton Victoria	2018/19	Redgate Rovers
1984/85	Heswall	2019/20	South Liverpool
1985/86	West Kirby	2020/21	Mossley Hill Athletic
1986/87	General Chemicals	2021/22	Mossley Hill Athletic
1987/88	Mersey Royal	2022/23	Mossley Hill Athletic
1988/89	Merseyside Police	2023/24	Mossley Hill Athletic
1989/90	Mersey Royal	2024/25	Bootle
1990/91	Poulton Victoria		

433

WEST LANCASHIRE LEAGUE

Season	Winner	Season	Winner
1889/90	Liverpool Stanley	1907/08	Helsby Athletic
1890/91	Bootle Athletic	1908/09	Sutton Commercial
1891/92	Kirkdale	1909/10	Clock Face
1892/93	Liverpool Reserves	1910/11	Morton's Recreation
1893/94	White Star Wanderers	1911/12	Stirling
1894/95	Liverpool South End		
1895/96	Toxteth	1920/21	Furness Withy
1896/97	Garston Copper Works	1921/22	Furness Withy
		1922/23	Furness Withy
1904/05	Garston Gasworks	1923/24	Furness Withy
1905/06	Prescot Wireworks	1924/25	Formby
		1925/26	Blundellsands

WIRRAL AMATEUR CUP WINNERS

Season	Winners	Season	Winners
1892/93	West Kirby	1909/10	Bromborough Pool
1893/94	Cleveland Athletic	1910/11	Lingdale
1894/95	Cleveland Athletic	1911/12	Central Vics.
1895/96	St. Johns	1912/13	Claughton St. Marks
1896/97	Seacombe Swifts	1913/14	Hoylake Trinity
1897/98	Wirral Railways Reserves	1919/20	Sutton Comrades
1898/99	Ellesmere Port	1920/21	Cement Works/Neston Comrades
1899/00	Ellesmere Port Reserves	1921/22	Bebington
1900/01	Melrose Reserves	1922/23	Port Sunlight
1901/02	Clarendon	1923/24	Poulton Rovers
1902/03	Rake Lane P.S.A.	1924/25	Victoria Lodge/West Kirby
1903/04	Valkyrie	1925/26	Brookville
1904/05	Liscard C.E.M.S.	1926/27	West Kirby
1905/06	Liscard Albion	1927/28	Brookville
1906/07	Bebington St Andrew's	1928/29	Shell Mex
1907/08	Lingdale	1929/30	Brookville
1908/09	Bebington St Andrew's	1930/31	West Kirby Southend

Season	Winners	Season	Winners
1931/32	Heswall	1967/68	St. Laurence's
1932/33	Heswall	1968/69	Bebington Hawks
1933/34	Heswall	1969/70	Cammell Laird
1934/35	Rock Ferry Social	1970/71	Bromborough Pool
1935/36	Heswall	1971/72	Willaston
1936/37	Heswall	1972/73	Harrowby
1937/38	Brookville	1973/74	Ashville
1938/39	Bowaters	1974/75	Poulton Victoria
1939/40	Port Sunlight Old Boys	1975/76	Poulton Victoria
1940/41	Silver Queen	1976/77	Heswall
1941/42	Shaftesbury Old Boys	1977/78	Poulton Victoria
1942/43	Park Villa	1978/79	Higher Bebington
1943/44	Eatham Athletic	1979/80	Shell
1944/45	Park Villa	1980/81	Mersey Royal
1945/46	Stork	1981/82	Burmah Castrol
1946/47	Newton	1982/83	Higher Bebington
1947/48	Stork	1983/84	Poulton Victoria
1948/49	Moreton	1984/85	Cammell Laird
1949/50	Moreton/Bromborough	1985/86	Vauxhall Motors
1950/51	Port Sunlight	1986/87	Heswall
1951/52	Moreton	1987/88	Higher Bebington
1952/53	Hoylake	1988/89	Shell
1953/54	Stork	1989/90	Stork
1954/55	Lobol	1990/91	Cammell Laird
1955/56	St. Laurence's	1991/92	Bromborough Pool
1956/57	Ashville	1992/93	Poulton Victoria
1957/58	Port Sunlight	1993/94	Ashville
1958/59	Moreton Rovers	1994/95	Stork
1959/60	Upton	1995/96	Heswall
1960/61	St. Laurence's	1996/97	Mallaby
1961/62	Birkenhead St. Anne's	1997/98	New Brighton
1962/63	Our Lady's	1998/99	Heswall
1963/64	Newton	1999/00	Cammell Laird
1964/65	Park Villa	2000/01	Mallaby
1965/66	Mersey Royal	2001/02	Castrol Social
1966/67	Shell	2002/03	Cammell Laird

Season	Winners	Season	Winners
2003/04	Heswall	2014/15	Willaston
2004/05	Willaston	2015/16	West Kirby & Wasps
2005/06	West Kirby	2016/17	Ashville
2006/07	Poulton Victoria	2017/18	St. Saviours
2007/08	FC Pensby	2018/19	Ellesmere Port
2008/09	Willaston	2019/20	Covid -19
2009/10	West Kirby	2020/21	Ellesmere Port
2010/11	West Kirby	2021/22	Hooton
2011/12	Ashville	2022/23	Ashville
2012/13	Mallaby	2023/24	Cammell Laird Reserves
2013/14	Ashville		

WIRRAL JUNIOR CUP WINNERS

Season	Winners	Season	Winners
1909/10	Gilbrook Mission	1932/33	Brougham Athletic
1910/11	Tranmere Institute	1933/34	St. Laurence's
1911/12	Hamilton Square	1934/35	St. Luke's Old Boys
1912/13	West Kirby CLB	1935/36	Port Sunlight Old Boys
1913/14	Port Sunlight	1936/37	Port Sunlight Old Boys
1918/19	Gilbrook	1937/38	Pensby
1919/20	Heswall	1938/39	West Kirby Central
1920/21	Liscard Co-op	1939/40	Brassey St. Institute
1921/22	Seacombe Conservatives	1940/41	Stanlaw Vics.
1922/23	Wheatland	1941/42	Eastham Athletic
1923/24	Ellesmere Port Prim M	1942/43	Birkenhead St. Anne's
1924/25	Port Sunlight Christ Church	1943/44	Park Villa
1925/26	Britannia	1944/45	Park Villa
1926/27	Britannia	1945/46	Port Sunlight Old Boys
1927/28	Heswall PSA	1946/47	Newton
1928/29	Britannia	1947/48	Shaftesbury Old Boys
1929/30	Birkenhead Nomads	1948/49	Birkenhead St. Anne's
1930/31	Birkenhead Nomads	1949/50	Moreton
1931/32	Shaftesbury Old Boys	1950/51	Neston Nomads

Season	Winners	Season	Winners
1951/52	Shaftesbury Old Boys	1988/89	Mallaby
1952/53	Claughton Villa	1989/90	Shaftesbury Old Boys
1953/54	Shaftesbury Old Boys	1990/91	Mallaby
1954/55	Heswall Amateurs	1991/92	Mallaby
1955/56	Moreton Rovers	1992/93	Seven Stiles
1956/57	Shell	1993/94	Seven Stiles
1957/58	Cup Withheld	1994/95	Malt Shovel
1958/59	Birkenhead St. Anne's	1995/96	New Brighton
1959/60	St. Laurence's	1996/97	Manor Athletic
1960/61	St. Laurence's	1997/98	Seven Stiles
1961/62	Birkenhead St. Anne's	1998/99	Seven Stiles Youth
1962/63	Our Lady's	1999/00	North Star
1963/64	Park Villa	2000/01	North Star
1964/65	St. Laurence's	2001/02	North Star
1965/66	Mersey Royal	2002/03	Abbotsford
1966/67	St. Laurence's	2003/04	Parkfield B A
1967/68	St. Laurence's	2004/05	Beechwood Social
1968/69	Labour Social	2005/06	Willaston
1969/70	Labour Social	2006/07	Bird in Hand
1970/71	Shamrock Celtic	2007/08	Universal Windows
1971/72	Mersey Royal	2008/09	Claughton Hotel
1972/73	Bowaters	2009/10	Birkenhead FC
1973/74	Ellesmere Port Youth Centre	2010/11	McGuinty's
1974/75	Bowaters	2011/12	Birkenhead Town
1975/76	Birkenhead Docks	2012/13	Birkenhead Town
1976/77	Wirral Celtic	2013/14	Birkenhead Town
1977/78	Shell	2014/15	Birkenhead Town
1978/79	Shell	2015/16	Mersey Royal Youth
1979/80	Birkenhead Docks	2016/17	Sutton Athletic
1980/81	Willaston	2017/18	Ellesmere Port
1981/82	Vauxhall Motors	2018/19	Avenue Vets
1982/83	Mallaby	2019/20	Covid-19
1983/84	Queens	2020/21	Capenhurst Villa Vets.
1984/85	Capenhurst Villa	2021/22	Hooton Vets.
1985/86	Meadows	2022/23	Poulton Victoria Youth
1986/87	Rake Social	2023/24	Mersey Royal Vets.
1987/88	Bebington Rangers		

WIRRAL SENIOR CUP WINNERS

Season	Winners	Score	Runners Up
1885/86	Bromborough Pool	3-1	Claughton
1886/87	Birkenhead Argyle	2-1	Bromborough Pool
1887/88	Bromborough Pool	3-1	Seacombe
1888/89	Tranmere Rovers	3-0	Primrose Rovers
1889/90	Bromborough Pool	3-1	Tranmere Rovers
1890/91	Tranmere Rovers	3-0	Tranmere Old Boys
1891/92	Tranmere Rovers	3-1	Tranmere Old Boys
1892/93	Tranmere Rovers	2-0	Tranmere Rovers Reserves
1893/94	L & N.W. Locos	2-1	Seacombe Rangers
1894/95	L & N.W. Locos	1-0	Bromborough Pool
1895/96	L & N.W. Locos	3-0	Melrose
1896/97	Melrose	4-1	L & N.W. Locos
1897/98	Tranmere Rovers	7-0	Hoylake
1898/99	New Brighton Tower Reserves	5-4	Seacombe Swifts
1899/00	New Brighton Tower Reserves		Seacombe Swifts
1900/01	New Brighton Tower Reserves	10-0	Wirral Railway
1901/02	Birkenhead	4-0	Melrose
1902/03	Birkenhead	2-0	Melrose
1903/04	Melrose	1-0	Port Sunlight
1904/05	Tranmere Rovers	3-0	Bebington Victoria
1905/06	Port Sunlight		Birkenhead
1906/07	Garston Gasworks	2-1	Prescot Wireworks
1907/08	African Royal	2-0	Garston Gasworks
1908/09	African Royal		Harrowby
1909/10	Burnell's Ironworks	1-0	Birkenhead North End
1910/11	Birkenhead North End		Hoylake
1911/12	Harrowby	1-0	Wallasey Rovers
1912/13	Bebington St. Andrews	4-3	Hoylake
1913/14	Tranmere Rovers	2-0	Wirral Railway
1918/19	Tranmere Rovers	2-1	Harrowby
1919/20	Harrowby	3-0	Ellesmere Port

Season	Winners	Score	Runners Up
1920/21	Ellesmere Port	2-1	West Kirby
1921/22	West Kirby		Ellesmere Port
1922/23	Bromborough Pool	1-0	Harrowby
1923/24	Ellesmere Port Cement Reserves		Bebington
1924/25	Chester Reserves		Ellesmere Port Cement Reserves
1925/26	Wirral Railways		Ellesmere Port Cement
1926/27	Shell Mex	3-2	West Kirby
1927/28	Harrowby	8-1	Shell Mex
1928/29	Planters	4-0	Neston Brickworks
1929/30	Planters	3-1	Ellesmere Port Town
1930/31	West Kirby	4-0	Shell Mex
1931/32	Shell Mex	2-0	Hoylake
1932/33	Shell Mex	2-0	Heswall
1933/34	Hoylake		West Kirby
1934/35	Shell Mex	1-0	Bromborough Port
1935/36	Rock Ferry Social	2-1	Heswall
1936/37	Hoylake		Bromborough Port
1937/38	Mersey Ironworks		Hoylake
1938/39	Heswall	5-1	Brookville
1939/40	Ellesmere Port Town		Tranmere Rovers
1940/41	Tranmere Rovers 'B'		Tranmere Rovers 'A'
1944/45	Graysons		Stork
1945/46	Ellesmere Port Town		Bromborough Pool
1946/47	Stork		Port Sunlight
1947/48	Shell		Hoylake Athletic
1948/49	Ellesmere Port Town		Stork
1949/50	Ellesmere Port Town		Stork
1950/51	Newton		Cammell Laird
1951/52	Stork		Ellesmere Port Town
1952/53	Port Sunlight		Bromborough
1953/54	Moreton		Ellesmere Port Town
1954/55	Moreton		Stork
1955/56	Stork		Ellesmere Port Town
1956/57	New Brighton		Tranmere Rovers

Season	Winners	Score	Runners Up
1957/58	Stork		Tranmere Rovers
1958/59	Ellesmere Port Town		Port Sunlight
1959/60	Port Sunlight	6-1	Stork
1960/61	Stork		Ashville
1961/62	Ashville	2-0	Bromborough Pool
1962/63	Stork	3-0	Newton
1963/64	Ellesmere Port Town		West Kirby
1964/65	Moreton	2-0	Port Sunlight
1965/66	Poulton Victoria		New Brighton
1966/67	Port Sunlight	4-1	Shell
1967/68	West Kirby		Port Sunlight
1968/69	Moreton		West Kirby
1969/70	Christleton		Harrowby
1970/71	Poulton Victoria		Hoylake Athletic
1971/72	Cammell Laird		Hoylake Athletic
1972/73	Poulton Victoria		Port Sunlight
1973/74	Newton		Poulton Victoria
1974/75	Poulton Victoria		Cammell Laird
1975/76	Poulton Victoria	1-0	Shell
1976/77	Cammell Laird		Poulton Victoria
1977/78	Cammell Laird		Poulton Victoria
1978/79	Cammell Laird	3-2	Poulton Victoria
1979/80	Cammell Laird		Poulton Victoria
1980/81	West Kirby		Bromborough Pool
1981/82	Hoylake Athletic	3-2	Van Leer
1982/83	Poulton Victoria	2-1	Vauxhall Motors
1983/84	West Kirby		Vauxhall Motors
1984/85	Heswall	1-0	Cammell Laird
1985/86	Mersey Royal		Cammell Laird
1986/87	Vauxhall Motors		Poulton Victoria
1987/88	Cammell Laird	5-2	Higher Bebington
1988/89	Higher Bebington	4-1	Mersey Royal
1989/90	Cammell Laird	2-1	Ashville
1990/91	Cammell Laird	2-1	Heswall

Season	Winners	Score	Runners Up
1991/92	Heswall	2-1	Bromborough Pool
1992/93	Capenhurst	2-1	Mersey Royal
1993/94	Poulton Victoria		Capenhurst
1994/95	Cammell Laird	2-1	Vauxhall Motors
1995/96	Heswall	1-0	Cammell Laird
1996/97	Heswall	4-2	Mersey Royal
1997/98	Heswall		Poulton Victoria
1998/99	Heswall	3-2	Stork
1999/00	Cammell Laird		Vauxhall Motors
2000/01	Poulton Victoria		Mersey Royal
2001/02	Cammell Laird		Poulton Victoria
2002/03	West Kirby		Mallaby
2003/04	Cammell Laird		Heswall
2004/05	Cammell Laird		Castrol Social
2005/06	Poulton Victoria		Ellesmere Port
2006/07	West Kirby		Heswall
2007/08	West Kirby		Heswall
2008/09	Cammell Laird		Newton
2009/10	West Kirby		Heswall
2010/11	Vauxhall Motors		Ashville
2011/12	Ashville		Heswall
2012/13	Vauxhall Motors		West Kirby
2013/14	West Kirby		Maghull
2014/15	Vauxhall Motors		Mallaby
2015/16	West Kirby & Wasps		Cammell Laird 1907
2016/17	Newton		Ashville
2017/18	Newton		Ashville
2018/19	Ashville		Neston Nomads
2019/20	Covid-19		
2020/21	Ellesmere Port Town	void	Heswall
2021/22	Cammell Laird 1907	3-0	Heswall
2022/23	Capenhurst Villa		
2023/24	Cammell Laird 1907		

SOURCES

Books

Aughton, Peter. *North Meols and Southport: A History.*

Baldursson, Arnie & Magnusson, Gudmundur. *Liverpool: The Complete History.*

Ball, Dave & Buckland, Gavin. *Everton: The Ultimate Book of Stats and Facts.*

Barnes, Tommy. *The Bootle Connection.*

Barnes, Tommy. *Third Time Lucky (Bootle Football Club).*

Barton, Bob. *Non-League.*

Bishop, Peter & Upton, Gilbert. *The A–Z of Tranmere Rovers.*

Brocken, Mike. *Liverpool City RLFC: Rugby League in a Football City.*

Brookes, Reg. *Never a Dull Moment: The Bootle Story.*

Brown, Jack Gordon & Ross, Philip. *England: The Complete Record 1872–2018.*

Brown, Paul. *The Victorian Football Miscellany.*

Channon, Howard. *Portrait of Liverpool.*

Collins, Tony. *How Football Began.*

Corbett, James. *Faith of Our Families: Everton an Oral History.*

Corbett, James. *Everton: The School of Science.*

Davey, Elizabeth. *Birkenhead: A History.*

Dykes, Garth. *New Brighton: A Complete Record of the Rakers in the Football League.*

Evans, Tony. *Two Tribes.*

Ferguson, Ryan. *Planet Prentonia.*

Floate, Mike. *Football Grounds of the Early 1900s.*

Gordon, Terry. *Non-League Football Grounds of Liverpool & Manchester.*

Howe, Martin. *Lives in Cricket: Frank Sugg – A Man for All Seasons.*

Hoole, Les. *The Birth of Rugby League 1895–1922.*

Hoult, James. *West Derby, Old Swan and Wavertree.*

Hughes, Simon. *On the Brink.*

Hughes, Simon. *There She Goes.*

Inglis, Simon. *League Football and the Men Who Made It.*

Inglis, Simon. *Football Grounds of Britain.*

Johnson, Steve. *Everton: The Official Complete Record.*

Johnson, Tim. *They Used to Play at Penny Lane.*

Kennedy, David & Kennedy, Peter. *Irish Football Clubs in Liverpool.*

Kennedy, David. *The Man Who Created Merseyside Football.*

Lenton, Barry. *Celebrating 125 Years: Marine Football Club 1894–2019.*

Macilwee, Michael. *The Gangs of Liverpool.*

McPartlin, Sean. *Golden Days: Falling for Southport FC in the Sixties.*

Metcalf, Mark. *The Origins of the Football League: The First Season.*

Murray, Scott. *The Title: The Story of the First Division.*

Onslow, Tony. *The Forgotten Rivals: A History of Bootle Football Club 1880–1893.*

Parrs Wood Press. *Lancashire Amateur Football League 1899–1999: Centenary History.*

Platt, Mark. *The Red Journey.*

Rees, D. Ben. *The Welsh of Merseyside.*

Sumner, Chas. *On the Borderline: The Official History of Chester City FC 1885–1997.*

Syers, Robert. *The History of Everton.*

Titley, U. A. & McWhirter, Ross. *Centenary History of the Rugby Football Union.*

Twydell, Dave. *Rejected FC, Volumes 1 & 3.*

Upton, Gilbert. *Tranmere Rovers 1881–1921: A New History.*

Walker, P. N. *The Liverpool Competition: A Study of the Development of Cricket on Merseyside.*

Walsh, Nick. *Dixie Dean.*

Williams, Glyn. *A Football Club in Prescot.*

Williams, Tony (ed.). *Non-League Club Directory (1978–1979, 1986, 1995, 2002, 2005).*

Wilson, Alan. *The Team of All the Macs.*

Wotherspoon, David. *The Mighty Mariners.*

Yates, John & Strickland, Stan. *Village Green Heroes.*

Young, Percy M. *Football on Merseyside.*

Guide to Southport 1849 by "J.S. (of Southport)."
History of the Lancashire Football Association 1878–1928.
News of the World Football Annual 1968/69.
Rothman's Football Yearbooks (various years).
The Cemetery End by Groundtastic.
Wirral District Football Association – Rules and Regulations.

Websites Used

Media / News
- 90min.com/posts/6597034-women-s-fa-cup-history-6-rogue-teams-to-win-the-competition-back-in-the-day
- bbc.co.uk
- champnews.com
- cheshire-live.co.uk
- dailypost.co.uk
- independent.co.uk
- liverpoolecho.co.uk
- southportvisiter.co.uk
- theguardian.com
- thefreelibrary.com
- walesonline.co.uk

Clubs (Current & Historic)
- chesterfc.com
- eastvillafc.co.uk
- evertonfc.com
- formbyfc.co.uk
- fulhamfc.com
- liverpoolfc.com
- liverpoolfeds.co.uk
- liverpoolramblersafc.com
- maghullfc.co.uk

- pilkingtonfc.com
- prescotcablesafc.com
- runcornlinnetsfc.co.uk
- sacrecoeur.co.uk
- southportfootballclub.co.uk
- tranmererovers.co.uk
- vauxhallmotorsfc.co.uk
- wooltonfc.org.uk

History / Archives / Research

- bluecorrespondent.co.uk
- bootlehistory.co.uk
- chester-city.co.uk/archive.asp
- chesterfootballhistory.com
- disused-stations.org.uk
- efcstatto.com
- eu-football.info
- evertoncollection.org.uk
- footballprogrammecentre.co.uk
- footballsite.co.uk
- football-stadiums.co.uk
- formbyfc.co.uk
- greyhoundracingtimes.co.uk
- historicalkits.co.uk
- liverweb.org.uk (via web.archive.org)
- liverpoolschoolsfa.org.uk/history-of-the-lsfa/
- petergould.co.uk
- playupliverpool.com
- ryanferguson.co.uk
- silkmenarchives.org.uk
- welshsoccerarchive.co.uk
- wfahistory.wordpress.com

Leagues / Governing Bodies

- cwfl.org.uk
- fulltime-league.thefa.com
- mitoo.co.uk (Liverpool County Combination archive)
- nwcfl.com
- pitchero.com
- thenationalleague.org.uk
- wirraldistrictfa.org

Fan / Blog / Miscellaneous

- burscough FC (mossleyweb.com)
- d2architects.co.uk
- footballpink.net
- hansard.parliament.uk (Football Grounds Improvement Trust, 1979)
- footballfoundation.org.uk (Football Stadia Improvement Fund)
- mossleyweb.com
- pyramid.info (Ground Grading)
- rakers1923.blogspot.com
- roy-mcdonald.co.uk
- shekicks.net
- thisisanfield.com
- troscirelandhome.wordpress.com
- tranmereroverspast.wordpress.com
- womensoccerunited.com
- womenssoccerscene.co.uk
- mcsfa.co.uk/about-mcsfa